THE
SHAPING OF THE
ELIZABETHAN
REGIME

THE
SHAPING OF THE
ELIZABETHAN
REGIME

Wallace MacCaffrey

JONATHAN CAPE
THIRTY BEDFORD SQUARE
LONDON

FIRST PUBLISHED IN GREAT BRITAIN 1969
© 1968 BY PRINCETON UNIVERSITY PRESS

JONATHAN CAPE LTD
30 BEDFORD SQUARE, LONDON, WCI

SBN 224 61701 X

PRINTED IN GREAT BRITAIN BY
EBENEZER BAYLIS AND SON LTD,
THE TRINITY PRESS, WORCESTER, AND LONDON,
ON PAPER MADE BY JOHN DICKINSON AND CO. LTD,
BOUND BY A. W. BAIN AND CO. LTD, LONDON

CONTENTS

ACKNOWLEDGMENTS

I owe numerous acknowledgments for assistance and advice in the writing of this book. Haverford College was generous in support from its Faculty Research Fund. The staffs of the Haverford College Library, the Dartmouth College Library, the British Museum, the Public Record Office and the Register of National Archives were very helpful. I am especially grateful to the Institute of Historical Research at the University of London within whose hospitable walls I spent so many fruitful hours. The History of Parliament Trust generously opened their files to me, and Miss Norah Fuidge of their staff was especially kind and helpful on many occasions. The Marquess of Bath and the Marquess of Anglesey kindly allowed me access to the Dudley Papers and to the Paget Papers. My colleague at Haverford, Professor John P. Spielman, was of great assistance in providing translations from difficult Spanish documents. Professor Lawrence Stone of Princeton and Professor Joel Hurstfield of London were kind enough to read the manuscript at different stages and to make valuable and penetrating comments, many of which are reflected in the final version of the book. Many conversations with Dr Patrick Collinson in London helped to shape my understanding of the period I was dealing with. Above all, I owe a very heavy debt to Professor Sir John Neale. At every stage he has been ready with assistance in the exploration of sources, with thoughtful advice and with helpful criticism. I have profited much from his great knowledge of the Elizabethan age and from his wise judgments. The final stages of preparing the manuscript were made easy for me by the skill and intelligence of Mrs Mildred Hargreaves. Finally I owe very much to my wife, for her steady encouragement and for her skilful criticism of the text.

ABBREVIATIONS

APC	*Acts of the Privy Council of England*, 32 v., edited by J. R. Dasent (London, 1890–1907).
BM	British Museum
CPR	*Calendar of the Patent Rolls Preserved in the P.R.O., Philip and Mary, Elizabeth, 1553–1572*, 9 v. (London, 1937–66).
CSPDom	*Calendar of State Papers, Domestic, 1547–1625*, 12 v., edited by Robert Lemon and M. A. E. Green (London, 1856–72).
CSPFor	*Calendar of State Papers, Foreign, Elizabeth*, 23 v., edited by Joseph Stevenson *et al.* (London, 1863–1950).
CSPRome	*Calendar of State Papers, Rome*, 2 v., edited by J. M. Rigg (London, 1916–26).
CSPScot	*Calendar of State Papers Relating to Scotland and Mary, Queen of Scots, 1547–1603*, 11 v. (Edinburgh and Glasgow, 1898–1936).
CSPSpan	*Calendar of State Papers, Spanish, Elizabeth*, 4 v., edited by M. A. S. Hume (London, 1892–9).
CSPVen	*Calendar of State Papers, Venetian*, 9 v., edited by Rowden Brown *et al.* (London, 1864–98).
Digges	*The Compleat Ambassador*, edited by Sir Dudley Digges (London, 1655).
Fénélon	*Correspondance Diplomatique de la Mothe-Fénélon*, 7 v., edited by A. Teulet (Paris and London, 1840).
Hardwicke	*Miscellaneous State Papers from 1501 to 1726*, 2 v. (London, 1778).
Hatfield	Historical Manuscripts Commission, *Calendar of the Manuscripts of the Marquess of Salisbury Preserved at Hatfield House, Hertfordshire*, Part I (London, 1883).
Haynes, Murdin	*Collection of State Papers . . . Left by William Cecil, Lord Burghley*, 2 v., edited by Samuel Haynes and William Murdin (London, 1740–59). Cited as *Haynes* for v. I and *Murdin* for v. II.

PRO   Public Record Office

ST   *A Complete Collection of State Trials and Proceedings for High Treason*, 42 v., edited by William Cobbett *et al.* (London, 1816–98).

Dedicated to

REGINALD FRANCIS
ARRAGON

Part One

THE NEW REGIME

1 *Prologue to a Reign*

FEW PERIODS in English history have attracted so much serious attention as the reign of Elizabeth I. Since the time of the great Froude a sequence of major historians have devoted their life's work to this age. In earlier generations Froude, Cheyney and Pollard worked on the grand scale, taking the whole course of national history as their subject. More recently their successors have turned their attention to specific men and to particular aspects of the era. Conyers Read's major biographical studies of Walsingham and of Cecil have illuminated the careers of Elizabeth's two greatest servants. Neale's work on Parliament has given new shape to our understanding of that institution and of the Elizabethan age. More recently still a group of able historians have concentrated their efforts on the institutions of government, on the lesser political figures and on the religious changes of these years, and on their social and economic history. Consequently, a word of explanation is needed to justify yet another stirring of soil so well cultivated.

The primary purpose of this book is to examine the fifteen years which lie between Elizabeth's accession to the throne and the death of the Duke of Norfolk in 1572. This was the testing-time of the regime—whether it was to live or to die. For contemporaries they were years of hope and despair, always shadowed by agonized uncertainties about the morrow. By 1572 the question of survival had been settled and the very struggle for survival had moulded the regime into a form which would endure almost as long as Queen Elizabeth lived.

The study of these years requires a dual perspective. From the shorter-term point of view of the sixteenth century they mark the last stage of a forty-year crisis which at times had threatened the very existence of basic political order in the English state. They brought to a close the alarming political disturbances attendant upon the English Reformation and, in a generation when much of Europe suffered from the terrible scourge of religious civil war, Englishmen were to enjoy domestic peace and general good order. This was no mean achievement; but it was one by no means on the cards when Elizabeth assumed power: the events through which a political stability lacking since the early decades of Henry VIII's reign was restored deserve careful attention and some reconsideration.

From the longer perspective of four centuries these years mark a fundamental turning-point in the history of English politics. Slowly and awkwardly England was turning away from the now archaic world of late medieval times, from a political universe paternalistic and dynastic in outlook, and since the 1470s very much royally-centred. In the era now beginning the magnetic pole of politics would not quite coincide with that visible and apparent centre of attraction, the throne, and as a consequence the very nature of political activity would change. By the early 1570s there existed in England a hybrid political order, viable but fragile, accommodating in uneasy partnership a still potent monarchy and an as yet ill-defined political elite. The first hesitating experiments in a new politics were being made at this time, in which the initiatives to action came not solely from the sovereign but also from partisan aristocratic groupings, linked loosely but effectively by the common ideology of Protestantism. It was the first painful stage of a process lasting over more than a century by which the power of the Crown would be gradually reduced and that of the aristocratic classes, especially the gentry, steadily augmented.

The mode in which this study is cast is one of compressed narrative, but the prime concern is not to rehearse once more the well-known events of these years so much as to understand their significance in the course of English political life. In the past these years have, perhaps unconsciously, often been regarded as a kind of prelude to the later triumphs of the Elizabethans. Posterity has been loud in its applause of those successes, and it has sometimes seemed as though they were predetermined, imprinted in the very fabric of history and in some sense self-explanatory. But to understand the Elizabethan achievement it is signally important to remember that the regime, during its first decade and a half, seemed to contemporaries to be a very fragile creation with a very precarious future. These men led lives conditioned by frightening and incalculable incertitudes. To them the sudden death of the queen, a ruinous marriage with Robert Dudley, privy conspiracy in favour of Mary Stuart, or even foreign invasion, formed the all-too-probable shape of the future. The worst of these fears were not realized, but their very existence is a vital fact of politics in these years. It is all the more important to forgo the delusive advantage given by four centuries of hindsight and to keep steadily before us the anxious forebodings with which contemporaries faced the grim uncertainties of these first Elizabethan years.

What was the outlook when Elizabeth succeeded her sister in November 1558? At the moment of accession there was both relief and rejoicing. Mary Tudor had died after an illness of some months. For the third time in less than a dozen years there was a change of sovereigns in England. In the sixteenth century such a change was at best an unsettling experience for the nation. In this case Mary's long illness had given warning of impending change, but the conventions of monarchy precluded any public preparation. Hence there was an air of crisis, an atmosphere of mingled apprehension and expectancy. Many feared disturbance, but at the centre of government the Council methodically took the usual measures attendant upon a royal death—the closing of the ports, alerting of garrisons, and other cautionary moves.

Thus the shock of Mary's death, when it came, was easily met; the new queen was proclaimed without incident and amid rejoicing that seems to have been more than merely conventional excitement; the shift of power to the new sovereign was swiftly achieved. Awkward and urgent problems had to be faced without delay. The country was still at war with France although active hostilities had ceased some months earlier. For weeks English commissioners in Flanders had been engaged in the painful task of negotiating a peace with France which could at the best be but a face-saving operation. The crushing defeat of the previous January had left England without a continental base, with negligible military resources and, indeed, without much will to continue the struggle. A little less urgent but more deeply troubling was the great question of religion. All England and half of Europe waited with nervous expectancy for the new queen's first moves in this all-important matter. Yet, for the moment, in the jubilance of her peaceful accession queen and subjects could pause to catch their breath.

During the years immediately ahead—between 1558 and 1572—England was to pass through the last phase of a grave political disturbance which had begun thirty years earlier with Henry VIII's 'great matter', the divorce from Catherine of Aragon. The original problem, difficult enough in itself, had soon snowballed into one of the major transformations of English history, with consequences, both religious and political, which reached far beyond the end of the sixteenth century. The first phase of this disturbance—up to about 1540—was largely one of institutional change. Under the ruthlessly efficient management of Thomas Cromwell the links

2

with Rome were quickly snapped, a new national ecclesiastical establishment set up, and—a by-product—the monasteries swept away and their wealth scooped into the royal coffers. Except for the lonely resistance of More, Fisher and the Carthusians, and the confused and ineffective protest of the Pilgrimage of Grace, the new order met no obstacles of any note.

Perhaps the ease of this first transition obscured the difficulties which lay ahead. Henry had hoped for a limited revolution, carefully restricted to jurisdictional and constitutional changes, untainted by any hint of religious heterodoxy. But unluckily for the king his rupture with Rome coincided with one of the great revolutions in Western Christian history. However much his servants might labour to draw distinctions between Henrician orthodoxy and Lutheran heresy, the flood of history was too much for them. The waters of the Reformation were about to overflow England, and the king by his actions in the 1530s had unwillingly and unwittingly opened the dykes.

Even the reluctant Henry, at the end of his life, began to sense that the break with Rome could not be confined to merely institutional changes but necessarily brought in its train a whole new religious order. Before his death there was the nucleus of a Protestant party in the realm, and under his successor the circumstances of a minority gave them the freest possible scope to realize their hopes. The resistance of the religious conservatives was no more effective now than in the 'thirties; the obstacles in the Protestants' path lay in their own uncertainties as to what new forms of worship should replace the now prohibited mass and on what doctrinal bases they should rest. The English Reformation threw up no Calvin or Knox to give focus or offer guidance to a new religion. When Edward's death in 1553 halted the development of English Protestantism in mid-career, there was little agreement among its adherents except in their wholehearted anti-Catholicism, i.e. their rejection of Rome's jurisdiction and of the Roman sacramental system. English Protestantism was not to find its focal point in a charismatic leader, in a confession of faith, or in a system of Church government. Its own individual character had yet to crystallize.

But the problems raised by the second stage of the long crisis lay not solely in the choice of a new national form of Christianity; they had larger dimensions still. These middle decades of the sixteenth century saw a profound transformation in the whole nature of English politics. The previous century had been one of open and violent disorder, in which brute force was repeatedly the final arbiter in the national political life. The revulsion against those unhappy times was deep and long-lasting, and a vivid

memory of the Wars of the Roses was an important element in Elizabethan attitudes. Monarchical leadership, more or less in abeyance since the
fourteenth century, was reasserted with great vigour by the Yorkist and
then by the Tudor kings. From the late 1490s down to the Pilgrimage of
Grace in 1536-7 England enjoyed a long generation of civil peace. The
official political doctrine of the Tudors naturally reflected these facts. The
old formulas of divine-right monarchy were given revived cogency even
before their vigorous use in royal defiance of divine-right papacy. The
alternative tradition of English medieval political thought—that the king
was subordinate to God and the law—receded into the background. Now
it was the monarch's divine lieutenancy which was constantly being
emphasized, in a simple and already rather archaic doctrine of right political order. This doctrine envisaged a ruler hallowed by divine sanction and
sustained by the facts of nature and history alike, who displayed an authoritarian but paternal solicitude for his people, and whose task was to ensure
their welfare and secure their best advantage. His subjects, on their side,
had the simple obligation of unquestioning obedience to God's nominee.

Such a theory of right order sharply trammelled political activity. The
ordinary competition for place or power was to be kept within limits laid
down by the king; disagreement or criticism were by logic excluded. A
ruler chosen from on high was supremely competent to make all decisions
affecting his people and in such an organic view of society the notion of
competing private or partisan thought or action was entirely abhorrent.
Under the first two Tudors the theory and practice of politics were not
far separated. These masterful kings monopolized to themselves all the
great political decisions of the realm, leaving to their ministers—even a
Wolsey or a Cromwell—the mere execution of royal commands. Seeking
a maximum freedom of action, the first two Tudors had made royal
service a career open to the talents, and had recruited widely from the
middle and upper middle ranks of society. However, they by no means
excluded the greater aristocrats from their service, and in their court there
was a mingling of new aristocrats of the robe and old ones of the sword.
But only a very few were admitted to assist in the highest mysteries of
state—in the making of policy and the issuance of commands. To enter the
royal service was to embrace the career of a bureaucrat not of a politician.

In this restricted political universe the course of the English Reformation
produced explosive effects. First of all there was the irony of chance circumstance which, at the very crisis of religious revolution, placed on the
throne first a child and then a woman of great personal courage but limited

political acumen. Such circumstances would in any event have seriously disordered a political world so pivoted on the monarch, but these seasonal storms were warnings of long-term changes in the whole climate of English politics.

In the first and most obvious instance the Reformation altered English politics by fostering faction. Over the previous half-century the power of the monarchy had pretty effectively extinguished the dynastic or semi-feudal factionalisms of the past; now the realm was threatened by internal disunity of a more serious and far more dangerous kind. Even before the death of Henry the nuclei of two opposing religious parties were forming in the court, and in the years after 1547 England was governed successively by two rancorously partisan regimes, Protestant under Edward, and Catholic under Mary. Each of these sovereigns thus became the leader of a religious faction, and the Crown's neutrality towards the major religious issues of the Reformation, which Henry with some success had struggled to maintain, was irretrievably lost. Elizabeth was left with no choice but to assume a partisan position at her accession. The question now was whether or not the Catholic party, left leaderless by Mary's death, could recover itself for a return bout to recapture power. To contemporaries this seemed likely enough, and fear of this possibility haunted Elizabethan ministers in the first decade of the new reign; the Catholic political failure is one of the themes dealt with in this book.

The triumph of the Protestant faction settled, at least for the present, the religious complexion of the nation, but implicit in it was a series of altera-tions in the nature of English politics, novel, bewildering and far-reaching. Even before Elizabeth's accession the intrusion of religious ideology into politics was introducing a perplexing confusion into the affairs of the English monarchy. In 1539 Parliament had, at Henry's irritable bidding, passed a bill hopefully entitled 'An act abolishing diversity in opinions'. It was an unavailing attempt to restore, under royal leadership, the kind of uniformity of faith which had hitherto been everywhere the norm of European life. But this particular Humpty Dumpty was not to be set up again in England, although the efforts of all the king's horses and all the king's men would continue to be engaged at the task. More important still, royal control over the delicate process of religious change, so boldly assumed in the 1530s, was, after 1547, fatally loosened. Initiative towards change had now shifted to a group of subjects; henceforward there was to be a constant tug between a Crown desperately struggling to retain reli-gious uniformity under royal auspices, and a forward party of Protestants straining and pulling to reshape the national religion according to their own strongly held convictions.

The very existence of such private initiative outside the control of the Crown was of course incompatible with patriarchal, divine-right monarchy. If England had remained under a Catholic monarch, the situation would no doubt have led to civil conflict and a developed theory of justified resistance to constituted authority, as in France. Given instead a Protestant and popular sovereign, there emerged a far more complex process – first, a rumbling discontent, erupting from time to time in real but inconclusive contests of will between the queen and the Protestant leadership; then, in the long run of three generations, a dangerous divergence between the monarch and a leading segment of his subjects.

The mere existence of a centre of initiative and action independent of the Crown was grave enough. But of even greater note was its ideological character. The old factionalism of the past had been personal, familial or dynastic in nature. The cement which held together this new grouping was ideology. Commitment to abstract principles of belief which were also a programme for action was, at least for laymen, something bewilderingly novel in the sixteenth century. But it was, as they were quick to discover, infinitely useful.

The use of the term 'ideology' in this context requires explication.[1] English Protestantism in the mid-sixteenth century was not governed by a tightly-knit and coherent body of doctrine. The most conspicuous features of its thought were not so much a body of positive assertions as its whole-hearted rejection of an outmoded and now despised system of belief. For most first-generation Protestants this meant a repudiation of 'idolatry', of obscurantism and mystery, and the liberating excitement of new knowledge, of a new enlightenment and a new freedom of intellectual movement. For some this experience was a highly private one, a spiritual conversion; they were indeed Pauline 'new men'. But to many other Englishmen the new faith signified a more public and external reformation, the reordering of public life on principles of a robust laicism. For those who sat at Calvin's feet in Geneva the new faith implied a very explicit and very radical doctrine. Few, even among the exiles, shared the intensity of vision which moved a Knox or a Goodman, but it is important to grasp that even such a wary trimmer as William Cecil or a political adventurer like Nicholas Throckmorton shared the vision of an enlightened Protestant polity and were no less contemptuous in their dismissal of an obscurantist Catholicism. They were prepared to compromise under

Mary, but once they held power under a Protestant sovereign there was
no turning back for them. In their eyes a Protestant polity was a *sine qua
non* for England's future.

An additional element in English Protestant ideology was its passionate
nationalism – or, perhaps more accurately, its xenophobia. The roots of
this feeling were ancient; its recent manifestations had preceded the
Reformation, but it fused quickly and easily with a cause which began by
repudiating external authority. Not until the 1560s would Foxe's great
work bring together in a full-blown mythology these nationalist and
religious strains.[2] But even earlier these feelings were given new shape as
Protestant England stood alone against its continental, Catholic neighbours. Anti-foreign and anti-Catholic sentiment blended, and the process
was hastened by Mary's unpopular Spanish marriage and the consequent
threat that England would become no more than a minor planet in a
Habsburg solar system.

This diffuse but potent ideology had another important characteristic.
It gave a vital new urgency and an unprecedented self-consciousness to
men's concerns with public issues; it became a focus for organizing their
views in these matters and thus served the purposes of a modern party
platform. In Mary's reign it provided a centre for the agitation against her
policies, domestic and foreign; after Elizabeth's accession it was a rallying
point for the Commons in their triumphant effort to establish the radically
Protestant Edwardian liturgy. In the next decade it would be a guide to
the Protestant leaders in their relentless efforts to influence the queen on the
succession, on her marriage, on the treatment of the Catholics and on
foreign policy. In short, as the new ideology came to permeate a large
segment of the aristocratic classes throughout the country, it would form
the matrix for a loose but potent body of public opinion on high matters of
state. Such an ideology, religious in terminology and concept, but political
in application and goals, proved extraordinarily serviceable to the needs
of the age.

In these decades there did not, of course, exist any formal party structure or, indeed, any continuity of organization. Ephemeral forms arose as
need or circumstance dictated – the co-operation of agitators in Mary's
and, later, in Elizabeth's Parliaments; the associations of exiles in Germany
and Switzerland under Mary; the alliance in Council grouped around
Cecil; or the rival, and more broadly based left-wing Protestant faction
led by Leicester. Ultimately there would appear the politically sophisticated
and well-organized Puritan movement of the 1570s and 1580s.

From the point of view of a traditional monarchy based on the patriarchal leadership of God's elect, all this was highly uncomfortable. It
meant that there now existed a focus of political belief and of action which
was not directly derived from the monarchy and — more significant still —
a standard of belief by which the monarchy could in fact be judged. John
Knox's ill-timed attack on the Marian monarchy and Christopher Goodman's even more dangerous pamphlet, published at the same time, were a
warning. At the moment of Elizabeth's accession Protestants rejoiced together at the wonderful working of God's providence, but it was soon to
be demonstrated that a Protestant monarch was no more immune from
the criticisms and the judgments of Protestant ideologues than her unloved
predecessor. None would follow Goodman in his angry denunciation of
the establishment and his call for revolution. But even those whose Protestantism was tepidly *politique* in character looked to the interests of the
Protestant party at home and abroad rather than to the royal will as the
basis of their views on public affairs. In the shrewdly analytical and profoundly political mind of Cecil a detached conception of English national
— as distinguished from royal — interest would blend into a thoroughly
secularized Protestantism.

He and his fellows would, of course, remain intensely royalist, but they
saw no incompatibility between their enthusiastic loyalty to the queen
and their straight-spoken admonitions to her on her political conduct. In
the end their enthusiasm for the queen was as much admiration for an able
practitioner of their own art as reverence for her royalty. There was no
question yet of challenging the royal direction of the national business; but
in the management of that business the queen had to take account more
and more of these cross-currents of feeling and opinion within the politically articulate classes; and indeed, within the Council, and the court itself,
she was soon to feel the pressures of these novel forces.

While these long-term trends were beginning to affect English political
life by 1558, other more immediate circumstances had intensified political
malaise. During the years since the death of Henry VIII there had been a
dangerous weakening of royal authority. Edward VI had not lived to
reach his majority, and the men who ruled the country in his name had
been reckless in their abuse of power. Two peasant revolts, one in Devon
and the other in Norfolk, and widespread rioting elsewhere had shaken the
social fabric in 1549, and it had taken a force of foreign mercenaries to
restore order. The Councillors of Edward indulged themselves in wholesale piracy in lands at the expense of Church and Crown. The climax of

this unhappy era came with John Dudley's desperate conspiracy to unseat the Tudors and usurp the throne for his family.

Mary's reign had opened with a loyal rally of the nation around the dynasty, yet within a few months that sentiment was so dissipated that a dangerous revolt, backed by powerful interests at court and in the country, attempted to thwart the queen's projected Spanish marriage. Even after the overthrow of the rebels, the country continued to display a fractious antipathy towards Philip and a rapidly cooling loyalty towards a ruler who shared so little in her subjects' warmest interests and aspirations. These unhappy years loosened the habits of obedience and of civic order built up slowly and painfully since the beginning of the century, and stimulated the revival of old practices of faction and intrigue. There was still a large fund of goodwill and loyalty towards the dynasty and a longing for the restoration of good order, but these impulses needed direction from a strong royal leadership. The reign of England's first queen regnant since the early Middle Ages had confirmed Englishmen's scepticism as to female government as they looked to the accession of a second woman ruler.

The political atmosphere in which Elizabeth acceded to the throne in November 1558 was deeply affected by the changes of the previous thirty years. The traditions of early Tudor monarchy were still strong, but they were beginning to assume a slightly archaic air, as they were gradually diluted by the novel political currents flowing from the Reformation. Beyond these general problems lay the uncertainties and the novelties produced by a change in leadership. The young queen was pretty much an unknown quantity; the men to whom she early gave her confidence were not entirely inexperienced but were untried in the tasks of supreme power. The potentiality of disorder – even of political disintegration – was all too apparent: there were the ill-starred legacies of the late reign; the intense religious feeling; and the dubiety with which men regarded another trial of feminine rulership. In the next few years the queen was to spread consternation in her court by her choice of the favourite on whom she fixed her affections, and then to exasperate her courtiers by a refusal to consider any of the more suitable matches which offered themselves. She was to anger and frustrate them by her unwillingness to provide for the succession. The two men who most fully shared her confidence – Leicester and Cecil – proved to be coldly hostile to one another, and a court faction, including leading noblemen, was organized in opposition to Dudley. Finally, the activities of Mary Stuart, especially after her arrival in England in 1568, led to conspiracy of the most dangerous kind and threatened to topple the regime.

And yet—in spite of all these impediments—by 1572 the regime had survived severe tests and clearly established itself. By no means were all problems solved, not even the most urgent question of the succession, let alone the longer-range problems posed by the great changes of the past generation. But a season of domestic tranquillity and political stability had opened which would last through the queen's lifetime and on into the 1620s, when the fierce quarrels between the Stuart kings and their Parliaments heralded the approach of a new storm. It was ruffled only once, at the close of her reign, in the Essex episode.

Any full explanation of this long epoch of domestic peace requires the work of social and economic as much as of political historians,[3] but the first step towards long-term stability lay in the re-establishment of a centre of political gravity. Workable and enduring relationships had to be formed at the summit of power before the confidence of the responsible political classes could be won and effective leadership restored to the nation. The process by which this new system of power was hammered out is the central theme of this book. That process was not an orderly or on the whole a very conscious one. It involved three disparate but powerful personalities—Elizabeth herself, Secretary Cecil, and the favourite, Robert Dudley. Naturally the process was affected in part by their own peculiarities of personality, particularly those of the queen, but it was shaped by the historical events to which they were compelled to respond in their roles at the summit of power. The queen, a traditionalist and a whole-hearted believer in the myth of monarchy, was coolly unsympathetic to most of the impulses stirring among her contemporaries; but she was endowed with a saving grace, an earthy political pragmatism which made her keenly aware of the limits of political possibility. Cecil and Dudley were conventional men of their time and place, ambitious courtiers, greedy of place and fortune, and hopeful of a posterity who would be great men in the land. But far more than their mistress they were responsive to the currents of new ideas and feelings around them. Part of their task was to draw her to a reluctant acceptance of this new-fashioned world.

Although these three were the leaders of the English state, they were not always initiators in the actions in which they moved. This circumstance was in part dictated by the general conditions of the time; western Europe was moving into the most terrible phase of the Reformation, an age of endemic civil and international war, fierce, bitter and hysterical, and England was borne along on this general tide. Many of the events which most affected the course of English politics arose outside the kingdom, in

Scotland, France or the Low Countries. But the relative passivity of English leadership arose also from the conservatism of the queen herself, from her profound unwillingness to take action until events forced it. This necessarily limited the actions of her servants, and only in a few rare cases were they able to take the lead in forward movement.

Thus, while the main attention of this book is given to these central and commanding personalities, it is necessarily diverted frequently to the great issues of foreign and domestic policy, all of which, as has been suggested above, cluster sooner or later around the magnetic pole of religion. The pattern of power relationships which ultimately evolved was strongly influenced by these larger forces. The new regime was consequently to develop a more complex and flexible character than that of the last preceding era of relative political stability—the reign of Henry VIII. The emergence of this pattern is the subject matter of what follows below.

2 *The Making of a Government*

AT THE moment of Mary's death and in the first hours of the new reign those at the centre of power trembled with fears of an opposed or troubled succession, but in a very short time it was apparent they had no reason to worry. Everywhere the queen was proclaimed with excited jubilation. But many difficult and some dangerous decisions had to be made within the next few weeks. First of all there was the delicate task of forming a new government, of choosing the ministers and servants of the new sovereign. Secondly, the ruinous war with France must be brought to a quick close, at whatever cost to pride and prestige. And, at the same time, the new government must face its first Parliament with a clear-cut programme for the national religious establishment. All these tasks were accomplished within less than six months. Hasty as these decisions were, they were bound to have long-term effects. The making of them forms the prologue to the reign and the stuff of our first chapter.

The most immediate task which faced the new queen on the day of her accession was the making of a new government. This modern phrase may seem anachronistic, but since constitutional theory held that most major offices of state and household were vacant on a sovereign's demise, the change of monarchs in the sixteenth century was as marked a caesura in the rhythm of government as a change of parties today. Then as now, it was a time for new men, new ideas, and new opportunities. There was the same air of excited expectancy that surrounds a modern Prime Minister as he makes his choices. But, free from the limits of party, the Tudor monarch was able to spread his selections more widely, so that incumbent as well as aspirant office-holders waited anxiously to hear their fate.

In another and important respect there was divergence from the modern pattern, since the queen was choosing not a ministry of departmental heads with specified functions and legal responsibilities, but something more like the staff of a great medieval household, a 'court' rather than a 'government'. Its outward and visible structure was rigid and even hieratic in character; inwardly it was far more flexible, informal, indeed 'amateurish' than any modern government, since the greater figures would have to fill as many different roles as the actors in a stock company. They would be in turn courtiers, diplomats, soldiers, administrators, and councillors, moving from role to role at the queen's pleasure. Some of them would enjoy the queen's utmost trust and confidence without ever holding an office of great consequence, while some of the most dignified officers of state might remain political ciphers. There was no necessary connection between a man's office and his place in the political firmament; from his relatively minor household post as Master of the Horse, Dudley would shine with more than planetary brilliance. Nonetheless, all the leading men of this reign would be found clustered in the Council and in the greater household offices directly about the queen's person.

The conventions surrounding the process of forming a new court were few; the queen's will was unconstrained. Nevertheless, it was taken for granted that a large proportion of the greater nobility (dukes, marquesses, and earls) would win appointments about the sovereign although, as has been said, this offered no sure entrée to the inmost circles of her confidence. As a matter of common sense, she would also choose others of her chief officers from the rather small body of experienced legal and administrative experts of the top level, men knowledgeable in the complex routines of state business, the 'permanent under-secretaries' of Tudor government. These again might become no more than glorified clerks, diligent executors of instructions like Sir William Petre (Secretary for nearly a decade), or they might be such linchpins of policy-making as Mary's late Chancellor, Bishop Gardiner, or her Lord Privy Seal, Paget. Up to 1558 it had been customary to draw heavily from the upper ranks of the clergy to fill many of the most important Crown posts.

Beyond this, little was certain. Even the function of Council, that all-important pillar of Tudor government, was hardly defined by contemporary practice. Although now firmly established as the executive instrument of the Crown, its corporate identity had emerged only rather slowly and quite recently, and its political importance had varied sharply under Elizabeth's three predecessors. Potentially it could serve not only as a continuing committee for central public business but also as a powerful policy-making body and as the fulcrum of active politics. Under Mary it seems to have served little more than the first of these functions. Whether it would again play a wider role lay in the future actions – and interactions – of the new Councillors and the intentions of the sovereign.

Elizabeth moved with speed and decision in the shaping of her government; between the morrow of her accession and her coronation day, January 15th, the work was in large part accomplished. By then the Council and the greater household offices were all filled. The new queen made plain her principles of selection in a succinct statement of her views, presumably spoken shortly after her accession:

—and as I am but one body naturally considered although by His permission a body politic to govern, so I shall desire you all, my lords (chiefly you of the nobility, everyone in his degree and power) to be assistant to me that I with my ruling and you with your service may make a good account to Almighty God and leave some comfort to our posterity in earth. I mean to direct all my actions by good advice and counsel. And therefore considering that divers of you be of the ancient nobility, having your beginnings and estates of my progenitors, kings of this realm and thereby [such] ought in honour to have the more natural care for maintaining of my estate and this commonwealth. Some others have been of long experience in governance and enabled by my father of noble memory, my brother, and my late sister to bear office, the rest of you being upon special trust lately called of her service only and trust, for your service considered and rewarded ... And for counsel and advice I shall accept you of my nobility and such others of you the rest as in consultation I shall think meet and shortly appoint. To the which also with their advice I will join to their aid and for ease of their burden others, meet for my service. And they which I shall not appoint, let them not think the same for any disability in them but that for I do consider a multitude doth make rather discord and confusion than good counsel and of my good will you shall not doubt, using yourselves as appertaineth to good and faithful subjects.[1]

Acting consistently on these principles, Elizabeth went about making her choices. Her sister's Council, of nearly thirty members, had been, as the new queen hinted, large and unwieldy. About a third of them were peers; a dozen were either administrative officials or law officers of the Crown; and four were clerics. A half-dozen household officers served on the Council, nearly all personal adherents of Queen Mary at the time of her accession and a number of them East Anglian squires by origin. Of this whole body barely a third were normally in attendance at Council during the last years of the reign. The regular attenders were largely drawn from the official and household element, the least weighty politically. The greater political figures of the Marian court were conspicuous by their long absences or, at best, spasmodic attendance.[2]

Elizabeth was ruthless in her excisions from the Council list. Less than a third of the old queen's Councillors remained to serve the new. Among the peers the rate of survival was highest; six out of ten were retained. Of those who were dropped, two (Hastings of Loughborough and Montague) were Marian creations and lords known for their warm Catholic sympathies; a third (Rich) very rarely attended at any time (six recorded attendances in the entire reign). But the fourth dismissal – that of Lord Paget – was a major political event. Since the death of Bishop Gardiner in 1555, Paget had been the most active and forceful member of the Council, the centre of policy-making and decision. He was widely held responsible for English entry into the unlucky war with France.[3] His dismissal necessarily shattered the existing structure of power within the highest political circles.

Among the commoners on the Council the mortality rate was much higher; only four were continued in office by Elizabeth.* All these were officials; one of them (Cheyney, Treasurer of the Household and Warden of the Cinque Ports) died before the year was out. These changes meant the elimination from the Council of all the commoners who owed their preferment to the late queen. Virtually the same condition obtained among the peers. William, Lord Howard of Effingham, owed both title and seat at the Council board to Mary, and the Earl of Derby had come to the body at the beginning of her reign as one of her ardent supporters; however, he rarely attended. The remainder of these noblemen dated their service to the Crown from earlier reigns.

This core of Councillors whom Elizabeth chose to retain is worth close attention. They fall roughly into two groups, one 'political' and the other 'official' in tone. To the first order belonged the lords Arundel, Clinton and Pembroke – and, for somewhat different reasons, the Earls of Derby and Shrewsbury. All save Pembroke were magnates of the realm by birthright; entrance to high political place had been theirs for the asking; political consequence had had to be won, but at least the terms of contest were easier than for those of lower birth. These men were winners at the game of high politics; in the court they had reached the highest rung on

* A fifth, Sir John Baker, Chancellor of the Exchequer, retained this office but died in December 1558. There is no evidence that he was to remain a Privy Councillor.

the ladder of power; in the country they were regional magnates of wide influence.

Arundel, holder of one of the oldest extant titles, had played a great role in Henry's court and campaigns and held the office of Lord Chamberlain at the end of the old king's life.[4] Under Edward he fell out with Dudley and spent an uncomfortable interval in the Tower in some danger of his life; his early and vital support of Mary restored him to high place, and he had been a man of first importance in her court. Clinton, another lord of long descent, had inherited a decayed family fortune, but his first marriage, with the mother of Henry's bastard son, Richmond, had taken him into the Henrician court circle; his second had been to a niece of John Dudley. In the French and Scottish wars he had won fame as a commander, and under Edward obtained the office of Lord Admiral; this post was lost temporarily at the opening of Mary's reign but recovered in 1557. He had sat in Council since 1550.

Pembroke, on the other hand, was an *arriviste* and the only illiterate on the Council. Descendant, through an illegitimate branch, of the old earls of Pembroke, William Herbert had his fortune to make; he had fought his way up step by painful step in the savage competition of Henrician politics, married into the Parrs, and then under Edward acquired both title and great fortune. Probably the greatest single beneficiary of the spoliation of Crown and Church in that reign, he was now among the half-dozen richest men in England.[5] At Elizabeth's accession Herbert was busily engaged in the building up of a great family position in South Wales and in Wiltshire.

The combination of experience, prestige and personality in each of these lords gave them a first claim on the new queen's consideration, to which she was quick to respond. Clinton remained Admiral under a life patent; Arundel was retained as Steward;[6] Pembroke, though holding no office, remained a major figure in Council and a diligent attender there.

Two other peers of ancient lineage, Derby and Shrewsbury, were also continued. Neither was a courtier, but their importance in the political life of the realm was hardly less than that of the three lords discussed above. Talbot, Earl of Shrewsbury, born in 1500, had long service under the Tudors and since 1550 had been Lord President of the North as well as Lieutenant of Yorkshire, Lancashire, Cheshire, Derbyshire, Shropshire, Staffordshire and Nottinghamshire. From his seat at Sheffield Castle in the West Riding he presided over a great cluster of estates extending through the counties of Nottingham and Derby, which made him, next to the

Duke of Norfolk, the richest peer in the realm.[7] Across the Pennines, Stanley, Earl of Derby, enjoyed a regional eminence in Lancashire and Cheshire comparable to that of the Talbots. Although holding no major Crown office, Derby too was retained on the Council as a sleeping partner. Common sense recommended cordial relations with these great lords, who, though seldom seen at court, enjoyed pervading influence across their remote countrysides. Even though they did not choose to play a great part at the political centre, their passive goodwill was vital to the Crown. In ordinary times it was imperative for the routine governance of society. In times of stress their support might spell the difference between survival and destruction for the regime.

Of the other peers held over from the Marian Council, one, Howard, was a special case. Deputy of Calais under Edward, he was appointed Councillor and raised to the Lords by Mary, but he had been a staunch and powerful friend to the Princess Elizabeth in her hours of hardest trial after the Wyatt Rebellion.[8] He was also her great-uncle. On him she bestowed the office of Lord Chamberlain of the Household. Howard, quite in contrast to his noble colleagues, was a court peer, with a very modest estate (perhaps not much more than five hundred pounds a year), to whom his Chamberlain's fee of one hundred pounds a year with additional perquisites was a significant increase in income.[9]

The last of the Councillor-peers to note is Paulet, Marquess of Winchester. Another *arriviste*, he had, as a royal administrator, climbed a somewhat safer and easier path than Pembroke. By 1539 he was rewarded with a peerage; in 1550 he secured the treasurership. Safely riding through all the gales of the 1550s, he not only kept his office but advanced in the peerage to a marquessate. He was now a very old man, probably an octogenarian. Although his great house at Basingstoke in Hampshire and his estates there made him a county magnate (his son Chidiock was Governor of Portsmouth), he was engrossed in the major administrative reforms he was carrying through in the Treasury and should be classed among the bureaucrats rather than among the great peers of the Council. Elizabeth confirmed him in his office in January 1559.[10]

The remaining hold-over members fell in the same category of officials. Mason, Treasurer of the Chamber since the preceding year, had a long career behind him, dating back to the 1530s. Originally he had taken minor holy orders, but in the 1540s he followed the same road as others, and crossed over into secular life. After a hopeful start under Henry, his career was rapidly advanced under Edward and he became a Privy Councillor in 1550; he continued there under Mary, charged with numerous important diplomatic missions. The story of his colleague, Sir William Petre, was not very different: a cleric initially (but then the founder of a county family),[11] an administrator under Henry, and then Secretary for a decade under the old king, Somerset, Northumberland and Mary. He had resigned that post in 1557 but continued a Councillor. A self-effacing man, he was the very embodiment of a hard-working, politically neutral bureaucrat. Nicholas Wotton, the third hold-over, was in some ways a more old-fashioned figure; still a cleric, he was a notable pluralist, holding the deaneries of both York and Canterbury among other benefices. But for all practical purposes he was a lay servant of the Crown and for two decades — except for a brief tenure as Secretary under Edward — had been almost uninterruptedly engaged in diplomatic missions. Even more than Petre, Wotton, withdrawn from the hurly-burly of politics, was the specialist civil servant. Thus of the continuing Councillors all but Derby had held high office before Mary came to the throne and had been intimate in the high political circles of her father's time.

Elizabeth retained briefly one other Marian Councillor, Archbishop Heath, who resigned from the chancellorship at the accession but until the end of the year remained in the Council. Her new appointments began with the first recorded Council of the reign, at Hatfield on November 20th, and were almost complete by Christmas. Two peers were added: Francis, second Earl of Bedford, and William Parr, newly restored Marquess of Northampton. Bedford had succeeded his father (a major political figure for several decades) only three years earlier and was well known as the most outspoken Protestant in the peerage. Parr, who had lost his title in 1553 for his support of Lady Jane Grey, was brother to Henry's last queen and brother-in-law to Pembroke. The commoners now appointed included the husbands of two cousins of Elizabeth on the Boleyn side. Sir Richard Sackville had been Chancellor of the Court of Augmentations until 1553. His career had been checked by Mary's accession, although he was able to salvage a handsome pension for his now extinct office; from early in the new year 1559 he was Under-Treasurer of England. A second cousin by marriage, Sir Francis Knollys, returned from exile in Protestant Strasbourg in January. Another new Councillor was Elizabeth's long-time steward, Sir Thomas Parry, now Treasurer of her Household. Sir Edward Rogers, a Somerset squire and Gentleman of the Privy Chamber to King Edward, was appointed to Council and Household (as Comptroller). Another country gentleman — but one without previous experience at court—was Sir Ambrose Cave, a Warwick-Leicestershire squire and a connection of Cecil's. He sat in the first Council on November 18th and a month later became Chancellor of the Duchy of Lancaster in place of the Marian Councillor, Waldegrave.* As Secretary the queen on the first day of her reign had chosen Sir William Cecil; to succeed Heath in the Chancellor's office she nominated the new Secretary's brother-in-law, Sir Nicholas Bacon, hitherto Attorney of the Court of Wards. This made a total of under twenty members, barely two-thirds the size of Mary's Council.

Several features of Elizabeth's new appointments catch the eye. First of all, far from being 'new men' in the world of government, they were almost without exception old hands. Two had moved in the highest ranges of politics; Cecil was returning to the post he had held in Edward's time, Northampton had been a Councillor and Chamberlain in that court. The others had not been quite so close to the centre of power. Rogers's service had made him intimate with Edward's inner court; Bedford had been important enough in that world to receive a special summons to the Lords in his father's lifetime and had been among the witnesses to the king's will. Knollys, son of a courtier of Henry VII, had himself served in Henry VIII's court and his son's, been knighted for service in Scotland, and been an intimate of the Edwardian Household. Bacon and Sackville, although ranking bureaucrats in two fiscal departments, had been outside the court circle itself. Sir Ambrose Cave was the only new Councillor who was a complete neophyte to high politics; once a Knight Hospitaller, he had retired on his pension at the Dissolution, to his native Leicestershire, there to flourish as sheriff, J.P. and knight of the shire in Parliament.

In age these lords and gentlemen were all considerably senior to their twenty-five-year-old sovereign lady. The youngest, William Cecil, born in 1520, was thirteen years older than his mistress, while among his colleagues no more than three or four were under fifty—in the sixteenth century the beginning of old age.† They were a very well-educated group;

* There was a re-shuffling of Household posts in early 1559. After the death of Cheyney, Parry succeeded to his office as Treasurer of the Household; Rogers replaced Parry as Comptroller; and Knollys replaced Rogers as Vice-Chamberlain. For Cave, see R. Somerville, *History of the Duchy of Lancaster* (Duchy of Lancaster Office, London, 1953), 395, under date December 22nd, 1558.

† This calculation excludes Parry, whose birth date is unknown, but since he was Clerk of the Peace in Gloucestershire in 1534 (*Letters and Papers, Henry VIII*, xx [2] [London, 1891], 82) he must have been born *c.* 1510. I owe this information to Miss Norah Fuidge of the History of Parliament Trust.

probably for the first time in English history, the queen's Council was dominated by university-trained laymen, products in large part of the new traditions of Renaissance humanist education. With the dubious exception of Wotton, not a single functioning cleric remained; several had begun a clerical career only to shift over in mid-course to the lay world. But the completely lay character of the Council marked the abrupt end of an age-old tradition in English government service.

In the circle around the queen there was a web of family groupings. The queen's own cousinage had two branches; one, the Boleyns, included Sackville and Knollys, both married to nieces of Anne Boleyn, and the new Master of the Wardrobe, John Fortescue, was a remoter cousin on this side—and also stepson to Mr Treasurer Parry. The vast Howard network (Elizabeth's grandmother was a Howard) was most directly represented by Lord William, the queen's great-uncle. The head of the family, the first peer of the realm, the Duke of Norfolk, was not yet a royal servant, except in his ceremonial capacity as Earl Marshal, but the Lord Deputy of Ireland, the Earl of Sussex, was a member of this clan through his mother. Arundel's deceased daughter had been Norfolk's first wife and mother to his heir. A more shadowy royal connection was that of the Parrs; Northampton was brother to Henry's last queen; Pembroke had married her younger sister.

A less aristocratic but more intellectually distinguished family was that of the Cookes. The father, Sir Anthony, was tutor to Edward VI and in exile at Strasbourg in the next reign; he was now member for Essex in Elizabeth's first Parliament. Two of his sons-in-law, Cecil and Bacon, sat in the new Council. The Dudley connection was not yet represented on the Council, but was well established in the court. The two sons of the late Duke of Northumberland, whose plot against Mary's succession had shaken the Tudor throne, were members of the Household—Robert as Master of the Horse and Ambrose as Master of Ordnance. Their sister's husband, Sir Henry Sidney, was shortly to be President of Wales; his sister was in turn married to Lord Sussex, the Irish Deputy. Family alliance did not necessarily mean political alliance, but these tangled genealogies serve to emphasize the tight-knit and rather ingrown nature of the high political world. The Elizabethan court was a small and very nearly a closed corporation.

In the middle of January the queen's dispositions were pretty much complete not only in Council but also in Household. A comparison between the coronation list of Elizabeth's Household and the funeral list of

Mary's reveals how much change had taken place since the accession.[12] At the top level there had been almost wholesale replacement; only Mason, Treasurer of the Chamber, was a hold-over from the previous reign. At the next level, among those who were the queen's regular personal attendants – gentlemen of the Privy Chamber, grooms, ushers and waiters – the turnover seems also to have been high; out of a total of some fifty in this category only a scattering of about a dozen survived from the preceding reign. In the 'private' offices of the Household, on the contrary, the continuity of personnel is marked. These civil servants, semi-professionals, continued to carry on the fixed routines of the domestic departments without break or pause. Similarly in the 'public' offices, the Signet, Privy Seal, and Council secretariat, almost all of the clerks were carried over into the new reign. Among the ladies attendant upon the queen, there was naturally a wholesale sweep; in the place of the Catholic ladies Wharton, Waldegrave, Cornwallis, Babington, Dormer and Southwell, there appeared the new queen's cousins, the ladies Knollys, Ashley and Cary, and the wives and daughters of the new courtiers, the ladies Cecil, Throckmorton, Warner, Benger, Cheke and others.

Outside the palace circle of great officers and courtiers there were additional changes. That key office, the Mastership of the Wards, passed from the hands of a loyal Catholic, Sir Francis Englefield, to those of Sir Thomas Parry; Sir Richard Southwell (a Marian Councillor) was removed from the Ordnance (although with a pension) to make way for Lord Ambrose Dudley, eldest son of the late Northumberland. Sir Walter Mildmay, a second-generation official in Augmentations and a close friend of Cecil, became Chancellor of the Exchequer in succession to the late Sir John Baker. Lord Cobham, a Kentish magnate, who had been in serious trouble during Wyatt's Rebellion, succeeded to the wardenry of the Cinque Ports on the death of Cheyney in December.[13] Away from the centre changes were fewer. Bishop Bourne was replaced as Lord President of the Marches of Wales by the ailing Lord Williams of Thame, an old civil servant, once an officer of Augmentations; ennobled by Mary, his claim on Elizabeth's favour may have been his gentle treatment of her during her detention in his house in 1554.[14] He died in October 1559, to be replaced after an interval by Sir Henry Sidney, brother-in-law to the Dudleys. The other great presidency, that of the North, remained in the hands of the incumbent, Lord Shrewsbury. Some changes in the Council at York, made at the opening of the reign, introduced several government officials into that body, but the real shift in power came with the commencement of hostilities on the Borders late in 1559.[15]

Noailles, the French ambassador, returning to London after an absence of several years, querulously complained that he hardly knew how to find his way about.[16] Certainly the immediate reshuffling of personnel had made great changes; yet, in fact, as has been suggested, there was more continuity than change, all things considered. The men called to service by the queen might be sorted into three general categories, the first consisting of those civil servants, skilled specialists, and political neuters whose careers had been unaffected by the convulsions of the past decade. A second was that of the active politicians who had been skilful enough to avoid losing their footing in the slippery scramble of those years. Finally, there were their less fortunate fellows whose advancement had been checked in mid-flight by the Marian regime and who were now able to resume their pursuit of political fortune. All three groups were comprised almost entirely of men who had already secured a foothold in the political arena under Henry or his son. In fact, they were in many cases second- or even third-generation servants of the Tudor Crown. To note only a few instances (putting those hereditary politicians, the peers, aside), three generations of Cecils, of Dudleys, and of Sidneys, and two of Knollys, Parrs, and Mildmays had served as many generations of Tudors.

Indeed, in the Elizabethan court it is the absence of newcomers which really catches the eye. A shrewd observer might have sensed a closing of the gates of political opportunity, a contracting process which was transforming the expansive, albeit dangerous, political world of Henry's time. The new queen's judicious choice of tried men and familiar faces was a pointer towards an era in which there would be less scope for new men or for the pursuit of bold personal ambitions, but a quieter life for those who by talent or by birth had slipped within the gates in time.

What was also evident was the strong anti-Marian cast of the court. Among the Councillors, Parr had lost his title in Lady Jane's cause; Rogers had gone to the Tower for his role in Wyatt's rebellion; so had the new Warden of the Cinque Ports. Sir Edward Warner, restored Lieutenant of the Tower; Sir Ralph Hopton, restored Knight Marshal of the Household; Sir William St Lo, now Captain of the Guard; Sir James Croft, Captain of Berwick; Sir Thomas Cawarden, Master of the Revels; and Cuthbert Vaughan, soon appointed to a command on the Borders, had been conspicuous in open opposition to Mary's government.[17] The Carewes of Devon, who had fled to France for their share in Wyatt's plots, were now

in favour and service again.* Sir Nicholas Throckmorton, whose trial for
treason (and acquittal) had been a *cause célèbre* in 1554, was now ambassador
at Paris. Last but not least, the two surviving sons of the arch-conspirator
himself, John Dudley, were almost immediately preferred to posts of trust,
Robert as Master of the Horse and Ambrose as Master of the Ordnance.

The religious tone of the new court was of course in sharp contrast to
Mary's. The committed Catholics of the former reign had disappeared to
a man. Yet the tone of the new establishment was initially more anti-
Catholic than positively Protestant. At the top level only Knollys, who
had gone into exile, and Bedford, who, after a brief imprisonment in
1553, had spent a winter in the bracing Protestant air of Zurich, were
outspoken adherents of the new faith. Among the rest there were none
who had sacrificed political opportunity for the sake of religion. Most of
those who had been involved in Wyatt's revolt had later made terms with
the regime and some had served it, often in positions of confidence. Whatever commitment they had had to the reformed religion had not been
allowed to stand in the way of political advancement. The keynote of the
new court was a political rather than an evangelical Protestantism, in
which hostility to the old faith and the regime which had promoted it was
as potent an ingredient as enthusiasm for the Gospel.

The queen had made her choices; it is instructive to compare them with
a list of proposed appointments made up by Sir Nicholas Throckmorton.[18] That such a list should be tendered by a mere subject to a Tudor
monarch is in itself cause for astonishment. But Throckmorton was irre-
pressible; under Mary he had by his own skilful defence cajoled a London
jury into acquitting him of treason, to the anger of the government. He
was a leading spirit among those most hostile to the old religion and its
political order, and his dispositions were much coloured by the hopes and
sympathies of that camp. He and his radical friends had much cause for
satisfaction when the royal appointments were complete. Throckmorton
had had the grace to offer the queen options, usually three or four, for
each post. The queen's choice of Lord Steward, Lord Chamberlain, Vice-
Chamberlain, Treasurer of the Household, and Secretary had fallen in each
case on one of Throckmorton's nominees. For the chancellorship she had
preferred Bacon to anyone on Sir Nicholas's list, but the new Lord Keeper

---

* George Carewe, the clerical member of the family, now had the Deanery of Windsor,
lately held by Mary's Secretary, Boxall (*CPR, 1558-60*, 339). Peter Carewe was employed
in the Scottish campaign and had a licence to import and export beer contrary to statute
(*CPR, 1560-63*, 1); Gawain Carewe was at least nominally a member of the Household
(PRO, LC 2/4/3).

had been included among those suggested for the mastership of the Rolls. Every new member of the Council appeared somewhere on the list. And of those rejected by the monarch for the specific posts proposed, many were chosen for other positions in her service. Randolph, put forward to be Clerk of the Council, was instead soon to be made Ambassador to Scotland. Sackville, suggested for the Rolls, became Under-Treasurer, and Cave, named for the treasurership, went to the Duchy of Lancaster. The great majority of those on Throckmorton's lists found some kind of post in the royal service, including, of course, the author himself in the embassy at Paris.

All this hints at the implicit limits which surrounded the queen's choices. The new establishment was in an important sense a partisan one. Its members were, of course, partisans of the new queen; but, more than that, they formed a party because of a common outlook on the political world and common association for loosely defined but clearly understood ends. Ever so slightly, the Crown had had to yield its freedom of choice on a vital decision and to accept a body of servants who were drawn together not solely by loyalty to the monarch but also by common political purposes that looked beyond the immediate interests of the sovereign.

Observers were watching not only for the queen's official decisions but also for her personal preferences in her choice of intimates. The figure of the favourite, singled out by the monarch for personal reasons, was a common enough phenomenon in late medieval and Renaissance monarchy. Such a person could be of major political importance or of none at all. In recent English history the politically significant favourite was infrequent. Henry VIII had showered a ducal title, honours, and wealth on Charles Brandon and even accepted him as brother-in-law, but there is little evidence that the Duke of Suffolk ever played a large role in serious matters of state. Edward was too young to have politically effective favourites; Mary concentrated her affections on her husband.

Elizabeth came to the throne without a known favourite; the scattering guesses as to a possible husband indicated that no man's name had been especially associated with hers. Robert Dudley seems not to have attracted attention before her accession, and he does not appear on Throckmorton's list, but in Cecil's notes of November 18th Lord Robert appears as Master of the Horse among the very first appointments of the reign.[19] In the next few months, he cut only a modest figure. Favour was granted to his older brother Ambrose by his appointment to the Ordnance, but Robert (aside from the high personal distinction of the Garter) received only secondary assignments (mostly commissions for minor purposes), some grants of land, and one licence to export wool. It was not until a year later, in November 1559, that he was appointed Lieutenant of Windsor Castle.[20] The full significance of the preference shown him was not to emerge until the second summer of the new reign.

Other than Dudley, the direct beneficiaries of the queen's favour were few. The creation of peers at her coronation was on a limited scale. Parr of Northampton was restored to his marquessate and given a grant of lands worth five hundred pounds a year.[21] Seymour's son was restored to the earldom of Hertford (but not to the Protector's dukedom of Somerset). Three new peers were created, St John of Bletso (Bedford's brother-in-law and Edwardian courtier), Howard of Bindon and Henry Cary, promoted to be Baron Hunsdon. The latter two were cousins of the queen; Hunsdon, nephew of Queen Anne Boleyn; Bindon the younger brother of the Earl of Surrey and thus first cousin to the queen; their promotions, like the appointments of Knollys and Sackville, were tokens of the queen's cordial but not extravagant regard for her mother's connections.

Taken all in all, Elizabeth's choices displayed a strong political common sense. She had drawn around her a solid bloc of her own adherents, but she had matched them with an equal number of experienced hands, both politicians and civil servants, who had served impartially each member of the dynasty in turn. The great regional lords of the North were given their due; so was Bedford in the West, Pembroke in South Wales and Arundel in Sussex. Norfolk, the greatest peer of all, was still without a post, other than his hereditary office as Earl Marshal, but he was young and inexperienced and had not served in any official capacity under the late regime either. Only two significant groups were clearly outside the circle of royal favour — the Catholic clergy, now excluded from any high post in government, and those laymen ardently and publicly sympathetic to the old faith.

3 The Opening Months

THE CORONATION past, the pause in English and in international affairs occasioned by Mary's death and Elizabeth's accession came to an end. The queen and her ministers had now to turn to the grave issues pending both at home and abroad. At Westminster the first Parliament of the new reign was about to gather and, at almost the same time, the adjourned peace conference at Cateau-Cambrésis, where English, French and Spanish delegates were met to re-establish peace in Europe, resumed its sessions.

The commissioners in Flanders had to deal with a piece of unfinished business left over from the last reign: the unpopular and unsuccessful war into which England had been drawn by Philip's insistence and with his doting wife's compliance. In 1557 there had been a brief spurt of glory when Englishmen shared in the Spanish victory at St Quentin, but in January 1558 England had suffered swift and agonizing defeat; in little more than a week Edward III's prize, the fortress seaport of Calais, springboard of English action in European politics and the last valued fragment of past empire, was snatched away by the French army. In their pained unreason Englishmen talked of treason in the English command at Calais, ready to grasp at any excuse which might gloss over the extent of English humiliation.

The negotiations at Cateau-Cambrésis marked an important stage in the secular struggle between Habsburg and Valois, but for the English commissioners the issues were all too dismayingly simple. Their task was to cut England's losses and to withdraw with what little dignity was possible under such circumstances. At home most advisors would have agreed with the veteran Councillor, Mason, who wrote to Cecil on November 20th that the 'first and principal point is to think upon the peace', and went on to urge that it was idle to 'stick upon Calais as though we had the Frenchmen at commandment'. A better way would be 'to conclude a peace *si non optimis conditionibus* neither of such agreement as we desire, yet by *mediocribus* and by such as we can get'. Mason felt there should be plain speaking with King Philip, who was to be told that 'our state can no longer bear these wars'. Indeed, he was prepared to accept a peace which made no mention of Calais.[1]

Englishmen might agree on these goals; Philip of Spain had no quarrel with them, since he was anxious to bring hostilities to a close; but the awkward question was what stance France would take. The Dauphin Francis and his wife Mary were the titular sovereigns of Scotland, and her mother, backed by French forces, regent of that realm. Worse still, Mary Stuart, as a descendant of Henry VIII's elder sister, was a claimant to the English throne—in Catholic eyes, the legitimate ruler. In the weeks immediately after Elizabeth's accession, rumours floated about both in the Low Countries and in Rome that France would seek to push Mary's claims.[2]

Actually Henry II of France was more anxious for peace than for a war to seat his daughter-in-law on the English throne, and through private and unofficial channels he made overtures to Elizabeth. His hope was to sow distrust between the English and Spanish allies; hers, to play off the continental powers one against the other and thus to free England from dependence on either.[3] Officially the English delegation, now headed by the veteran courtier, Howard, fluent in French and personally acquainted with the leading French delegate, the Constable Montmorency, was told to stand firm. It soon became clear that while Spain would make no effort to recover Calais, she would not abandon the English to threats of French aggression. Under these conditions the English soon accepted a face-saving formula put forward by the French. Calais was to remain in French hands for eight years; at the end of that term, France was to yield the port or else pay an indemnity. The Council were unanimous in urging the queen to accept this solution.[4]

Details were worked out fairly quickly, but in the last stages of the negotiations their course was deflected for a few days by a flash of royal anger.[5] The Spaniards were still dealing directly with the French and passing proposals between them and the English. In discussions about one particular clause Philip's commissioners reported a question raised by the French. What was the meaning of their obligation to the Crown of England when it was so uncertain who was rightful possessor of that Crown? The question was apparently raised as a legal speculation rather than as a diplomatic ploy and was not exploited by the French. It was against her own agents rather than the French government that the queen directed her wrath.

The English commissioners had dealt with it as a legal problem, discussed its bearings, and referred their doubts to England. The queen's answer was short and harsh. Whatever the ministers of other Crowns might say, she was deeply displeased that her own servants would allow others so to speak 'without due reprehension or misliking' or that they should be so foolish as to ask her pleasure in a matter 'which might have been performed by any of you, that we may nor ever will permit any over whom we have rule or may have to make doubt, question, or treaty of this matter'. Mason afterwards reported, with a courtier's exaggeration, that the recipients of this rebuke would carry its marks to the grave. The unlucky commissioners had touched on a raw nerve of their new mistress. The very fact that a shadow actually did hang over her title made Elizabeth doubly determined to assert her dignity, her authority and her royalty. Her flaring anger was a token that, though a woman, the new ruler had inherited the forceful and dominating personality of her father. She would not hesitate to use it as a weapon in her struggle to impose her female sovereignty on a masculine world.

By March 22nd the queen could write of the treaty as settled. It was clear gain to have this unfinished business settled, however harsh the treaty's terms. At least the government could claim to have made a dignified retreat from a disaster not of its making. For the time being English relations with the two great continental powers were stabilized without England's being closely tied to either. Nevertheless, the rapprochement between France and Spain which followed Cateau-Cambrésis troubled the English leaders. They saw in it the possibility of united action by the two Catholic governments against the Protestant cause; indeed, in these months were sown the seeds of a conviction which was to flourish vigorously and long—the belief in an international Catholic plot to launch a general crusade against the heretic world. In that vast intrigue the French ducal house of Guise (of which Mary Stuart was a member through her mother), the Habsburgs and the pope were cast in the key roles.

The meeting of Parliament presented the new government with issues both novel and awkward. It was the first confrontation of the new sovereign with the nobles and gentry of England mobilized in Parliament. That relationship was an ancient one, but the terms on which they met in 1559 were disturbingly uncertain and full of only half-defined novelties. In her grandfather's time, a meeting of Parliament hardly ruffled the rhythms of political life. Nor were matters much different under the second Tudor, although in the 1520s Commons had been ominously

restive when Wolsey sought to alter the accepted conventions of the tax-
ing process. In the 1530s the two houses had been generally willing accom-
plices of the king in his revolutionary attack on the ancient religious order.
But appetite comes with eating, and after the years of extraordinary activity
under Henry, Commons showed a disconcerting wilfulness before which
the hesitant and ill-guided governments of Edward VI and Mary had had
to retreat. In the latter reign Commons had, in effect, driven a bargain
with the Crown over the vital question of monastic lands.

Underlying these surface manifestations were subterranean shifts in
political geology. The great transactions of state which had opened with
the statutes of the Reformation Parliament were working an obscure and
but dimly understood revolution in politics. Henry's pursuit of his 'great
cause' had two far-reaching consequences. It drew Englishmen, who had
hitherto felt only the outer eddies of the religious maelstrom, fully into
the soul-shaking debates of the Reformation. Secondly — a less visible process — there was the emergence of Parliament as a major integer in national
politics. A third stage, the fusion of religious and constitutional unrest, lay
largely in the future.

As early as 1539 a bemused Henry VIII had discovered the political
dangers inherent in religious innovation and had tried to clamp the lid
back on Pandora's box through his Act to end diversity in religious
opinion. After the old king's death the sanguine men who ruled England
in his place welcomed discussion and encouraged diversity, and religious
uniformity was shattered beyond repair. By the end of the 1550s the
initiative in religious matters was no longer fully within the grasp of the
Crown. The nature of right religion had become a matter of conscience
for individual Englishmen and a political problem for the whole nation.
And in this very process the nature of politics was rapidly changing. The
articulate nucleus of ardent supporters of the new faith, a minority in the
nation, but now strongly represented among the gentry, in many towns
and in the new court, formed a loosely defined movement of men firmly
resolved to see another religious revolution when Parliament met. Its
more ebullient members regarded Mary's death and Elizabeth's accession
as nothing less than a sign of Providential intervention and hailed the new
monarch as England's Deborah.[6] The new queen herself gave unequivocal
hints as to the general course she proposed to follow — by her choice of
advisors, her preference in preachers, her withdrawal from the Christmas
mass at the elevation of the host, to cite but a few instances. But the precise
shape of the new religious order remained a matter for intense speculation.

The new government confronted a novel and rather baffling set of circumstances. For the first time an English government had to deal with an organized movement of public opinion which sought to achieve an ideological revolution, and whose impulses to action came not from the Crown—as in the 1530s—but from powerful elements within the country. While sympathetic to a change, the leaders of the government were uneasily uncertain about their relations with this unorthodox political force and, at the same time, nervous as to the extent of a determined Catholic opposition.

At least four formal statements of advice on these great questions were addressed to the queen at the beginning of the reign.[7] The very fact that private citizens were offering unsolicited advice to the Crown is a matter for astonishment and another token of the growth of an informed, sophisticated and partisan interest in high politics outside the immediate entourage of the sovereign. We may regard them as among the earliest efforts in English political history at assessing the state of public opinion. The busy Throckmorton, in his advice on appointments, had promised a second instalment to deal with policy matters. The other self-appointed counsellors, less eminent and less bold, confined themselves to more general problems of state. All these statements were composed by writers of a Protestant bent of mind, yet all agreed on one thing: all urged the greatest caution in making changes in religion. Throckmorton suggested continuing Mary's Council in office for the time being, although Goodrich, a left-wing Protestant lawyer, counselled active measures against both clerical and lay dignitaries of Catholic persuasion. In any case these men clearly envisaged the probability of Catholic resistance to the new regime if it attempted to interfere with the existing Roman order. Bishops, Privy Councillors, J.P.s and prospective members of Parliament needed to be watched and, if necessary, checked in hostile action. The anonymous author of the paper called 'The device for the alteration of religion' was clear-sighted enough to suggest danger from the other extreme also, from those 'who could be content to have religion altered but would have it go too far'. They, seeing 'that some old ceremonies shall be left still or that their doctrine which they embrace is not allowed and commanded only, and all other abolished and disproved, shall be discontented and call the alteration a cloaked Papistry or a mingle mangle'. Amidst these cloudy uncertainties the new government sought to find its way.

With the meeting of Parliament there could be no further hesitation; the queen must take her measures and show her hand fully. The writs for

Parliament had gone out on December 5th; summoned for January 23rd, it actually began to sit two days later. Whether or not it was packed by the government was once a subject of great contention, since Catholic historians believed that it had been. It now seems that there was pretty clearly no packing in the grossest sense of that term; indeed, the Council seems not to have sent out the circular letters used by the late government to encourage the election of suitable members. Nevertheless, there was careful management by the new government. A Tudor House of Commons was of course not a politically organized body in the modern sense; the Crown and its Councillors thought not in terms of mustering a majority but of providing an official nucleus to serve as a strong pole around which, particle-like, individual members would cluster. Lately, in the Marian House of 1555 a counter-pole had appeared, an embryonic 'opposition' which had embarrassed the Crown and on one or two vital issues checked the royal will. Elizabeth's government was resolved to avoid such an embarrassment.

In the 1559 House the official nucleus was a strong one; all the commoners in the Privy Council sat, all but one dignified by the prestige of a county constituency. Petre, Mason, Cave and Rogers had sat in the Marian Parliament of 1558 for Essex, Hampshire, Warwickshire and Somerset respectively.[8] Cecil and Parry now joined them as knights for Lincolnshire and Hertfordshire. (Sir Francis Knollys, returning late from the Continent, was accommodated, presumably by the Earl of Arundel, in the borough seat of Arundel.) The Councillors were afforced by a sprinkling of high officials, like Mildmay, Chancellor of the Exchequer, or Gargrave, Vice-President of the Council of the North (shortly to be Speaker). The Councillors were the Crown's direct spokesmen in the Commons, but there was another more or less official element, consisting of at least fifty to sixty courtiers and royal officials, holding seats and including, among others, Robert Dudley, as county member for Norfolk. Many of these recently appointed place-men had not sat in the last Commons of Mary's reign and their appearance in the new House was obviously not fortuitous. They were a bloc on which the Councillors could normally count as responsive to direction from above.

Outside these 'government' supporters one could detect some vaguer, but distinguishable, groupings in the House. The Parliamentary patronage of magnates was no curiosity in the sixteenth century. In this particular Parliament two noblemen certainly exercised such influence on some scale. The Duke of Norfolk enjoyed immense prestige in two areas, in the smaller Norfolk boroughs and in a second group of Sussex seats, where Howard influence was a matter of tradition. The Earl of Bedford[9] doubt-less had to make a more conscious and deliberate effort to exploit the newly founded eminence of the Russells in the West, but he was strikingly successful. Other peers had lesser spheres of operation. Arundel could find seats for both Francis Knollys and for the courtier Thomas Heneage in his home borough; it is hardly surprising to find a Paget sitting for Lichfield or a Hastings for Leicester, since these towns were dominated by Lord Paget and the Earl of Huntingdon. Around every luminary in the counties was a penumbra of younger brothers, sons, or family dependants who would follow their patron's lead. In the 1559 House, the government had cause for cheer since the important borough-patron, Bedford, was a Councillor, while his colleague at that board, Arundel, exercised strong influence over his son-in-law of Norfolk. It needs to be reiterated that power was not to be reckoned in this setting by the counting of heads but by the weighing of influence. A Crown which enjoyed the active loyalty of the weightier members of the aristocracy could be assured of the sup-port of the lesser satellites.

The important thing was to be certain that no alternative pole of attrac-tion existed, as it had in the 1555 House. Elizabeth's ministers had considered this matter, for one striking fact about the new House was the absence of all the leading Marian Councillors from the seats they had filled a year earlier. We cannot tell what form intervention against these gentlemen took; discreet backing for an opponent – the mere fact of a royal appoint-ment – would have weighed heavily enough with the leaders of county opinion. Catholics were certainly not excluded; Dr John Story, soon to be an exile and later a martyr for his faith, sat for the Wiltshire borough of Downton. But, more to the point, the men who might have led at least a delaying action for the old faith were conspicuously absent, almost certainly by the deliberate pleasure of the Crown.

Was there, on the other side, an organized Protestant faction within the House? The record is too sparse for a satisfactory answer to be given. There were plenty of ardent backers of the new faith present. Bedford had exerted his regional influence with the clear intention of bringing up to Westminster a corps of like-minded Gospellers. Essex was represented (in the place of the Catholic Councillor Waldegrave) by Sir Anthony Cooke, barely returned from Strasbourg. Vice-Chamberlain Knollys was an even more eminent representative of the exiles. And looking to the future one notes a substantial number of names soon to be famous among the Puritan protagonists of later Parliaments – Francis Walsingham, Paul Wentworth, William Strickland and a handful of the famous 'choir' of the 1563 House were already sitting in 1559. Left-wing Protestants were numerously and strongly represented, but unluckily we do not possess the evidence to tell the full story of their actions in this first Parliament of the reign.

The actual events in this Parliament, whose work was to remain so fate-fully enduring, are and must always remain tantalizingly obscure. Of late much light has been shed by the persuasive and brilliant arguments of Sir John Neale, and it is his general interpretation of events that is fol-lowed here.[10]

According to this reconstruction, the Parliament falls into two distinct periods – the first lasting from the opening session on January 25th to Easter (late in March), the second running through April up to adjourn-ment on May 8th. During the first interval the Crown brought forward its ecclesiastical legislation, a cautious programme aimed merely at restor-ing the royal supremacy and turning the clock back to where it stood at King Henry's death. An additional bill, authorizing communion in both kinds, which remains embedded in the final act, was probably intended originally as a stop-gap measure to bridge over the interval until an act of uniformity could be brought forward in a second session of Parliament. Neale argues that this act of uniformity would have been built around the semi-Catholic First Prayer Book of Edward VI.

This official programme was attacked on both sides. In the Commons independent action was taken by the leaders of the reform party, who early brought forward their own proposals for liturgical change and then went on to amend the government's supremacy bill to include an Act of uniformity which embraced the radically Protestant Second Book of 1552. These amendments foundered in the Upper House, where the bishops, with some lay supporters, were opposed not only to these but to all changes. The bulk of the lay lords were docilely prepared to go along with the government's original intentions and sent back to Commons the simple Act of supremacy first put forward. The Commons gave grudging approval and it was this act the queen was about to sign when, dramati-cally, over Easter week-end (March 25th–26th), she changed, or was persuaded to change, her mind.

Official settlement of the peace was now completed at Cateau-Cambrésis, which meant that France had accepted, at least for the time being, the new English regime. The queen, no longer threatened by foreign intervention, could take larger risks. She could also assess a home situation which was a good deal clearer than at the beginning of the year. On the one hand was the evident strength, determination and organization of the reform party. Even after their first failure to bring in radical liturgical change, they had pushed through Commons a second measure which would in effect have tolerated Protestant nonconformity. It seems certain that it was the reformed party leaders rather than the Privy Councillors who dominated the House on the issue of religion. True, they had failed, as their successors were to fail in future Parliaments, in their efforts to force the Crown's hand. But the queen's situation was a very difficult one. She had not only to deal with recalcitrant left-wingers pushing her along the road away from Rome but also with a united right-wing refusal to go even one step with her on that road. From the beginning Elizabeth probably had few illusions about the compliance of the whole episcopate, but, looking at the records of some of the incumbents, she might reasonably have hoped to gain at least part of them. Heath, after all, had stuck to his see under Edward until 1551; Thirlby, promoted from Westminster to Norwich in 1550, had served through the whole reign; Tunstall at Durham had held his see up to the very last period of the reign. Most of them had in the earlier stages of their careers accepted the royal supremacy of Henry VIII. Perhaps with a conservative liturgy to salve their consciences, some might do so again.

Their behaviour in Parliament revealed both the strength and weakness of the episcopate. They could not follow the path of their Henrician predecessors; the hazy spectrum of religious colours of the 1530s was now pretty well resolved, by the whole course of events, into two sharply contrasting shades. The speeches of Bishop Scot and Abbot Feckenham set forth a strong and clear-cut doctrine of the pope's Petrine supremacy.[11] Nevertheless, the bulk of the Marian episcopate were men reared in the service of the Tudor monarchy and deeply rooted in habits of obedience and loyalty. Hence, although they would not vote for the new order in the Lords, nor deviate from Roman orthodoxy in the Chapel Royal or in the coronation mass, they would also take no lead in active resistance or disloyalty. They were content with a passive refusal to approve the new order.

Nor did there emerge an organized lay Catholic resistance to the new measures. Lay Protestant leaders co-operated closely with the reformed clerics now pouring back from the Continent or emerging from retirement. But the potential lay leaders of a Catholic opposition, such as Lord Montague, contented themselves with discharging their consciences by

4

a vote against the uniformity bill in the Lords.[12] They too were mostly long-time servants of the Tudors and too well-disciplined to break with the habits of a lifetime. The contrast with the Protestant leadership is sharp and clear. Where the latter were quick to take the initiative, swift to organize and bold in pushing their views, the Catholics were passive, tied to old habits of obedience to the Crown, conservative and cautious in all their reactions. Only one major lay member of the late government, Sir Francis Englefield, was prepared to make even the sacrifice of exile (self-imposed in his case). No one else was ready to take any risks at this point. Whatever their interior discomforts the nobles and gentry who had backed Mary's ardent Catholicism supinely accepted a series of measures, legislative and executive, which overthrew the old religion in every essential aspect.

Hence it was that the queen found the Catholic opposition, the source of so much nervous apprehension a short time ago, in fact little to be feared. Nevertheless, the unbroken opposition of the episcopate meant she would have to turn out the incumbents and to re-staff the whole upper ranks of the Church. Since a Protestant establishment would necessarily draw its bishops from leaders who had been in exile or were sympathetic to the exiles' views, the queen had little bargaining power as to the religious orientation of the new establishment. Whatever her personal preferences, she had to meet the reformed party at the furthest point they were willing to go, that is, the Second Book of Edward VI.

This is, of course, assumption – unprovable, but a reasonable guess. All we know is that after Easter there was first a rigged colloquy on questions of liturgical change, managed in such a way as to humiliate the Catholic bishops. This was followed by a new government bill of supremacy (with the queen's title changed from Supreme Head to Supreme Governor) and a new bill of uniformity containing the Second Book of 1552. It was unaltered except in two famous passages – the Words of Administration and the 'kneeling' rubric. Just how these changes came about is a mystery. But what is clear is that the liturgy now established by law was a radically Protestant one – not so radical as zealous Genevans might hope, but well to the left in its position on the central issues which divided Protestant and Roman Catholic. When the settlement of 1559 came under attack from the Protestant left it was not for doctrinal deficiencies, but for its retention of Roman ceremonial observances. The Book of Common Prayer of 1559 placed the English Church squarely among those of the Reformation tradition.

This in turn powerfully affected the pattern of English politics, for every political question, foreign or domestic, would henceforth be shaped by this central fact. Already, enthusiasts anticipated further reform at home and looked to the queen as the champion of an international Protestant cause. Men already took for granted the new regime's political alignment with the causes of the new faith. It was a decision from which there was no turning back. For it was a choice made not, as in the 1530s, by the sovereign alone, obediently followed by a docile realm. In 1559 the queen was backed in her decision by an enthusiastic party of radical Protestants, rooted in the aristocratic classes, strongly represented at court, and not hesitant in prodding the queen farther along the road of change than she would of her own will have travelled. The sovereign, willy-nilly, found herself in alliance with a party of her subjects. On most great matters her interests and theirs coincided, but where opinion as to action differed, they were not backward in expressing their views or in urging them upon the monarch. Thirty years earlier Henry by his own wilful act had set in motion the machinery of religious revolution. His daughter's religious settlement, coming a generation later, was initiated by the sovereign, but took final shape as a compromise between her wishes and those of a powerful, determined and organized party of her own subjects. Another step had been taken, half-consciously, in reshaping the English political order. A great decision of state—a resoundingly important one—had been made, not only by compromise between Crown and Commons, but also to accommodate the spiritual—and political—predilections of a major group of the queen's subjects.

Yet it would not do to over-emphasize the immediate extent of change. The circumstances of 1559 were very special and not likely to recur. The Commons had been able to play a large role in reordering English religion; but Parliament met only rarely and at the pleasure of the sovereign. What the most hopeful enthusiasts of 1559 perhaps overlooked, in the excitements of the moment, was that the new settlement left the structure of ecclesiastical government untouched. Designed to serve the purposes of a highly centralized monarchical papacy, it had now passed intact into the control of a secular ruler. Executive government of the Church was firmly in the grasp of the queen herself, and without her co-operation future change in religion would come to pass only with the greatest difficulty.

With the official adoption of the new liturgy in June 1559, the opening phase of the new reign was complete. The unfinished business of the old regime was cleared up by the painful but necessary surgery of Cateau-Cambrésis. On the central issue of religion the new government had made a full 180-degree turn. It was still too early to foresee the consequences of this action or to do more than guess as to particular features and individual personalities in the new political order. But the contrast with the late Marian court was apparent in one striking respect. Then it was the queen, single-minded in her Catholic orthodoxy and unswervingly loyal to Habsburg leadership, who led the way. Ministers, courtiers and Parliament, however reluctant, dismayed, or even recalcitrant, followed in her wake. Now, under the new dispensation, there was a royal personality no less courageous and far more commanding than that of her late sister, and Elizabeth displayed a sureness of political touch which Mary never possessed. Nevertheless, the vital centre of belief and of action in the nation was not any longer in the monarch but diffused among her ministers and, even more important, among a determined band of enthusiasts formed both of court and of country elements.

Part Two

THE YEARS OF ADVENTURE

4 *The Shaping of the Regime*

THE YEARS between the summers of 1559 and 1563 were formative ones for the new regime. The actors in this new drama now came forward to take their places on the stage, and it soon became apparent who would play the stellar parts and in what roles each would be cast. At the same time events, both within the realm and outside its borders, began to shape the plot and push the protagonists into action.

The queen herself, although clearly of a princely presence and widely popular at her accession, was still an unknown quantity as a ruler. In these years she revealed something of her many-sided angularity of character, her vitality and force and her intelligence; yet she remained in some important ways a withdrawn and half-mysterious personality. Among her servants the first to assume a major and clearly defined role was William Cecil, and in the first year of the reign he bade fair to dominate the whole stage. But he was soon to find a rival in Robert Dudley. The cautious sparring of the minister and the favourite for the royal confidence soon became a main theme of action.

In 1559–60 and again in 1562–3 England's leaders committed the country to two great foreign enterprises. The first—the intervention in Scotland—was forced on them by events outside their control; it ended in dazzling success. The other—the expedition to aid the Huguenots—was initiated largely by their own free choice and ended in flat failure. The Treaty of Edinburgh, which concluded the struggle in Scotland, opened up the brightest possibilities for the future; most of them were soon dimmed, in part by the queen's hesitancy to gamble in the uncertainties of Scottish politics, but also in part by the turn of fortune which brought the widowed Mary Stuart home again. The intervention in Normandy failed either to recover the lost march of Calais or effectively to assist French Protestantism, yet England escaped almost every disastrous consequence which so signal a failure might have entailed. With it ended the spurt of adventuresomeness which had characterized the regime up to this point; the years after 1563 were one of cautious isolationism in foreign affairs. Correspondingly the focus of English politics was to move to British issues — to the questions of marriage and succession in England and Scotland.

The years between 1559 and 1563 went far in defining the character and goals of the new regime. The anti-Roman position taken in the religious settlement of 1559 was underlined by English action abroad in support of foreign Protestants and at home by watchful observation of potential Catholic leaders and determined suppression of any slight move towards Catholic revival. In all these episodes — in regard to Scotland, to France, and within the English court circle — the drive for action and for change came from the servants of the Crown, alternately harassing and cajoling a reluctant queen, herself timid of action and indifferent, even hostile, to the passions, secular and religious, which moved the men about her.

Up to the summer of 1559 the political character of the new English court remained inchoate. The general direction of the new regime was made clear enough by the legislation of the 1559 Parliament, but we know next to nothing of the roles played by individual members of the government in that episode. Most of the lineaments of the new political canvas were yet to be revealed. But men now knew their ruler to be a princess endowed with a queenly personality and vigorous political common sense.

Her Council, in spite of its strong veteran contingent, had yet to cohere as a political entity. The queen had deliberately excluded from that body the man who had been the fulcrum of policy at the end of the last reign — Lord Paget. The survivors of the Marian Council were — with the exception of Arundel — weighty rather than dynamic politicians, men whose support would count heavily, but who were themselves unlikely to take the initiative in important action. The new ministers were as yet untried in meeting the supreme responsibilities which now fell to them; their talents remained to be proved. Their individual views, their relations to one another and to the new queen, their mistress — in short the whole structure of power in the new court — were yet to be shaped by events. These were not long in coming; the short-fused politics of Scotland exploded once again in the spring of 1559 and the resulting year-long crisis spread rapidly to involve England, France and ultimately Spain as well.

The facts of this situation were plain enough. Since the days of Henry VII English policy had sought by alternate bouts of conciliation and of bullying to draw Scotland into the orbit of English power. Henry VIII had not lacked statesmanlike vision when he proposed a union of the realms through the marriage of his son to the infant Scottish queen, Mary, but the over-sensitive feelings of the Scots towards their aggressive neighbour and the quicksilver uncertainties of Scottish politics required the nicest kind of diplomatic handling. Henry's bludgeoning methods only resulted in driving the Scots into the arms of the French. The engagement of Mary Stuart—and, in 1558, her marriage—to the heir of France produced a kind of melancholy parallelism in the fortunes of the sister kingdoms. In both instances, the monarch's foreign match led to a state of dependency, although in Scotland's case the situation was more extreme since in that realm there were an absentee sovereign, a foreign regent, and a foreign garrison to back her. In England Mary Tudor's opportune death probably forestalled an explosion of injured national feeling against alien dominance, but no such lucky event interposed to prevent such an eruption north of the Border. There, resentment of the foreigner was allied with religious radicalism when a group of Protestant magnates calling themselves Lords of the Congregation rose against the Regent Mother, Mary of Guise, in the spring of 1559.

In that summer the sudden death of Henry II (July 10th) brought Mary's husband, Francis II, to the French throne. The young couple were flexible instruments in the hands of Mary's uncles, the Guises, whose dynastic ambitions had no limits but whose allegiance to the Catholic faith was fixed. They were now masters in France and Scotland; English statesmen feared they would soon seek to add England to their domains. Their niece's hereditary claim to the English throne, linked with her unimpeachable Catholic orthodoxy, would provide an ideal excuse for such a venture. If the French regent crushed the rising of the Protestant lords, it seemed all too probable to the English government that the new French regime would not be content with victory north of the Tweed but would follow it by pressing with all possible means Mary's claims on the English Crown. Indeed, in some Englishmen's eyes the Guises were not merely opportunistic and ambitious political adventurers, but the spearhead of a deep-laid move to restore Catholic ascendancy throughout Europe, a move which was to be inaugurated by striking down the new Protestant regime in England.

The English response to this challenge had the effect of crystallizing the political divisions of the new reign. All the English Councillors admitted the gravity of the problem; the rub came in finding agreement on how to deal with it. One member of the Council took the lead in offering a radical solution; as early as August 1559 Secretary Cecil had set forth in a momentous state paper his clear analysis of the situation and the bold policy he proposed for meeting it.[1] Starting with the premise that the 'best worldly felicity that Scotland can have is either to continue in a perpetual peace with England or to be made one monarchy with it', he proposed a programme. The Scottish nobility led by the Hamilton family, as next heirs to the Crown, should be backed by England; once in control, they should enact a series of reforms designed to ensure the complete freedom of their country from French control so long as their queen was also Queen of France. Authority should be vested in a council elected by the Scots Parliament with full powers to make appointments (no Frenchmen being allowed to hold any Scottish office), and to expend the national revenue. The Three Estates in Parliament were to abolish 'idolatry' as had been done in England. If Mary and Francis did not accede to these de-mands, the governance of the realm might be transferred to the next heir. Under these conditions, the way would be open for enduring accord between the two island realms.

Cecil argued that there existed a unique opportunity, not likely to recur. As he wrote at the time, 'Any wise kindle the fire, for if quenched, the opportunity will not come in our lives.'[2] In the looming shadow of all-too-obvious French domination, older Scottish fears of English overlord-ship dwindled, while at the same time there appeared in Scottish politics a party held together by the strong cement of a common religious ideology. Such a party offered a potentiality for continuing unity hitherto beyond reach. Since this Protestant ideology was in large measure shared by the party now dominant in England and since English national interest urgent-ly required the elimination of French rule in Scotland, there was a fragile but viable base for Anglo-Scottish co-operation.

This was the policy the Secretary now sought to implement by un-remitting pressure on his sovereign and on his fellow Councillors. His tenacity was initially rewarded when the queen, in the autumn of 1559, consented to clandestine aid in money and munitions to the Scottish rebels. When that proved inadequate, she grudgingly agreed first to the dispatch of a fleet to the Firth of Forth, and then, in the spring of 1560, of an army which was to cross the frontier and collaborate with the rebels in the siege of Leith, the fortress in which the French had concentrated their forces.

During these months France wavered between all-out military support for their garrison and conciliatory negotiation with England. Winter weather frustrated the first alternative, and the uncertainties of French politics pushed them towards the second. In the spring Spain weighed in by sending an embassy of arbitration with the proposal that Spanish troops replace the French in Scotland, thus maintaining the Catholic ascendancy there but alleviating English fears of the French presence. This move was skilfully neutralized by Cecil, who exploited the differences between the resident ambassador of Spain, the ardently Catholic Bishop De Quadra, and the special envoy, a Low Countryman more concerned with the economic effects of a possible war on the Flemish economy.[3] In the end, in spite of English military ineptitude before Leith, circumstances at home and in Scotland were too much for the French; the death of the Regent Mother in July 1560 was the final straw; they threw in their hand and agreed to a withdrawal of all but the merest token forces from Scotland.

Cecil's policy had triumphed, but not until the first battle for power of the new reign had been fought out in the court. It was a three-sided struggle; Cecil fought to win the support of his fellow Councillors; at the same time he and his collaborators strove to bring the queen into line with their plans. As early as August 1559 Cecil prepared a memorandum in which he sought to bring his hesitant mistress to his own way of thinking. It is quite different in argument from the state paper of almost the same date which set out his own hopes (and plans) for a Scottish revolution. He began simply by declaring that the disposition of the French to conquer England was well known. He then arrayed all the arguments which sustained this proposition: the attempt to conclude a separate peace with Spain at Cateau-Cambrésis; the doubts cast on the queen's title at the same conference; French attempts to have Elizabeth declared illegitimate by Rome; their usurpation of the arms of England on the hangings and plate of the royal French couple and on a Scottish Great Seal used by them.[4]

This was a skilfully conceived essay in persuasion, designed to convince the queen of a grave risk to her throne. Cecil had already sensed how unwilling she was to venture on the dangers of open war. Only the immediate threat of invasion from the North, directly aimed at possession of the English Crown, would—so he guessed—wring a reluctant consent to intervention in Scotland from his hesitant sovereign.

Characteristically both Cecil and Throckmorton, his eager collaborator at Paris, took care to bring to the queen's attention every piece of evidence that the Franco-Scottish royal couple were using the arms of England. Even Challoner, the ambassador at Brussels, was pressed into service to uncover evidence of such action.[5] Obviously such displays by the French

royal pair could be a clue to their policy, but it was also an action peculiarly calculated to touch the most sensitive nerves of the Queen of England.
As she had shown in February, she was especially susceptible to any
slightest aspersion on her title to the throne. Nothing was so likely to
arouse her suspicions and her animosity towards France as this particular
device.

There was no duplicity here in Cecil's actions; he believed strongly
enough in the Guises' hostile intentions and in a great Catholic conspiracy
against England, but above all he saw that only by emphasizing the immediate danger to Elizabeth's Crown from French action could he move
her to act. During the late summer and early autumn, from the first
appeal of the Congregation to their dismal failures in the field in October
and November, the queen allowed herself to be persuaded to a flirtation
with their cause but never to whole-hearted commitment. Money was
doled out sparingly; general promises were made; Arran, the heir of the
Hamiltons and proposed leader of the revolt, was graciously received. But
the queen's doubts about wholesale support remained. What their causes
were has to be gleaned by indirect means.

The very first royal objection which Cecil, in his memorandum of
August, sets out to counter, reads, 'It is against God's law to aid any
subjects against their natural princes or their ministers.' This maxim, so
dear to Tudor political thought, was to the queen no mere platitude but a
prime law of nature. How much it influenced her policy is indicated in
the instructions sent to the Scots lords when the queen eventually consented to some additional aid;[6] their tenor throughout emphasizes that
Elizabeth is prepared to aid the Scots nobles only because of the threat to
England. In the suit to the queen which Cecil framed for the Scots lords,
they are made emphatically to declare their loyalty to their own queen,
'in no wise withdrawing their hearts from their sovereign lady'. Coupled
with this is a clause urging Mary not to 'delight in this unjust and dis-
honourable usurpation of the arms, style, and title of other kingdoms'.
Elizabeth, in the very act of alliance with her neighbour's disloyal subjects, reasserts the general law of obedience not only in her own favour,
but also in protection of her rival's just rights. It is worth noting that the
hints dropped in Cecil's original state paper about pushing either the
Hamilton claim to the Scots Crown or the pretensions of Mary's bastard
brother, Lord James Stuart, quite vanished.

Secondly, the queen had strong objections to the religious aims of the
Congregation. The very name of their prophet and spiritual guide, John

Knox, was odious to the queen, after his ill-timed assault on feminine rule, and his associates were *personae non gratae* at the English court.[7] In Cecil's original proposals the establishment of Christ's religion in Scotland is set forth as the first step towards permanent reconciliation and future co-operation, but in the Scots petition of November (Cecil's own work) no single word about religion is allowed. No doubt the need to avoid offend-ing the Catholic sensibilities of Spain was kept in mind, but this diplomatic necessity chimed well with the queen's own indisposition to appear as the sponsor of radical Protestantism.

Cecil's difficulties were not only with his reluctant sovereign. Initially the matter was handled by an inner committee of Pembroke, Clinton, Parry and some others, who were persuaded by the Secretary's arguments, but in discussions among the whole Council, a little later on, there was less unanimity. At the end of October Cecil wrote worriedly of the opposi-tion to his proposals: 'For here be many more letters [hinderers] than ye would think, some not liking the progress of religion, some not so angry with the French good fortunes as I am, some doubting other successes, as in marriage and such like, if prosperity should follow there, and so with some more difficult aid is granted than seemeth convenient.'[8]

In the opening arguments in full Council, Bacon, Winchester, Petre, Mason and Wotton were doubtful about an expedition into Scotland (clandestine aid by this time was a *fait accompli*) while Arundel was com-pletely opposed. These were, of course, with the exception of Bacon, Marian hold-overs. Against them, backing Cecil, stood the three veteran peers, Pembroke, Clinton and Howard, and the Councillors of the new dispensation, Northampton, Parry, Rogers, Knollys, Sackville and Cave. Neither the Earl of Bedford nor the magnates from the North, Shrewsbury and Derby, were present.[9]

The opposition's views were summed up in a speech by Lord Keeper Bacon. Should the Scots nobility be openly aided in expelling the French? Bacon's answer was a qualified no; his reasons, several. England could not fight a war; France, four times larger, not only had men and money but could hire German mercenaries, while England—and here he echoes many contemporaries—was depopulated and impoverished. Not only did the queen lack the funds to pay her debts, but her nobility, gentry and com-mons shared this poverty. At home there was much to fear from those of rank, discontented for religion's sake—a formidable array—and 'those who take themselves to have had their credit or living decayed'. Abroad, England was without reliable allies; Philip was pressing the suit of his cousin, Archduke Charles of Austria, for Elizabeth's hand; he might use this opportunity to force it on the queen or alternatively be tempted by French offers into their camp. Reckoning that France could not act with major force in less than eighteen months, he ended by recommending indirect and secret aid to the Scots through the next summer.

In the end Bacon and his fellows—except Arundel—allowed themselves to be persuaded out of their doubts. Without abandoning their original objections, they were nonetheless convinced the Guises would never cease to advance Mary Stuart's title against the queen and with that view would make war as soon as it suited them. Hence, after urging honourable marriage on the queen, they proposed the raising of money to pay for an army in the North and a fleet in the Forth. Since the French would be impeded by winter weather in shipping cavalry to Scotland, the queen should act speedily to crush the French garrison as quickly as possible. These recommendations were interlaced with interjections of fear and anxiety and with expressions of reluctance; nevertheless, the Councillors nerved themselves to take the gamble. Cecil had persuaded them of the reality of a Guisan menace to the regime. Perhaps one additional factor weighed in their judgment: the repeated rumours of Mary's bad health, the unlikelihood of heirs, and the possibility of her early death. All parties could share this cheerful hope.

The hints about marriage referred to a train of events which formed a counterpoint to the main theme of the Scottish entanglement. Everyone assumed the queen would marry; no one took seriously her modest avowal to Parliament that she would prefer to remain single; the only question was whom she would choose. Philip had offered himself and been declined; the Swedish dynasty had made a determined bid but also had failed. The most serious candidate, politically speaking, was the Archduke Charles, younger son of the Austrian Habsburgs. In April King Philip was already instructing his ambassador to forward such a match with his cousin, and in May an imperial envoy, specially accredited for this purpose, arrived in London.[10] At the end of June he had an ambiguous refusal but the two Habsburg ambassadors remained hopeful; and in September the archduke's prospects brightened when Lady Sidney, a confidante of the queen and sister to Robert Dudley, intimated to the Spanish ambassador, Bishop De Quadra, that it was a propitious moment for pressing his candidate's claims anew. The bishop recommended the archduke come to England himself; for a time Habsburg stock soared, but it had declined again by mid-November.[11]

In fact the comedy of this wooing, one of the first in so long a series, veiled a set of manoeuvres which the Spanish ambassador only half understood. As relations with France worsened, the obvious diplomatic ploy was to turn to the Habsburg powers; favourable consideration of a match Philip favoured was a convenient and inexpensive way of keeping open diplomatic lines with Spain. At the same time the match had very real attractions for an important segment of English politicians. Those who thought Cecil's policy would only lead to as disastrous and wasting a war as the last regarded a marriage with the Austrian archduke and the consequent renewal of the Habsburg alliance as a much better way of securing the queen against the Guises than backing the Scots rebels. No less a person than the Duke of Norfolk told De Quadra that he had begun to oppose the war openly and to support the Austrian match. Since the end aimed at, namely, the defence of the country, could be attained much more easily by this means, there was no reason to go to war. An echo of this same view came from the English ambassador at Brussels, the timid but experienced Challoner. Always an advocate of the Austrian match, he summed up his hopes – and those of many others – in a letter of December 1st. Hoping that war might be delayed for two or three years, he added, 'Marriage and the fruit thereof as a sure pawn to bind all men's hearts; time gained to put our things in order and settle things begun but not achieved; with a thousand other accidents that the time itself would discover for occasions to take hold upon, do draw one down to that side.'[12]

There was another and very delicate reason which influenced the supporters of the archduke. The favour enjoyed by Lord Robert Dudley had been a matter for comment since the spring; resentment against the favourite inevitably began to rise. During the autumn of 1559 his most outspoken critic at court was Norfolk, and the duke was by no means solitary in his resentment.[13] In any case the advocates of an Austrian marriage and a Habsburg alliance found their hand strengthened by support from those who feared a Dudley match.

Cecil's difficulties with his unconvinced colleagues continued. In early April there was still pressure for following the Habsburg lead: apparently Sir John Mason was the principal Councillor advocating such a move; there is a hint that Paget, the one great politician who had lost his footing altogether at Mary's death, was moving behind the scenes to achieve the same end. These moves coincided with the arrival of the special Spanish mission. Arundel, Petre, and even possibly Parry were supporters of these manoeuvres. Outside the Council, Cecil had the warm but possibly some-what embarrassing good wishes of the extreme left-wing Protestants. Such an ardent evangelical as Lord John Grey, who had nearly lost his head for his part in Wyatt's Rebellion, roundly condemned the conservatives as practisers against God and their country and applauded the Secretary as a maintainer of God's causes, and the protector of his country and sovereign.[14]

The struggle continued to be a hard one, and at one time Cecil had been driven to the extremity of threatening resignation of all responsibilities for Scottish matters. The queen, moreover, remained unconvinced and became increasingly irritable. Her first response to the Council's proposals for outright intervention had been a flat negative. But on individual measures she slowly yielded grudging consent. Admiral Winter was allowed to sail northward to the Forth to blockade the French. He was under solemn instructions to state that he acted only for himself and not for his mistress, a deception which deceived no one but the deceiver herself. So, by slow degrees, her piecemeal moves added up to a *de facto* acceptance of the whole programme. But many about the queen still urged a halt. Nicholas Wotton, the veteran diplomat asked by Cecil to draw up a memorandum when Spanish intervention seemed a real possibility, suggested that the queen reconsider her Scottish commitments and, if necessary, compromise on a reduction of French forces in Scotland, on the question of a French regent and on the matter of religion.[15] It was this willingness to compromise the interests of the new faith which was infuriating to left-wing Protestants; for Cecil such a policy would have undercut the essential goals of the whole risky venture. But such proposals as Wotton's reflected the nervousness of the older generation at the prospect of English isolation. Their country's position seemed to them too fragile to permit her to act separately from one or another of the greater dynastic powers.

The last and worst stage of Cecil's sufferings came after the dismaying failure of English arms before Leith in May 1560. The queen, already edgy and hesitant, alternated between anger and pessimism. A distracted Cecil declared, 'I have had such a torment herein with the Queen's Majesty as an ague hath not in five so much abated.' The diplomat, Henry Killigrew, reported her as having renewed the opinion of Cassandra. Clinton, the Lord Admiral, feared the queen's reaction to the news from Scotland and wrote a vigorous letter urging again that England's basic security was at stake and nothing should be spared in the effort to evict the French from the island. Perhaps hinting at disagreement in the Council, he declared, 'Whosoever shall say contrary shall never be able to lay any grounded reason to maintain his opinion nor I think a good Englishman can ever consent that France should have the upper hand in Scotland.' The Council itself fired off a declaration of confidence in the northern Lieutenant, the harried Duke of Norfolk, and urged him to redoubled efforts. Their immediate fears were allayed; the queen approved the sending of reinforcements and new supplies for another effort, but Cecil pessimistically observed, 'The Queen's Majesty never liketh this matter of Scotland; you know what hangeth thereupon; weak-hearted men and flatterers will follow that way.'[16]

Cecil needed as much support and sympathy as he could muster, for he was about to take the most dangerous plunge of his career. By May 22nd it had been determined that he and Wotton should go north as the heads of a commission to negotiate with the Scots and French at Edinburgh. Both Cecil and his friends were dubious about this decision. 'My friends in Council', he wrote to Throckmorton, 'think it necessary for the matter and convenient for me; my friends abroad think I am herein betrayed to be sent from the Queen's Majesty.' Both Killigrew and Throckmorton shared this anxiety. The former, praising Cecil's patriotism, doubtfully added, 'I would the Queen's Majesty would love her country as well.' In reality, Cecil had no choice; if peace were to be made, it must be his work; he must run the risks of absence from the court.[17]

The reasons for the concern of Cecil's friends emerge only dimly from the veiled references of their letters. The nucleus of resistance in the Council was still Mason, but that rather bruised Councillor wrote a letter to Cecil on the latter's departure, bewailing his treatment, and declaring his intention not to frequent the court in Cecil's absence. He would be satisfied, he wrote, with a peace which included a promise from Philip to back England should France break the agreement. Of the Councillors, Pembroke and Clinton were singled out by the knowledgeable Killigrew as steadfast supporters of Cecil, and he added Norfolk's name to the list.[18]

The real difficulties lay with the queen herself. Once the preliminary stages of negotiation were past, when her army was moving across the Border and chest after chest of her money trundled northward—in short, once events began to develop their own momentum—the queen's irritability and hesitations mounted. A sense of her own powerlessness to control what was relentlessly happening on those distant frontiers both infuriated and agitated her, and the royal impatience for peace grew apace.

5

In this uncertain mood she was the despair of all her Councillors. Throckmorton summed up their feelings in a letter to Cecil. Although anxious
for Cecil to be at the making of the treaty, he was worried by the Secretary's absence from court. 'Who will speedily resolve the doubtful delays?
Who shall make dispatch of anything?'[19]

In this unhappy frame of mind Cecil set out on a mission which in its
conclusion was to prove spectacularly successful. The French conceded,
directly or implicitly, all that Cecil had laid out as his programme nearly
a year previously. Yet in that very hour of triumph he was brought up
short by an impetuous change of mind on his mistress's part. The treaty
had already been signed and proclaimed in Edinburgh when the English
commissioners were appalled by receipt of a letter from the queen commanding them to hold up the entire treaty until they obtained both Calais
and with it five hundred thousand crowns to soothe the wounds to her
dignity caused by French use of her title and arms. Fortunately, the new
instruction was to hold only if peace had not been already concluded.[20]

What lay behind this radical shift of royal policy was a proposal brought
to the queen, presumably from Huguenot sources, after Cecil's departure
from court. It was an offer to deliver certain towns in Normandy or
Brittany to Elizabeth in return for her assistance. Cecil had written urging
delay, but there had been a second approach, and it was this which moved
the queen to raise the issue of Calais. Cecil's reply mingled his relief that
the royal letter had not arrived in time with his alarm that Elizabeth
should have considered such a policy. To have risked force and treasure
in such a bottomless pit would have been to duplicate, indeed magnify,
the French mistake in Scotland. A foreign intruder with no claim to support except 'a devotion popular upon matters of religion', she would have
been expelled so soon as Francis II made concessions to the Protestants.[21]
Cecil's keen sense of the limits of English interest — and of English power —
is evident here. In Scotland there was a happy coincidence of both English
and Scottish state interests with those of Protestantism, but in France an
alliance with the Huguenots would have been short-lived since it directly
threatened French national safety.

The circumstances of this great crisis were the product of outside forces
— the revolt of the Protestant lords in Scotland and the ambitions of the
Guises. But the character of the English response had been determined in
large part by the English Secretary. It was he who came forward with a
programme at once comprehensive and detailed, tailored to the existing
facts of politics but aimed at achieving long-term effects. The queen her-

self had offered no lead; in the day-by-day thrust and parry of diplomatic exchange she had demonstrated an almost instinctive skill, but when it came to the making of irreversible decisions she had trembled indecisively, and her impetuous bid for Calais in July 1560 displayed more than a touch of unsureness.

It was Cecil who had forced events to his own shaping, drawing the queen reluctantly step by weary step to follow the path he laid out. He was able to win her piecemeal acceptance, not by any appeal to the long-run interests of the English state or those of the Protestant faith, but only by convincing her of a real and immediate threat to her own possession of the throne. But he might not have succeeded in his policy had he not been able to draw with him the weightiest part of the Council. He might reasonably have hoped for the backing of the new members; some, like Knollys or Bedford, clearly shared his policy aims; all were closely tied to the fortunes of the new regime for any hope of political advancement or, indeed, of survival. And, with the single exception of Bacon – and possibly Parry – they rallied to him from the start. Nor was it surprising that the opposition to his aims arose from among the hold-over members. These long-time servants of the Tudor monarchy, survivors of the decade of disaster that followed Henry's death, were all too conscious of English weakness and the extreme risks of a forward policy. They were – except for Arundel – men of the robe rather than the sword, cautiously neutral on the religious issue, and by habit and out of experience they clung to the safer, smoother paths of diplomacy and the sheltering umbrella of Habsburg protection. They feared the rough violence of open intervention proposed by the Secretary and, even more, the risks of isolated action.

It was therefore of the greatest importance that the Secretary was able to swing to his side the three veteran politicians of first rank on the Council – the Lords Pembroke, Clinton and Howard. These men were nobles of the sword; soldiers who had held great commands as well as practised politicians, they had played greater – and, more dangerous – roles in the theatre of politics than the prudent diplomats and bureaucrats who opposed Cecil. Their rank, experience and prestige must have weighed heavily in persuading the queen to adopt the course proposed by the yet untried and unproved Secretary. So long as this weight was thrown to his side, Cecil could feel hopeful that no effective counterforce of opposition would prevail against him within the Council. The queen could – and did – refuse for the moment to accept the Council's advice, but she could hardly stand out indefinitely against the pressure of their united opinion.

The overwhelming success of Cecil's policy transformed his status; from being merely a newcomer of promise and competence, he vaulted into the first rank of contemporary politicians and to what must have seemed a decisive position of leadership in the circle of Councillors close about the throne. No one could rival his talents either as maker of policy or man of business. He might seem about to move along the road to that high and special ministry which only Wolsey and Cromwell had hitherto exercised under the Tudors.

But the outward pomps of success veiled the inner ambiguities of the whole position. Cecil had set out to achieve — and had achieved — a stroke of grand policy. He had seen not only a once-for-all chance to eliminate the threat of a France which stood 'bestriding the realm, one foot in Calais, the other in Scotland',[22] but also the possibility of a new epoch in British history, the emergence of a new-found co-operation between England and Scotland, based on a common faith and a common political interest. His vision was shared in various degrees by others. Some, like Throckmorton, let their imaginations leap ahead to the hope of an English hegemony in a grand alliance of Protestant states; others, like Admiral Clinton, rejoiced simply in a victory over the ancient enemy — especially in such a reversal of recent misfortune. Others yet, such as Lord John Grey, more piously disposed, saw the victory as that of God's cause. In any case this clear-cut victory was a major gain for the regime. This striking repulse of French ambitions might be held to more than offset the Marian disaster at Calais. The new regime had taken a long step forward in securing its own stability and strengthening its hopes for survival.

The architects of this triumph thus seemed about to give a strong ideological bent to English national policy; within the Council they had beaten out their conservative opponents, who thought in terms of a cautious reliance upon Philip's friendship and minimal risks of English resources. More important still, they had nudged their reluctant mistress into the role of Protestant champion within the island and by implication in a larger theatre. But these fair prospects were as uncertain as the brightness of an English summer morning and the elements of the situation as volatile as the weather of an English August.

For the queen's ministers had learned that she shared few of their visions for the future. Her basic position was that of her father, a view of the world already more than a little old-fashioned. She took literally the tenets of divine-right monarchy; she stood firmly on her own dignity, as much angry at the outrageous pretensions of the Guises' niece as fearful of their assault on her power. But in her keen feelings for the infrangible rights of monarchs she distinguished clearly between her rights in England and those of her rival, Mary, in Scotland, and looked with deep distaste on any dealings with rebels against Mary's just authority. A great gulf separated her from those of her servants who looked beyond the immediate threats to the queen to the larger threat to the nation and, farther still, to the opportunities for England's safety and glory in the indefinite future — even to a time when Elizabeth would have been gathered to her fathers.

For her the episode had been a painful one, forced on her by unavoidable circumstance. She had been respectfully but relentlessly urged along a road which she did not wish to travel. Much against the grain, she had become the patroness and collaborator of a group of disloyal conspirators against their lawful sovereign. She had also — much against her disposition — contributed to the establishment in the northern kingdom of a thoroughgoing Protestantism whose clerical leaders were anathema to her authoritarian tastes. The queen had endured these unwelcome constraints on her freedom because circumstance was too strong for her, but once the spur of ineluctable events was removed, she would be free to exercise her own untrammelled will again. Just possibly the bid for Calais was a gesture of independence by the queen once her resolute tutor was away in Edinburgh. She was soon to have wider opportunity to flaunt her independence.

The course of events during the Scottish enterprise had, of course, produced some shifts in the personnel of high politics. One magnate alone — Arundel — had stood out against Cecil's suasions; his obstinate adherence to a policy of collaboration with the Habsburgs left him odd-man-out in the Council, soured by his fall from the great place he had held in the politics of the late reign.

His son-in-law of Norfolk had moved in another direction. When it became necessary to establish a high command on the Borders, the duke was selected as Queen's Lieutenant in the North. The role this young grandee was to fill was a showy but circumscribed one, since he was surrounded by a bevy of councillors and experts. Since Norfolk had been a critic of Cecil's policy, it was a shrewd stroke to draw him into collaboration; a suggestible and inexperienced young man, he was readily attracted into Cecil's orbit of political friendship. Another figure at court, Lord Robert Dudley, no doubt rejoiced at seeing his most outspoken and formidable critic removed to a safe distance from the scene.

Real power in the North was entrusted to a kind of 'Minister of State for Scottish Affairs', the experienced Sir Ralph Sadler. He was another Edwardian (Master of the Wardrobe and Privy Councillor under that king) who had gone into virtual retirement under Mary. Summoned to Elizabeth's first Councils he seems to have sat only a few times and does not reappear at that board again until 1566. A prominent figure under Henry, he had been that monarch's agent in the negotiations of the Scots marriage treaty and probably knew more about Scottish affairs than any other Englishman. Thoroughly sympathetic with Cecil's aims, deeply committed to the new faith, he was an ideal collaborator for the Secretary.

The appointment of Sadler and Norfolk to chief charge on the Border had worked a minor revolution in the regional politics of the North. The Earl of Northumberland had been removed from his wardenry of the East and Middle Marches and the reflux of Percy power in that area encouraged by the late queen thus roughly checked. Lord Dacre, the Warden of the West March, was deliberately kept at court as much as possible since he was hardly more trusted than Northumberland.[23] The death of Shrewsbury, the old Lord President at York, followed the Treaty of Edinburgh by less than three months; in January 1561 the second Earl of Rutland was appointed to that office. This Midlands potentate had held the wardenry of the East and Middle Marches under Edward VI; at the opening of Mary's reign he was briefly imprisoned although he was restored to favour later on, but not to a Border post. The wardenry of the East Marches passed to the old commander, Lord Grey of Wilton, lately general of the English forces in Scotland; but that of the Middle Marches had been given to Percy's enemy, Sir John Forster,[24] a local squire. The effect of these shifts of office was to throw into disarray the traditional Percy hegemony in the North-East and to entrust the critical Border commands to men who had close links to the new regime.

5 The Emergence of Dudley

IN THE summer of 1560 the party in the English court which had pushed a forward policy with such success in Scotland looked hopefully towards its continuation. Throckmorton, perhaps the most ebullient member of the group, envisaged the queen spending twenty thousand pounds a year on Scottish pensions and at the same time building up her navy, while the Guises, he thought, might be entertained with blandishments until relations with the new Scotland were tightly knit. Parliament could be summoned to provide money, and, one supposes, to put pressure on the queen to continue this policy. Cecil, sympathetic but less expansive in his views, limited himself to prodding the queen to spend money on pensions across the Border.[1]

The party was brought up sharp by Elizabeth's cold indifference to its programme and by her unwillingness to distribute any rewards to those prominent in the late enterprise.[2] Cecil moaned in a letter to Throckmorton that he would be worse this seven years for his northern service, for which he had had no reward, while Norfolk, that *columen familiae reginae*, was sent home without allowance in credit or promise. Worse still, the queen showed no disposition either to provide for the needy Scots lords or to summon a Parliament. The men who had dominated policy for the last year suddenly discovered the contracted limits of their influence once the spur of immediate danger and the urgency for some kind of action were removed.

But the immediate issue of Scotland faded into an even larger concern as the summer waned. Since the day of Elizabeth's accession, men had looked forward eagerly to the queen's marriage; Parliament had been almost as much concerned with it as with religion; courtiers, ambassadors, the Privy Council, all had ceaselessly urged matrimony upon their mistress. If Elizabeth died at this juncture, the succession would be claimed by the Franco-Scottish Mary Stuart, backed by the Guises abroad and the Catholics at home. The most likely English claimant was the obscure and childless Lady Catherine Grey, cousin to the queen, but there were other, more distant, claimants, the Protestant Earl of Huntingdon or the Catholic Countess of Lennox, for example, who might well put forward their candidacies. Civil war was altogether too likely a result.

But, even leaving these doleful possibilities aside, there was an immediate necessity for a royal marriage. Men looked to the queen to settle a political situation which remained in restless agitation. No one could envisage a kingless realm, ruled by a virgin queen; she must choose a husband and by that choice give shape and direction to English politics which only a man could provide. Nothing less would offer stability for the present and security for the future.

The Scots lords boldly offered as a bridegroom the Hamilton Earl of Arran, next heir after the Stuarts to the Scottish throne. They were assuming either that Mary would die childless or that she could be set aside; hence the match would result in the union of the kingdoms. They looked to a future in which, Ireland subdued, the queen would be 'the strongest princess in Christendom upon the seas, and establish a certain monarchy by itself in the ocean, divided from the rest of the world'.[3] But Elizabeth would, of course, not listen to a proposal which so flagrantly challenged the rights of her royal cousin and opened up the possibility of renewed struggle.

The queen had turned her eyes towards a more favoured candidate; since Amy Dudley's death by accident in September 1560, her widower had become an open contender for the royal hand. Even before that event, the queen's intimacy with him had become a matter of the widest publicity. In mid-August the Essex J.P.s were questioning a woman of Brentwood who had gossipped up and down eastern Essex about the pregnancy of the queen by the Lord Robert.[4] If gossip of this kind had reached the peasantry of these villages, it obviously already had wide circulation in more important circles. Indeed, a crisis of frightening proportion had been precipitated in the English political world, even before the shock of Amy Robsart's death and the terrible suspicions which were immediately voiced. Dudley had been an increasingly disturbing factor in English politics for some months past. In the previous December there was gossip in the court of Brussels about him and a stirring of open criticism at home, led by Norfolk; in March 1560 De Quadra reported that Lord Robert might divorce his wife.[5] Up to this point Dudley seems not to have played any part in high state policy. An occasional letter of courtesy between him and Cecil are the only indications of his relations with the Secretary. But, at another level of politics, the favourite was very active indeed. From early in the reign his influence with his mistress was well known to suitors to the Crown. Men of all ranks turned to him to obtain personal favours from the queen. Even the fragments of his correspondence which are all that survive reveal half the English earls, cap in hand, at the favourite's door, asking his aid or pledging their hopeful friendship — Derby, Pembroke, Westmorland, Rutland, Arundel, Huntingdon. It is significant that he figures largely in ecclesiastical patronage. The ultra-Protestant Bedford writes to him urging Aylmer as Dean of Winchester (but without success); while the new Bishop of Worcester, Edwin Sandys, is profuse in thanks for favours done and in offers to defend Dudley's reputation against the malicious. The Spanish Count Feria (lately Philip's envoy in England) and the present Spanish ambassador were also among his suitors.[6]

At the same time Lord Robert was looked to by anxious Roman Catholics as a benevolent protector. Their intermediary at court was a gentleman of the Privy Chamber, Francis Yaxley, scion of a Norfolk family. He maintained a correspondence with Mary's Councillors, Boxall, Cornwallis, Wharton, Bourne and Montague. Cornwallis, particularly, had sought and found favours by this route. Dudley seems to have encouraged Yaxley's attendance on him and to have been the source of various small favours to the Catholic gentry.[7]

Lord Robert spread his correspondence widely: Sir Henry Paget, son of the eminent Marian Councillor, now travelling on the Continent, was a useful source of information; Gresham and other correspondents provided Low Countries news; the English ambassador to Spain wrote both to seek favour and to provide information. Croft, so long as he was Captain of Berwick, was a link with Border matters.[8]

Dudley's prospects as a royal bridegroom were cloudy as long as his wife lived, and he had to tread with delicate step where royal matrimonial possibilities were concerned. In the preceding autumn, he had played a principal part in matrimonial intrigues about the queen. His sister, Lady Sidney, had approached De Quadra with assurances of her brother's strong support for an Austrian marriage. By November the favourite had backed away and was reported favouring the Swedish candidate. The ambassador thought the queen in fact intended to marry Dudley and was using the archduke and the Swede for a delaying action until Dudley should be a widower. Possibly this was the case, or Dudley may — at one point — have thought the Austrian match likely enough to have been worth backing.[9]

In December 1559 there was a mysterious episode, of which only the barest outlines are visible. Captain William Drury, a soldier employed by the queen on a 'military aid mission' to the Scots lords, was arrested, along with his brother Drew, Esquire for the Body, allegedly for plotting against Lord Robert. There is a letter from William Drury to Dudley, begging pardon for 'words spoken' when 'moved by nature, not by malice'. The Drurys remained in custody until October 1560.[10]

Up to this point Dudley—so far as one can assess his actions—seems to have taken a discreet and shrewd line. His position was a very delicate one, since it depended solely on the uncertain favour of the queen. Noblemen and courtiers might shower kind words on him, seeking to exploit his influence with the sovereign, but he could have no illusions as to their behaviour should that favour be withdrawn. Even more difficult would be his situation if circumstances drove the queen to marriage with a foreign prince.

Hence he kept cautiously in the background of great events, while conducting himself so as to avoid offending his mistress. He had at once to nourish the royal partiality, to build up a credit balance with her which could be lavished in maintaining good relations in as many directions as possible, and to avoid conduct which would raise up powerful enemies. His strategy must be to keep as many doors as possible open, for a quick shift of ground or a sudden retreat. Hence his array of antennae reaching at once towards Catholic gentry and Protestant divines, towards all possible sources of information or influence at home and abroad.

But in the summer of 1560 he had taken a bolder tack and begun to play for the highest possible stakes. Perhaps the occasion for this change of course was his wife's failing health.[11] If she died, marriage with the queen would no longer be a mere shimmering mirage on a distant horizon but a near and concrete possibility. There can be little doubt that the queen, on her side, gave him strong encouragement during these summer months. Even before Amy Dudley's death on September 8th, her husband's ambitions had had a disintegrating effect on court politics. Cecil in a very sour-tempered mood was already talking of resignation in August although he hoped that he might be replaced by Throckmorton, who would of course pursue much the same general policy. But the depth of Cecil's distress was revealed in an outburst to De Quadra in early September before the death of Lady Dudley.[12] This was probably meant to reach Elizabeth's ears; the Secretary could say to the ambassador what he dared not say directly to his mistress. He declared his intention to retire since the queen's intimacy with Lord Robert would bring ruin to the realm in any case. He urged the ambassador to warn the queen of her misconduct and declared that Dudley would be better in paradise than here; he ended by hinting that the favourite would kill his present wife; it was only a day later that the queen herself told the bishop of Amy Robsart's death.

The weeks which followed were ones of painful uncertainty for all. No letter of Cecil's survives for this critical period; Throckmorton found him warily ambiguous in correspondence, but the Secretary patently did not pursue his threats of resignation. Like others, he hung on, racked by ague bouts of fear. The ambassador at Paris was in a perfect agony of desperation and at the end of October wrote Cecil, urging him 'to do all your endeavour to hinder that marriage; for if it take place there is no counsel or advice that can help'. He added, 'God and religion will be out of estimation; the Queen discredited, condemned, and neglected, and the country ruined, and made prey.' At home rumours of a nobles' revolt as the consequence of such a match floated about the country. De Quadra picked up fragments of an intrigue to make the Earl of Huntingdon successor, and Lady Margaret Lennox, a descendant of Henry VIII's sister, Margaret, by her second marriage, began to stir.[13]

The queen, amidst the flurry and embarrassment of her councillors, diplomats and divines, equivocated and delayed. About mid-October Cecil told a sceptical De Quadra that the queen had said she would not marry Lord Robert. But uncertainty continued to pervade the court; and a month later the Spanish ambassador was relaying home the story of a secret marriage.[14] Among the greater politicians there was a cautious and subdued jostling; Throckmorton, with his customary forthrightness, broadcast widely the views he had expressed to Cecil.[15]

At the end of November his secretary, Jones, crossed over to England; a report sent by the latter from court gives a vivid impression of the situation at that moment.[16] Both Robert Dudley and the queen pressed Jones as to his master's views and as to the gossip of the French court. (Throckmorton had already reported Catherine de Médicis's remark that Elizabeth was to marry her horse-master.) The queen took in good part this and other not very flattering reports but was earnest in her defence of Dudley's innocence in his wife's death. Among the courtiers there was nervous uncertainty. The lords of Council—Pembroke, Clinton, Bedford and Northampton are mentioned—seemed to approve Throckmorton's insistence on relaying unfavourable opinion to the queen, but they were very guarded and showed no disposition to back the ambassador's protests openly. There had been a hint earlier that Pembroke and Northampton might be encouraging Dudley. Parry had been his supporter; he was now ill, of what proved to be a fatal malady. Killigrew, the courtier, now an adherent of the favourite, told the secretary that 'Lord Robert shall run away with the hare and have the Queen'. Nevertheless, Jones's own conclusion was that Dudley would not have her hand; the queen, he reported, had cut up the patents drawn up for Robert's creation as a peer. 'And yet,' he added, 'the favours be great which are shown him at the Queen's hand.'

These uncertainties did not altogether resolve themselves with time; at the year's end Throckmorton was still full of passion on the subject. 'But if Her Majesty do so foully forget herself in her marriage as the bruit runneth here, never think to bring anything to pass, either here or elsewhere.' He went on to warn Cecil, 'do not think you do enough because you do not further the matter'. No one of weight was bold enough to speak out to the queen against the marriage, while other Councillors were busy in forwarding it. But Throckmorton's angry letter must have crossed in the post one from Cecil, who, in a discreet postscript, wrote, 'Whatsoever reports or opinions be, I know surely that my Lord Robert himself hath more fear than hope and so doth the Queen give him cause'.[17]

At the turn of the year several events altered the pattern on the chessboard and opened the way for new moves. In early December 1560 Francis II ended his brief reign after a short illness and Mary Stuart found herself a cipher in French politics; the Guises were ousted from their eminence, and all was fluid again at Paris. The Scottish situation, on the other hand, so favourable to the English since the preceding summer, was now again blurred and out of focus as the Scots lords waited uneasily for their widowed sovereign's next moves. At home Mr Treasurer Parry died just before Christmas, leaving his two posts open; courtiers waited expectantly for musical chairs to begin. They had not long to wait for the first move, since on January 10th Cecil was appointed Master of the Wards.[18] Parry's other office as Treasurer of the Household went unfilled. Cecil's appointment was a move of great importance; in the previous autumn he had seriously doubted whether he could remain in office. The queen ignored his advice and showed herself coldly indifferent to his services in Scotland, and he regarded her infatuation with Dudley as spelling ruin to the state. His new post was lucrative and important and his appointment a clear sign of royal approbation. The frighteningly

dangerous interval since the previous summer, during which the breakdown of confidence between the sovereign and the leading group of her
Councillors seemed to threaten a general disintegration of political
coherence, was now past.

But Dudley had by no means given over his hopes for the royal hand
in marriage. In January Sir Henry Sidney, acting as his brother-in-law's
agent, and then Lord Robert himself waited on Bishop De Quadra with
a startling proposal. According to this pair, the queen was much inclined
to marry Robert; if De Quadra could persuade his royal master into
backing the match, the favourite and his mistress would undertake the re-
establishment of Catholicism by means of a General Council. The ambassador was understandably sceptical. Dudley insisted that the queen stood
behind him. She would take no initiative herself, but if the bishop brought
up the matter, he would find her responsive. The pious De Quadra
roundly told Sidney that the matter of religion should be a matter of
conscience, not of political expediency, but he offered a qualified promise
of support with the queen.[19]

When the ambassador raised the question directly with Elizabeth, she
coyly admitted, after a good deal of circumlocution, her preference for
Lord Robert—although she had not decided to marry him or anyone
else—and asked what Philip would think if she married one of her servi-
tors; on the following day Robert again urged De Quadra to press the
queen, asserting that with only a little more push, she could be brought
to a favourable decision. The ambassador, at once baffled and hopeful,
wrote off in haste for instructions.

What are we to make of this curious intrigue? Are we really to believe
that the queen in her infatuation was willing to sell herself both to Spain
and to Rome to secure marriage with Dudley? Obviously, we can only
speculate, but some such hypothesis as follows may be put forward.

The queen was for once really tempted to marriage. Dudley had a great
attraction for her and now that he was free she was more than half-
persuaded to the possibility of matrimony. But her political sense did not
desert her, however strong her passion. She knew that Dudley excited
not only the natural resentment aroused by any favourite, but also the
intense odium felt towards his upstart and inordinately ambitious house;
men could not forget his father's bid for sovereign power. Clearly she
could not choose him as husband unless there was some strong backing
from the magnates of Council and court. Hence she looked expectantly
towards them for a sign; if there had been a move of any strength to back

Dudley's candidacy, it is a fair guess that marriage might have followed. So far as we can tell, only her old servant Parry, and just possibly the trimmer Pembroke, promoted it. The main body of Councillors stood sullenly aloof, unwilling to stir in Dudley's behalf but afraid to risk their own futures in open opposition. From the wings Throckmorton and Norfolk vehemently opposed the match. The result was stalemate; the queen's mood of indecision deepened, and Dudley anxiously cast about for new leverage. An appeal to De Quadra was natural; as representative of the Habsburg interest, his support would undercut Norfolk's opposition and perhaps persuade some of the conservative Councillors to Dudley's side. But he would need to be offered specially tempting bait. The Council of Trent was about to reconvene; an invitation to England was in the air; here was ready-made opportunity. Dudley could (and did) promise the sending of a delegation.

From his point of view all this was risky but not absolutely perilous. No doubt he thought the queen nearer favourable decision than in fact she was; the ambassador's influence might be decisive. Promises were cheap, and the circumstances of English and of international politics would offer plenty of opportunities for retreat later on. The great object was to win the prize now. The queen's role at this stage was altogether slighter. Whatever her deeper hopes or intentions, she had overtly done little more than hint at her affection for Robert, speculate on marriage with a subject, and defer decision to the future. Elizabeth loved diplomacy for the sake of the game and was learning to love courtship for the same reason. Here was the chance to indulge all those pleasures—to play the delicious game of wooing with Dudley, to fence with De Quadra, probing out possibilities without making any commitment, and perhaps to do a little humdrum business in connection with the forthcoming General Council.

It was, however, the oblique intervention of the queen which ended this stage of the intrigue. At her bidding Cecil took over the initiative in dealing with De Quadra, and although the Secretary proposed that Philip be induced to write suggesting that Elizabeth marry soon, and choose one of her own subjects, Dudley clearly interpreted this royal move as a check. There was even a rumour that he proposed to offer an ultimatum to the queen—with the backing of Pembroke and Sidney—demanding she marry him or else license him to go abroad in the Spanish service. A courtier's letter reported, 'I hear she hath answered him that marry him she will not but will not only not license him to go over according to his political desire but will make him able to withstand the malice of his enemy.' At any rate the question of the match rested for the nonce and Bedford could report that 'the great matters whereof the world was wont to talk are now asleep, having had some fits both hot and cold'.[20]

Dudley's highly personal intrigues had, however, now become entangled with a public issue of supreme importance. The Tridentine Council was about to reconvene and it was rumoured – and then confirmed – that the pope would send a nuncio to Elizabeth in the hope of persuading her to send representatives. Cecil and his supporters hoped to build a backfire by winning French co-operation in an effort to delay further meetings of the Council, and Bedford was sent off to Paris to exploit his connections with the Protestant or Protestantizing nobles there.[21]

De Quadra thought he saw a chance in the Dudley intrigue for furthering Catholic aims. The bishop, in many respects a conventional ecclesiastical diplomat in the Habsburg service, was also a man of uncomplicated piety and was accordingly shocked by what he saw about him in England. Since in his eyes the interest of the Catholic faith and the Habsburg dynasty were always identical, he had no hesitation in pushing for a reversal of the English decision of 1559. With this in view he had always kept in touch with those men whom he regarded as the leaders of a Catholic party.

He hoped now that the intrigues of Lord Robert would make it possible to press the queen into receiving the nuncio and then perhaps into authorizing English representation at the Council. While remaining wary of any firm commitment, he was cordial towards the favourite and even hoped their intimacy might alienate the Protestants from the Crown. Indeed, he felt compelled to reassure Lord Montague, the leading peer of Catholic sympathies, and Heath, the late Archbishop of York, as to his intentions. Cecil, fully aware of the situation, countered by suggesting discussions between the ambassador and the Archbishop of Canterbury, no doubt hoping to entangle De Quadra in controversy and thus to bog down the whole negotiation in a marsh of theological disputation.[22]

In fact, the English Councillors were rather worried as to the queen's intentions now that the nuncio was actually in Brussels and making application for a passport. Throckmorton, with his usual impetuousness, fired off a dispatch to the queen which was a state paper in itself. He bluntly told her that were she no otherwise stirred with religion than Numa Pompilius or Sertorius, she might not alter the religion for her safety and policy's sake. He went on to urge that her whole strength rested on her adherence to Protestantism; to change her faith would merely reduce her to the same dependence and involvement abroad as her late sister. Secretary Cecil, also alarmed, was more discreet in his methods of dealing with the matter. 'The Bishop of Aquila', he succinctly observed, 'had entered into such a practice with a pretence to further the great matter here (meaning principally the Church matter, and perchance, accidentally, the other also) that he had taken faster hold to plant his purpose than was [my] ease shortly to root up.' But once the centre of gravity shifted from the question of marriage to that of religion, Cecil had an opening which he could (and did) exploit. The Secretary continued to hold the ambassador in discussion, giving the impression that differences between them were not ones of substance. Dudley went much farther in hopeful agreement with the bishop and wrote a friendly and encouraging letter to Montague. The queen remained aloof, avoiding direct mention of the religious question but speaking hopefully of the nuncio's reception.[23]

Then suddenly Cecil pounced. A chaplain of Sir Edward Waldegrave, lately a Marian Councillor, was seized on his way to Flanders. Compromising letters and the information extracted by a conciliar examination led to the arrest not only of Waldegrave and his wife but two other Marian Councillors, Wharton and Hastings of Loughborough, along with Arthur Pole, nephew to the late cardinal. The prisoners were examined by Cecil and Bacon with great thoroughness, with much questioning as to their views on the Scottish intervention and the re-marriage of the Queen of Scots. Enough was discovered to convict the accused of violating the religious statutes and they were fined and forced to take the oath of supremacy. Additional information about communications among the Catholic gentry, the Spanish ambassador, the imprisoned Marian bishops and the Catholics who had gone into exile abroad helped to create the impression of Catholic conspiracy. As Cecil rather brutally put it to Throckmorton, 'he thought it necessary to dull the Papists' expectation by discovering of certain Mass-mongers and punishing them'. He added, 'I take God to record I mean no evil to any of them, but only for the rebating of the Papists' humours which by the Queen's lenity grow too rank. I find it hath done much good.'[24]

These discoveries were highly effectual in puncturing De Quadra's hopes. A minute of Council unanimously advised the queen not to admit the nuncio. The document exploited fully the late arrests, pointing out that the very rumour of the nuncio's coming had disturbed the peace of the commonwealth. Doctrinal disputation was avoided, but the political hostility which subsisted between the papacy and England was made very explicit.[25]

To untangle all the threads of these intertwined intrigues is beyond our powers, but it is possible to make some speculative judgments about the principal actors. Robert Dudley's is probably the easiest role to assay. Eager and hopeful about his marriage, he thought the queen needed only a little more pressure to take the plunge; the Spanish ambassador and his royal master would provide it. While he would no doubt have preferred that pressure to come from political allies within the court, he knew by the year's end that was a vain hope; but the backing of a great foreign power which was traditionally a friend of England might influence both the sovereign and the more conservative elements in the political world. Dudley had no scruples about making promises to the Catholics since they were all necessarily post-dated. He did not win the prize he hoped for, but he made the happy and exciting discovery that even though the queen refused him her hand in marriage, her favour and protection remained steadfast. Hence, paradoxically, in spite of his defeats, both in the marriage intrigue and the affair of the nuncio, his position at court was strengthened. It was now plain for all to see that Dudley, secure within the immunity of the royal favour, was not subject to the usual penalties for political irresponsibility. He could do no political wrong; he could play fast and loose with the greatest issues of national life and yet fear no harm. Men would now have to count on Dudley as something more than a mere closet favourite; they would have to treat him as a serious political figure, albeit one whose movements were predictable by none of the set rules of political calculus.

Cecil's role is no harder to understand. He now stood firmly among those committed to the new religion, although he did not share all the political aims of its more ardent adherents. Their outlook was widely expansionist, and they dreamed of their own country playing a great role as the fulcrum of an international Protestant alliance, built around England, Scotland and France. Since they saw the steady Catholic orthodoxy of the Habsburgs as the great unchangeable fact of European politics, any shift of their queen towards alliance with that dynasty seemed to spell disaster for all their hopes.

Cecil shared their fears and some of their hopes — at least in regard to Scotland. More especially he feared and distrusted a revived Catholic party at home. To him that possibility seemed much more real and menacing than we, with the hindsight of history, can appreciate. Even the hapless Councillors of the late queen seemed to him a threat. And the possibility of a renascent Catholic party crystallizing around the irresponsible and all-powerful favourite was without doubt a nightmare to the Secretary. He was grimly determined to end the intrigue and choke off Catholic hopes. Hence he was not too nice in his methods and the unlucky Councillors of the late queen suffered accordingly. He had fought this battle with the clear-cut support of his brother-in-law, Bacon, and Lord Northampton, and he had won the whole Council to oppose the admission of the nuncio. It was a satisfying reassertion of his leadership in policy-making, but he must have been unpleasantly aware that he had not eliminated the favourite and that this rogue male of the political herd might, when he thought the time opportune, break loose again.

Of all the protagonists none is so difficult to fathom as the queen. The evidence is scantier than for the others, and hers was a personality of greater complexity and deeper ambivalence. In the months between summer 1560 and spring 1561 Elizabeth cast off the restraints of duty and convention and gave rein to her feelings in a way which disconcerted and dismayed her advisors. For an interval English affairs were threatened with the fearfully destructive kind of experience which overtook Scotland a few years later, in the wake of the Darnley murder and the Bothwell marriage. The queen seemed ready to risk all for love—almost but not quite all—for she never entirely ceased to listen to the voices of her servants. The shocked outcries of some and the distrustful silence of many others warned her how great the risk of such a marriage would be. The hard-won gains of the past two years would be sacrificed. Elizabeth's effortlessly royal personality had won the respect of hard-bitten politicians and calculating courtiers, and to some extent overcome their deep-rooted convictions as to feminine incapacity. All this would be lost, and worse still the kind of unbridled factionalism which lay just beneath the surface of English politics, and which a woman ruler was particularly hard put to suppress, would break forth with dangerous virulence.

All these things she probably saw and understood, yet the temptations of a match with Lord Robert remained strong. In this ambivalent mood she was not prepared to take any action herself, but not disposed to hinder Dudley's doing so. Hence her willingness to countenance the favourite's intrigues with De Quadra. The thought of falling back on Philip, of covering herself with his shield and carrying through the marriage with Habsburg backing, may have had a momentary appeal. But, as for her own part in the intrigue, she remained prudently cautious, probing and hinting but making no commitment. Nor was this mood long-lasting. When she admitted Cecil to the intrigue, probably in early March, she must have known its character would change, given his hostility to a Dudley marriage. The Secretary's cue would be to complicate and proliferate the issues of discussion until the whole matter died away in fruitless debate. And indeed, from that point on, the question of marriage fell into the background and discussion with the ambassador turned to the question of the nuncio, although Dudley kept the former issue alive as long as he could.

Elizabeth's attitude on the religious issue at this juncture is less troublesome to analyse. In the Chapel Royal she gave rein to her own preferences; there Catholic ornaments of crucifix and candles remained on the altar, to the scandal and indignation of left-wing Protestant circles. The queen's practice in this instance was a token of her antipathy towards their ideological rigidity rather than an indication of any strong religious leanings to the right. There is no evidence to suggest that the queen had any intention of changing her faith. Throughout the discussions she herself refrained from the hints or half-promises which Dudley lavished so profusely, and confined herself to the matter of the nuncio's visit. Cecil's real alarm makes it more than possible that the queen might have admitted the papal agent. Elizabeth valued highly the freedom from external intrusions on her authority guaranteed by the settlement of 1559, but she regarded this freedom as protecting her not only from papal intervention but also from the interference of her own subjects in this high matter. The symbols in the Chapel Royal were indicative not so much of a religious preference as of the royal determination to keep as wide as possible her freedom of action. The maintenance of some kind of dialogue with Rome was an element in that freedom, for it allowed room for manoeuvre, both at home and abroad.

The queen was, in fact, more old-fashioned in her views than her ministers. They accepted readily the sharpening of distinctions, the drawing of lines, between Catholic and Protestant; their faith in the new order made them confident in its triumph in any trial of strength; she, of course, would have preferred the blurred lines of her father's times, with the greater flexibility which they offered the Crown. She was, moreover, indifferent to the strong religious enthusiasm of the left wing and could not share their passionate partisanship. Cecil's agility in striking down the Catholics and the Council's consequent firmness in rejecting the nuncio's application for a passport, manoeuvred the queen once more along a road which identified her more firmly with the international Protestant cause.

The net result of these dangerous months of intrigue was to leave English politics in a state of heightened tension. Cecil, and indeed the whole Council, must have been profoundly shaken by this crisis. After all, they shared most of John Knox's views on the unnatural character of female government, even if they deplored his style of exposition; Mary Tudor's political conduct had gone far to confirm this prejudice. And now, in the second year of her reign, the new sovereign showed the same alarming symptoms. Indeed, the potentialities of the situation seemed even more worrying since Elizabeth had fixed her affections upon a man whose antecedents were the worst possible and whose accession to power promised faction in its ugliest guise.

When Cecil spoke to De Quadra of resignation and compared himself to a sailor fleeing to port before a storm, he was being more than merely rhetorical. If English politics dissolved into unrestrained faction-fighting and open violence, Cecil's own position would be acutely perilous. He had not yet had the time to build up a great interest of his own in landed estate and local influence, and his chances of remaining politically afloat in a great storm would have been poor. More than the great mansion he was so proudly building at Stamford would have come to a halt; Cecil's whole ambition for himself and his family would have been checked in mid-flight.

In the midst of such a gale, Elizabeth's appointment of Cecil as Master of the Wards must have been an immensely reassuring token of fairer weather to come. De Quadra wrote that Cecil had sold out to Dudley in exchange for the office; Throckmorton's secretary, Jones, thought as much although he afterwards modified his judgment.[26] Neither saw the matter very clearly; Cecil was no more converted to a Dudley adherent than before. But the award of this lucrative office was a substantial indication that the queen was prepared to advance the career of one of Dudley's known opponents; the favourite was not to enjoy a monopoly of the royal confidence. Coupled with the growing probability that—at least for the present—there would be no marriage, it went some way to re-establish a sense of balance and stability in the badly shaken fabric of the political world. When in March the queen gave Cecil free rein in dealing with De Quadra, he and his colleagues must have felt that their ship was once more on an even keel.

But reconciliation and peace had to be paid for. The queen was willing to forgo – or at least postpone – a marriage with Dudley, but his place in the royal favour was in no way diminished, while his position in the firmament of high politics was, as events would soon demonstrate, to be greatly enhanced. Before the recent convulsion there had existed only one focus of action within the court – the advanced Protestant party centred around Cecil. Now, there was, in Robert Dudley, a second nucleus. It was, of course, of entirely different character since Robert Dudley stood for no one except Robert Dudley; as yet he had taken up no ideological stance or policy position. But the drawing power of this pole of attraction was nevertheless potent since its force came from the Crown itself. How Dudley would use his power remained to be seen, but the fact that he was an established feature of the English political landscape had to be accepted – however reluctantly – by all Councillors and courtiers alike.

6 *The Newhaven Adventure*

FROM THE late spring of 1562 to August of the following year, the great preoccupation of the English government was its intervention in Normandy in favour of the Huguenots. But before that episode opened up fully, there was played out the first scene of a play which was to have many acts—Mary Stuart's attempts to win a place in the English succession. With the death of Francis II in December 1560 a new phase opened both in French and in Scottish politics. From the English point of view, the change in Paris was at first a hopeful one since the Guises went into at least temporary eclipse and the formal link between France and Scotland was now completely snapped. But when they looked northward, they had less cause to rejoice. The favourable pattern of Scottish politics which had been taking shape under the guidance of Lord James Stuart and Secretary Maitland now rapidly fell apart, all the pieces once again in confusion. The work of Cecil and his collaborators stood in jeopardy.

More important still, the Queen of Scots's relation to English politics was now radically altered. As Queen of France she had been a threat to English interests because she could be used as a pawn by the French monarchy, but her domestic importance was slight so long as she was the consort of a realm which was traditionally England's chief enemy. Disencumbered of her French throne, Mary had to be seen in a new light. Her claims to the English succession now began to gain real political weight. In this respect Scottish sovereignty was an asset since union with the weaker kingdom was already much in the minds of English leaders; the more sober-minded saw it as a means for removing a standing threat; for the bolder it was a glorious opportunity to expand English power.

The succession question was a murkily uncertain one. The leading Protestant contender, Lady Catherine Grey, had been revealed during the summer of 1561 as the secret wife of the Earl of Hertford, son of the Protector Somerset, and was now about to bear his child. The queen's anger knew no bounds; both the culprits went to the Tower, while the legality of the marriage was attacked with every weapon the queen could bring to bear.[1] Elizabeth would no doubt have preferred to see her cousin remain a virgin; a married heiress presumptive offered too many problems to a virgin queen. But her fury was perhaps not unmixed with satisfaction that Lady Catherine had discredited herself, thrown a blight of illegitimacy on her offspring, and effectively exiled herself from court.

All this tended to raise the stock of the Queen of Scots; whatever the legality of her claims, she was undeniably a queen, unattached for the present, and possessor of the rich dowry of Scotland. All turned on the way she conducted herself now, when for the first time in her life she was no longer the instrument of others. There followed some months of uncertainty as Mary canvassed marital prospects on the Continent, while carefully feeling out the leaders of Scottish opinion. In the end she decided on a return home and on the shrewd policy of collaboration with the Lord James and Maitland, reserving her own rights to practise the Catholic faith but leaving untouched the Protestant ascendancy already established in her kingdom.

Elizabeth lost the first round in the sparring which began with Mary's return home; she attempted to trade a passport to travel through England for Mary's ratification of the Treaty of Edinburgh. That treaty had never been formally accepted by the Scottish Crown. But Mary evaded such proposals and took the risk of sailing directly for Scotland in August 1561 just before an ungracious and belated permission to pass through England was granted.[2] But once it became clear that Mary did not propose to disturb the tenure of Maitland and Lord James as the political leaders of Scotland, tension between the two cousins subsided. The questions in dispute were allowed to drift; for the time being the grave issues at stake were left to sleep.

In both courts this welcome relaxation of tension endured to the end of the year. In England the summer's progress of 1561 was marked by the queen's entertainment of Lord Robert, whose favour with his mistress continued to wax. There are glimpses of the queen's romps in this light-hearted season. She and Lord Robert, entertaining the Spanish ambassador, teased the embarrassed prelate with the suggestion that he be the minister of their nuptials. On another day the queen stole in disguise to watch Dudley shooting a match in Windsor Park. There was much company at court, the Duke of Norfolk frequently among those present, not always friendly to the favourite, but smiled upon by the queen.[3] The beams of royal favour streamed down steadily on Robert; there was less talk of marriage but more public acceptance of his prime place in the royal affections. What had seemed a dangerous and agitating scandal a year ago was gradually beginning to be looked upon with wary acceptance as a fact of the political universe. Subtly the relationship itself altered as the fever of first love subsided into a more settled affection. Dudley himself still entertained high hopes; in January 1562 he again sounded out the Spanish ambassador, asking for a letter of support and hinting that the French were willing to provide one. The queen herself told De Quadra she would not marry sight unseen, and hence would probably choose an Englishman, 'in which case she thought she could find no person more fitting than Lord Robert'.[4] At this stage Elizabeth was content to drift comfortably with events, allowing Lord Robert to play his own game, with just enough encouragement to keep up interest but not enough to alarm his watchful antagonists.

This holiday mood gave little satisfaction to men of a sober cast of mind. Cecil fretted that he was not listened to; the Lord Treasurer Winchester gloomily totted up the royal debts; others mourned over lost opportunities to make provision for the future. Meanwhile the Scots lords were united in an unaccustomed harmony around their personable mistress. Knox's stern disapproval of their compromise with Mary on religion weakened their alliance with the religious radicals and forced them to reluctant co-operation with their queen in her schemes for her own advancement. The centre of their strategy was to frame an accord between the two queens in which Mary would formally surrender all claims to the English throne during the lifetime of Elizabeth or any of her heirs; in return she was to have an acknowledgment of the Stuart place in the English succession if Elizabeth's line failed. Their siege plans were well laid. The Duke of Guise, Mary's uncle, pushed the scheme with Throckmorton at Paris, promising that his niece would not marry without English approval. Lord James Stuart (now Earl of Moray) brought to bear the weight of his sobersided statesmanship in a letter to Queen Elizabeth, suggesting that the isle might be bound in perpetual friendship if Elizabeth provided for his mistress's rights in lawful descent from Henry VII. The subtle Scottish Secretary, Maitland of Lethington, arrived in England, heralded by a perfect snowstorm of persuasive letters. All his considerable art was lavished in an attempt to win Cecil's support. The English ambassador at Edinburgh, Randolph, was put under similar persuasions, with hints of a Scottish pension and a Scottish wife. He wrote, 'This trade is now clean cut off from me; I have to traffic now with other kind of merchants than before. They know the value of their wares and in all places how the market goeth.'[5] This was, of course, just the point; the Scots, hitherto dependants in relation to England, now found themselves in a strong bargaining position. Mary's immediate claims to the English throne had little more than nuisance value in the market for the moment, but dealings in her future were highly attractive speculations.

For the English court the situation was embarrassing and rather difficult. Cecil told Throckmorton that the Council was divided on the matter and admitted his own fear of touching it for fear of wrong construction. The ambassador had earlier expressed his own uncertainties but thought that not to deal at all was too dangerous, in view of their own queen's childlessness. The Scots in the meantime pressed their case a stage further by urging a personal interview between the two queens, insisting that on the vital question of religion Elizabeth alone might draw the Scots queen from her old allegiance. Maitland found Cecil reserved in the matter and complained of his 'brief and dark sentences'; finally he himself appeared at the English court to press the case in person, and by July 6th he had won his battle: an agreement was drawn up, signed by him and Lord Chamberlain Howard, on the precise conditions of the meeting.[6]

The decision to go forward with the interview was in fact a royal one. The queen had in this matter directly contravened the Council's views. In Cecil's words, 'This interview is hardly got of this Council; only the authority of the crown had got consent thereto and it is strange to see the vehemency of Her Majesty here.' The French ambassador heard not only that the whole Council was against the interview but that Maitland had used Lord Robert to convince the queen.[7]

The Councillors' position was peculiarly awkward. The Scots baited their proposals for the meeting with the offer of a formal and full-scale alliance, but only if Mary's claims to the English succession were recognized. True, she would succeed only after the issue of Elizabeth, but there lay the catch—the queen had neither husband nor child. Sudden death was all too familiar to the sixteenth century; the ministers had but to note the two recent examples in France. And to all supporters of the reformed religion and of the international polity which they envisaged as its secular counterpart, this meant irrevocable catastrophe: a Catholic sovereign at home, dependence on a Guise-ruled France abroad. And yet, the perilous problem of succession could not be evaded by responsible Councillors, and the Scottish proposals were not without attraction, as Throckmorton noted.

In the meantime Catherine Grey had borne her child in the Tower; but the queen's anger showed no abatement. Another possible claimant to the succession, Margaret, Countess of Lennox, descendant of Queen Margaret's second marriage, had overreached herself in intrigue, with the result that her husband, the exiled Scottish Earl of Lennox, was in the Tower and she herself under restraint at Sheen. Her eager plotting for the benefit of her son, Lord Darnley, had been uncovered, and the government had not hesitated to pounce upon her.[8]

Why the queen finally accepted the interview is not at all certain. If Lord Robert was Maitland's ally and pushed the meeting, there is one explanation which might hold water. Robert might well calculate that once Mary's rights were established, the anxiety of the English Councillors to see the queen married and with child would override any personal objections they entertained towards him. There were, of course, diplomatic reasons for accepting the proposal since an outright refusal would have given the Scots a legitimate grievance to play upon. And, if one looks at dates, it seems probable the queen had, at the moment of acceptance, already in hand a watertight excuse for postponement. By early July an Anglo-French crisis, simmering for some months, was reaching boiling-point.

The background to this international crisis lay in the circumstances of French domestic politics. The French body politic was infected by the same virus of religious disagreement which afflicted England and Scotland, but its symptoms were different across the Channel. In England circumstance had wedded the dynasty to firm acceptance of the new faith; in France the reigning house wavered between a determined acceptance of the old faith and a mediatory role between the two. Two strong factions found opportunity for development, one linked to the political interests of the Catholic Guises; the other, to those of the Protestant house of Châtillon. The rough balance maintained since the death of Francis II by the alliance of the King of Navarre with the Châtillons broke down when that potentate shifted his support to the Guises, who appeared in force in Paris. The Protestant leader, Condé, responded by summoning his followers in arms and the two sides confronted each other, in expectation of open fighting.

The English queen's first response was a proposal that her ambassador mediate between the contending parties. But Throckmorton already was looking forward to a more ambitious intervention in French affairs. To the queen he urged the danger of Spanish intervention on the Catholic side and dropped the hint that it might chance in these garboils that some opportunity would offer to regain possession of Calais, or some other place of consequence on the Continent. To Cecil he wrote the same day (April 17th) a franker letter. 'Our friends, the Protestants,' he wrote, 'must be handled and dandled,' so that, should Spain intervene, they, 'For their defence, or for desire of revenge or affection to the Queen, may be moved to give her possession of Calais, Dieppe, or Newhaven, perhaps all three.' (Le Havre was known to the English as Newhaven.) Sir Nicholas drew a comparison with the Scottish situation in 1559 and then, moving from persuasion to action, sent his servant, Middlemore, to conduct a secret agent of the Châtillons to England.[9]

There was a pause while, through the late spring and early summer, France alternated between hope and despair, one day offering peace, the next dashing all hope, and the third reviving it. Fighting actually broke out late in June; the Protestants were not fortunate in the field and were soon constrained to seek help abroad.

The English response at this juncture of affairs strikes a note of sharp contrast to the comparable situation in Scotland three years earlier. Then, in the first year of the reign, most English leaders had been hesitant and uncertain, doubtful of their country's ability to run any risks. But now, in 1562, with the Scottish success behind them, they had little hesitation about taking a bold and chancy plunge. The *dramatis personae* had also changed with time. In that first episode in Elizabethan foreign relations, the centre of all thought and action was one man, William Cecil; his was the driving force throughout. This time the impulse to action came from a different quarter. One strong influence was the ambassador in Paris, whose dispatches, streaming in steadily, alternately persuaded and exhorted his government to active support of the French Protestants. But far more important was the role of the favourite. What is almost certain is that Lord Robert Dudley was the moving spirit in this whole enterprise. Dudley had been in communication with the Châtillons in the preceding winter (without Throckmorton's knowledge), seeking an alliance for mutual advantage.[10] From May on he was actively involved in the government's negotiations with the Prince of Condé, the Huguenot leader; it was Dudley's brother-in-law, Sir Henry Sidney, who went as special emissary to France in that month.[11] It was also his adherents and servants who were the principal English agents in France during the earliest stages of the enterprise — Henry Killigrew, Edward Horsey and Thomas Leighton. At the same time there was a reconciliation between Dudley and

Throckmorton. Sir Nicholas's outspoken criticism of the favourite in the winter of 1560–61 had made them enemies. Previously Bedford had offered to patch things up, but the intermediary now was Sidney. Letters were exchanged by the principals, and the treaty of peace ratified when Dudley acted as godfather for Sir Nicholas's youngest child.[12] It was hardly accident that at this particular moment Lord Robert went out of his way to conciliate the man who stood at the very centre of Anglo-French relations.

Dudley had been receiving very substantial marks of continuing royal favour. At the height of his dealings with De Quadra had come the first really large grant of land, principally out of his father's attainted estate. But it was in 1562 that the stream of largesse began to flow abundantly. During that summer a series of patents licensed Dudley to export eighty thousand undressed white cloths over the next few years (the Merchant Adventurers' yearly quota was only thirty thousand) with the assurance that no one else would be granted such licence. These licences could of course be sold to exporters and were one of the most prized forms of royal beneficence. The spring did not cease to flow even after this flood; in October the queen added an annual pension of one thousand pounds, charged on the customs of London, to be enjoyed by the recipient until such time as he had lands of equal value. The terms of this patent recited the 'queen's great favour where she has declared him worthy above the rest of men on account of his many excellent virtues and gifts of mind'.[13]

There had been rumours that Dudley would be raised to the peerage; although he was not so favoured in his own person, his elder brother Ambrose was in fact restored to their father's earldom of Warwick in December 1561. This was followed in April by a generous grant of his father's land, including the castle, manor, and borough of Warwick with much other land in that vicinity.[14] This meant a great deal to both brothers. Restoration to the select circle of earls not only cleared the taint of 1553 from their name (so far as royal action could do it) but gave them the special aura which attached to peerage in that rank-conscious world. Moreover, it gave them a landed base, a place in local society; they ceased to be mere court exotics and began to take on the appearance of sturdy native flora, rooted in town and countryside. With these tangible and public evidences of continuing royal backing, Robert Dudley was ready to push himself forward into the great issues of state. The Newhaven expedition was to be his first essay in the great game of statesmanship.

The mystery of this episode is, of course, Secretary Cecil's role. The surviving evidence is dismayingly slight; only one policy paper remains from his pen.[15] In this document of late July he analyses in very gloomy terms the consequences of a Guisan victory in France — French alliance with Spain, a match between Mary Stuart and the prince of Spain, and a concerted attack on the English regime by a combination of foreign Catholic invaders and domestic Catholic rebels. But he does not follow his analysis with any proposals for action. Earlier in the year he had backed a scheme for collaboration with the German Protestants for the general defence of Protestantism. Later he favoured mediatory efforts in France, and in July hoped for a German army, paid for by England, to enter France on the side of the Protestants. But from then on he appears solely as the man of business, planning and organizing finance and supply for the expedition, but never as the maker of policy. Nor is there any recorded echo of his earlier opposition to just such an intervention in France when it was proposed in July 1560.

Dudley was apparently successful in carrying the Council with him; only a hint of Mason's scepticism mars their seeming harmony.[16] The queen too — in sharp contrast to her hesitations in 1560 — seems to have agreed without hesitation to the whole scheme. Events began to move in mid-July when the full Council was summoned and when orders for military preparations began to flow out, but it was late August before actual agreement was reached with the Huguenot leaders. Condé was to receive a subvention of 140,000 crowns; he was to yield Newhaven, to be held by Elizabeth until Calais was handed over. English forces were to be dispatched to Dieppe and inland to Rouen to aid the Protestants.[17]

An English commander had now to be appointed; when the choice was made, contemporaries were taken aback. Norfolk had been among those sent for in July and, since he had commanded the last major expedition, might be chosen again. The French ambassador heard it would be Bedford, but by early September it was known that Ambrose Dudley was the man. His past military service was limited to participation as a gentleman volunteer in the English army sent to Flanders in 1557. It was not surprising that the French leaders rather nervously inquired what old captains came with the earl.[18]

Warwick was given a freer hand than either Norfolk or Grey had enjoyed in Scotland; he was accompanied by a council of war of experienced captains but there was no 'minister of state' like Sadler at his elbow. The earl's choice of advisors was signally important, for he turned to the religious party of the extreme left. His clerk of council was Thomas

Wood, a Marian exile and an elder of the Genevan congregation. And with him, as chaplain to the earl, came Wood's brother-in-law, William Whittingham, another member of Knox's circle and a man who as yet hesitated to accept the 1559 settlement. Two other clerics, both Knoxians, Keith and Bradbridge, filled out what has been aptly called a Calvinist 'cave of Adullam'. There was even talk of bringing over Christopher Goodman, the ultra-Calvinist divine, who dared not enter England. Safely outside the bounds of English law, in Newhaven, these divines could – and did – use a variant mode of worship, more consonant with Calvinist liturgical ideas than the imperfect Prayer Book. Warwick's principal lay advisors were men of the same stripe. Cuthbert Vaughan, the Comptroller, complained during the winter that the forthcoming Parliament would do nothing to complete the reform of the Church. Sir Adrian Poynings, the Marshal, was a Hampshire squire, one of the few gentry in that county who were fully and publicly backing the new faith.[19]

The Dudley brothers worked in close collaboration, so these dispositions of Ambrose unquestionably had the approval of his brother, Robert. After his long flirtation with De Quadra and his cultivation of the English Catholics, Dudley was now veering about a full 180 degrees to a course which brought him into close association with the most advanced wing of the Protestants and commitment to the expansive foreign policy of the radical politicians. The family tradition was, of course, one of political alliance with the advanced reformers, and Dudley's role in the distribution of ecclesiastical patronage had placed him on good terms with a large number of eminent clerics, most of them of the exilic tradition.[20] Now – at least as early as January 1562 – he had reached out for a link with French Protestant leadership.

Dudley's motives and aims can only be guessed at, but his actions show a growing independence and a boldness tempered by shrewdness. For the time being a royal match was out of his reach, but he had grasped the all-important fact that even though the queen withheld her hand in marriage, she was still unstinting in favours and in support for him. He was quick to see that this opened possibilities for a new orientation of his ambitions. He could hope now to free himself a little from royal control and to launch his own bark in the mainstream of English politics. By a daringly conceived strategy he began with a flanking movement which challenged the leadership of the religious and political left. Hitherto its most articulate spokesman in high places had been Cecil.

Dudley was now appealing to two different, though overlapping, groups on the radical end of the spectrum of opinion. The first consisted of those political figures who advocated an aggressive foreign policy aimed at the advancement of international Protestantism under English leadership—a programme of religio-political nationalism. The second group, more clerical in character, was more purely interested in further reform within the English Church on the model of Geneva. At the moment the issue was one of foreign policy, but it is important that the Dudleys chose also to go out of their way to patronize the clerical malcontents and thus to stake out a claim as grand patrons and protectors of the far-out radicals.

Warwick arrived to take up his command at the end of October; actual occupation of Le Havre and Dieppe had taken place at the beginning of the month. The climax of the French civil struggle came quickly, in the battle for Rouen, held by the Protestants against Catholic siege. The queen warily held the bulk of Warwick's forces in Newhaven, and only a few hundred English participated in the defence of the Norman capital before its fall in late November. Dudley's friend and protégé, Henry Killigrew, lay badly wounded in the city, a captive in Catholic hands.[21] The fall of Dieppe followed hard on that of Rouen, and the English found themselves confined to Newhaven with a hostile hinterland behind them. The French parties by now had begun negotiation again, and the centre of activity swung back from the battlefield to the court.

At the very beginning of the venture Elizabeth had appointed a new ambassador to Paris, Sir Thomas Smith, who had been nominated the preceding November (1561).[22] Throckmorton had long sought recall; he must have known that his high-vaulting ambitions could never be realized unless he was nearer the centre of the political universe. His successor was a man of altogether different stripe. Smith, Edward's Secretary of State, had fallen with Somerset, and had not re-emerged to employment of any importance under Elizabeth until now. A Cambridge graduate, and later Vice-Chancellor of that university, he was, like Mason, Petre or Wotton, an amphibian, half-layman, half-cleric. Although now married and established as an Essex squire, he still claimed the deanery of Carlisle under an Edwardian grant. Smith was Protestant enough in his religious outlook, but his angle of view was much closer to the cautious Cecil's than to that of the impetuous Throckmorton. From the first he enjoyed a close relationship with the Secretary. The new ambassador lacked the self-confidence and dash of his predecessor and was in a much more dependent relation to Cecil. This moderate and peaceable man was to prove a more satisfactory collaborator to the Secretary, especially now that Throckmorton was moving rapidly into the orbit of Dudley.

Throckmorton did not in fact vanish from the French scene so soon as was planned since he managed to fall first into the hands of the Huguenots, and then into those of the Catholics, and returned home only in January 1563. English policy through these winter months vacillated uncertainly while the French parties jockeyed for position, slowly and fumblingly drawing towards agreement. The capture of Condé and of Montmorency, followed by the deaths of Navarre and then of Guise and his two brothers, weakened the factions and opened the way for reconciliation. The increasing unsureness of English policy during this period reflected a certain lack of coherence. In striking contrast to the Scottish venture three years earlier, English aims were cloudy. In Scotland national and religious interests had coincided on both sides. In France there was an embarrassing incompatibility between the high purposes of a professed religious solidarity and the obvious conflict of national interests. The most ardent French Protestant could hardly reconcile himself to the English grab at Calais.

This embarrassment disappeared quickly enough when the French parties made peace among themselves and united in common action against the alien intruders at Newhaven. English policy could then aim solely at the straightforward goal of forcing the French to disgorge Calais in return for Le Havre. But how much should England risk in pursuit of this goal; how much money, how many men and ships? This was the decision to be made in the spring of 1563 as the armies of the French monarchy converged on the lonely garrison of Newhaven. The choice of resistance was probably inevitable; too much was invested in men, money and pride to retreat at the first French summons. And there was the will-o'-the-wisp hope that some new rupture of the fragile French compromise might throw the Huguenots again into English arms.

While the issue within France was in doubt, England's two ambassadors — Throckmorton had returned in February on a mission to Protestant headquarters — pulled in opposite directions. Throckmorton was all for encouraging Protestant intransigence; Smith, on the other hand, followed a generally mediatory line, seeking to find a formula for religious compromise. Throckmorton gradually fell under royal displeasure for lingering too long in the Huguenot camp. (In the end he was unlucky enough to fall a prisoner into Catholic hands again.) Elizabeth declined to follow Warwick's urgings that she make a maximum military effort in France, while French affairs were still disorganized; she even refused to provide

money for fortifications at Le Havre. After the religious peace was concluded in France, the English government continued to hope against hope
that some change might still occur in their favour, but the French forces
advanced steadily. Nature herself intervened against the English at this
juncture with the appearance of plague among the garrison in June 1563.
There was some effort to provide reinforcements by sea, but the weather
baffled this, and in the end there was nothing for it but surrender. The
French allowed the wounded Warwick and the battered remnant of the
garrison to return to England, where they promptly spread the infection
of the plague which they brought home with them.

English statesmen could now meditate at leisure on the events of the
last year. English interest in keeping the French Protestants intact and in
breaking Guise control of the French court was satisfied, although English
actions had relatively little to do with this outcome, but the speculation
that Calais could somehow be extorted from a distracted France had been
altogether ill-founded; and England had neither the force nor the skill to
maintain Newhaven against the whole power of France. Dudley's scheme
for combining the old-fashioned goal of securing a foothold on the
Continent with the new-fashioned hope of succouring true religion had
come to nought. Yet, humiliating as the outcome had been, no vital
English interest was touched. France was in no position to take further
steps once the English were ejected from her soil. Lives and money had
been poured out uselessly; a bid to re-establish an English position on the
Continent had failed; yet England's relative international position remained unchanged, neither substantially better nor substantially worse
than in the spring of 1562.

But the Dudleys, with a kind of perversely good fortune, far from
suffering from the ill-fated enterprise which they had sponsored, continued
to flourish with unabated vigour. In October 1562 Robert had won the
coveted prize of a place at the Council board although his pleasure at this
promotion may have been alloyed by seeing another new appointee there,
his old critic and ill-wisher, Norfolk.[23] No doubt the queen thought it
wise to offer this appeasement to the favourite's resentful rivals. Dudley's
faithful attendance and regular attention soon drew him into the heart of
all state business. In June 1563, just as the disaster at Newhaven was
approaching its climax, the queen endowed Robert with a princely gift
of lands, including Kenilworth Castle and a great clutch of holdings on the
Welsh Border and inside the principality, including the old Marcher lord-
ships of Mortimer and Denbigh.[24]

7

Cecil had remained throughout an active participant in all business connected with the expedition but cautiously reserved in his policy views. In December he urged Throckmorton to do what he could to make peace, 'for the charges of these wars will eat away the fruit thereof'.[25] But, if he had his doubts, he loyally followed his mistress's policy of holding on at Newhaven until hope was gone. During these months the working alliance between Cecil and Throckmorton, which had subsisted from the beginning of the reign, began to dissolve. As Throckmorton involved himself more deeply in French Huguenot affairs (to the royal displeasure) and pushed hard for an extremist policy, Cecil found himself more sympathetic to the irenic Sir Thomas Smith. As early as January, Throckmorton accused the Secretary of indifference to his plight, and relations did not improve with time.[26]

Dudley's new flanking position on the extreme left of the English political spectrum was beginning to pay off. This new magnet was drawing those ardent spirits who chafed impatiently for bolder action. Cecil, who without changing his own views had been shoved a stage to the right, to a middle-of-the-road stance, was forced to readjust his position accordingly.

The first outlines of a Dudley faction were just visible in the men grouped around the favourite, dependent on his favour and agents of his will. The most eminent and able member of this group up to 1562 was Henry Killigrew, a Cornish gentleman, plotter and exile under Mary, and from the earliest months a diplomatic agent for the new regime. His adherence to Dudley in the crisis of 1560–61 had sealed their attachment and Killigrew had had his reward in a tellership of the Exchequer, granted to him in June 1561.[27] Now, with the recruitment of Sir Nicholas Throckmorton, Dudley was drawing a larger fish into his net. The adherence of so able a politician as Sir Nicholas was another token of the favourite's new stature in the world of politics.

The return of Warwick's plague-stricken veterans to England marked the end, not only of the ill-fated enterprise in France, but also of a stage in English political affairs. Elizabeth had burned her fingers rather painfully and would not give her consent to another adventure in foreign affairs until the very end of the decade. The preoccupations of the Habsburgs and of France in their own tangled affairs made possible this period of isolation from continental matters. It also meant that the focus of English politics over the next half-dozen years would be found in the English and Scottish courts.

The stage just closing was one which had witnessed the development of important alignments in the English court. William Cecil had been the first to assume his place. By persuading his mistress to assist a revolutionary regime in Scotland to power, he had manoeuvred the queen into the position of protectress of radical Protestantism north of the Tweed and excited the hopes of all those who looked toward the emergence of a Protestant internationale in western Europe. He himself stood out as the advocate of a forward policy for England, one of bold initiatives in favour of the new religion. At home his ruthless attack on the English Catholics and his resolute determination to prevent any resurgence of the old religion were clear indications of his anti-papal views. Nevertheless, as Cecil had made clear to his mistress in the summer of 1560, his views included quite calculated limits as to the scope of English action and he had little interest in active collaboration with Protestants outside the island of Great Britain. The confidence, albeit somewhat grudging, shown by the queen, and the more enthusiastic backing he received from his fellow-Councillors seemed for a moment to give promise of a stable regime, focused on Cecil's role as leading minister and on the policy he advocated.

Any such calculations were quite overturned in the summer and autumn of 1561 by the rapid rise of Dudley to high political place. The favours lavished on Lord Robert and the cold shoulder turned towards Cecil seemed to portend a season of royal irresponsibility and to threaten political anarchy. This did not in fact ensue, but the unbalance created by the royal partiality to Dudley only very slowly righted itself. Cecil's appointment to the Wards and the opportunity which Elizabeth offered him to put a spoke in Dudley's intrigue with De Quadra were encouraging tokens. But Lord Robert's continuing role in promoting the French expedition and his success in carrying the queen with him in this risky scheme, at once ultra-Protestant and expansionist in aim, must have been galling to Cecil. However, by the summer of 1563 something like a balance had been struck between the rivals. The Secretary gradually recovered influence in the last phases of the Newhaven affair with the appointment of Smith to replace Throckmorton and with the royal refusal to make any determined effort to retain a foothold in France. The favourite was showered with gifts and reassured as to his privileged place in the queen's esteem and in the English political firmament. But the policy, which he had pushed, of involvement in French internal affairs by backing the Huguenots was to be dropped.

So as things stood by the summer of 1563 the queen's government rested on an ill-assorted triad of leaders – Elizabeth herself, Secretary Cecil, and Lord Robert Dudley. The queen had demonstrated her command of supremely important capacities as a ruler; she could master her own passions and subordinate them to the overriding needs of political stability, and she could hold in a firm rein a team of two mutually incompatible but able servants. Both remained her loyal servants but each was reluctant in his collaboration with his fellow-Councillor. Their roles were of the first importance since they had each successively taken the lead in drawing their mistress on to important commitments of English power and to a significant shaping of English policy.

Each had revealed by now a good deal of his particular personality. Cecil embodied all the qualities of a permanent civil servant – great industry, wide knowledge of affairs, infinite discretion and a willingness to bow obediently to royal decisions. Dudley, the glittering favourite, was showing surprising evidence of great political shrewdness, adaptability, and a useful competence at public affairs. The flamboyant Master of the Horse and the sobersided Secretary could hardly have contrasted more widely in personality. But on matters of policy their views were not so far apart. Both stood well over on the Protestant side of the religious spectrum, but Dudley well to the left of Cecil. The Secretary represented a cautious, limited and essentially *politique* kind of Protestantism, conditioned primarily by his anxiety to retain maximum autonomy of action for England, amounting to a kind of isolationism. Dudley, for his part, was no more personally pious, but he was already in close touch with the clerical radicals of the extreme, Genevan left, and sympathetic to a bolder, more expansionist foreign policy which blended in uncertain quantities a zeal for the international Protestant cause with rather vague dreams of renewed English prestige on the Continent. One could certainly not speak of party, and perhaps not even of faction as yet, but these two leaders were clearly the focal points around which ideas and men would tend to group themselves.

At the conclusion of five years of power the regime had chalked up one great victory for England – the expulsion of the French from the island – and by its policies at home and abroad identified itself with the aspirations of the Protestant interest. Alliance with the most coherent, vital and organized element in English society was a firm basis for future stability. Nevertheless, the regime was still terrifyingly fragile since the absence of royal husband or royal heir and the total uncertainty as to the next claimant to the throne cast lengthening shadows. The queen's partiality for Robert Dudley sent tremors through the system and boded ill for any satisfactory solution to the marriage problem. Worse still, a near-fatal royal illness in October 1562 opened for a horrifying moment vistas of ultimate chaos. Until some kind of answer to these questions of marriage and succession was provided, the political future must necessarily remain more than doubtful.

Part Three

MARY AND ELIZABETH

7 Succession and Marriage: The First Phase

THE TREATY of Troyes, signed in April 1564, marked the restoration of diplomatic civility between England and France. For the next four — nearly five — years England was to be free of serious involvement with a continental power. The queen, whose willingness to gamble on the Newhaven venture sharply contrasted with her hesitations in 1559–60, now fell back into her characteristic dislike of enterprises which imperilled her own freedom of action. Fortunately for her, both France and Spain had their own preoccupations during these years and little time to spare for British affairs. Since the beginning of the reign English political action had been largely shaped by outside circumstance — the rising in Scotland, the reassembling of the Council of Trent, the French religious war. The one great exception was, of course, the Dudley affair. Now, in the next phase of the reign, the centre of action would be in the island and in essentially domestic problems — the royal marriages, both English and Scottish, proposed or actual; and the delicate question of the English succession. The islanders were to make their own history in these years, little influenced by outside forces.

Events between 1562 and 1568 fall into two major phases. The first, lasting up to the marriage of Mary Stuart and Henry Darnley in the summer of 1565, was characterized largely by the negotiations over a possible husband for the Scottish queen. She rather abruptly solved this problem by marrying her cousin. Then, for a time, it was the English queen's courtships which dominated events. In the last stage the centre of action was again in the North, where events accelerated into the breathless melodrama of the Darnley murder, the Bothwell marriage, Mary's imprisonment, deposition and escape, and finally her arrival in Cumberland in May 1568.

These developments led to changes in the character of English political life. The problems of this phase were different from those of the early years of the reign, and a number of new actors took their places on the political stage. The central issues of marriage and of succession were not new problems, but they now took on more urgency and gravity. Earlier, they had seemed simple enough; the queen would marry and, God willing, produce a male heir. Her choice of husband was naturally a matter of concern, but the list of possible candidates seemed long and varied enough. But by 1564 the problem had assumed more than one level of complexity. In its most obvious aspect it could be grasped by the most simple-minded. If the queen died without issue and with no settled succession arrange- ments, there would probably be civil war—a return of the Wars of the Roses made even more dreadful by the acid hatreds of rival religions. Therefore, as a matter of public policy Elizabeth should marry with all dispatch. And so Councillors and Parliaments unrelentingly urged their sovereign over and over again through these years. There simplicity ended.

First of all, the queen's maidenly reserves about matrimony, treated initially as a matter of mere form, now began to assume an air of serious- ness. Secondly, since 1560, it was clear that if there were to be a royal husband, the queen's choice would be Robert Dudley, probably the most cordially hated man in the court. And even her partial disengagement, when she offered him to her cousin of Scotland in 1564, did little to alleviate the situation. The Earl of Leicester (a peer since 1564) was not likely idly to watch the prize withheld from him fall to someone else's lot, since this would mean not mere loss of favour but utter ruin to him. And, as time went by, anti-Dudley feeling hardened into an organized anti-Dudley faction, led by the Duke of Norfolk, Privy Councillor since 1562, and his cousin, the Earl of Sussex, who joined the ranks of major political figures on returning from Ireland in 1564. They had the discreet backing of William Cecil.

Thus the marriage problem, simple enough in its basic form and pre- sumably tractable, had become in fact hopelessly entangled in the bitter personal antipathies and the resulting factionalism engendered by the favourite. When a campaign was mounted to bring about a marriage be- tween Elizabeth and the Archduke Charles of Austria, it was easy to argue on high public considerations his eminent suitability as a candidate and the manifest advantages of such a match. It was harder to disguise the fact that the campaign was also a determined assault on Dudley by his enemies. Hence the events of these years must be seen both as a serious effort by responsible Councillors of the Crown to provide for the threat- ened security of the state through a suitable royal marriage and as a bitter, highly personal, and often sordid, episode of political in-fighting at the highest court levels.

But if the marriage question hopelessly entangled public policy and personal antipathies, the succession problem was even knottier. Elizabeth's steady evasion of matrimony naturally drove her subjects to think more and more of the advantage of a settled succession, and thus of Mary Stuart. Mary's unblemished descent and her unquestioned royalty — not to mention the existence of a male heir — made her very attractive, not only to those who shared her Catholic convictions, but to that larger class who longed for the security which her assured rights in the succession might bestow on their future. Here again circumstances complicated simplicity.

The force of Protestant religious feeling in the country became apparent in the resistance to the vestiarian decrees in 1565 and in the spread of the newly self-conscious Puritan movement. It was heightened by events in France and the Low Countries, which dangerously threatened the very life of the reformed religion on the Continent. And inevitably the great political questions of the day were transmuted into new forms as they came to be measured against the overarching demands of religious ideology. The issue took concrete form in the negotiations for the archducal match. Was it possible, in order to secure the manifest advantages of such a marriage, to exempt Charles from the anti-Catholic statutes and allow him personal freedom to hear the mass? The question became much graver when men began to doubt that their consciences would permit them to yield obedience to a Catholic queen in a future reign. This was a dangerous matter on which to divide Englishmen. Here the alignments rested not only on the merely personal hatreds and dynastic jealousies of the court magnates which separated Leicester's friends from his foes. There was a deep gulf between those for whom the new religion in some form was a *sine qua non* of English national life and those *politiques* who cheerfully hoped for Mary's easy conversion or trusted that some workable compromise satisfactory to those of both faiths would be found. These years were a restless, irritable, faction-ridden time, heavy with the threat of open violence, when men desperately anxious about the future became impatient for solutions. They were also a time when initiative in action came very largely from the queen herself. After five years in which either Cecil or Dudley had taken the lead in formulating policy and in urging action on the sovereign, the roles were reversed. At least until Mary's marriage in 1565 and to a large extent thereafter, it was Elizabeth who called the tune to which her servants, however unwillingly, danced.

It was the succession problem which first held attention. The law regulating the succession was anything but clear. By strict hereditary descent, right lay in Mary Stuart as descendant of Henry VIII's older sister, Margaret, wife of James IV of Scotland. By this same argument the next heir after Mary would be Margaret Douglas, Countess of Lennox, daughter of Queen Margaret's second marriage. But in some quarters the ordinary line of descent was held to be reversed under terms of the will Henry VIII made by virtue of statutes of 1536 and 1544 in which Parliament authorized him to determine the succession by testament. This instrument devised the Crown (upon the death of the last of his children without issue) to the heirs of Mary, Duchess of Suffolk, Henry's younger sister, represented now by the luckless Lady Catherine Grey. Unhappily all kinds of difficulties dulled the effectiveness of this document. First of all, there was great uncertainty as to the whereabouts of the original. Secondly, there was, for a variety of legal and constitutional reasons, scope for radical disagreement among the lawyers as to its validity.

The prevailing unease on the subject might have continued to rumble on subterraneously but ineffectually; it was brought to the surface by a terrifying event in October 1562. The queen fell ill with the dreaded smallpox, and at the crisis of the disease hung for some hours between life and death while the Council hovered in agonizing indecision. The only contemporary witness as to actual events in the palace is De Quadra, whose information was second-hand and whose judgment was biased. His picture is one of utter confusion and wide disagreement, with almost as many opinions as there were Councillors, but with three main positions emergent. Some wanted to stick by Henry's will and proclaim Catherine Grey should the queen die; others, among whom he lists Cecil, Dudley, Bedford, Pembroke and Norfolk, backed the Earl of Huntingdon, the nearest Protestant male in line. A third, smaller, group led by Lord Treasurer Winchester, urged delay while the legal experts were called in to give judgment. This was understood to be a move favourable to a Catholic heir, since the senior members of the bar were thought sympathetic to the old faith. The queen, De Quadra reported, upon recovering consciousness, urged them to make Lord Robert protector of the realm.[1]

There is no effective way of checking the accuracy of this account. The Spanish ambassador had been reporting Huntingdon as the candidate of the extreme Protestant party for some time past, although there is no corroborative evidence from other sources. His claim was a remote one, a White Rose descent in fact, from Edward IV's brother, Clarence. His commitment to the left-wing Protestants was a strong one; he was also brother-in-law to Lord Robert Dudley. But a few glimpses we catch of him at this stage of his career are of a modest and unambitious young man.[2] Catherine Grey was a safer choice since her claims, though contested, rested on a legal base. The fly in the ointment here was the clandestine match with Lord Hertford, recently declared null by the ecclesiastical courts. Neither the infatuated Catherine nor her flighty husband could have appealed very strongly to hard-headed politicians. It is important, as De Quadra unhappily noted, that no one dared openly advocate a Catholic candidate at this juncture.

These were in any case panic choices, presumably representing no firm or considered convictions. The cooler judgment of Cecil and other Councillors is probably represented by an abortive bill prepared for the Parliament of 1563.[3] By its terms the sovereign power would pass to the existing Privy Council should the queen die without parliamentary provision for the succession. That body would continue to govern the country until Parliament should choose a successor. The constitutional interest of this proposal is obvious; in its immediate political context it is surely to be seen as an anti-Catholic move. The existing Council was dominated by strong Protestants, and a Parliament in the same frame of mind as that of 1563 would hardly have chosen a Catholic successor — or would, at the very least, have insisted on exacting conditions. We may guess that Cecil (and others of the Council) hoped by this measure to throw the decision on the succession into their own hands should the queen die without issue.

But the succession problem cannot be separated from that of marriage — of two royal marriages. Men in power had to calculate the probable actions of a widowed (and childless) queen in Edinburgh, eager for marriage but restricted in her choices, and a virgin queen to the south, increasingly indifferent if not positively antipathetic to matrimony. In 1562 and 1563 their attention necessarily focused on the Scottish queen since her English cousin seemed out of the matrimonial market.

The actions of this decorous drama were to be played on two stages with a multitudinous cast and a maze of sub-plots. At home the English lords and gentlemen in Parliament exhausted themselves in an effort to bring their queen to promise marriage. The queen of Scots's ministers pressed almost as hard to get recognition of their sovereign's rights in the English succession while at the same time eagerly searching to find her a husband. The Cardinal of Lorraine, her uncle, thought he had found a suitable match in the Archduke Charles, but Mary and her advisors hunted bigger game. De Quadra, in the last piece of public business of his life, intrigued with Maitland to match the Scots queen to the Prince of Spain, Philip's son. Cecil and his mistress, keeping a keen eye on their northern neighbour, sought to impose an English veto on any choice she might make. The queen mother of France, a wary observer, watched for whatever chance might serve her ends. Amidst the rush and bustle of these greater personages the Countess of Lennox worked unceasingly to exploit for her son the modest but centrally strategic advantages possessed by that family.

It is convenient to begin by tracing out Lady Lennox's career up to the summer of 1563. Since she had more than one string to her bow, she could vary her strategy as circumstances altered. Her first object had been to end the family's exile from Scotland by regaining the earldom of Lennox and Angus, now held for many years by their rivals, the Hamiltons. This was to be a first step in destroying the Hamilton claim to be next successors after Mary Stuart to Scotland's Crown and the reassertion of the Lennox claim to be right heirs. Her intrigues in Scotland in 1559–60 were uncovered by the English government, but the Lennoxes got off lightly. In October 1560 when they approached both the French and Spanish ambassadors for help in pushing their cause, there was a stern reprimand from the English Council, well aware, as they told the earl, that he looked 'for a higher feather' than mere recovery of his lands.[4]

The death of Francis II opened up new and exciting possibilities. Lord Lennox's claim to the Scottish succession was a doubtful one, but Lady Lennox was a daughter to Queen Margaret of Scotland and hence stood in the English succession. As long as Mary was still Queen of France, the consort of a hostile neighbour, Margaret Lennox kept alive her claim as next heir after Elizabeth, especially courting the Roman Catholics. In their remote Yorkshire house, the Lennoxes continued to practise the old faith and to make this fact known among Catholics. But once Mary Stuart was a widow, Margaret shifted her ground. Now that the Scottish queen was an acceptable claimant to the English succession (and one with a better claim than Lady Lennox) the latter began to push forward her son, Henry, Lord Darnley, as a suitor for Mary's hand. Their marriage would merge the two Scottish claims to the English succession. And although the Lennoxes, as descendants of a second marriage, stood behind Mary in the strict line of descent, they had certain advantages to offer. Darnley and his mother were English-born, while it was alleged against Mary that no foreign-born person could accede to the English throne. Darnley's birth and upbringing would make him acceptable to considerable parties in both kingdoms. Mary and Darnley, as wife and husband, would offer strong legal claims and an attractive political combination in the bidding for support. Lady Margaret's initial approaches were not very warmly received in Edinburgh, but Darnley's name crept more and more frequently into the endless speculation about Mary's suitors.[5]

Lady Lennox's somewhat amateurish intrigues did not escape the sharp eye of Cecil; in the winter of 1561-2, he pounced first on her agents, and then, with the evidence in hand, he scooped up the lady and her family. They were ordered south; Lord Lennox went to the Tower and his wife, with her son, into house arrest at Sheen, in the custody of the Sackvilles. Lady Margaret had intrigued in both English and Scottish courts, though not with anyone very high-placed. She had made some foolish remarks about her rights to the throne and said some unpleasant things about the queen. She had dealt, not very circumspectly, with the Spanish ambassador. It was a petty matter for the most part although the government could have made much of it had they wished, but in the end the Lennoxes were let off very easily. Lord Robert and Pembroke, both reputedly hostile to the Greys, may have promoted this move; it also checked enthusiasm for Mary Stuart by pushing forward her competitor. The earl subscribed the required submission and was released from the Tower in November 1562. In another six months they were not only re-admitted to the royal presence but made much of by the queen, who listened complaisantly to the young Darnley's efforts on the lute. In the autumn they were allowed to return north to their Yorkshire home.[6]

This interlude was playing itself out when, in the early weeks of 1563, some three months after the queen's illness, Parliament met. It was four years since the last summons. There had been rumours of a meeting in 1561 when the unpaid debts of the Scottish expedition gave the Lord Treasurer sleepless nights, but land was sold, more than £250,000 worth. With the coming of the Newhaven crisis, there was no alternative to a summons, and it was included among the items on Cecil's agenda of July 1562.[7]

The government's programme for the session was very limited; the main concern was to secure a subsidy. It also intended to put through a bill stiffening the laws against Catholics. The government came well armed with instances to back such a measure. In the preceding autumn the late Cardinal Pole's nephews, presuming upon their White Rose descent, had fecklessly plotted to secure armed aid from the Guises for the purpose of proclaiming Mary Stuart queen. Arthur Pole was married to a Percy and was the protégé of the Catholic Lord Hastings of Loughborough. He visited both the Spanish and French ambassadors, neither of whom took him very seriously although both held out some hopes of support if the brothers migrated to the Continent. The Poles and their associates were soon prisoners in the Tower and a bill of attainder was one of the pieces of Parliamentary business. The foolish little plot provided the government with a very timely demonstration of the Catholic menace. And if that were not enough, they went on to stage a raid on the Spanish and French embassy chapels on Candlemas day, to ferret out any English Catholic communicants.[8]

If these raids were intended to warm up anti-Catholic feeling they were quite unnecessary, for, as Cecil discovered, the 'humours of the Commons House be such as they think nothing sharp enough against Papists'. The cry against the Papists had been raised by the Dean of St Paul's in his sermon at the opening of Parliament. At the same time the dissatisfaction of the more advanced Protestants with the settlement of 1559 took concrete form in their efforts to push through Convocation a programme of reforms, particularly of the ceremonial prescribed in the Prayer Book. This first assault on the settlement of 1559 was defeated by only one vote. In the Commons the sentiments of this party expressed themselves in their hostility towards the Catholics. The ardent Knollys, the queen's ultra-Protestant cousin, headed the committee, which produced a bill of harsh character. Those who refused the oath of supremacy were to fall under praemunire on the first refusal and treason on the second. The categories required to take the oath were much extended, and in effect Catholics were excluded from a future House of Commons, although not from the Lords. Reluctantly, the queen accepted this measure, much as she disliked its extreme character. She moved almost immediately to use her prerogative to protect the Marian bishops, the intended first victims of the measure.[9]

The Houses also romped off in another direction – pursuing the burning question of the succession. Cecil had predicted this development, and indeed little else had been talked about in court and capital since the queen's illness. Almost certainly there were informal meetings among the nobles to discuss the issue, and arguments were being drawn up in support of the various claims. Maitland was on hand to watch out for his mistress's interests and to forward them as much as he could.[10]

Under these circumstances the queen could not refuse to listen to the

Houses, however distasteful their discussions of her marriage or of the succession might be to her. Two successive delegations and two petitions came up from each House, dealing with each of these questions but emphasizing that of succession. They were received calmly and courteously and in her replies the queen deployed all her reserves of tact and charm. In a winning display of rhetoric she gracefully acknowledged their petitions, consented to consider them, hinted at action being taken, and sent them home. Cecil had never had any expectations that she would be moved, and there is a note of bleak resignation in his remark to Smith, 'I cannot see any effect will come of the earnest suits made by the Three Estates to Her Majesty either for marriage or state of succession.'[11]

He – and no doubt his mistress – were glad to see the last of Parliament. Like their predecessors of 1559 these gentlemen had come up to Westminster primed with their own opinions on matters of state and with an unrestrained zeal for expressing them. They had hardly waited for the ceremonial preliminaries to be past before plunging into such arcane mysteries of state as the succession. The queen had no difficulty in blocking off any parliamentary action on this delicate question, but she could not prevent the publicity which now illumined all too brightly its every facet, nor could she impede the spread of discussion and speculation to every corner of the kingdom, as M.P.s journeyed homewards. On the issue of religion the queen had once again found herself pushed farther to the left than she wished to go, into a more rigidly anti-Catholic stance and into a more partisan Protestantism.

On April 10th, 1563, Easter Eve, Parliament ended, and ministers were free to turn once again to the darkening fortunes of their expeditionary forces at Newhaven. It was not until late July that the wounded Warwick and his plague-stricken garrison returned dismally home. In the meantime the English government had to deal with the problems of the succession on other fronts. Of these the most pressing was that to the North. After the abortive plans for the meeting of the two queens, there was a lull during which Mary was preoccupied with Scottish affairs. Maitland had his sources of information in London, and was quick to write, shortly after the queen's illness, noting the rumour that someone else than his mistress had been intended as successor 'which I cannot think to be true, seeing none is more worthy for all respects nor hath so good a title'. If religion were alleged against it, let them but observe her behaviour in Scotland where indeed the new religion flourished more than ever.[12] In the year or more since Mary's homecoming Maitland's position had swung

8

steadily around the compass so that he was now the devoted servant of the princess whose return he had once dreaded. He remained faithful to the reformed religion and to his statesman's vision of a united Britain, but his political hopes were completely at odds with those of the English ministers. Two years earlier he had been willing to contemplate the deposition of the Stuarts and Arran's marriage to Elizabeth as the means of union. Now he was fighting hard for a Scottish succession to the English throne which, he hoped, would make his mistress one day queen of the entire island. He and Cecil, perhaps more alike in cast of mind than any other two men in the island, were now cautious enemies, sparring at each other from hostilely opposed postures.

There followed, between the summers of 1563 and 1565, a long duel between the two queens. It is they personally who monopolize action at this time; their servants fall into the background as men who come and go at the bidding and pleasure of their mistresses. On the English side Elizabeth's aim was first to hold off the remarriage of her cousin for as long as possible and secondly to dictate Mary's choice if marriage there must be. The queen of Scots, on her side, sought a match which would most effectively promote her ambitions in England – at the least, the succession; at the best, immediate possession of the throne.

Mary began with a survey of possible continental husbands, a manœuvre which the English government watched nervously. During the winter the Cardinal of Lorraine, her uncle, had put out feelers for a match with the Archduke Charles, quondam suitor to Elizabeth. Maitland knew this when he set out for London and Paris in late winter, but the immediate purpose of his mission was to obtain Guise aid for a match with Charles IX of France. The death of the Duke of Guise about the time of Maitland's arrival in the English capital spiked hopes of achieving much in that direction. And as the Scottish Secretary told Bishop De Quadra, the archduke was too poor and too inconsequential to suit. What Mary hoped for was a husband weighty enough to be an effective instrument in pushing her English ambitions. Catherine de Médicis was quick to check any moves towards a match with her son. And, indeed, Mary's hopes were already turning in another direction.

Maitland's visit to the Spanish ambassador was not merely one of courtesy. His real purpose was to propose a match between Don Carlos, the Infante of Spain, and his mistress. The Scottish statesman sketched a glowing picture of Philip's future mastery over the British Isles, and on the awkward question of religion assured De Quadra that toleration for

Catholics could be arranged. In a later interview with the ambassador Maitland disclosed conversations with several English peers who were favourable to Mary's candidacy for the English succession but who emphasized the desirability of a Spanish marriage. The Scottish Secretary, in his determination to secure the English succession, was hopeful of constructing an English party to back him up. De Quadra faithfully reported these conversations to his master, and Philip, after the usual long delay imposed by communications with Spain, gave a very half-hearted consent to secret negotiations, expressing his continued preference for a match between Mary and the archduke. In the meantime Catherine de Médicis had persuaded the Guises to back a match with Archduke Charles in preference to Don Carlos. Philip's willingness to countenance a suit for his son was conditioned by his fears of another Franco-Scottish match and when the queen mother made it plain that this would not eventuate, the Spanish king's interest rapidly cooled. This wrote finis to Mary's dream of a match with the Infante.[13]

How much of Maitland's dealings the English government knew at this time is not certain. Randolph had reported the Austrian proposals in May. Apparently the English also had an inkling of the Spanish scheme since in June, on Maitland's return from France, Elizabeth declared to him that a marriage between Mary and any Habsburg, Spanish or Austrian, would force England to regard her as an enemy. And in August Randolph was instructed to repeat to Mary quite bluntly that a match with any member of the emperor's family would be regarded as an unfriendly act and one which would affect Mary's chances of being recognized heir in England. The English queen was not ready to take a lead of her own, but he was to add that Elizabeth hoped her cousin might marry some Englishman of noble birth 'having also conditions and qualities meet for the same—yea, perchance such as she would hardly think we could agree unto'. It was to be strongly hinted that such a match would further the acknowledgment of Mary's claims on the succession.[14]

Randolph returned to Scotland and presented his message, which was somewhat coldly received. Nevertheless, Mary returned a polite answer and expressed her willingness to listen to Elizabeth's advice on marriage. Randolph made another trip south, returning north at the end of 1563. This time his instructions were both more and less candid. He was to spell out the limits of Mary's choice; no son of France, Spain or Austria would be acceptable to English policy. Elizabeth would plainly prefer an English nobleman. The written instructions went no further than that, but it was an open secret in London which nobleman the queen had chosen for her cousin's hand. When Maitland was in London the previous winter, the queen had startled and embarrassed him by naming Lord Robert—or alternatively his brother—as a suitable match for Mary. The ambassador had turned the conversation and nothing more was then said, but by the ensuing autumn Lord Robert had been settled on as Elizabeth's official candidate for the Scottish match. Randolph, however, was not to mention the name directly to Mary. The queen hoped it would come from her cousin's lips once the general conditions were stated.[15]

There followed a protracted diplomatic comedy. Randolph laid out all his arguments—grave or trivial—in favour of a decision. Mary backed and filled, liked to hear of marriage, and then talked of the felicities of widowhood. Nor would she believe this was all Elizabeth had to say. 'Let me know plainly what your mistress' mind is that I may the better devise with myself and confer with other and so to give a more resolute answer than by these general words spoken by you I can.' Randolph could only fall back on the argument that his mistress did not wish so to limit Mary's choice. The Scottish ministers, anxious for a marriage, and well-disposed towards an English one at this juncture, pressed him equally hard, and, guessing names, most usually hit on Darnley. The frustrations of the unlucky ambassador were almost too much for him. When he was finally given an answer to carry back to England, it was such as might have been given 'the first or third day' as at the end of three months—as general and as evasive as the English proposal.

So at last the English queen had to give in and instruct her ambassador openly to propose Dudley's name to Mary. The offer itself only opened the way for more procrastination; Mary raised the obvious questions—should she marry a subject? What advantages could she expect from such a match? Finally she asked that special commissioners be sent—Lord Bedford, then Governor at Berwick, was mentioned—to negotiate further on so weighty a matter.[16]

Probably no episode in Elizabeth's career is so puzzling to the modern observer. For three years the queen had publicly lavished on Robert Dudley one token after another of her favour and affection—estate, wealth, the highest place in her counsels, unbounded confidence in his public abilities, uncritical partiality for his private qualities. If she had denied him marriage, it was from politic concern for the consequences, not from any opinion of unworthiness in him, and she had made plain to the world that if she would—or could—marry, this would be the man of her choosing.

Now, suddenly, without any diminution in her affections, she proposed this man as a husband of the cousin-rival, whom she both feared and disliked. Dudley, whose excellences were lauded now more warmly than ever, was to be the link between the two realms and the two sovereigns. Elizabeth strongly implied—although she did not promise—that she herself would not marry and the happy couple—or their children—would be the inheritors of both kingdoms. In her latest offer she went so far as to envisage an extraordinary *ménage à trois*, all three sharing a single household, but Elizabeth bearing the whole charge of the 'family'.[17] The imagination boggles—or turns to Freudian wonderings.

What, then, are we to make of this extraordinary proposal? The simplest explanation is that it was intended to drag out negotiations and thus delay any marital decision by Mary. Convention required that it be treated with all due seriousness, and it provided the plot for a courtly comedy lasting for many months. Viewed strictly as a piece of diplomacy, the scheme had a certain logic to it. English state policy and the sovereign's personal feelings chimed together in one aim—to limit, and, if possible, to dictate Mary's choice of a second husband. The English were determined to prevent altogether any marriage with a continental prince, for it was a cardinal aim of English statesmen to block off any renewal of Scottish ties with any power outside the island. So far they could take satisfaction in the course of events. Political circumstances on the Continent had doomed Mary's scheme there; Maitland's efforts to find a French or Spanish husband for his mistress had been checked. The Queen of Scots, swayed by her advisors, made the best of her bad fortune and brought herself to accept the limitation of her choice.

But this development, although a gain for the English, posed a dilemma. Suitable candidates within the British Isles were few in number, and each bore special liabilities. Arran, the Hamilton heir, had excited Mary's antipathy at first sight and had in any case now declined into madness. The only other candidate of the blood royal was Darnley. In Scotland the renewal of his family's feuds might topple the precarious balance of power among the nobles; in England his Catholic connections rendered him suspect among all good Protestants. No other noble of suitable rank was available.

Hence Elizabeth's nomination of Dudley had a certain political logic. In Scotland he would be an outsider, acceptable at least to the Protestant faction; while his high place in the English queen's confidence would make an ideal link between the two courts. If the marriage were seen in purely political terms, here was the man best suited to achieve a harmonious union between the two realms. And, even if—as was probable—Mary rejected the proposal, the very process of negotiation (in which the onus of refusal would be on the Scot) would buy more delay.

But when the argument was transferred from the impersonal political level to that of personal relationships, its implausibility—even ludicrousness—became apparent. Randolph, the ambassador who was saddled with the task of convincing Mary, put the difficulties with characteristic candour. Dudley's place in his mistress's affections was manifest to all the world. Could he with any honesty—or honour—abandon such a place? Informed Scots opinion, 'knowing both their affections and judging them inseparable', could only 'think that no such thing is meant on my sovereign's part and that all these offers bear a greater show and face of good will than any good meaning'.[18]

It is hard to disagree with this assessment; one may assume that Mary Stuart and her advisors operated from such a premise and regarded the move as yet another attempt to stall off a marital choice by the Scottish queen. Yet, in Elizabeth's labyrinthine and oblique consciousness, something more may have been half-intended. Elizabeth was in one aspect a cool, hard-headed and intuitively skilful politician, and this 'business' side of her personality is much the easier to penetrate. Yet her relationship to Mary had also a personal element in it, singularly hard to assess. She accepted the Scottish queen as her only equal within the island and almost certainly regarded her as the rightful English successor. Her attitude towards her cousin-rival was coolly detached and contained little spice of active malice; what she demanded of Mary was acceptance of the harsh terms which Elizabeth offered. To an observer these terms might seem so onerous and so humiliating as not to be borne under any conditions. But Elizabeth was a supremely ruthless egotist who not only demanded but in fact received from everyone within her orbit of experience the full surrender of his personal feelings, wishes and ambitions. In a world viewed through these uniquely royal spectacles, there was nothing odd in Dudley's submission to the Scottish marriage, and possibly the queen saw no reason why Mary should not make the same sacrifice, especially since it would bring such advantageous prospects. This subjugation of others to her will was the only kind of human relationship Elizabeth knew or understood. Hence in her view of things the scheme for a match between her favourite and her rival may have had a fantastic kind of plausibility. But if some such feelings did animate the queen's actions, they were but half-conscious, half-coherent, even to herself, and inextricably mingled with more hard-headed considerations of day-to-day politics.

The other principals undoubtedly saw the matter in a somewhat different light. Mary, intensely proud of her unblemished royal descent and of the great splendour of her first marriage, had no intention of marrying an English politician of such dubious antecedents and one who would appear as the cast-off favourite of her rival. Nor did Dudley—and there is evidence to support this—much relish the precarious dignities of a Scottish consortship.

From her ministers' point of view the offer of Dudley to Mary Stuart was an exercise in royal initiative which they must execute on instructions. What Cecil's views were we are left to guess. Maitland complained of a coldness and a certain indifference in the English Secretary's pursuit of the matter. Certainly Cecil was anxious that no promise be made to the Scots queen on the vital question of the succession. Here at least he and his mistress were on common ground. She was determined to have no legally appointed heir to become a focus of intrigue and opposition; he was equally resolved to prevent any commitments to a Catholic successor.

This was, of course, exactly what Mary and her ministers were determined, if possible, to obtain. Throughout the long comedy of negotiation, however many courteous arguments were elaborated, the path always led back to the one meaningful question of guarantees. Would the English queen arrange legal—preferably parliamentary—provision to secure Mary's rights in the succession? To this wearisomely repetitive question there came always the same tedious reply. Mary must rely on the affection of her cousin and the close relations which would follow from the marriage. Under these circumstances the negotiations were doomed from the beginning, yet both sides were perhaps content to let them drift on; neither could see very clearly what would come next. The break, when it came, was dramatic and unexpected. It was now Mary's turn to seize the initiative; the move she made was hardly less surprising than Elizabeth's offer of Dudley.

A year earlier, in June 1563, Elizabeth, having re-admitted the Lennoxes to her favour, had asked Mary to license the earl's return to Scotland. Her motives are not altogether clear; possibly, since Mary was husband-hunting on the Continent at that time, Elizabeth wished to emphasize the Lennox claims to the English succession as a warning against a continental commitment by the Queen of Scots.[19] Permission was slow in coming and, when it did, in the summer of 1564, Elizabeth's intentions had changed. At this point Lennox's appearance in Scotland in the midst of the marriage negotiations could upset her scheme, and at first she refused him leave to go. But, as the Scots were quick to point out, it was she who had first asked for his return; there was nothing to do but give way, and in September he arrived in Edinburgh. Moray and Maitland were content to see him return (their enemy Hamilton was his old foe); Mary had her own purposes in mind, as we shall see. In October 1564 the official proclamation of Lennox's restoration to rank and lands was made at the town cross of Edinburgh. Even before that event a knowledgeable Scottish correspondent told Randolph flatly that his countrymen would not accept Dudley, but 'if you will earnestly press it, you may cause us to take the Lord Darnley—otherwise it will not be'.[20]

And as Lennox was travelling north, Sir James Melville was on his way south as Mary's emissary to London, ostensibly to improve somewhat frayed relations with Elizabeth but also to obtain permission for the young Lord Darnley to come north. In this enterprise he found an ally in Sir Nicholas Throckmorton, now unemployed and at a loose end, but no less busy in great matters than before. Throckmorton had been favourably impressed by Mary when he dealt with her in France after the death of her husband. By 1564 he was acting as an unofficial counsellor to her and advising her agent how best to advance her cause in England. Since he was at this time a close confidant of Leicester—some said he was the earl's 'director'—he may well have been acting for the favourite. The latter (Earl of Leicester since September) confided to Melville (probably with some truthfulness) his great unwillingness to marry Mary, and added (with less veracity) that the scheme was invented by his enemy, Cecil. The latter was not so prodigal of his views, but the Scot thought he was opposed to the marriage of either queen. If we may believe Camden, Leicester took the further step of advising Bedford, the commissioner for negotiating the match between Mary and Dudley, not to press it. In February, he used his influence to procure a licence for Darnley to join his father in Scotland.[21]

By the end of the year the English had in fact played out their hand; the negotiations between Bedford and the Scots lords at Berwick in November had revealed the impasse; Mary would not take Leicester without a promise of the succession; Elizabeth would never yield the point. After the conference Cecil expressed his doubt that the match would ever come off and a month later wrote that while Elizabeth seemed zealous for the marriage, she was 'remiss of her earnestness for the conditions'.[22] Both Cecil and Dudley advised their mistress to license Darnley's journey, Leicester probably with some relief; Cecil possibly with some uneasy doubts as to the future. He and his mistress probably thought the risks of a match between Mary and Darnley slight. Up to this point Mary had allowed herself to be guided by the two cool heads of Lethington and Moray who were unlikely to push such a marriage. Finally, since Darnley was an English subject, with English lands and fortune, Elizabeth could interpose her authority to summon him home if need arose.

The licence was granted to the young lord and he arrived in Scotland early in February 1565. Only Randolph, at this point, was worried, and even he probably did not realize the Queen of Scots's determination to take the reins in her own hands and work a revolution in Scottish policy by turning her back on the alignments of the past four years. Events moved fast. In April there was a falling-out between Mary and her half-brother which resulted in Moray's leaving the court. At the same time Maitland was dispatched southward. Randolph seems not to have known the nature of the mission, but by mid-April he was writing in alarm about the favours shown Darnley and the consternation of the Protestants. In the meantime Maitland, in London, revealed his instructions. He was to say that since Queen Elizabeth would not guarantee Mary's title to the succession as a condition of the Leicester match, she would not proceed, but in accordance with the English wish that she not marry on the Continent, the Scots queen now proposed the name of Lord Darnley as her bridegroom. The English government, highly alarmed, reacted by rushing Nicholas Throckmorton to Scotland to see if it were still possible to halt such a match. He went provided with all kinds of inducements to change Mary's mind. If she would have Leicester, Elizabeth would consent to inquiry into Mary's title and due publication of the results. Failing Leicester, Mary could have any other nobleman of England (Norfolk and Arundel were mentioned) with Elizabeth's goodwill, but without any declaration of title. But if she married Darnley, she need not expect Elizabeth's approval or goodwill.[23]

Throckmorton executed his mission in due form but all to no avail. Randolph could do little but wring his hands as he watched the familiar lineaments of Scottish politics fading about him. Mary went about her business with dispatch. Moray's refusal to support the marriage ended in his exile from council and court; Maitland found himself coldly regarded and his advice neglected. In June Darnley was ennobled in several titles; in July the royal nuptials took place. Moray was by now driven to take up

arms, along with Argyll; after unavailing attempts to find adequate support, they were forced into retreat, first to the west Borders, and then, in
October 1565, over the frontier into England.

In a few short months a revolution had occurred which overturned the
pillars on which English policy had rested since the Treaty of Edinburgh.
Abroad, the close-working alliance with a Protestant and Anglophile
Scots regime was shattered, its chief Scottish architect in exile. Mary,
throwing off her brother's and Maitland's tutelage, had taken up a defiant
stance. The effect on English domestic politics was hardly less far-reaching.
The marriage between the two Catholic claimants to the English succession stirred up grave dangers and panic fears. English politics seemed
about to undergo a radical regrouping. But as these great matters came
to a head, English statesmen had also to keep their eyes on other major
alterations in English political affairs.

Bishop De Quadra died quite unexpectedly on August 26th, 1563. His
career in England was about ended in any case since the English government had already talked of asking for his recall. He had essayed to be not
only ambassador of Spain but protector of his co-religionists, and pursuing that end had sought too actively to intervene in English domestic
affairs—hence Cecil's determined enmity to the bishop; in 1561 the
Secretary had triumphed over him in the matter of the nuncio, but he was
determined to pursue every possible advantage against the ambassador.
In the following year chance—or skilful intrigue—put into Cecil's hands
a powerful weapon against his enemy with the defection of the envoy's
secretary to the English. The secrets thus uncovered became the basis for
a formal protest to De Quadra, the purpose of which was to discredit him
with the queen. He was alleged, among other things, to have written a
sonnet about her and Dudley.[24]

Later in the year the English minister found another stick with which
to beat the bishop in the shape of the Pole nephews' plot; even though De
Quadra had behaved with discretion, it was easy enough to draw the
connection between the Spanish embassy and treason, as Cecil took care
to do in Parliament. Chance played against the ambassador when a hired
assassin took refuge in the embassy; the embassy servants resisted English
officers pursuing the man and he escaped by the back door. The English
used this as an excuse for putting in their own doorkeeper. (Durham
Place, the embassy, was a royal house and hence the government could
claim a right to intervene.) They pounced once again by raiding the
embassy chapel during the Candlemas mass, searching for English Catholic

communicants. In January 1563 Elizabeth had written to Philip asking that De Quadra either be ordered to desist from his interference in English affairs or else be recalled.[25]

The effects of all this on the English Catholics were disastrous. Their position after 1559 was at the best painful and any path of action choked with briars. Probably the most obvious one was to imitate their Protestant counterparts in France by forming a faction in the hope of future victory, or at least of privileged toleration. Such a fear was clearly in the minds of the Protestant Councillors and motivated their energy in crushing any slight appearance of Catholic revival. Hence their attitude towards the proposed visit of the nuncio and their watchful hostility towards the Queen of Scots and the Lennox family.

The presence of an ambassador who, as Cecil wrote, 'seemeth to neglect all other affairs and rather serveth, as may appear, like a nuncio of the Pope than the King's ambassador',[26] only worsened the Catholics' situation. Imperceptibly he had assumed the post of their leader; in the spring of 1561 he negotiated with Dudley over a proposed Catholic restoration (taking care to reassure the English Catholics as to his intentions). Later he dealt with the Irish rebel, Shane O'Neil, with the Countess of Lennox and with Geoffrey Pole. It may well be that the more cautious Catholic magnates like Lord Montague grew more chary of dealing with him; his contacts with them seem to diminish after 1562. But when Parliament met in 1563 he was in close touch with Catholic members and discussed the possibility of pushing the Scottish queen's claims.[27] Most of this was known to the watchful Cecil, and although the Secretary's general political role in 1562 and 1563 was a rather reserved one, in this matter he was alert and active, both in undermining the ambassador's position and in driving home the connection between this alien agent and the English Catholics. The latter thus fell stage by stage under the terrible taint of treason; Cecil and his collaborators saw with grim satisfaction the discredit cast on their foes; yet they could still not assuage their restless fears of a revival of Catholic power in the realm. All this, of course, powerfully assisted the rapid growth of an intense anti-Catholic feeling in the country. Councillors and courtiers were perhaps not wholly aware how potent a force this was becoming.

During these years the Catholic claimants to the English succession were not the only ones whose supporters were working to advance their interests. A counter-offensive by the more zealous Protestants was mounted in an unexpected quarter. The Lady Catherine Grey had been a prisoner since 1561 although, when the plague struck after Newhaven, she was allowed to leave the Tower and live in the care of her uncle Lord John Grey of Pirgo. She was certainly among the possible successors considered by the Council during the queen's illness in October 1562; and there was probably discussion of her rights to the succession in the Parliament of 1563. Perhaps as early as the meeting of Parliament—certainly by April—a book was written defending in detail the Suffolk claim and attacking strongly the claims of Mary Stuart and Margaret Lennox.[28] It was the work of John Hales, Clerk of the Hanaper of Exchequer, a middling bureaucrat of pronounced Protestant views. It was not printed, but manuscript copies circulated fairly widely and came to the attention of the government. Hales was sent to the Tower, not only on account of the book but, even worse, for having procured foreign legal opinion that Catherine Grey's marriage to Hertford was legal. And greater men were touched: Lord John Grey was in deep trouble; Lord Keeper Bacon was forbidden the court; and Cecil was not free of suspicion. The queen's anger ran high, for her contempt and dislike for the Greys was deep. She was particularly incensed that any subject should have meddled in this whole dangerous question of the succession. Bacon was a long time in purdah, and the revival of the succession question in this fashion may have contributed to the prorogation of Parliament, which had been generally expected to meet in 1564. Hales and his friends suffered for their zeal, but they sparked off a chain reaction. Hales's book or abridgments of it must have circulated fairly widely, and the other side was not long in answering. In fact, the somewhat defensive form the argument takes in Hales's hands suggests that the Scottish claim had already been put in some ordered form. At any rate public opinion was deeply stirred upon the issue, and the underground disturbances rumbled on, to explode when Parliament met again in 1566.[29]

While the succession battle was being fought on its various fronts, the ordinary changes of day-to-day politics sputtered on. The sun of Dudley fortunes reached a zenith in the summer months of 1564. Ambrose, the hero of Newhaven, was generously rewarded in June by a grant of lands, largely in North Wales, reputedly worth five hundred pounds a year.[30] In September the negotiations with Mary provided sufficient excuse for the elevation of Robert to the peerage as Earl of Leicester and Viscount Denbigh. The event had been long forecast and had nearly happened on previous occasions.

The following autumn saw the eclipse of another great courtier. The

Earl of Arundel in a fit of pettishness had surrendered his staff as Lord High Steward 'with sundry speeches of offence towards the Queen's Majesty'.[31] He was confined to his house for a time, although he suffered no worse penalty. Arundel had had large hopes at the opening of the reign, lifting his eyes, some thought, to a royal match. He was a one-man minority at the time of the Scottish expedition, and later reported to be on bad terms with Dudley. But at least for the present his resentment towards the newcomers about the queen and his wounded *amour propre* found no sympathetic echoes in the court, and he was left to sulk alone.

8 *Succession and Marriage: The Second Phase*

By the summer of the Darnley marriage, the new English regime was in its seventh year; the queen had already reigned longer than either her brother or her sister. The new court had developed a distinctively patterned life of its own, fashioned about the habits and tastes of its royal mistress. But it was at the same time throwing out tendrils and sinking roots in the larger aristocratic world of the counties. Marriage, family, friendship and business were creating countless ties between the court world and the nobles and gentry of the counties. Less conscious links — common habit, sympathy of outlook, shared ambition, and agreed way of life — provided powerful underpinnings for a compact and well-knit aristocratic community, embracing both court and shires.

Elizabeth's court had by now distinctive qualities of its own; it was conducted with an ordered and decorous magnificence which centred on the queen's person. Every routine activity, every public movement of the sovereign was regulated by a severe and gorgeous etiquette designed to exalt her person and office to a semi-hieratic status. The splendours of ritual banished from the churches were lavished upon the sovereign. Yet Elizabeth's court was saved from a too severe formality by the personality of the queen herself. The variety of her charms — her wit, her high spirits and a certain condescending graciousness which she could assume — enlivened the court atmosphere without dissolving its dignity.

This was not an extravagant court, compared with its predecessors. Annual expenses, jealously watched by Cecil, were kept at an even level in a period of rising prices and rather below those of Edward's or Mary's reign.[1] Money was spent lavishly for robes, hangings, uniforms — for the immediate setting of ceremonial — but very little went to the far more costly purposes of building. The splendour of the court setting was meant to impress the subject with the power and the unique status of the ruler. Yet it was not the Byzantine setting of an unapproachable autocrat, a distant being enshrined in the overwhelming splendours of an Escorial or a Versailles. There was a certain familiarity in the surroundings. The rambling, overgrown manor houses in which the queen spent much of her year were not very different in kind from the residences of many noblemen or gentlemen. Indeed, the great building spree of the century, fairly under way by the 1560s, was already throwing up mansions which matched and surpassed the royal residences.

And, in fact, the queen, for considerations of both policy and pleasure, moved freely and frequently among her people. The ordinary rotation of residence, from one royal house to another around London, made her a familiar figure in some half-dozen or more south-eastern counties. Each summer she extended her range and went on progress across two or three more distant shires. In the first years of the reign these peregrinations were limited pretty much to the ring of counties immediately around London. In 1560 she visited Hampshire and in the following year ventured into Suffolk, but it was not until 1564 that she went farther afield. In that year the queen travelled as far as Cambridge, Huntingdonshire, Northampton-shire and Leicestershire; in 1566 she was to visit Coventry, Oxford, Stamford and Kenilworth.[2] These visits were expensive privileges for those who entertained her, but they brought the sovereign in direct touch with a significant part of the English aristocracy. Once she had been seen by half the population of a county and met by most of the notables, she was no longer a distant, awesome presence but a voluble, smiling lady, princely but gracious.

The organization of the court itself also served to keep it in close touch with the country. Of the more than a hundred ladies and gentlemen who served in the Chamber or among the Gentlemen Pensioners, only a frac-tion were in attendance at any one time. In the intervals they travelled back to their own homes, all over the country, bearing the news and gossip of the court with them. They served as useful links between the court and an aristocracy whose concerns were still largely local. Men like Clement Paston, the Gentleman Pensioner; Roger Manners, Gentleman of the Chamber; or Thomas Markham, Standard-bearer of the Pensioners, kept open a line of communication between their families in the distant shires of the Midlands or East Anglia and the busy world of the court.

Around the core of serving courtiers there was a penumbra of 'courtiers extraordinary', called upon for special service from time to time. For example the coming of the French ambassadors to ratify the Treaty of Troyes in 1564 required the attendance of over forty gentlemen and a dozen noblemen, only a handful of whom were properly courtiers.[3]

Some, like Sir Hugh Paulet, or Sir Henry Neville, were in attendance because they knew French; others were gentry of Kent, who were to attend the Frenchmen from Dover to Greenwich; yet another group were knights of standing called up from the various counties to add dignity to the occasion—Sir Robert Tyrwhitt from Huntingdonshire; Sir William Dormer of Buckinghamshire; three Essex knights, Francis Jobson, Anthony Cooke, and Edward Capell; another Paulet, Sir William (from Hampshire); and a Norfolk squire, Sir Thomas Lovell. Most of these were men of substance who were J.P.s, deputy lieutenants or who held other official posts in their counties, but who changed hats and appeared as courtiers—at their own expense—for such an occasion. Sometimes they were called on for foreign service, forming the suite of some nobleman sent on an embassy of honour to award the Garter, to condole, or to congratulate. If the meeting between the two queens had eventuated, some hundreds of English ladies and gentlemen would have been mobilized to attend their sovereign.

The court reached out into the country unofficially as well as officially. Privy Councillors were not only ministers of state but influential country magnates. Cecil was rapidly building up his position in Northamptonshire and Lincolnshire as his great house at Stamford grew and as his weight was felt in the affairs of both counties. In the latter county he shared influence with Lord Admiral Clinton, whose seat was at Sempringham, while in Northamptonshire, Cecil's old friend, Sir Walter Mildmay, Chancellor of the Exchequer although not yet a Privy Councillor, was settling in at Apethorpe. Warwickshire was a Dudley preserve with one brother at Warwick Castle and the other at Kenilworth, but Sir Ambrose Cave, Chancellor of the Duchy, shared the Lord Lieutenancy with Robert. Cave himself was also a Leicestershire notable. Dudley influence was strong in North Wales and Cheshire. In the latter Leicester had replaced the Earl of Derby as Chamberlain of the County Palatine in July 1565.[4]

In the south conciliar influence was widely spread. Bedford, Lord Lieutenant in Devon and Cornwall, with great estates and a great parliamentary influence, was unchallenged as patron of the West Country, while his house at Chenies in Buckinghamshire made him a familiar presence in that county as well. In Somerset Sir Edward Rogers, the queen's Comptroller, represented conciliar interest, and in Oxfordshire Sir Francis Knollys was settling down as a landed proprietor, with generous gifts from the Crown.[5] The immensely wealthy Earl of Pembroke was seated in Wiltshire, but his large interests in South Wales and around

Avonmouth made him a great figure in those regions as well. The Marquess of Winchester enjoyed a solitary eminence in Hampshire; Sussex, on the other hand, was rather too crowded with magnates. In that small county, Sackville, Howard of Effingham and Arundel all jostled one another. In Kent, Cobham as Lord Warden was not only the official representative of the Crown but an unofficial outpost of the conciliar circle. In Essex, aside from the half-retired Petre, Mildmay and Cooke were links with court and Council. In East Anglia, the vast regional influence of the Duke of Norfolk was drawn into the official orbit by his councillorship. In nearly half the English counties, the presence of the court was made felt through the residence, for some part of the year, of a Councillor.

Recently the great provincial offices had been reshuffled. The Earl of Rutland, who had succeeded to the presidency of the North in January 1561 when the old Earl of Shrewsbury died, had followed his predecessor to the grave in 1563. It was shortly reported that Warwick would be appointed to the northern presidency,[6] but his health did not permit this, and the office was finally given to Thomas Young, Archbishop of York (May 1564), the first Elizabethan prelate to hold high civil office. In the meantime Bedford had already been nominated Governor of Berwick and Warden of the East Marches and in August 1565, hot on the heels of the Darnley marriage, he was appointed Lieutenant General in the North, an office vacant since the Scottish campaign of 1559–60.[7] In 1563 Lord Dacre, the Catholic Warden of the West Marches, had died and been replaced by another North Country peer, more politically reliable, Lord Scrope, brother-in-law to Norfolk.[8] This meant that the government was strongly represented in the North by one of its major Councillors; it also meant that the traditional rulers of the North, the Earls of Northumberland and Westmorland, were bypassed entirely.

Within the court circle new ties were binding together men who had now been working together in the queen's service for more than half a decade. In November 1565 the marriage of Warwick, a widower since 1563, with Bedford's daughter, Anne, was celebrated with great pomp. Besides bringing together two great court figures, it may be seen as another step in the shift which was carrying the Dudleys into the left-wing reformers' camp.

Cecil had been casting his lines out also; his sister had married Ambrose Cave's nephew, Roger, in 1561.[9] The Secretary had made his first alliance with the peerage—albeit a modest one—by the marriage of his son,

9

Thomas, to Dorothy, daughter of John Neville, Baron Latimer, in 1564. Sir Henry Percy, husband to the bride's sister, may have had some role as middleman in arranging this match.[10] Both Lady Cecil and Lady Bacon, those formidable sisters, acquired a new brother-in-law when the courtier, Henry Killigrew, Leicester's protégé, married the third Cooke daughter in 1565. Sir Francis Knollys was also busy in building marital alliances for his numerous offspring. It was during these years that his daughter, Lettice, married Walter Devereux, Viscount Hereford, while his son, Henry, was wedded to Margaret Cave, daughter and heiress of the Chancellor of the Duchy, in 1565.[11] Another tie within the court circle linked an old and a new family with the marriage in 1563 of Charles Howard, the Chamberlain's son, to Anne, daughter of the queen's cousin, Lord Hunsdon.[12] The climber, Pembroke, cemented his position by a double match, marrying his son, Henry, to Shrewsbury's daughter, Katherine, and his daughter to Shrewsbury's son in 1563.[13]

All these events are tokens of a political world gradually settling down and taking form as the newcomers to the inner circle were accepted and absorbed, made their marriages, built up their estates, and assimilated themselves to magnate status. But in the back of everyone's consciousness there remained the terrifying uncertainties that hung over the whole political future. So long as the queen remained unmarried, the question of the succession was a major one, and, until that matter was settled, no one's future was safe. The marriage of the Queen of Scots and the possibility—which became a probability as the year waned—of issue to that marriage, raised these matters again in a most acute and uncomfortable form.

Just how much the Darnley marriage had frightened English leaders is revealed in Council resolutions of that troubled summer, which represent the views of the entire body, except for the dissident Arundel.[14] The analyses of individual Councillors differed in detail, but there was wholehearted agreement as to the dangers the match presented. It was, in their eyes, a move aimed at the English succession, and to many the revival of a conspiracy set on foot at the beginning of the reign, first manifest in the use of the English title and style in 1559. Frustrated 'by God and the Queen', Mary Stuart had, so to speak, gone underground, hiding her purposes and biding her time. Now, with power in her grasp again, she was resuming her old course. Hence the Darnley match was another move in the deep-laid, long-conceived plans of an international Catholic leadership set in its determination to wreck the heretic English regime.

Many went further and believed that Mary aimed not merely at the succession but at present possession of the English throne. Even before the match came over the horizon, they argued, there were signs of a strengthening Marian party in the country, grown 'bold and stout' throughout the realm, 'yea, seen manifestly in this court, both in hall and chamber'. The survey of the J.P.s made in the previous year had demonstrated that barely half of them were sound in religion, and it was on religion that Mary's claim hinged. Here was the crux of the matter. The Catholics in the realm had fastened on Mary and Darnley as their best hope and now looked to them as the leaders who would bring about a Catholic restoration. The phantom which had haunted the Elizabethan Councillors since the opening of the reign seemed about to take solid form, and they gloomily anticipated intrigue, disturbance and open violence.

Worse still, as Cecil and others pointed out, the new situation would be fatally attractive to others besides Catholics. All who looked on the Queen of Scots as the rightful successor would be confirmed in their leanings, and if there were a child, 'heir to both kingdoms and augur of peace', the long-term attractions of such a succession would even make them indifferent to the marriage of the English queen.

The gloom of the Councillors reflected in part the facts revealed by the inquiry of 1564; this survey of religious loyalties made by the bishops showed that only about a half of the incumbent J.P.s could be counted as reasonably enthusiastic supporters of the new religion, while a core of some 150 (out of about 850 in the survey) were positive adherents of Catholicism.[15] To add to this there was the disarray among the possible Protestant claimants to the succession. In this very summer Lady Mary, the younger Grey sister, provided a kind of parody of her elder sister's behaviour by a secret marriage to the Sergeant Porter of the court. Since he was the tallest man in court, and she a dwarf, her action was not only indiscreet but ridiculous. Lady Catherine remained in forced seclusion by the queen's order; Elizabeth's implacable resentment did not soften with time.

Diagnosis was simple enough; but remedy was not so easy to find. One prescription was obvious, if only the patient would take heed. By prayer to God and supplication to the queen the Councillors hoped to bring her to marriage. And in this area there was cause for hope, as was soon evident. More immediately, they counselled various steps. Religion had suffered recently because the bishops by royal commandment 'had ... dealt straightly with some persons of good religion because they had forborne to wear certain apparel and such like things, being now of form and of accident than of any substance'. They suggested a public statement which would reassure all that no change in the established religion was intended. Other measures recommended were the re-imprisonment of the Marian bishops and pressure on the judges and lawyers, who were thought to be more than partial to the old religion. There was the somewhat timid suggestion that Lady Catherine might be more mildly treated.

These proposals linked the succession problem to the current tensions within the English Church. Early in 1565 Archbishop Parker was ordered by the queen to take strong measures against the prevailing diversity of practice among the clergy. Many parish priests were openly ignoring the directions of the Prayer Book as to ceremonial usages and clerical vestments, each adopting his own variant of a simpler — and Protestant — style. The royal sense of decorum was offended. More important, such diversity struck at the very principle of effective royal supremacy over the Church, as a social — and political — institution. There had been strong resistance to these orders among those of the left wing who regarded the Prayer Book as very imperfectly purged of Catholic remnants and saw the traditional vestments, however simplified, as 'popish rags'.[16]

Against the archiepiscopal authority they had turned for protection to Leicester and his fellow-Councillor, Knollys. The Primate had been able to oust Humphrey and Sampson, the two radical leaders at Oxford (who had received personal assistance from Leicester and his brother-in-law, Huntingdon) but he was unable to gain royal support for the regulations he drew up for general application. According to one story, it was Leicester who persuaded the queen to refuse her signature. At any rate the queen's resolve to maintain outward uniformity had opened a fissure in Protestant ranks and a division within the highest political circles. A deadlock had ensued; now, in the strain of the Darnley crisis, the left-wing magnates saw a chance which might be exploited to the advantage of their side.[17]

But these, at least, were domestic matters and within the scope of effective political action. What was to be done about the recalcitrant Queen of Scots? There were easily agreed steps such as the increase of garrisons in the North and the dispatch of a Lieutenant-General. Norfolk or Shrewsbury was suggested for this post; in fact it was the militant Protestant Bedford who was appointed.[18] Some were for stopping short here and negotiating; others were prepared to press on to general hostilities, if necessary. The latter question became acute when the Scots opposition lords, led by Moray, were forced to flee from Edinburgh and took refuge at Dumfries, in early September. The whole Council was again summoned to debate this question, and there was clearly disagreement. Moray and his associates, backed by Randolph at Edinburgh and Bedford at Berwick, were begging for both money and men. Initially the queen authorized a thousand pounds for Moray and instructed Bedford covertly to send three hundred soldiers from Carlisle to aid the rebels in defending themselves. By the end of the month, she was back-tracking, preparing to treat with Mary and withholding the three hundred troops. Within a fortnight the Queen of Scots was in Dumfries and the rebel nobles in Carlisle.[19]

What was behind this change of front is not entirely clear. Leicester seems to have been hot in backing Bedford; rumour had it that he was supported within the Council by Cecil and without by Throckmorton. Norfolk was thought to head the opposition; it may have been the duke's doing that his kinsman, Sussex, newly returned from Ireland, was proposed as commissioner to the Queen of Scots.[20]

Cecil's — and probably the queen's — mind on this matter is reflected in a paper in the Secretary's favourite tabular form. The risk, that a triumphant Mary would make a league with France and excite endless disturbance south of the Border, was admitted. But over against these considerations was the delicate question whether it was politic to support other princes' rebels, especially in this case; and, secondly, there was the matter of money. War was costly nowadays, as Newhaven bore witness. On balance Cecil opted for armed and watchful waiting while negotiations were continued. Mary talked boldly of leading her troops to London, but the French ambassador, who reported the remark, doubted her ability to make good the boast. Her troops, he pointed out, were a hodgepodge force, drawn together momentarily by the flux of Scottish politics but not permanently at her command. At any rate Elizabeth gave the command to hold off all hostilities, publicly rebuked the exiled lords and made moves to negotiate with her cousin.[21]

The queen had sent an agent to Scotland just after the marriage, with instructions couched in a hectoring style, expressing Elizabeth's strong displeasure. He received as good as he gave, and his return to England was delayed by his refusal to acknowledge a safe-conduct signed by Darnley as king. By now Elizabeth was preparing to make the best of a bad situation by acknowledging the marriage if Mary would pardon the exiled nobles and guarantee the existing religion. Instructions were drawn up in November for commissioners to treat in Scotland, but no one was sent. The winter passed away without decisive action since Mary showed little disposition towards compromise. By January it was known that she was with child. Early in March the Scottish situation veered suddenly and violently. Bedford and Randolph wrote to the queen, Cecil and Leicester of a plot afoot between Moray and his associates on the one hand and a band of nobles at the Scottish court, leagued with Darnley, on the other. The matter was speedily dispatched; Mary's Italian secretary, Rizzio, who had aroused the jealousy of her estranged husband, was dead by March 11th. Within the week Moray, now returned to Scotland, was in receipt of a generous supply of money from Elizabeth and in a few days reconciled to his sister. The curtain was rung down on the first scene in Mary's married life with Henry Darnley while a violent shifting of stage settings went forward.[22]

In Scotland the royal marriage dissolved political life into bloody melodrama. In the more stable and sedate atmosphere of the English court its solvent effect upon the existing political order worked more slowly. In fact that political order, more or less static since 1561, was already in motion. Renewed discussion of the queen's marriage ante-dated the Darnley match. For three years the matter had lain dormant since the queen's public partiality for Dudley necessarily paralysed any other possible suit. Courtiers as highly placed as Norfolk could and did grumble; Cecil maintained a cold, watchful neutrality; but they could do nothing to break the stalemate. It was the queen's nomination of Leicester as her choice for Mary's hand that subtly but perceptibly altered the situation. Whatever her own motives in this move, it was an oblique but public withdrawal on her part. By offering Dudley to her cousin, the queen opened up at least the possibility that she might marry someone else. A small but useful area of manoeuvre was now available for those who hoped to prise the queen and the favourite apart—and beyond that looked to a suitable royal marriage.

This meant another shift in the rhythm of English politics. Since the conclusion of peace with France after Newhaven, the queen had dominated the scene pretty exclusively, keeping well within her control the negotiations with Mary over the latter's marriage. Now, the magnates were able to take a hand. The threat from the North was now so acute that Elizabeth could hardly refuse to face seriously the possibility of marriage, especially since she herself had turned away from Leicester when she offered him to Mary.

Cecil's keen eye detected these possibilities early in the game; even before the end of 1563 he made the first moves to revive the abortive candidacy of Archduke Charles for the queen's hand. There were no direct diplomatic relations with the court of Vienna, and the cumbrous machinery of the imperial government worked slowly at best; it was a long time before Cecil's artificial respiration began to work, and it was not until well into 1565 that the Austrian suit was fully revived.[23]

Leicester was no less quick than his antagonist to see the alteration in his position and alert in planning a counter-move. If he himself was being jostled aside as a suitor, he could at least set up a rival to the Austrian. Since the Treaty of Troyes in April 1564 which cleared up the aftermath of the Newhaven episode, Anglo-French relations had been amicable. When the English court put out feelers in the spring of 1565, hinting Elizabeth's willingness to be wooed by Charles IX, Catherine de Médicis, the queen mother, chose to respond favourably. There is no certain proof but there is at least a strong possibility that it was Leicester who had persuaded Elizabeth to the first advances as early as December 1564. In any case he now came forward as a warm friend to the French and a strong supporter of the match. Throckmorton acted as his intermediary with the French envoy, De Foix, with Killigrew sometimes standing in for Sir Nicholas.[24] The move was shrewdly conceived. First of all, any real possibility of a marriage between the fifteen-year-old Charles and the thirty-two-year-old Elizabeth was slight. Apart from the ludicrous difference in age, any match between the queen and another reigning sovereign was likely to have the same unhappy consequences for English independence as the late queen's marriage to Philip of Spain. Cecil was the first to voice such doubts, and Leicester could count on his rival's checking a French marriage. Secondly, French backing could be — and was — turned to good account by Dudley. Once it became certain — after a weary summer of protracted negotiation — that Elizabeth had not the slightest intention of marrying the King of France, his court was glad enough to throw its weight behind Leicester as an alternative to a Habsburg husband for the English queen.[25] In addition — an uncovenanted benefit — the Spanish court, coldly sceptical of the queen's intentions towards the archduke, instructed its ambassador to give all reasonable assistance to his imperial colleague, but, once the Habsburg match became hopeless, to switch his backing to the favourite.[26]

The summer of 1565 was largely consumed in an elaborate diplomatic farce; the queen gave audience to the respective ambassadors; ministers met for hours of discussion; dispatches poured from their pens; and couriers travelled backward and forward to Paris or Vienna. They had little enough to show for their pains. By August the French had concluded — as they had suspected all along—that the queen was not serious in her intentions towards Charles IX and shifted their diplomatic backing to Leicester.

The Austrian negotiations dragged their slow way through the autumn and winter. In February 1566 a concerted effort was made—with Cecil's backing—to rally the court around the archduke's candidacy and to bring pressure on the queen to forward the suit. Norfolk went directly to Leicester to insist that he keep to a promise of the previous summer and throw his full support behind the archduke, relinquishing any desires of his own. The duke promised that Leicester's interests would be duly protected. The earl had no choice but to acquiesce; the conventions demanded that, and his own interests required that he establish civil relations with a royal husband, should one by chance emerge. Bacon, Winchester, and others were drawn into the group. Shortly afterward Leicester left court for a short time, an unusual event, since the queen rarely allowed him to be absent from her side. From Buckinghamshire he wrote he was glad to hear the queen had decided to marry.

Whether or not as a result of this pressure, the queen shortly thereafter agreed to send an English agent to Vienna. In previous discussion of a mission, rumour had it at one time that Cecil and Throckmorton would be paired in this task. But this time, after several possible nominees had been rejected, the choice fell on an obscure cousin of Lady Cecil's, Thomas Dannett, a man talked of once before as a possible ambassador at Paris. He set off in May; it was late summer before he returned with the emperor's ambiguous answer. The Habsburgs stuck both on their religion and on their dignity, and for a time hopes were dimmed among the archduke's supporters; and they revived, and talk went on through the winter of 1566-7 of some great personage being sent in embassy to Vienna.[27]

One member of the Howard alliance had in the meantime opted out of politics altogether. Arundel had given up the wand of the High Steward a year earlier in a fit of pique and suffered house confinement for a short time. Since then he had refused to take part in Council proceedings and lived retired in his country house. Now he sought to go abroad, to visit the spas of Italy; by the end of 1565 he had departed, but in a parting interview with the Spanish ambassador he declared his neutrality as to any of the candidates for the succession. He also affirmed his respect for King Philip and his desire for close contact with the Spanish court.[28]

In the meantime there was developing in the English court a bitter struggle between Leicester and his enemies; much hitherto covert hostility became open and declared. A new focus of anti-Dudley feeling now appeared in the figure of Thomas Radcliffe, Earl of Sussex. This nobleman had been the governor of Ireland (either as Deputy or Lieutenant) since 1556 and only occasionally present in England. But in May 1564 he left Ireland permanently and was soon a familiar figure at the court. Sussex belonged to the pre-Tudor nobility, although his wife was Sir Henry Sidney's sister. More important to him was his connection, through his mother, with the vast Howard clan. 'My lord of Norfolk loveth my lord of Sussex earnestly and so all that stock of the Howards seem to join in friendship together', wrote Cecil.[29] This alone might well have drawn Sussex into the anti-Dudley camp. Civil relations between the duke and Leicester had broken down again in the spring of 1564. This outbreak of unpleasantness had occurred when the earl, playing at tennis, had borrowed the queen's napkin to mop his brow. The duke had broken out in a fury and been rebuked by the queen. But Sussex soon had his own causes of quarrel with the favourite. The original subject of dispute was Sussex's conduct in Ireland. Leicester implied that the Deputy had had dealings with the Irish rebels. The latter responded angrily; temperatures rose rapidly; and in June 1565 both earls and their followers were carrying arms at court and threatening open violence. Sussex protested to the queen that his life was in danger; it was the nearest the Elizabethan court had yet come to naked violence.[30]

Sussex and Norfolk entered into alliance not only against their common enemy, Dudley, but as joint managers of a campaign to advance the Habsburg match. In June 1565 Sussex interviewed the Spanish ambassador, seeking support in forcing Leicester to back the archduke's cause. In July arrangements were made for Norfolk to have prior knowledge of the emperor's answer to his ambassador's note. When the courier did return, the ambassador sent straightaway for Sussex, who, with Cecil, came to confer on the contents of the note and how it should be communicated to the queen. From this time on, Norfolk and Sussex worked hand in glove with the imperial representatives to push the marriage of their sovereign with Archduke Charles.[31]

Within the court the faction quarrel rumbled on, usually below the surface but periodically erupting into open unpleasantness. In the autumn of 1565 it flared up again and the Lord Chamberlain Howard and Lord Hunsdon were reported to be allies of Sussex, although Cecil pooh-poohed the seriousness of the issues. In January 1566 there was a very bad sign indeed; the followers of Leicester and those of Norfolk took to wearing ribbons as insignia of their respective factions—purple for the earl and yellow for the duke. Again in the early summer there was trouble; this time the two earls of Leicester and Sussex exchanged challenges and would have fought but for their mistress's mediation. At her urging a reconciliation was effected and for the balance of the summer they remained on public good behaviour.[32]

With the court in at least outward good temper the queen could settle down to the real business of the season—a long progress which took her to Cecil's house at Stamford, the Admiral's at Sempringham, round to Dudley's Kenilworth, and then homeward by way of Oxford. Even now there was skirmishing along the route as some courtiers sought without success to dissuade the queen from visiting Leicester's house.[33]

Throughout these ill-tempered exchanges Cecil remained aloof from active partisanship. But his feelings towards Leicester were not very well concealed beneath a veneer of civility. Rumour often reported their mutual hostility although Cecil took care to deny it. Dudley was also correct in his public attitude but in private did not scruple to vilify the Secretary. He laboured to poison the mind of Guzman de Silva against Cecil when the new Spanish ambassador first came to England, and Throckmorton while dealing with the French ambassador spoke of the Secretary as the earl's enemy. Cecil took care to emphasize his belief that the queen would not marry the favourite and went out of his way to praise Norfolk, the earl's principal opponent.[34]

Leicester now worked in close alliance with Sir Nicholas Throckmorton; the latter often acted as the earl's representative, and some thought that he managed the favourite. His ambition—and the earl's for him—was a seat at the Council board. Once, in September 1564, they almost accomplished their end; Leicester boasted to the Spanish ambassador that the appointment was made, but then had to admit it had fallen through; Cecil, he said, was the cause of it. In June 1565 there was another effort to place Throckmorton on the Council. Cecil's blandly malicious comment to Sir Thomas Smith was, 'Great means is made for Nicholas Throckmorton to be of the Privy Council; and so I wish you both.' Sir Nicholas remained outside the charmed circle.[35]

On another Council appointment Cecil had his way. Sir Richard Sackville died in April 1566 and his place at the board was filled, before October, by Sir Walter Mildmay, Chancellor of the Exchequer, who in the next January also received Sackville's old office as Under-Treasurer. Mildmay was a long-time friend and close collaborator of Cecil, and his appointment was clearly a satisfaction to the Secretary. Sir Walter was a deeply committed Protestant of the left wing and thus added his weight to that of his co-religionists already on the Council.[36]

Whatever Cecil's public position in regard to the favourite might be, he had no doubt at all privately that a marriage between the queen and the earl would be an unmitigated disaster. Probably it was in April 1566 when Dannett was setting off for Vienna that the Secretary drew up one of his pro/contra tables on the subject *De Matrimonio Reginae Angliae cum extero Principe*.[37] The pro column was headed 'Reasons to move the queen to accept Charles', while the contra list stood under the rubric 'Reasons against the E. of L'. The archduke was of such rank as to do honour to the queen; he would head no faction within the nation; hence he would be completely dependent on the queen. 'No prince of England ever remained without good amity with the house of Burgundy.' This marriage would secure Philip's friendship at a time when France's was doubtful; when a foreign queen pretended a claim to the English Crown; and when the pope and his followers were 'watching adversaries to the Crown'. Leicester would bring neither riches, estimation, nor power; defamed himself by his wife's death, he would defame the queen; and his study would be but to enrich his friends. The Secretary's discretion was monumental and perhaps no eyes save his saw these notes, but they bear clear witness to Cecil's feelings.

Through all these storms the queen pursued her enigmatic way. Even when the wooing of both Habsburg and Valois was at its hottest, almost all observers, English or foreign, remained sceptical of her intentions. Some still thought she would choose Leicester; others doubted whether she could be moved to marriage at all. Perhaps she was for once honest when she told Guzman de Silva, 'If I could appoint such a successor to the Crown as would please me and the country, I would not marry, as it is a thing for which I have never had any inclination. My subjects, however, press me so that I cannot help myself or take the other course, which is a very difficult one. There is a strong idea in the world that a woman cannot live unless she is married, or at all events that if she refrains from marriage she does so for some bad reason ... '[38] Quite probably Elizabeth's basic antipathy to marriage, shaken for a time by her preference for Dudley, had now taken on new strength, and the resolve to reign and die a virgin was fast hardening. But circumstances cruelly pressed her. The alliance of the two Catholic claimants threatened her safety, and she had to face the fact that marriage might become an unavoidable political imperative. But, until the very last moment, she was resolved to procrastinate, using every possible excuse to gain time.

The summer of 1566 was marked by the birth of the Scottish prince. There was at least formal rejoicing at the English court, and this event, like the Rizzio murder, served to improve relations between the queens, although the underlying causes of hostility remained unchanged. Sir James Melville came to England to announce the birth and to test once again the queen's willingness to yield ground to Mary's right to the succession; here he made little headway. But he had another mission – to sound out the English notables; his brother, the resident ambassador, had already been so zealous in this activity as to win Elizabeth's demand for his recall. Prospects were promisingly bright. Not only Leicester and his political ally, Pembroke, but their opponent, Norfolk, were all warmly cordial towards Mary. This was probably not the first hint of Leicester's friendliness. In the autumn of 1565 Throckmorton, the earl's confidant, had sent a letter of counsel to Mary. In it he was urgent in emphasizing her need to win the confidence of those Protestants who thought her the right heir but distrusted her religion. With this end in view, he advised her to pardon and restore Moray and his confederates and take care to play down her relations with France and Spain. Events had since forced her to follow the first part of this advice.[39]

These cross-currents of interest intensified the complexities of the English political world but perhaps, by the very ambiguities they created, averted head-on factional confrontation. The campaign to forward the Habsburg marriage was, of course, also an anti-Dudley movement, which matched the two noblemen, Norfolk and Sussex, with the quiet backing of Cecil, against the favourite. Their intense dislike of Leicester was common ground although the sources of that antipathy were somewhat different. Cecil displayed a cold distaste towards the man whom he saw as a self-seeking adventurer and whose accession to supreme power would lead to a public calamity. Norfolk and Sussex entertained a more personal passion towards a man 'who could produce no more but two ancestors, namely his father and grandfather and these both of them enemies and traitors to their country'.[40]

Thus the magnet of the Habsburg marriage held together one grouping of particles; but when the counter-pull of a Stuart succession was felt, they clustered in a different configuration. In this second case Norfolk, Sussex and Leicester found common ground in their anxiety to hedge against a future in which Mary — a decade younger than her English cousin — might be the next sovereign of England. There was a strong feeling in influential circles that Mary was the rightful heir, failing another Tudor. Sussex, who was perhaps a fair representative of this school of thought, had put his point of view a year earlier. He would have had the queen accept Mary's proposals, trading acknowledgment of the Stuart claims against a present renunciation. Recognition of Stuart rights was, he argued, but just and reasonable.[41] But Cecil sternly withstood the allurements of the Scottish Circe. However appealing the stability of a guaranteed succession, Cecil believed the price of a Stuart succession too high to be paid. To him Mary's unbending Catholicism, her Guisan relatives and her potential attractions to the Spanish house were intolerable conditions. Hence, on this great issue, Cecil stood apart from the Howard allies; while they, in turn, found themselves in unaccustomed affinity to Dudley.

Elizabeth herself, although determined to make no commitment, would surely have preferred Mary to the Greys, and in November 1566 when Bedford went up to Edinburgh to represent the queen at her godson's christening, he carried instructions to seek a reconciliation. He was to suggest a reformulation of clause five of the Treaty of Edinburgh by which, in return for Mary's renunciation of present claims, Elizabeth would reciprocally engage to protect Mary against claims to the English succession prejudicial to hers. The English queen would not go so far as to recognize Mary's claims outright, but in token of her good faith she emphasized the severity with which Hales's indiscreet effort had been punished.[42]

Leicester's role was an especially difficult one. For the first time in the reign the queen had displayed signs of coolness towards the earl. She may well have had some inkling of his dealings with Mary Stuart's agents and may even have blamed him for promoting Darnley's cause. Leicester was certainly showing signs of increasing independence both in his patronage of the Protestant radicals and in his attitude towards Mary. At the same time he was fighting desperately to prevent the Habsburg match; a bridegroom who was the candidate of Norfolk, Sussex and Cecil would hardly be his friend. And, casting an unsentimental eye upon the future, Leicester needed to ensure the goodwill of the possible successor. To keep all these balls in the air at once required a display of most uncommon political virtuosity.

Mary chose neither to follow Throckmorton's advice nor to respond to Elizabeth's tenders of conciliation. She and her husband had early in their married life sought out the protection of King Philip. Their dubious agent was Francis Yaxley, a busybody English courtier, once a liaison man between the Catholics and Robert Dudley, later a meddler in Lady Lennox's plottings. Imprisoned for this latter escapade, he had been released and fled abroad, only to turn up at the Scottish court in the summer of 1565. Winning the confidence of the royal couple, he had been sent off to Spain as their agent. Philip entrusted him with a small sum of money and assurances of his avuncular interest in the royal pair, but on the way back Yaxley was drowned off the Northumberland coast.[43] Philip was now becoming interested in backing the Stuart claim to the succession, and Mary's policy was gradually gravitating towards this powerful protector. In the meantime she dabbled in trifling conspiracy with such stray Englishmen as the Yorkshire squire, Lascelles, or the vagrant debtor, Rokesby, the latter a creature of Cecil's. She also sent an indiscreet letter to the Earl of Northumberland, already a much suspect nobleman.[44] All these moves deepened Cecil's suspicions; none of them was calculated to win support in England, where she needed it, among the solid gentry who made up the Commons and filled the J.P.s' bench. But for the season Mary and her prospects had to yield second place to English hopes that their queen would marry.

In this atmosphere the oft-prorogued Parliament elected in 1563 met once again, just after Michaelmas 1566. Whether or not this session would actually take place was highly uncertain until late in the summer. The government had hesitated to summon it out of well-grounded fear that the Houses would broach once again the delicate matter of the queen's marriage, and, even worse, the dangerous question of the succession. The accumulated debts of the Crown were a heavy burden and without parliamentary taxation could not be cleared away. Yet even under these pressures, the Council hesitated, and the French ambassador heard they had discussed the possibility of adjournment without a grant, if discussion of the succession went forward. His Spanish colleague reported that no supplies would be voted unless the queen either married or proclaimed a successor, and earlier wrote that Leicester was behind the agitation for discussion of the succession, hoping thus to distract the queen and upset the archduke's applecart. Cecil's parliamentary agenda included a royal instruction that the Parliament should not have long continuance nor deal in unnecessary matters. But no one could doubt, even before the members assembled at Westminster, that in their view the latter rubric would not extend to the succession question.[45]

The Lords and Commons came to this new session all too well briefed on this issue. It was during the previous session of Parliament that Hales, member for Lancaster borough, had produced his now famous defence of the Grey claim. The defensive phraseology of that pamphlet suggests that the author aimed at countering an already formulated argument. The Hales tract had circulated in manuscript and a manuscript answer had been written, probably by Justice Anthony Browne, a Catholic member of the bench. This in turn was followed at the end of 1565 by a printed anti-Stuart tract which was answered early in the next year by several defences of the Scottish queen's claims, one of which may have appeared in print. This pamphlet war had made familiar the substance of the legal arguments as well as the half-articulate constitutional debate which grew from them.[46]

There were two central questions around which these arguments revolved. Mary's claim rested on her descent from the elder daughter of Henry VII; by the ordinary rules of the common law her claim to inherit would take precedence over all others. Against this the adherents of the Greys made two assertions: the first, that Henry VIII by his will had set aside the Stuart claim and appointed the descendants of his younger sister, Mary, to follow his own issue. By a second and independent argument they assailed the Queen of Scots by asserting that her foreign birth invalidated her right to the English throne. Their authority here was a general rule of the common law against inheritance by aliens.

Around these positions the polemical war raged fiercely. The Marians' strongest argument was that the will of Henry VIII was invalid. Their attacks varied in character; some stuck to the more narrowly legal contention that Henry had signed with a stamp instead of his hand, thereby contravening the statute which authorized him to devise the Crown. Others took the larger ground that he was bound to leave the Crown only to persons morally fit to inherit; the corollary argument to this was the alleged illegitimacy of Lady Frances Brandon, daughter to the Princess Mary and the Duke of Suffolk, as well as the conduct of Lady Catherine Grey in her relations with the Earl of Hertford. The same kind of argument was used against the Lady Lennox who, although born in England, was alleged to be the fruit of an adulterous union.

The whole argument over the will was complicated by the fact that the document was apparently missing. Both sides resorted to legal and historical proofs to establish either the effectiveness or the nullity of the instrument, and in both instances the main line of dispute trailed off into a bewildering labyrinth of antiquarian intricacies.

Mary's defenders wisely stuck to law and history so far as possible, avoiding the crucial question of religion. Even the ardently Protestant Dean Sampson noted that Englishmen 'are led by known and allowed law as their late sticking to maintain the title of your sister Queen Mary and yours also against the attempt of the Duke of Northumberland doth sufficiently declare'.[47] Mary's strongest position rested precisely on the appeal to the traditional rules of descent and unquestioned royalty which had saved Mary Tudor's throne and which loomed so importantly in the thinking of all educated Englishmen. These were the men, loyal, moderate and law-abiding, whose defection to the Queen of Scots Cecil so dreaded.

The anti-Stuart pamphleteers, while going to great trouble to answer their opponents' legal arguments, did not hesitate to sound another note. Contemptuous antipathy was the traditional English attitude towards the Scots, and it was not very difficult to conjure the imaginary horrors of another Norman conquest with the attendant calamity of foreign oppression. It was probably in the previous session of Parliament that Sir Ralph Sadler, the greatest English expert on Scottish affairs, had made a powerful speech in much the same vein. Nature and history barred the succession of a Scottish prince to the English throne. No Englishman could consent to subjection to an alien ruler: ' ... our common people and the stones in the street would rebel against it.'[48]

A second line of attack—on the grounds of religion—was more cautiously pursued, although it was pretty bluntly stated by the end of 1565.[49] Many of those who supported the Queen of Scots—the argument ran— were but 'dissimuled or hypocritical Protestants' who wished to wash their hands in the blood of the faithful in a general return to idolatry and cruelty. In these same months before the meeting of the Houses another pamphlet issued forth, probably the work of the anti-vestiarian Thomas Sampson, deprived Dean of Christ Church, who, after exhorting the queen to marriage and to consideration of the succession, went on to suggest in rather strong terms that if the queen did not listen to the counsel of Parliament, the Houses should not hesitate in pushing their views. 'They must neither for faintness nor flattery let slip their duty in this behalf. Wherefore if there should be such difficulty in the Queen that she would not of herself incline to help this misery then is the wisdom and power of the Parliament to be showed so that they do what may be done to have this matter of succession decided.'[50]

Public debate on a great state question and the creation of excited public opinion among the aristocracy were utterly deplorable circumstances from the point of view of any Tudor government, for this was an intolerable intrusion into the *arcana imperii*. It was made much worse by the fact that the Protestant and anti-Stuart bias of much of the aristocracy clashed head-on with the prejudices of the queen. Although fixed in her determination not to declare formally an heir, her own preferences ran strongly in favour of Mary's claims. For the Greys Elizabeth entertained feelings of unconcealed contempt; Mary she viewed as an equal, incontestably royal, and possessed of rights which deserved protection. Through the haze of endless bickering, suspicious resentment and intense jealousy which for ever clouded relations between the cousins, Elizabeth never lost sight of these fundamental facts. Once her anger over the Darnley match died down, she resumed her efforts to maintain civility between them and restated her willingness to protect Mary's claims so far as she could without actually confirming them.

These circumstances meant that Parliament met in 1566 under conditions unusual under the Tudor dynasty. It was inevitable that the members, excited by public and private discussion of a great public issue, maintained at fever pitch for more than a year, would adopt a position which cut athwart the purposes of the sovereign. The assault upon the queen began, in fact, with an extra-parliamentary move. Parliament met on September 30th and the Speaker-Elect was presented to the queen on October 2nd, but little business was done for a fortnight. In the meantime at a Council meeting on October 12th the Duke of Norfolk took the lead in reminding the queen of her promises in the 1563 session and in urging her to allow the present meeting to discuss both succession and marriage. The queen rounded on him, angrily declaring that, for the first, she had no desire to be buried alive and to see them repeating to the seat of her heir the journeys they had made to Hatfield in Queen Mary's time. As for the marriage—they saw well enough that was not far off. With that she left them.[51]

Checked in the Council, the offensive was soon resumed in the Commons. There a motion made by John Molyneux, member for Nottinghamshire and just possibly a creature of Leicester's, to take up the suit for succession made in the earlier session was very favourably received. Not even the queen's declaration—delivered through Cecil and Knollys—that she was about to proceed with her marriage would turn the Commons's determination. Moreover, they proceeded with all deliberation to hold back the subsidy bill until they had some answer from the queen. Their next step was to propose a delegation from both Houses to urge their case upon her. In fact it was a delegation of peers only which went to see the sovereign; the Lord Treasurer declared their case, while the others, headed by the Duke of Norfolk, each individually supported the argument. Winchester put quite bluntly the situation of the Commons, whose stalling tactics were holding up the subsidy and halting all legislation. He implored the queen to declare her views on the succession or else to dismiss Parliament and allow them all to go home. The queen again took a high line, dismissed them curtly as a set of featherbrains, and declared she would take the views of a half dozen of the ablest lawyers.

But once again her tactics failed to deter the Parliament. A resolute Commons pushed on, pulling the somewhat more hesitant Lords behind them, resolute for a joint petition. The queen decided then to forestall their action and sent for a delegation from each House, the Speaker choosing those from the lower House. Her answer was one of the great masterpieces of Elizabethan royal rhetoric, charged with indignation and barbed with sarcasm. It supplemented in a public and more dignified manner the tongue-lashing she had already administered to the lords of the Council in private and the even sterner discipline she laid on Leicester and Pembroke by denying them admission to court. Nevertheless, she bent with the storm so far as to promise marriage in the near future. On the succession issue, she sternly forbade any further discussion, but promised to deal with the problem as soon as conditions safely permitted.[52]

This speech, conveyed though in much softened tones to the Commons, was without avail; debate on the succession continued in the lower House. The queen, driven to her last weapons, now expressly prohibited further discussion. The command had to be repeated a second time. The House of Commons thereupon took a new tack by debating whether the queen's command violated their liberties and ended by drawing up a gently worded but daringly conceived petition on this constitutional issue. The queen at last yielded—or half-yielded—withdrawing her commands, but understanding that she would not be further pressed.

This crisis was hardly ended before another, less major in consequence, but hardly less painful, arose. A member of the House, during the debate on their liberties, seeing a copy of a poem recently published in Paris celebrating the birth of James, Prince of Scotland, *England, and Ireland*, discharged his indignation at this libellous work with some damaging reflections on the Scottish claim to the succession. Melville, Mary's representative in London, was quick to object; Dalton, the member in question, denied the gravest of the allegations made against him, and after an abortive conciliar scheme to send another royal message, rebuking the House, the matter was allowed to drop.[53]

The queen found that in order to secure the passage of a subsidy bill some further concession yet was necessary; she now relinquished the proposed third payment on the subsidy. The House received this gesture with appropriate delight but went on to alter the terms proposed by Cecil so as to reduce the rate of assessment below that of 1563.[54] Since the government had begun rather timidly at the opening of the session by asking for only one tenth and fifteenth instead of the two given in 1559, the total receipts from this parliamentary grant were dismayingly low.

As if the record of this Parliament were not already dismal enough, yet another cause of discord arose in the final weeks of a very long session. The reforming party in the Church, backed by the bishops, attempted to push through an act confirming the articles of religion passed by the Convocation of 1563. One effect of such a measure would be to squeeze whatever remaining Marian clergy had not yet formally submitted to the new faith. Commons was enthusiastic in approval, but the bill was stopped in the Lords by a royal prohibition while the queen summoned the archbishop and some of his colleagues to scold them for having introduced a bill on religion without her consent. The Commons played a delaying game, first holding up the subsidy bill before sending it to Lords and then blocking government legislation to renew certain acts expiring with this Parliament. On this final note of discord the session of 1566 ended and with it—by dissolution—the life of the Parliament itself.

Cecil's views of this unhappy session were contained in a memorandum which was largely a litany of things not done, including: the succession not answered, the marriage not followed, the bill of religion stayed to the comfort of adversaries. It ended with a note of 'dangers ensuing'—general discontentments, the slender execution of the subsidy, and danger of sedition in the summer by persons discontented.[55]

There was small cause for content. A determined aristocracy, mobilized in Parliament and Council, had faced an angry monarch in a stormy confrontation; in the upshot each had thwarted the other. The Lords and Commons had failed to coerce the queen into accepting their demands, but her doubtful victory had cost the government heavily. Yet the dust of this head-on collision obscured the cloudy ambiguities which lay behind. The political elite of the nation were agreed in their demands that the queen marry and that the succession be settled. But harmony as to ends was hardly matched by accord as to means. Whom would they have her marry? Who was their choice for heir presumptive? The conservative nobles, Norfolk, Sussex and their friends, were prepared to accept a Catholic husband or – in Mary – a Catholic successor. But how many of the gentlemen of the shires who had voted for the Articles of Religion or nodded approval to Dalton's attack on Scottish presumption would go along with such a programme? Had the leaders among the nobles and gentlemen of court and Parliament somehow won the queen to accept their petitions, they might have lived to regret their success, for the temporary alliance between conservatives and radicals – trimmers and sectaries – to force a royal marriage only papered over the deep differences between them.

9 The Downfall of Mary Stuart

IN FEBRUARY 1567 England and all Europe were startled by the news of the murder of Henry Darnley. The Queen of Scots had been on cool terms with her husband since the murder of Rizzio, but during the early winter of 1566–7 Scottish affairs had seemed tranquil enough to outsiders. In truth, such stability as Scottish politics had enjoyed under Mary had vanished with her marriage. Since then the government had been conducted under severe limitations. The Queen of Scots had to be satisfied with protecting her own person and independence without much hope of exacting effective obedience from her subjects. Nevertheless it was by her own volition that Mary plunged into the wildest adventure of her life when she proposed to marry her husband's murderer. Politically it was madness and spelt utter ruin to her Scottish career. When it became apparent what her intentions were, her most cool-headed councillor, Moray, departed for Italy. The more supple Maitland found himself dragged, reluctant but powerless, in the wake of her passionate determination to marry Bothwell. Her alliance with the most feared and hated figure in Scottish politics crystallized an effective opposition as no other move could have done. The result was a bouleversement which had plenty of precedents in Scottish history but which took contemporary observers by surprise.

The English court watched with mingled feelings the rapid course of events from the murder at Kirk-o'-Field in February to the deposition of Mary and the coronation of James VI in July. The opening act, Darnley's murder, immediately shifted the balance in relations between the sovereigns in Elizabeth's favour. Since Mary's marriage the initiative had lain with her; Elizabeth could do little but grumblingly protest at the marriage and at Moray's expulsion; the Rizzio plot had had English approval but had done little to re-establish English influence at the Scottish court. Elizabeth's last proposals, in November 1566, had gone as far to conciliate Mary as the English sovereign could go. But now, with the appalling suspicions which hung over the Queen of Scots's head, it was easy for Elizabeth to seize the advantage. The queen assumed an air of cold and condescending sympathy and urged Mary to solve the mystery of the murder and to vindicate her own honour. But the Scots queen went her reckless way to the utter shipwreck of her fortunes; the marriage, the revolt which followed, and Mary's imprisonment in Lochleven in July 1567 ensued before Elizabeth, now deeply disturbed, stirred herself to action.

Her initial move was to write a letter which began with a bald rebuke on the folly of the marriage but went on more comfortably to promise intervention in Mary's behalf. Within a few days Sir Nicholas Throckmorton was on his way northward with instructions which expressed very emphatically Elizabeth's views. The queen (he was to say) found it incredible that the ranking nobility of the realm could offer such violence to their sovereign as to imprison her. Whatever her faults, it was not the business of subjects to reform a monarch. The queen was willing that Bothwell be charged, that a divorce follow, and that the Queen of Scots be hedged in by conciliar checks, but the cardinal condition was to be Mary's liberation from prison. Elizabeth was genuinely anxious to see Mary free but on terms which would make both the Scottish queen and the Scottish lords dependent on English support.[1]

Throckmorton soon discovered the impracticability of such terms. The Scots lords were in an advantageous position and meant to exploit it. Their queen safely locked away, they intended to bargain for the best terms they could get from either England or France. Throckmorton was frank with Cecil, 'for when all is done, it is they which must stand her [Elizabeth] in more stead than the Queen her cousin'.[2] But the English queen was adamant in insisting on the release of Mary. For her, one of the greatest social principles was at issue, and her ministers' representations as to the dangers of French intervention left her unmoved. But Throckmorton's pleading did not avail even to an interview with the captive queen; the Scots lords pressed ahead and on July 29th, having extracted an abdication from his mother, crowned James VI at Stirling. One accomplishment probably was to be credited to Throckmorton's mission. For a few days the Queen of Scots's life was in real danger; Throckmorton's appeal perhaps turned the tables in her favour; Robert Melville at least thought so.[3]

Through this crisis Leicester and his follower Throckmorton were accounted firm friends of the Scottish queen; Sir Nicholas had the reputation of being a secret friend of Mary for some time past. His aims for the present — aside from preserving Mary's life — were to obtain English custody of the young James; but, as he emphasized to his patrons, Leicester and Pembroke, the Scots lords would agree to this only if there were explicit acknowledgment of James's future rights in the English succession. Elizabeth showed no disposition to budge in her refusal to make commitments on the succession. Cecil looked on the situation with grave concern, fearing the likelihood of a Scottish rapprochement with France. For him the remedy lay not in rescuing Mary but in supporting Moray as Regent. The Secretary had done all he could to hasten the latter's return from the Continent. Once the earl was established as Regent the divorce between the realms would be 'rather in terms than in hearts'. Cecil's confidence in Moray lessened his fear of foreign intervention in the northern kingdom. The formidable Scot seemed to English eyes a little larger than life; even Throckmorton wrote of him as one who 'seeks to imitate rather some which have led the people of Israel than any captains of our age'.[4]

There were other Englishmen who felt unabashed satisfaction in Mary's downfall. Richard Bertie, husband to the outspokenly Protestant Duchess of Suffolk, noted bluntly that the Scots lords now had the wolf by the ears, and was hopeful she might never again exercise power. Sir Walter Mildmay, newly appointed Privy Councillor, put the Protestant view more piously: 'She hath accorded to this resignation of her estate in marvellous tragedy if a man repeat it from the beginning, showing the issue of such as live not in the fear of God.'[5]

The queen would have none of this; her fury with the Scottish lords grew and was held in check only when her ministers pointed out that too much pressure might push the Scots lords to kill Mary, with fatal consequences to Elizabeth's own reputation, since this event would be ascribed to her machinations. She did, however, much against the advice of her ministers, order co-operation with the Hamilton faction which was now arming in Scotland against the Regent — this in the face of Throckmorton's estimate of the Hamiltons: 'their behaviour so inordinate, the most of them unable, their living so vicious, their fidelity so fickle, their party so weak, as I count it lost whatsoever is bestowed upon them.'[6]

In fact the Regent's vigorous action reduced Dunbar, which was holding out against him, by the beginning of October, and the Hamiltons were compelled to a resentful quiescence for the time being. Autumn passed away into winter; the Queen of Scots remained in her island prison, and Anglo-Scottish relations in frozen suspense. By September the renewed religious wars in France had rendered that government impotent to intervene in Scotland, and in October the northern Border was reckoned quiet enough to allow the recall of Bedford from his lieutenancy of the North. Sir William Drury, Marshal of Berwick, remained in charge.[7]

English policy, throughout these critical months, had been conducted by the queen personally and on principles of high political morality rather than considerations of state. Without very much effort and by the expenditure of a little money Elizabeth might have rid herself of her Scottish rival for ever. At the very least she might have installed a government at Edinburgh devoted to English interests and dependent on English support. But to Elizabeth the issue was a straightforward one. Mary had behaved in an unqueenly way, as Elizabeth did not hesitate to tell her. But rebuke from a fellow-sovereign and cousin was within the canon; when the Scottish lords undertook to judge, even worse to imprison and dethrone, their ruler, they had overstepped the bounds laid down by God and established in nature. It was no mere bias of another sovereign that moved Elizabeth, so she declared, but the universally acknowledged principles of right order. The English queen, already disturbed by the tumults that racked Flanders in that uneasy summer and the prospect of renewed civil war in France, was deeply angered by events in Scotland. Her fury was approaching an hysteria which her advisors were able to check only by invoking an even more cherished principle. If Mary were murdered, an imputation would be cast upon Elizabeth which would never be lived down. This argument had a duly sobering effect and Elizabeth brought herself to acquiesce in events and to recognize that it was not in her power to release Mary. But she would not compromise herself by any recognition of the new Scottish regime.

The melodramatic events in Scotland had preoccupied the islanders during this summer, but on the Continent matters of greater moment were transpiring. The smouldering discontent of King Philip's Low Countries subjects had broken out in open revolt. The Spanish ambassador watched the English court narrowly for signs of collaboration with their co-religionists across the Channel. The queen herself was forceful in her expressions of indignation towards the rebels, and the ambassador was disposed to believe in her sincerity. Refugees flocked across to England, but there was no evidence of English intervention in Flemish affairs.[8]

When renewed troubles broke out in France, there was more temptation to take a hand. The English representative in Paris was now the inexperienced Sir Henry Norris, the Oxfordshire squire who had replaced

Cecil's brother-in-law, Hoby, when the latter died in the French capital after a short tenure of the embassy. That ancient war-horse Throckmorton, remembering his own days in France, wrote anxiously to Cecil suggesting Norris's replacement by Henry Killigrew, who might be more able to speak 'some grateful things on Her Majesty's behalf' to the Protestants there and to prevent their being overthrown.[9] But this time the English government did not yield to these dangerous temptations, and continued to pursue a correct and cautious policy towards French affairs even though that very summer the eight years' French occupation of Calais stipulated by Cateau-Cambrésis had come to a close without any satisfaction being rendered to Elizabeth.

In the meantime, amidst all these excitements, the negotiations of an Austrian marriage dragged on their weary, halting way. During the early months of 1567 the advocates of the match very nearly gave up. The Spanish ambassador heard that all hope of any marriage had been abandoned, and Lord Chamberlain Howard, a warm advocate of the archduke, confessed that he did not think Sussex would ever be sent to Germany. The matter had again become intertwined with the Leicester–Sussex rivalry, which broke out anew in the spring. This time the issue was the presidency of Wales, which Sussex sought; Leicester had promised his support, but now Sidney, the latter's brother-in-law, was to be continued in his Welsh office. Pembroke intervened and managed to patch up a settlement.[10]

That nobleman, the close ally of Leicester, was advanced at Easter to the office of Lord High Steward, vacant since Arundel's impulsive resignation in July 1564. The latter earl returned from his continental travels a few weeks later, at the royal command, and his friends hoped for his restoration to office and influence. He spent the summer with the court but retired in disgust to his country house in August. Leicester in the meantime continued to cultivate good relations with Guzman de Silva, and even to play the role of protector of Roman Catholics, using his office of Chancellor of Oxford to that end. But even the hopeful Guzman had to acknowledge Leicester's thorough-going Protestantism. The Privy Council, he lamented, had now not a single Catholic sympathizer; Pembroke, once thought to be of the old faith, had now been drawn over by Leicester to the new. The chief hope of the Roman Catholics lay now in the Duke of Norfolk, who at the end of 1566 married the widowed Lady Dacre, a strong Catholic. There were also Catholics in the ducal household and there was hope of his conversion.[11]

About Eastertime of 1567 the queen at last brought herself to the decision to send Sussex to the imperial court, carrying the Garter and the long-delayed response to the previous imperial proposals of the autumn of 1566. The stumbling-block was religion. So far the Habsburgs had insisted on the archduke's right to the public exercise of the mass. The English instructions declared that the queen could allow no exceptions to the religion established by law but then added rather uncertainly that here was a general toleration for subjects living otherwise quietly, which the archduke would of course enjoy. Sussex was to make confidential inquiry as to just how seriously the archduke meant these demands (with the implication that they were diplomatic camouflage). The earl himself was in some perplexity, as he confessed to Guzman de Silva. What in fact was the religion established by law? Sussex believed that the English held by the Augsburg confession (and he was instructed to tell the imperial court that this was the case), but nevertheless Calvinism was being taught and preached everywhere. In this somewhat uncertain frame of mind Sussex set out for Vienna.[12]

The negotiations in that distant capital proceeded almost as slowly as they had at Westminster and it was October before the arrival of Henry Cobham (younger brother to the Lord Warden) with dispatches from Sussex gave any clear indication of what was going forward. The discussions still turned on the single but crucial issue of faith. The archduke and his imperial brother still insisted on one essential condition – that the bridegroom have the use of his religion. They were willing that this should be entirely private, that no Englishman should attend under legal penalty, and that the archduke should attend public service with the queen. These conditions secretly promised, the archduke was willing to come to England without further discussion; if the queen then rejected him, it could be given out that the cause was religion.[13]

The concessions made by the Habsburgs put the issue squarely up to the queen and her Councillors for decision. Consultation and debate followed; in the Council itself there was said to be division, with Leicester, Pembroke, Northampton and Vice-Chamberlain Knollys opposed while Lord Chamberlain Howard, the Admiral Clinton, Cecil and Comptroller Rogers supported a marriage on these terms. Norfolk was too ill to come up to court but the queen sent to ask his opinion.

In replies to both the queen and Cecil, the duke urged accommodation with the Austrians. He was certain that the archduke made conditions about religion merely for bargaining purposes and to give him an out if he were rejected for other reasons. No doubt, once married, he would be brought over to the established English faith. Against this *politique* argument the opponents of the match marshalled the threat to the Protestant faith implied by such concessions to a royal husband. Norfolk and Sussex both expressed their contemptuous scepticism as to the piety of their opponents and ascribed more selfish and worldly motives to them. But, in the event, it was the opposition to the marriage which triumphed. The queen made her decision in letters sent off to Sussex on December 10th. In them she again refused to concede separate worship for her husband, partly on the grounds of law ('which cannot be altered without the consent of the Estates of the realm') and partly on the grounds of her own conscience.[14]

To all practical purposes that was the close of this unromantic wooing, although Sussex lingered on through January, bestowed the Garter, and departed on civil terms. The earl was back in England in March, still hopeful, and Cecil remained uncertain as to what the queen's intentions were. No final step was taken, occasional echoes were heard, but as the spring advanced and more urgent matters intervened, the Habsburg suit faded into oblivion. The season had proved unpropitious and the once promising fruit remained unripe to rot upon the tree.

This was the end of the Habsburg match, which had preoccupied English politicians for more than four years. The motives of those who had pushed it were obviously mixed, but the main impulse came from the most sober and responsible of English statesmen. For these men the royal marriage was a straightforward problem in politics; the need for a royal husband and an assured succession was obvious to all. Among the possible candidates, the archduke had by far the most to recommend him. He was a scion of the greatest of European royal families, but the Austrian connection would not involve England in any entangling alliances. On the other hand, it would provide a useful link with the Habsburg interest, and generally amicable relations with that dynasty—the inheritors of the old Burgundian alliance—seemed to many Englishmen still to be the foundation of English foreign policy.

This *politique* view of the situation was sound so far as it went; what it omitted was the intentions of the queen herself. For four years she had confounded those who knew her most intimately; probably she herself was far from certain. Earlier the notion of marrying Robert Dudley had for a time an immense, sometimes almost overpowering, attraction. And —had it not been for another dimension of her personality—she would have plunged into marriage with as much abandon as her Scottish cousin twice displayed. But Elizabeth was quite as capable of appreciating the political dimensions of her situation as any of her most cool-headed ministers. She knew as well as Cecil that such a marriage would bring the appalling consequences he sketched in his memorandum of 1566, and, beyond these, the ultimate disruption of the Tudor state's hard-won stability. She knew, too, that any marriage would mean a sharing of the power which she so greedily treasured. And so gradually the allurements of the Dudley marriage faded, flaring up for the last time in the spring of 1564. The pleasures of flirtation remained no less delightful, but it was henceforth to be flirtation and no more.

She now turned to a colder consideration of the problems of her marriage. As she witheringly told the parliamentary delegation of 1566, the perils facing the nation were plain to the most simple. And she was probably not entirely insincere when she expressed her willingness to marry for the sake of her realm. But in her own mind this eventuality remained a remote—indeed, almost an abstract—possibility. For a time, after Mary's marriage to Darnley and the birth of James, it seemed as though circumstances might transform mere possibility into constraining necessity. No doubt this was the hope of Cecil and his associates in 1567. But in fact circumstances turned against them. The debacle in Scotland thoroughly shattered Mary's career, and when she was immured in her lake-bound prison the once acute pressures on the English queen rapidly lessened. The latter was again free to indulge the deep-seated antipathy to any marriage which had been growing in her for some time past. The game had gone against Norfolk, Cecil and their friends and left them with a worthless hand of cards. Leicester could breathe easier now that fortune had delivered him from the threat of a royal husband.

In rejecting the archduke, the existing law, which only Parliament could change, had been pleaded. This was a convenient diplomatic ploy; but it also reflected a new but potent fact of English political life. From the beginning the question of the archduke's religion had posed a difficulty. Until the end of the negotiations it was not very clearly faced. The religion established by law bound the ordinary subject, but it did not touch ambassadors; that had been tacitly conceded from the beginning of the reign. Neither did it fully bind peers of Parliament; the oaths required by the penal Act of 1563 did not include lords. And in Edward's time it had been found very difficult to bring a princess under the rubric of such statutes. In Scotland the startling experiment of a sovereign differing in religion from her subjects had been tried for half a dozen years with surprising success. These were the inconclusive guides offered to the English court when negotiations with the Habsburgs opened. As the record has shown, the opposition to the marriage was determined and persistent, yet it was not until the final crisis of the treaty that the religious question was openly raised as an objection to proceeding further.

It was true that among the adherents of the Habsburg match, there had been some difference of attitude. Most of the supporters of the match were so anxious for its fulfilment that they were willing to push the question of religion into the background. Doubtless most of them, like the Duke of Norfolk, thought that once the archduke arrived on the scene, he would himself accept the English state religion as they had done. Sussex, thinking more specifically about the matter, once told the Spanish ambassador that if the archduke would accompany the queen to public service, he could have the mass in his own apartments, and those were of course the terms put forward by the Austrians at the crux of the negotiations. Cecil was more concerned about the religious problem, perhaps because of his wife's urging, undoubtedly because of his own commitment to the new religion.[15] But in his thinking, as in that of all the backers of the match, there was a strong *politique* element, a disposition to evade the religious issue and to solve it by some convenient compromise.

But farther away from the court circle, the ever-growing intensity of Protestant feeling created a different atmosphere in which any concessions would be regarded as betrayal of the faith, a bowing to Antichrist. Strong echoes of this were heard in the Parliament of 1566, and the Councillors who pushed this point of view in December 1567 had behind them a great force of public feeling. Norfolk's hesitant advice to the queen began by acknowledging the overriding importance of religion and the necessity for elaborate safeguards. The events of 1567 on the Continent had done much to heighten Protestant feeling in the country. Altogether, the *politique* compromise proposed by Sussex was probably already unworkable. The queen's religious scruples were a diplomatic fiction, but those of a potent part of the English nation were real enough, and to have secured any parliamentary approval for a compromise arrangement would have been painfully embarrassing — perhaps impossible.

The faction-ridden years now coming to an end were a time of unusually confused and turbulent political life. But if we glance backward briefly several features become apparent. Initially, Elizabeth, challenged by Mary Stuart's determination to take another husband, had undertaken a prolonged delaying action. In this phase the queen was necessarily in complete command; her servants followed, however reluctantly, the policy she laid down. She failed to prevent a marriage of which she disapproved, yet it was the Councillors more than the queen who were shaken by the Darnley match; the queen was prepared, after some grumbling, to make the best of it. Then and later she sought some kind of *modus vivendi* with her cousin. Elizabeth's policy was in fact coolly consistent throughout. She viewed the political universe from the Olympian heights of a divine-right monarch. In this clear air the problem seemed quite uncomplicated. The rules governing royal succession were simple, straightforward, and unchangeable. Mary's descent in the senior line from Henry VII and her own undoubted royalty made her the sole possible claimant as ultimate successor in England. Other considerations were, from Elizabeth's unique point of view, irrelevant; other candidates, mere impostors. Consequently the English queen was willing to support the Stuart claim to the extent of suppressing any rival bids for recognition as heir. Acting on the same principles, she was also prepared to protect Mary's royal rights in Scotland after the enforced abdication. The Scottish nobles' assault on these rights was nothing less than a violation of the natural order. But in less exalted and very practical terms Elizabeth made it clear that Mary's rights in England were entirely of a contingent nature and that during the present reign the Scottish queen must expect to bend to the will of her cousin just as much as any other dependant.

This royal view, which brushed aside the central question of religion and left so open-ended all arrangements for the future, was hardly acceptable to her anxious subjects, whose worries about their own futures were not shared by their mistress. Hence in 1565-6 when Mary's marriage, the birth of her son, and her temporary triumph in Scotland seemed to bring her several steps closer to the English throne, the alarmed English Councillors took the initiative in urging their queen to marriage with the Archduke Charles. For a moment it looked as though the pressures would be great enough to force a very reluctant Elizabeth into a marriage of self-protection. But the queen played desperately for time, abetted in every device of delay by the anxious favourite, Leicester, and in the end escaped the net. Mary's own waywardness and her inability to handle the unruly Scottish nobles relaxed the pressures at the crucial moment. By the time Sussex's embassy set off to Vienna, Darnley was dead and the whole scandal of Bothwell about to break; by the time negotiations with the Habsburgs were broken off, Mary was a prisoner in Lochleven.

The promoters of the marriage had every cause for dismay. Not only had the match not come off, but their detested antagonist, Leicester, was better off than ever. Since the process of marrying Elizabeth to Charles necessarily involved the elimination of Robert Dudley, the latter had fought hard in self-defence. In the course of this skilful action he had appreciably bettered his own position. He was already the protector of the religious radicals, now in uneasy discord with the establishment, and in a larger sense the grand champion of the Protestant cause in England. But in opposing the proposed marriage with the Catholic archduke, his explicit advocacy of the new religion had become more pronounced. His opponents, in turn, by their willingness to compromise on the Habs-burgs' religious demands, were pushed into an uncomfortable and ambiguous position where at the very least they seemed indifferent to the interests of Christ's religion.

Hence, the net result of these years of intense intrigue and threatened violence was to leave the queen as free of matrimonial bonds as ever, to enlarge the political stature of the Earl of Leicester, and to leave the central issue of the political future—who would be the next sovereign of England—as far from settlement as ever. The most suitable foreign candidate for the queen's hand had now been rejected, and the possibilities of her marrying at all were fast diminishing. It is not surprising that politically astute men began to turn from the question of marriage to that of the succession.

In 1568 England stood on the eve of a great and prolonged political crisis, which would put every political career in jeopardy. Even earlier, events had created dangerous and tricky cross-currents in the stream of politics and made navigation difficult for the most experienced hands. Among them none had been so consistent or single-minded as William Cecil. Never doubting the necessity for the queen to marry, he had pressed her in season and out, and once the fever of her attachment to Dudley had sufficiently cooled he had moved with speed and decision to back the Austrian match. The reverse of this coin was his unwavering opposition to a Dudley marriage, although he had the political tact to avoid a confrontation with the favourite and worked through the agency of great and less vulnerable courtiers. Yet Cecil was at the best pessimistic about the outcome; he knew his mistress too well to expect that anything but the harshest force of circumstance would bring her to accept the archduke.

That disillusioned cynic, the Earl of Arundel, had declared that the Secretary did not really wish his mistress to marry at all since he would lose too much power if there was a royal husband. The queen herself, in the harassments of the parliamentary session, had flashed out that many who professed themselves anxious for marriage in fact wished the contrary.[16] Neither observation need be taken at face value but they hint at what must have been a half-acknowledged thought in Cecil's, and others', mind. The present political order, fortified by habit and embedded in vested interests, had lasted a decade; a royal husband might shatter its structure. However cogent the well-rehearsed arguments for speedy marriage, they were unconsciously eroded by the inertia of success.

But in Cecil's views on the succession there were fewer half-lights. His opposition to the Stuart claim was rock-like; he was convinced beyond all shadow of doubt that a second Mary on the English throne would repeat all the blunders of the first. She would draw the country once more into the orbit of one of the great Catholic powers; the cause of religion and – what counted most for Cecil – English independence would be lost again. On the awkward question of an alternative line of succession, Cecil probably saw no clear path; he was often accused of being an adherent of the Grey–Hertford line, and perhaps, if the terrible contingency of succession had had to be faced, he would in desperation have opted for a house so unquestionably Protestant and English. But he was prepared to be patient, to hope against hope for the miracle of a marriage, and in the meantime to preserve a mask of impenetrable discretion.

These were years in which the constraints of circumstance hung heavy and left Cecil with little room for manoeuvre. Although he was the key man of business within the government, holding all the threads of administration in his fingers, he had not the status outside the court to jostle on equal terms against a Norfolk, a Pembroke, or a Sussex, or openly to assail Leicester. His share in the royal confidence was large but not to be compared with the queen's undiscriminating and inexhaustible regard for Leicester. Hence Cecil's role in affairs between 1562 and 1569 was one of cautious and reserved constraint, his actions usually indirect and circumspect. Much of the time he was fighting a defensive battle – staving off Leicester's schemes for self-advancement, holding back the advances of the Stuart party, checking the intrigues of De Quadra, or discreetly backing the Howards. There was little opportunity for the bold and forceful leadership of 1559–60.

The new shape which the religious question took displays his problems. Where the Catholics were concerned, he was direct, determined, even ruthless. But Protestant dissent offered an awkward dilemma. On the one side were his own undeniable sympathies for the new faith; on the other the direct commands of the queen, resolute in her insistence on the goal of uniformity but waveringly uncertain as to enforcement. As principal administrator, Cecil was in an unenviable position since he could only carry out his mistress's orders. This unhappy conjuncture won him both the reproachful complaints of the harried Primate and the blunt disapproval of the Protestant ultras. The latter blamed him as 'one of the chief instruments and procurers of the present calamity'.[17]

His noble colleagues on the Council and in the court were freer to act and correspondingly more flexible and more open in the paths they followed. On the marriage question Norfolk and Sussex were guided not only by the urgent need for a settled succession but also by their angry detestation of Dudley. From time to time the fires of their hatred blazed up into open defiance of the favourite and had to be damped down by the queen. With these uncomplicated views they had no hesitation in pushing with all their force for the archducal marriage. The question of his religion hardly seemed important since they assumed Charles would have the same adaptable conscience that they possessed; the great thing was to prevent the ultimate catastrophe of a Dudley match.

They could also afford to be more flexible on the succession question. Although they shared in the general alarm which the Darnley marriage first conjured up, once the infant James was born they began to relax a little in their attitudes towards the northern dynasty. After all, a Duke of Norfolk or an Earl of Sussex would still be a great man in a Stuart court (although a Cecil might be nobody), and they had to make their calculations about the future accordingly. Hence their willingness to conciliate Mary and to think well of her claim to be the recognized heir, an attitude which in their minds cast no shadows on their loyalty to the present sovereign.

Nor did they feel so strongly on the issues which troubled the English Church. Sussex voted with the Catholic contingent in the House of Lords against the bill for confirming the validity of episcopal authority in the Parliament of 1566.[18] In 1567 Norfolk for dynastic reasons concluded a marriage with the widowed Lady Dacre, a lady of strong Catholic convictions, a match which rejoiced the hearts of the supporters of the old faith. Neither of these lords was himself a Catholic, but neither of them felt that commitment to Protestantism was a matter of conscience, or, like Cecil, a *sine qua non* of the national interest.

Leicester's position was for obvious reasons a more difficult one. The

11

prospect of marriage with Elizabeth diminished steadily during these years, but he never quite gave up hope. In any case her marriage to anyone else would be at the best a humiliating defeat and at the worst an irretrievable disaster for him. In addition he was the most cordially hated man at court. It took more than common skill to steer a course which would countervail the backers of Archduke Charles, keep him on good terms with his mistress, and rally as much support within the court as was possible—all this within the allowable bounds of convention and of decorum.

Backing the French bid had been a useful ploy during 1564 and 1565, but during late 1565 and much of 1566 Leicester had had to deal with the first bout of royal displeasure to mar their relationship. His enemies were of course hopeful, but Cecil's dry comment probably summed up the true state of affairs: 'I think the Queen's Majesty's favour to my Lord of Leicester be not so manifest as it was to move men to think she will marry with him and yet his lordship hath favour sufficient.'[19] The cause of this coldness is not immediately evident; it may have arisen from the queen's awareness of his cordiality towards Mary and the suspicion that he had forwarded Darnley's prospects to free himself from a Stuart match. At any rate it proved to be only the temporary coolness which occasionally chequers the course of long friendship rather than the rupture which Dudley's enemies fondly hoped for. He never lost the magic talisman of royal favour.

Leicester's relations with the Scottish queen were of course shaped by the uncertainties of his position in England. Like the other peers of the Council he was now a great landed magnate; but like Cecil he was very much a creature of the present regime. Lacking the ballast which the Secretary's considered views of national policy gave him, Leicester was more politically volatile, more willing to look ahead into the future when Queen Elizabeth might no longer be alive. Hence he was to be found among those politicians who were willing to cultivate the Scots queen.

But it was on the great question of Protestant discontent with the settlement of 1559 that Leicester's actions were most interesting. In contrast to his usual prudent fence-mending, he was here willing, even eager, to take a bold and risky line. His patronage of individual divines was fast turning into the leadership of a cause. His protection in 1565 and 1566 had not been sufficient to spare many of them the penalty of deprivation, but his persistence in pushing their cause was effective in blunting the edge of the Primate's efforts to secure uniformity. Leicester's advocacy was now becoming a more and more public one; in 1566 he had aligned himself with the bishops in their unsuccessful efforts to get the Thirty-Nine Articles turned into statute, a move which aroused open royal contradiction. He even went so far as publicly to take communion in the French church in London in early 1568.[20]

These moves had, of course, political value; they won him allies on the Council, where both Knollys and Northampton joined in his opposition to the archducal marriage. Indeed, slowly but surely, Dudley was building up a following. In 1566 Cecil's list of Dudley's 'own particular friends' included only a handful of first-level politicians: his brother, Ambrose; his brother-in-law, Sidney; and the courtier-diplomat, Killigrew.[21] He perhaps should have added Throckmorton; certainly by 1568 both Sir Nicholas and the veteran magnate, Pembroke, were firmly in the Dudley camp and Knollys and Northampton disposed to co-operate. Leicester had seen the end of the Habsburg threat to his position, had recovered the full favour of the queen, was established as a court magnate with powerful allies; above all, he was the public and acknowledged patron of the most articulate and insistent force for change within England.

The interrelationships among these great persons had formed the fluid but not entirely irregular pattern of English political movement during these past years. It had never lost the basic triangular configuration established early in the reign – based on the queen, Cecil and Dudley. Specific episodes had often found them grouped in a two-versus-one combination. In external policy the queen and the Secretary shared the same wary suspicion of foreign involvement while Dudley pushed for more daring initiatives abroad. But at the time of the proposed match between Mary and Robert Dudley, the Secretary and the favourite were uneasy co-operators – with different motives – in discouraging such a marriage. On religious matters they were generally in accord, even though Dudley was likely to be bolder in supporting the Protestant cause. When the Habsburg match was pressed on the queen, she and Leicester were implicitly allied in an effort to stave it off. In general, one might argue that the ordered steps of this court minuet made for healthy political stability. The political world was kept in constant but fairly predictable motion. For each protagonist it provided both adequate liberty and salutary checks. To the queen it meant that however much one combination of Councillors might press her to a course of action, she could always find backing for an alternative course from another. On the Habsburg marriage, for instance, she could count on Dudley and his Protestant allies to raise the convincing argument of religion. Hence she could not be borne down by the sheer weight of united Council pressure. Only occasionally, as on anti-Catholic measures, did she find herself carried along by an irresistible tide of opinion. Dudley, although checked in his central ambition of marriage, found himself protected by the queen against attack on his vital interests and yet with enough independence of status to oppose the queen on religious questions. Cecil, in turn, trusted by the queen and loosely allied with the Norfolk–Sussex interest, could feel a sense of security in his own position and satisfaction in the general course of policy.

In any case it was a flexible enough arrangement to allow the queen's two servants a share in the making of high policy and freedom to disagree with one another without endangering their whole careers. Only once or twice, when the Leicester–Sussex quarrel flared up to the danger point, did this balance of forces seem threatened. It is hard to gauge this danger — was it play-acting or the real thing? In each instance the queen's firm intervention was sufficient to quell the immediate disturbance. It is unlikely that either protagonist wished to risk a real showdown. The melodrama of threatened duels and partisan badges offered a suitably flamboyant but essentially irenic substitute for actual violence.

But the stability of the regime was threatened in 1568, as five years earlier, by the underlying failure to provide security for the future, and when discussion of the question shifted from marriage to succession, danger loomed ahead. The Queen of Scots had hoped to establish a party of her own in English politics, at least since the Darnley marriage and, indeed, since she returned to Scotland. Recently she had received excellent advice from that skilled practitioner, Throckmorton, and friendly responses from a number of notables. But her capacity to understand the mysteries of English politics was no greater than that displayed by her descendants in the next century. She could not grasp the necessity for building a broad base of support which would include religious neuters and at least a sizable proportion of the active Protestants. She thought only in terms of her co-religionists and her tactics were those of petty intrigue. In Scottish politics she had shown promise, but after the Darnley match she frittered away her opportunities by yielding to one feckless impulse after another.

Moreover, as public debate on the issue indicated, her religion was a more and more awkward obstacle to her ambitions. The floodtide of Protestant feeling was rising in England, a flood which rose not by any government prompting but from deep springs of popular religious sentiment. Stridently anti-Catholic, anti-clerical and anti-foreign, the movement was now given positive form in the faith of the Puritans. Although such views were not popular with the queen, there was strong backing at court, powerfully supported by such magnates as Leicester and Bedford, and a broad base among the country gentry and greater townsmen. Anxious as the political classes were for a settlement to the succession problem, they were no less insistent that the future of the English nation should be an unequivocally Protestant one.

And yet Mary's ambitions presented a real political danger. Up to this point the alignment among the great politicians had provided a rough balance in the court. Cecil, Norfolk, Sussex and their allies offset but did not outweigh Dudley, backed by Pembroke, Throckmorton, Bacon and others. But even before the arrival of Mary Stuart in England, there were alarming tokens of a reshuffling of alignments. Leicester and Pembroke seemed to be outdoing Norfolk and Sussex in their civilities to the northern queen. Cecil alone, with the lesser backing of Knollys and perhaps Bacon, held out determinedly against Stuart wiles. These new and surprising combinations were signs of a gathering storm of great force.

The tenth spring of the reign marked the end of an epoch. The abortive attempt of the English nobles to arrange a marriage for their mistress suitable to the national needs was fading out; in February the wretched Lady Catherine Grey died, still in confinement, leaving Hertford two children. Her luckless sister, Lady Mary, was pining away in country confinement; the Grey claim was about to pass into a political twilight.

The Queen of Scots was still close prisoner in Lochleven castle although romantic stories of her attempted escapes began to spread. Rumours circulated that Moray planned to release and marry her to one of the younger Stuarts, or that French troops might land in Scotland to liberate her. The Hamiltons were still unreconciled to the new regime, and in the very nature of Scottish politics it was unlikely that Mary could be kept locked up indefinitely. Hence when news of the melodramatic escape of the Queen of Scots arrived early in May, it may not have much surprised the English court.[22]

The queen's reaction was to take up again the policy frozen in the previous year. She wrote to congratulate Mary on her freedom and to offer her aid in recovering her throne.[23] The conditions set were that Mary should allow Elizabeth to act as arbitrator in composing Scottish quarrels — with the understanding that if the lords failed to come to heel, English force would be used to support Mary. The latter must also eschew all French aid. What reaction might have come from Mary we cannot know;

within a fortnight of her escape, the hastily assembled forces of the Hamiltons were broken by the Regent's superior power. After a few days of harried flight, Mary crossed the Solway firth with a tiny train. On May 16th, 1568 she landed at Workington in Cumberland. The Queen of Scots's arrival in England on that spring evening was the opening event in four years of intense crisis, the great testing-time of Elizabeth's reign.

Part Four

PRELUDE TO CRISIS

10 *Mary in England*

IN THE year 1568 three clusters of events vitally affected the security of the English state and forced grave decisions on the English leadership. In the spring Mary Stuart arrived in England and there followed the series of intricate negotiations with her, with the Regent's government and with the Hamilton faction in Scotland, which ended in December. In the summer the French civil war burst out again, and the appeal of the Huguenots, now entrenched in La Rochelle, moved England to her first limited re-entry into French affairs since 1563. Finally, in the mid-winter of 1568–9 England quite deliberately challenged Spain by her seizure of the Spanish treasure ships carrying funds to Alva.

In all these matters there is strong evidence of renewed initiative from Elizabeth's ministers, particularly from Secretary Cecil. The queen was hesitant in her attitude towards Mary of Scotland and at least half-disposed to assist in a restoration. The Council seem to have been unanimous in their opposition; they were able to persuade their mistress to a series of decisions which by the end of the year had severely damaged Mary's reputation, weakened her supporters in Scotland, and made it clear that she was a prisoner rather than a refugee in England. On the other great matters the same general harmony seems to have prevailed among the Councillors; Leicester, assisted by Throckmorton, put some pressure on Cecil to aid the Huguenots, and the Secretary was willing to accept such a policy, provided English commitments were narrowly limited. The Spanish affair seems to have been very much Cecil's doing, although until the new year of 1569 he seems at least to have met no opposition in the Council.

These actions add up to a renewal of a forward and active policy after a long period of relative quiescence, even isolationism. The Scottish matter was of course forced on the English by circumstance, but the two other enterprises resulted largely from deliberate English initiative. Cecil was moved to action by the strong conviction that the whole Protestant cause, and more particularly the English regime, was faced by a grave assault on its very existence. There was, in short, a sharp change of mood and of tone in English policy. The undertakings abroad were risky, but the leadership in court and Council seemed united in supporting them. There was also seeming harmony as to what should be done with the Queen of Scots. One must emphasize the word 'seeming', for at the very end of 1568 and in the first weeks of the new year, ugly and alarming fissures began to appear in the Council and in the court.

Mary Stuart's unexpected arrival on English soil opened this new epoch in the political history of the reign. The first phase of her English career lasted from her arrival, in May, down to July 1568. The first English official to deal with her was a Cumberland squire, Richard Lowther, deputy to Lord Scrope, Warden of the West Marches. This gentleman acted with dispatch and decision, provided for the exile and her party, first at Cockermouth and then at Carlisle, where Lord Scrope and his wife (Norfolk's sister) hastened to attend on her. He also sent off to the court at the earliest moment news of her arrival. The government acted with unaccustomed haste; before May 22nd Vice-Chamberlain Knollys had been appointed to wait upon the Queen of Scots; by May 25th he was in Cumberland.

In the meantime the Earl of Northumberland had been eagerly hastening across the hills from the North Riding. Cockermouth was a lordship of his, and when his officers there advised him of the queen's arrival he made an effort to reach her, intending to take her under his charge. He even obtained letters from the Council of the North to back him up, but Lowther sturdily declined to yield up his charge, and Knollys's arrival quenched the earl's hopes. The Vice-Chamberlain roundly told off the offending nobleman and counselled him to go to court to explain his conduct. The crestfallen earl retired homeward; Knollys and Scrope were firmly in possession of Mary's person and in control of her movements. It was none too soon since there were authoritative warnings of her popularity in the North and of the excitement at her coming.[1]

Mary was in the English grasp, but what was to be done with her? The Queen of Scots had chosen her ground skilfully, appealing to Elizabeth as a refugee sovereign, driven forth by her rebellious subjects, and seeking aid for her restoration. She anxiously desired to hasten to the English court to explain her affairs and quiet any doubts about the past yet lingering in Elizabeth's mind. The English queen may momentarily have considered receiving the fugitive—the French ambassador heard as much—but the impulse was checked. Perhaps Elizabeth did for an instant long to meet her royal cousin, nearest kinswoman and most dangerous enemy. There were politic reasons why she should not; there were almost certainly personal ones also. The queen may well have shrunk from encountering her only equal in the island; nor was she likely to forget the inevitable comparisons which the whole court would draw between her and her younger rival. Elizabeth was not unsympathetic to her cousin's plight and not unwilling to help her, but dealings between them were to be at a distance and through intermediaries. The choice of Knollys as the first such intermediary was important. His wife was the queen's first cousin; he himself was a courtier of decades' experience, reliable, disciplined, and devoted. An outspoken, left-wing Protestant (and a Genevan exile), he could not be suspected of any partiality for the Catholic Mary, but he would treat her with the courtesy and honour which service in the court had taught him. He could be counted on to be firm in handling Mary and honest in reporting her conduct. He had the queen's confidence, but his own views more nearly reflected those of the Council.[2]

It was easy enough to find immediate grounds for declining an interview and for keeping Mary in honourable detention, but what longer-term policy was to be followed? The facts of the Scottish political situation were plain enough. The queen's follies had ended the relative harmony and unaccustomed stability which had lasted from her return from France down to the Darnley marriage and which had been founded on her alliance with Moray and Maitland. Scottish politics now reverted to their usual ragged disarray—a state of semi-feudal anarchy in which ever-shifting personal or family alliances produced endemic chaos. But there were some disturbing novelties in the current situation. Moray was the stalwart champion of the Protestant faith, and the rallying-point for all its committed adherents; his opponents comprised a coalition of many elements, but included among them were most of the scattered forces of Scottish Catholicism. The division was made even sharper by the fact that each party was gathered about opposing claims to legitimate sovereignty—the queen's or the infant king's. For the present, Moray's strong personality and vigorous efficiency gave to his party a coherence which his opponents, the feeble Hamiltons, could not hope to match. They still clung to the fortress of Dumbarton, but their forces elsewhere were broken and, putting their hopes in foreign assistance, they wrote off to Alva, the Viceroy of the Netherlands, to ask for help.[3] Moray naturally looked to England for countenance and support. He took hope from the fact that during the latter months of Mary's imprisonment a kind of *de facto* recognition had been extended to his government by England, at least for Border relations.

At the English court rather widely variant views were taken of the new situation created by Mary's arrival. The queen was still primarily concerned for her cousin's restoration; the cardinal fact of rebellion and the need for the re-establishment of right order loomed large in her mind. Yet her views had shifted from what they were in the previous summer when Mary was deposed. Elizabeth was now disposed to give some acknowledgment to the interests and even the rights of Moray and his party. She was at least prepared to hear a statement of their case, although it was they who were to appear as the defendants—accused of unlawful rebellion and called upon to explain their aberrant behaviour. This was the line taken in the first approach to Mary at Carlisle. But there were times when the English queen swayed back to her older antipathies to the rebels and proposed an unconditional restoration of Mary—provided the latter agreed to eschew French or Spanish aid.[4]

Against this second course of action the Council reacted vigorously. To them Mary's downfall and her consequent flight to England were almost miraculously opportune events. England's most dangerous enemy was now in their grasp; to allow her to return to Scotland (or even to go abroad) would only offer her free scope to resume her relentless pursuit of the English throne. Even to restore her on terms to Scotland, in title and name only, without the realities of power, would be to court disaster. She had already proved her untrustworthiness in 1565; how could anyone trust her now? The Councillors were emphatic: 'Her Majesty can neither aid her, permit her to come to her presence, or restore her, or suffer her to depart before trial.'[5]

Cecil, mulling over the matter in his accustomed way, spelt out the alternatives even more grimly. If she went to France, she would revive the 'auld alliance' and set about reviving her claims to the English succession, at a moment when England, standing alone in international affairs, would be ill prepared to withstand French pressure. Remaining in England, she would practise with her friends here for the English Crown and at the same time recover her hold on Scotland, 'for no man can think but such a sweet bait would make concord betwixt them all'. Returned to rule in Scotland under the old terms, she would end the English alliance; James would have no long life and the queen herself would soon disappear amidst universal anarchy.[6] A temperamental pessimism seemed to grow in Cecil with age, and on the Queen of Scots he was always prone to the gloomiest views; yet this paper does reflect the respect he entertained for Mary's political capabilities, a respect which Knollys was soon reluctantly echoing from the Yorkshire moors.

To any proposal that she should justify herself by answering the charges of Moray, Mary strenuously objected. She talked boldly of returning to Scotland or of going to France. In the atmosphere of the Borders this was not entirely an idle boast. Hence the Council were anxious to move her away from the Papist shires of the North to the safer milieu of the Protestant Midlands, at Tutbury or Fotheringay, but this she stoutly resisted and in the end the English government had to compromise on Bolton Castle in Wensleydale, a house of Lord Scrope, farther removed from the Scottish border than Carlisle but still, in Protestant eyes, only a meagre improvement. Before leaving Carlisle in early July, Mary appealed again to Elizabeth either to let her go to France or, failing that, allow her to return to Scotland with the promise to receive no foreigners without Elizabeth's consent. The English queen for the moment hesitated, but the persuasions of the Council and her own feelings swayed her to a refusal. Mary finally yielded to the proposal for a hearing; Moray had already accepted, so that arrangements could now go forward.[7]

Various considerations moved Mary to this vital concession. Her hand had been a weak one from the beginning, although she had played her few cards with skill. Her personal appeal to Elizabeth, which might have succeeded could they have met, had failed. Hopes of France dimmed as the religious civil wars, damped down in the spring, showed signs of blazing up again. The only other alternative — return to Scotland — became less and less feasible, once her adherents had lost control of the west Borders and access to Dumbarton thus became hindered.

Elizabeth's decision to follow this course doubtless stemmed in part from the considerations her Council put to her, particularly the risk to England were the Queen of Scots either at home again or in France. But it also suited her personal taste; for she was now cast again in the role she had once before essayed to play in Scottish affairs. In 1565 she had sought to impose her will on her cousin, providing a husband of Elizabeth's choosing and reducing Mary to another satellite in the Elizabethan solar system. Now again in 1568, while intending Mary's restoration and the humbling of her rebellious nobles, the English queen proposed to assert her will over the Scottish sovereign. Mary, acknowledging past misdeeds and promising future amendment, was to return to her throne a chastened queen, bowing to her rival's superior wisdom and princely grace.

Mary had made a great surrender, although its magnitude was perhaps veiled by the ambiguities which surrounded it. In Mary's understanding of her position there was to be no prejudice to her honour, Crown, position, or any rights she might have in England. At the hearing she would be in her place as sovereign, her opponents there as subjects. Her agent, Lord Herries, wrote that if the Scots lords' 'allegiance were not found worthy', i.e. if their actions were not justified, Mary would be restored unconditionally with full authority, immediately. And 'if all were not so well as she [Mary] would wish it' she should still be restored, but under tutelage of a council. Reports of such favourable terms were widely circulated in Scotland, so much to the distress of Moray's party that finally Elizabeth herself wrote to the Regent. She made it clear that should Mary be found guilty of the alleged crimes, 'it should behove us to consider otherwise of her cause than to satisfy her desire in restitution of her to the government of that kingdom'.[8]

Other views of the forthcoming negotiations were reflected by Sir Ralph Sadler, one of the newly appointed commissioners for the hearing. Sadler urged that some men of learning accompany the commissioners, for there was bound to be much discussion of the nature of tyranny, the rightfulness of deposing a tyrant, and such-like questions. But he went on to say bluntly that if their business was 'to persuade that at least she may have the name of queen, and other the government', the results of their labour would not last long. Sadler was a Privy Councillor; he knew the English Council's views; they hardly coincided with the expectations of Mary and her partisans. Cecil, writing to another commissioner, the Earl of Sussex, was succinct, and less oracular than usual: 'It is not meant if the Queen of Scots shall be proved guilty of the murder to restore her to Scotland, how so ever her friends may brag to the contrary: nor yet shall there be any haste made of her delivery until the success of the matters of France and Flanders be seen.'[9]

The interval between Mary's surrender in July and the assembly of the commissioners at York on September 30th was an uneasy time, during which both Scottish parties jostled restively for position. The Queen of England had named as commissioners the Duke of Norfolk, with Sussex and Sadler as his colleagues. The choice is of some interest. In August Cecil had drawn up a list of names of possible choices; he included – besides the three chosen – Bedford, Arundel, Leicester, Mildmay and Throckmorton.[10]

The Secretary must have taken some satisfaction in the final choice. Sussex had just been appointed Lord President of the North (in July); this earl had been for some time a sympathetic associate of Cecil's; there was mutual trust and a common point of view, and he was, of course, still the leading opponent of Leicester. Norfolk, the ranking member of the commission, had earned Cecil's enthusiastic commendation in the preceding year and was also a leader of the anti-Leicester party. Sadler, the most experienced of the three, had just been appointed Chancellor of the Duchy of Lancaster. Cecil approved heartily of this appointment although Leicester claimed credit for it.[11] It was a group on which Cecil could rely confidently; it significantly excluded both the Earl of Leicester and Sir Nicholas Throckmorton.

The commissioners carried instructions with them which reveal the expectations of the queen. Moray and his associates, it was thought, might refuse to make their charges against Mary on the grounds that Elizabeth would in any case restore her. To this the English were to answer that if there were plain proof, Mary would not be thought worthy of a kingdom, but if it were a matter merely of suspicion and conjecture, which 'somewhat diminish her reputation', Elizabeth would consider how to restore her without danger of relapse. The negotiators were then to proceed to details. If, by chance, Moray did formally charge his sister, the whole matter was to be referred back to Elizabeth. But most of their instructions dealt with the details of the tripartite treaty—among Elizabeth, Mary and James—which was envisaged. The specifics need not concern us, but their whole intention was to establish the Queen of England as permanent umpire over Scottish matters and to emphasize the future dependence of the restored Queen of Scotland upon her neighbour. The perspicacious Sadler had few expectations of any long-term stability arising from such a treaty.[12]

The proceedings which followed brought on to the stage either at York or later at Westminster virtually all the major political personalities of both kingdoms. The Regent Moray and his ally Morton were on hand. Mary was represented by the forceful Herries and other familiar counsellors, but the leadership of this band passed to a new figure, John Leslie, Bishop-Elect of Ross, soon to be Mary's prime agent. Secretary Maitland was present, nominally in the Regent's train, but he was already more than half engaged in the Queen of Scots's service. The transfer of proceedings from York to Westminster drew in the whole English Privy Council, afforced by the whole body of English earls. From early October to

Christmas conference followed conference while accusations, denials, counter-accusations, proofs and counter-proofs piled up, as the two Scottish factions wrestled for the support of the English 'umpire'.

The jumble of competing Scottish interests became more coherent when the protagonists met at York. Moray's party was the more organized; an ideological rallying-point, possession of the machinery of government, and a strong leader were substantial advantages. Yet there was a haunting spectre in the background; let the infant king die and most of these advantages would vanish in an instant. There would remain merely a Stuart faction, fighting for its claims to the throne against a Hamilton faction. Awareness of this harsh possibility could never be far from Moray's mind.

The deficiencies of the Marian party were all too apparent. Their captive leader could exercise effective control only over her personal following, but the main strength of her party in Scotland lay with the Hamiltons, uncertain allies rather than loyal followers. For them the issue at stake was their claim to power (and their hopes for the succession) rather than Mary's rights. Their leader (usually known by his French title, Duke of Châtelherault) saw himself as a protagonist equal in stature to Mary or Moray.[13]

The Regent had thus two alternative openings before him—the first, some kind of accommodation with Mary and her followers which would cut out the Hamiltons altogether. The struggle had become too fierce now to allow him much room for concession; to concede the queen any real power would be fatal to him and his closest allies; the most they could offer was an empty title, a pension, and a public acquittal from charges connected with Darnley's murder. The other alternative was a bolder one—to try to sweep the whole board. This meant bringing up their heaviest artillery, the whole body of evidence, above all, the 'casket letters' by which they hoped to implicate Mary irrevocably in her husband's murder. Once these charges and the supporting evidence were laid on the table, the English government would be compelled either to admit Mary's guilt, to undertake a formal trial of the Scottish queen, or else to abandon altogether its posture of mediator and to throw its weight arbitrarily behind a Marian restoration. Clearly it was the latter which Moray feared, in spite of Elizabeth's reassurances, and he dared not attack directly until he had promises for the future from England.

Moray, determined to put the English to the test after a few days of preliminary sparring at York, bluntly demanded whether Elizabeth's commissioners had power to pass judgment as to Mary's guilt and, if she were found guilty, what attitude would be taken to the present Scottish regime. The English commissioners had of course to refer back to their principal, and in the interval negotiations stalled. The queen in response summoned Sadler, Herries (for Mary), Maitland (for the Regent), and Kilwinning (for the Hamiltons) to her court. She added an important clause to her letter, 'You shall have good regard that none of them gather any doubt of the success of her cause, but imagine this conference principally meant how her restitution may be devised, with surety of the prince her son, and the nobility adhering to him.'[14]

The English government had now to make the decision which had been avoided ever since Mary's arrival at Workington. Although there was no formal presentation of the evidence against Mary, the English commissioners saw informally some of it and were convinced of Mary's probable guilty involvement. Sussex forthrightly asserted that under existing conditions much the best policy for England was to adjudge Mary guilty, continue to detain her, and recognize the new Scottish government, but he foresaw impassable obstacles to any judicial proceedings. Mary's denial of the letters produced against her would block any further action or else resolve the case in her favour. A composition without threat of a trial seemed to him the sensible course and if that would not bring the Queen of Scots to a surrender of her powers, England must fall back on Moray. There again it would be necessary to square the Hamiltons so as to prevent their turning to France. And, if the worst came to the worst, he was prepared to back Moray against Châtelherault and let the latter do his damnedest. Norfolk and Knollys were in substantial agreement with this. Cecil's views were not much different; a continuation of the present situation seemed to him the best, although not the easiest way for England to follow.[15]

What the queen's views were at this time is unclear; her instructions when summoning Sadler, Maitland and the others to London seem to indicate no change from her previous position. But Norfolk had by mid-October formed other views of Elizabeth's intentions. When he and Maitland rode out from York to Cawood one October Saturday, the duke informed the Scottish Secretary that the queen would make no judgment now but would encourage the Regent to make his weightiest charges. Her intention was to disgrace Mary in English eyes and so mar her cause in England. Elizabeth, he predicted, would make no judgment on the matter but would remove Mary farther into the interior. Maitland

— whether with Norfolk's knowledge or no — passed this information on to the Bishop of Ross with the further counsel that Mary take a soft and submissive line with her cousin.[16]

As events turned out, this was a remarkably accurate prediction, and the duke may have been speaking with knowledge of a Privy Council meeting a few days earlier. There the active core of the Council (Pembroke, Leicester, Clinton, Howard, Cecil and Sadler) had advised the queen to answer Moray's questions by promising that if Mary were found guilty she would either be delivered to the Regent or kept prisoner in England and that the new regime would be given sufficient backing. The queen apparently approved this and ordered that Moray be secretly informed. At the end of the month the same Councillors (with the addition of Bacon) set the stage for the next act.[17] Mary's commissioners were, if possible, to be tricked into participation in the proceedings without understanding how far their mistress would be maligned. Moray's agents were to be encouraged to bring forward the direct charges with the same assurance presumably already imparted to the Regent. Since, in the leaky English court, Mary would almost certainly find out much of this before the proceedings were complete, she was to be prevented from escaping by removal to Tutbury. (She hinted to Huntly and Argyll her plans for escaping over the west Border.) These were weighty matters so they should be shown to the entire Privy Council, the senior earls, the Primate, and the Bishop of London.

The intention to proceed boldly against the Queen of Scots, damaging her reputation as much as possible while strengthening her opponents in Scotland, undoubtedly displayed the settled convictions of the leading Councillors. Leicester, Cecil and Pembroke, probably the most influential politicians at this point, as well as the weighty Clinton and Howard and the veteran Sadler, were working in close agreement. Norfolk was still at York; Arundel not yet at court; none of the other Councillors was likely to make a defence of the Scots queen. Steps to implement their policy followed with fair speed. Norfolk and Sussex were summoned back to London and a new commission issued on November 24th for the hearing of Mary's cause. It included the former three incumbents but added to their number Bacon, Cecil, Leicester, Arundel and Clinton. This new commission began business on the 26th and the same day Moray and his associates received the official reply to their questions of October, substantially that which had been given unofficially several weeks earlier. Without further delay, the Scots lords announced their intention of

proceeding to formal accusation and proof and laid before the English commissioners their allegations and evidence. Mary's representatives fell back
on the instructions she had originally given them that, if her honour were
touched, they should insist that she herself appear in the presence of the
queen, the nobility and the foreign ambassadors to give answer. The
scene now shifted to the court, where, in the presence of the whole Privy
Council, the Scots queen's agents pressed her claim to appear in person.
Elizabeth eluded their demands by arguing that Mary's personal appearance would give to the accusations a likelihood which she herself (Elizabeth) did not find in them. The fiction that the Regent was the defendant
was still maintained and he was now required to lay out his full proofs.
The following day he produced the casket letters and a mass of other
relevant documents.[18]

The queen now summoned the Earls of Northumberland, Shrewsbury,
Huntingdon, Westmorland, Worcester and Warwick to join with the
Privy Council in hearing a full account of all the proceedings both at
York and Westminster, including the incriminating documents produced
in the previous week by the Scots. They were informed that the queen
now felt more strongly than ever the position she had taken last summer
– that so long as the Queen of Scots laboured under so terrible an imputation she could not be received at court. These imputations were now much
strengthened, and *a fortiori* the queen's unwillingness to see her cousin.
The notables, polled as to their opinions, duly registered approval of their
mistress's actions. The Scots queen's representatives were then told that
no further action would be taken until Mary had answered the specific
charges made against her either by agent or by herself to noblemen sent
by the queen. It was highly unlikely that Mary would ever consent to
this; Knollys guessed rightly that Mary's notion of an answer was simply
to deny the accusations 'because that she in the word of a princess will say
they are false'. The English Council, moreover, were anxious to end these
semi-judicial proceedings, and when Mary asked for copies of the evidence
against her they warned that she could have them only by submitting herself to Elizabeth's judgment.[19]

As the official proceedings dragged to a halt, Cecil was able to persuade
his mistress to seek a shorter way of ending the matter. It was a simpler
version of a scheme he had conceived in November. Knollys and Scrope,
acting as if on their own, were to soften Mary up for a proposal which the
Bishop of Ross would then formally present. Mary would resign the
Crown to James anew, thus clearing up any legal deficiencies; Moray

would be acknowledged Regent and James would be brought to England for his education. Mary was to remain in England at Elizabeth's pleasure while the whole scandal of the Darnley murder would be buried in oblivion. Presumably Cecil and his mistress thought the damage done to her cause by the revelations of the Scots lords had broken her spirit. If so, they reckoned badly, for she stoutly rejected any such notion, declaring her resolve to die a queen.[20]

Shortly after this, in January 1569, Elizabeth gave order for the removal of Mary from Bolton to a more secure place, Tutbury Castle in Staffordshire, deep in the Midlands, while providing a new keeper for her, the Earl of Shrewsbury, whose own seat, Sheffield Castle, was not far distant. Elizabeth was at last taking Knollys's oft-repeated advice to place her rival under the care of a local magnate. Shrewsbury, in the midst of a familiar countryside which he dominated, would have the loyalty of his tenants and dependants to support him in his difficult task while Mary's adherents would find it much more difficult to carry on intrigue or plan escape.

Mary's affairs had reached the end of the phase which began with her arrival in England. Elizabeth's hesitant consideration of backing her cousin's return to Scotland was at an end. The device of a semi-judicial hearing, which the queen may originally have intended to be an instrument for reconciling Mary and her rebellious subjects, had become a powerful weapon for crippling the Queen of Scots. In May the terrible allegations of Mary's complicity in her husband's murder were but rumour and hearsay; now they were charges backed by weighty proofs solemnly made before the Privy Council and the earls of England. Mary must have known by now that her best hopes for redeeming her broken fortunes lay in another direction—still within England, but not with her cousin.

This new and hopeful turn in her fortunes had its beginnings in certain conversations of the previous autumn. When the treaty at York began, Knollys, assuming his mistress still intended the restoration of the Scottish queen, considered how some security for her good behaviour might be obtained once she was home. He hit on the notion that she might be married to some reliable Englishman, possibly one of the queen's Boleyn cousins, at any rate someone favourable to the Gospel.[21] Whether through his suggestion, or independently, the same notion took root in other minds among the Scots and English lords at York. The full extent of those speculations was not to be revealed for some time to come, and there is little evidence of how much was known to the English Council. But in

November the French ambassador got hold of the story that the negotiations had been shifted from York to Westminster and the commissioners augmented because Norfolk was thought to be too favourable to the Queen of Scots and indeed even to have intrigued for a marriage with her.[22] Norfolk had certainly acted as a channel for getting information to Mary by his conversation with Maitland, noted above. And, in January, the French ambassador reported that Mary was being supported in the English Council by Norfolk and Arundel.[23] Arundel did certainly write to the queen urging a settlement before the Regent's return to Scotland and criticizing her efforts to persuade Mary to abdicate. 'One that has a crown can hardly persuade another leave her crown because her subjects will not obey. It may be a new doctrine in Scotland, but is not good to be taught in England.'[24] With these stirrings opening up new ranges of opportunity, the quick-witted Stuart queen had no reason to be entirely down-hearted when she left Bolton for her new residence at Tutbury.

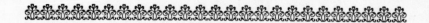

11 *French Protestants and Spanish Gold*

THE SAME year which saw the downfall of Mary Stuart in Scotland was marked by the resumption of civil war in France, and the attention of English statesmen was drawn distractedly across the Channel. French crises had by sheer repetition acquired a certain familiar pattern; it was easier now to size up situations and to assess the men involved. The English government was deeply concerned by the movement of events in France, but there was a greater ease in the handling of affairs and a clearer sense of proportion than during the Newhaven episode.

England was represented in Paris by Sir Henry Norris, a young Oxford-shire squire, member of a courtier family on whom the queen smiled and whose house at Ricote was a favourite visiting place of hers. Inexperienced in diplomacy, he played largely the role of observer, reporter and trans-mitter. The essential transactions between his government and the French Protestants were to take place in London rather than in Paris.

Rumours of impending trouble were circulating in the summer of 1567; open collision occurred by the end of September. English policy remained reserved and cool. This was all the more notable since Norris was feeding his government with a steady diet of alarmist rumours that a general Catholic conspiracy was afoot there; the French Protestants were to be the first victims; the British, the next. The ministers were more agitated than their sceptical queen, and at one time they feared an invasion by the heir of France—the Duke of Anjou—to free Mary, and at another the arrival of Châtelherault with a French garrison for Dumbarton.[1]

At the end of August 1568 matters came to a head in a short, sharp Anglo-French crisis. The Huguenots were now masters of La Rochelle, a major Atlantic seaport, and a strong base for their operations, particu-larly at sea. Its strategic location gave them access to one of the main sea routes of western Europe; it also dominated an area with which England dealt extensively in salt and wine. Throckmorton, busy again with his old French connections, conducted a Rochellois Protestant to court. The queen seemed to threaten intervention, and the French court dispatched a special envoy in alarm. In the upshot the queen softened her words and explained away her earlier threats; the temperature cooled quickly.[2] Shortly afterwards Cecil, pressed by the urgencies of Throckmorton, came up with a solution for the Huguenot problem, at once neat and workable. The French Protestants would receive the support they needed, partly in money, partly in military supplies; in return they would give value for value in the form of salt and wine, the products of the Rochelle district. The exchange would be cast in the form of a contract between the Merchant Adventurers and the Rochellois and be handled solely by them except for the ordnance and munitions which Admiral Winter would convey over in queen's ships. Officially Cecil knew nothing of this: Winter was cruising against pirates in the Channel; and Norris was instructed to deny any English aid to the rebels although, the Secretary disingenuously added, 'If in case of merchandise for salt or wine, the prince's [Condé's] ministers can borrow things of our merchants, I do not know to remedy secret bargains where merchandise is in use.' The secret was an open one, and the French ambassador reported the circumstances of Winter's voyage quite accurately to his government.[3]

The new French ambassador, de la Mothe Fénélon, was cordially received and was soon reporting to his government that they need have no fear of open English intervention. Secret aid in supplies would continue, but he believed that Cecil and Leicester, although strongly Protestant, were united in a pacific policy towards continental affairs. They were, he thought, apprehensive of some movement among the English Catholics, increasingly restless and disposed to seek some recovery of the old faith.[4] On these contradictory notes of amity and enmity Anglo-French relations remained poised at the new year of 1569.

This chapter in English policy forms an instructive contrast with the events of 1562-4. The basic view of the English leadership had not changed. Cecil's sympathy for the French Huguenots was politic and carefully regardful of English interests; he was co-operating now with the activists, Leicester and Pembroke, but it was the Secretary who set the tone of the agreement. The queen's distaste for aiding other princes' rebels was as strong as ever and her cold indifference to their religious views, the same. But the Councillors' understanding both of their mistress and of their co-religionists overseas was keener and shrewder than half a decade earlier. The venturesome abandon of the Newhaven episode was replaced by a calculating caution and a careful conservation of resources.

Aid to the Huguenots was kept within limits manageable by the English government without putting a strain on its supplies. There were no unsecured loans as in 1563 but a neat commercial transaction. There was a much more thoughtful estimate of English strategic needs and of available English means. It is the cautious moderation of policy towards France which contrasts so startlingly with the boldly defiant English attitude towards Spain during these same months.

For a decade relations with Spain had drifted uncertainly. Philip's attempt to intervene in the Scottish embroilment of 1560 had ended abortively and since then he had given only spasmodic attention to English matters. His first ambassador, the Bishop of Aquila, had entangled himself in a network of intrigue which finally made him *persona non grata* at the English court, but the envoy's opportune death had eased the situation. Philip's next representative, Guzman de Silva, was both subtler and more flexible and relations sweetened during the years of his service. Trade relations with the Low Countries had been troubled; for a time in 1563-4 the government at Brussels had tried by embargo to break the power of the English government, which it regarded as the fountainhead of heretical conspiracy and the patron of political discontent. The embargo was ended when Flemish discontent forced the dismissal of Cardinal Granvelle by Philip. Trade was reopened in late 1564 and after long negotiations an inconclusive trade treaty was signed at Bruges in 1566. The issues were not settled, but Guzman could fairly write in February 1568 – when seeking transfer – that 'since things here being quiet, the friendliness of the king undoubted and Flemish commercial affairs arranged', someone else could easily take his place.[5]

Yet in fact, Anglo-Spanish relations were far from easy, and the sense of estrangement between the two countries was growing. In part the difficulty was a mechanical one, arising from the inadequacies of the English diplomatic service. Still embryonic in form, its permanent establishment consisted of a Paris embassy regularly maintained, an Edinburgh mission only spasmodically staffed since the Darnley marriage, a few floating diplomats, most notably Henry Killigrew and Thomas Randolph, and a half-forgotten ambassador in Madrid. The latter post had been established when Philip left the Low Countries in 1559, the representative in Brussels then being recalled. The first two appointees to this post, Chamberlain and Challoner, were men of some diplomatic experience but of little weight – a striking contrast to the able and vigorous men assigned to the embassy in Paris. Nor had the home government paid much attention to their activities. Communication across the stormy waters of Biscay and the rugged mountains of northern Spain (or by the long route through France) was bad enough, but the home government allowed months to pass without sending information or instructions, and the isolated envoys in Madrid had a justified sense of neglect. The post was peculiarly unattractive and Chamberlain and Challoner, each in turn, clamoured for recall. When Challoner was relieved in 1565, he was replaced by John Man, Dean of Gloucester. Man was a cleric of no great distinction and little experience in public affairs. Head of a house at Oxford in Edwardian times and later chaplain to Archbishop Parker, he seems to have been clearly identified with the Protestant party although the queen spoke of him once as a religious conservative.[6] Altogether he was a rather curious choice for the Madrid post. To send a Protestant cleric to the court of the Catholic king was either an act of bravado (perhaps to counter the clerical diplomats sent to London) or a kind of carelessness which seems uncharacteristic of Elizabeth's government.

The seeming indifference of the English government towards Spain reflected in part the very limited range of English diplomatic conceptions. Traditionally they had not comprehended more than France and the Low Countries. Spain's emergence as a single power at the end of the fifteenth century had made her a useful counterweight against France; the dynastic link between the Low Countries and Spain had perpetuated the relationship. From the point of view of English statesmen—and in their political terminology—it was a Burgundian alliance and the Habsburgs were primarily Burgundian rulers, who periodically disappeared over the horizon to visit their remote Spanish dominions. But a Habsburg who dwelt permanently in Spain and the focus of whose policy was Mediterranean—as Philip's was increasingly becoming—was outside the scope of traditional English diplomatic thinking. As long as Philip remained in Spain—and most Englishmen assumed his stay there would be temporary—England could afford to be an indifferent spectator of his activities in the peninsula or on the European and African littorals of the Mediterranean. Once his attention was again drawn to his Low Country dominions, English interest in his actions would revive. But even now, it was Brussels rather than Madrid, so remote and inaccessible, to which the English court looked. There Gresham served as a semi-official representative; English merchants provided copious information; and periodic exchanges of special embassies were used to negotiate on trade matters.

Under these conditions matters had jogged along, each sovereign pre-occupied with his own local difficulties. Yet one fatal difference was gradually poisoning all their relationships. Twentieth-century experience has made plain the singular difficulties of diplomatic intercourse between nations of profoundly differing ideologies, where each regards the other's basic principles of conduct with abhorrence and with fear. In the 1560s relations between Catholic and Protestant states presented a profound and perplexing novelty. The rules of diplomacy themselves were too new to offer much guidance, but the basic notion of an ambassador's personal immunity — as his sovereign's immediate representative — provided a workable ground rule for the conduct of ordinary business. In the relatively liberal atmosphere of the English capital this was interpreted to mean that Catholic ambassadors could maintain chapels within their residences, daily hearing the mass the celebration of which was otherwise forbidden within the realm. And in fact the English authorities usually looked the other way when the queen's subjects attended mass at an embassy chapel, although from time to time they descended on the Catholic embassies to harry English communicants. In Madrid, however, the rigorous views of that orthodox court made the position of the sole heretic embassy a very difficult one. Quite probably the first two Elizabethan ambassadors were less than half-hearted in their observance of the religion established by law at home during their service in the Spanish capital.[7]

How deep the gulf between the two societies was becoming is revealed by a letter of Guzman de Silva. Urbane and cosmopolitan as he was, he could yet write of the dangers of long exposure 'to so much freedom and bad conversation. This gives great and constant anxiety ... because the failure to attend regularly at church and perform the sacred offices and duties, cools devotion and causes a greater fall still and, for this reason, the long-continued residence of the ministers in this country is a matter to be deeply considered.'[8] Guzman found the atmosphere of London greatly trying, but at least he kept his head. De Quadra, his predecessor, unable to restrain his feelings, had come to confuse his role as the King of Spain's representative with another one, that of champion and defender of the true faith oppressed. The consequent loss of perspective and judgment on diplomatic matters had made him a worse than useless, indeed, a dangerous servant to his master's interests. His amateurish dabbling in plots only served to convince the edgy English court of the malevolent intentions of the Habsburgs while his dispatches to his masters in Madrid and Brussels fed them month in and month out with his own distorted suspicions, fears and prejudices.

Moreover, although the Spanish envoys received more attention and more direction from their own government than the English, geography lengthened the distance between them and Madrid and threw them much upon their own discretion. Situated as it were in the enemy's camp, at one periphery of the far-flung Spanish battlefront, their own sense of proportion was affected and they tended to think of England as the very focus of the whole struggle while to their royal master it was only one of the lesser theatres of conflict. The ambassadors doubtless exaggerated the importance of England's role; perhaps Philip a little underestimated it during the 1560s.

For the time being, however, there remained a fund of dispassion in both courts which countervailed the worst effects of growing hysteria. The official policy of each sovereign towards the other remained one of ambiguous goodwill, characterized by wary civility. In London this awkward relationship was made easier by the skill of Guzman de Silva, whose good judgment and quick perception enabled him to strike just the right note of low-keyed goodwill and to win the liking of the queen and the respect of Cecil. His conduct accurately reflected Philip's attitudes at this period. In a letter written early in 1568 the king asked his ambassador to keep him advised of any changes which might hint at the queen's 'coming to her senses' by abjuring her heresy. Philip resignedly added that he had little hope of such a transformation but if he could help it he would do so with all his heart. In the same letter he urged Guzman to make plain in the strongest terms his friendship and kindliness towards the queen.[9] At this stage in affairs Philip was able to harmonize unshakable disapproval of Elizabeth's religious conduct with a more worldly disposition to wait on events, while, in the meantime, maintaining civil relations. Basic to his position was the decision made when Alva was sent to the Low Countries in 1566 — to focus all efforts on restoring royal power and the Catholic faith in those provinces. The corollary to this was carefully to refrain from any embroilment in English affairs which might dissipate Spanish strength.

In September 1568 Philip rewarded Guzman de Silva's faithful and able service by acceding to his request for a transfer to a climate both meteorologically and spiritually more congenial, and appointing him to Venice. Elizabeth seems to have been genuinely sorry to see this urbane diplomat leave, especially since his departure coincided with an awkward turn in her relations with Philip. In April the king had written to Guzman flatly declaring that John Man's attitude towards the Catholic faith made him *persona non grata* at the court of Spain. He was not to be received any longer at the palace and was immediately packed off to enforced residence in a village outside Madrid. The English response was one of natural irritation, but Guzman was able to soothe this and even, in June, to obtain the queen's order for Man's recall. Her complaisance was perhaps secured in part by Philip's willingness to recall a book recently printed in Spain and containing some passages highly uncomplimentary to Elizabeth.[10]

That same summer was one of disturbances in Flanders which clearly portended a coming strain in Anglo-Habsburg relations. Alva's efforts to crush Protestantism in the Lowlands were reaching a climax; streams of refugees poured across the North Sea with their tales of woe, and many of them were using the English coast as a base for their resistance to Alva. The queen was under heavy pressure actively to assist the Protestant cause in Flanders. However, the ambassador's representations were met with officially correct responses; a proclamation was issued against use of English bases by Flemish rebels. Guzman continued to watch and to report upon the collection of money to aid the Flemings and Leicester's suspicious connections with the Prince of Orange. But he sounded no note of urgency in his reports home.

Nevertheless, the English leaders had viewed with increasing unease the heavy concentration of Spanish military power just across the seas from them. For the moment Alva was busy in the task of pacification, but that enterprise seemed nearly complete. His large forces would soon be free for other activities. Old fears of a Catholic crusade revived in England, and in France the Huguenots, fearful of a Guise–Habsburg conspiracy against them, were again in arms.[11]

It was in these circumstances, increasingly difficult but not yet alarming, that the new Spanish representative, Guerau De Spes, arrived on the scene. A diplomat who much more resembled the late Bishop of Aquila than his immediate predecessor, he was to have scant opportunity to settle into his new surroundings, for within a very few weeks a storm of hurricane intensity began quite suddenly and unpredictably to blow. In the latest phase of the French civil wars, in February 1568, the Huguenots had gained control of La Rochelle and thus added a new dimension to their power, since they could now sweep the main sea route of western Europe across Biscay and up into the Channel. This was a striking gain to the general Protestant cause, but at the same time it meant graver problems for all the maritime states since the offshore seas of the Atlantic coast were now delivered over to the general anarchy which was spreading from the Pyrenees to the Zuider Zee. Ships sailing under the commission of the Huguenot princes claimed the privileges of belligerency and the justifications of a holy war. What resulted was the spread of unrestricted piracy which made these seas unsafe for merchants, whether Spanish, French, English or Flemish. The English government, in order to protect the wine and salt trade, had to resort to convoys under royal naval protection.[12]

In this very season of danger the Spanish government sent north by ship a large consignment of funds for Alva's government at Brussels. The money, new-minted, had been borrowed in Genoa. The carrying fleet had to run the gauntlet of Protestant pirates swarming in the Narrow Seas. On November 23rd De Spes in London learned that some of these ships had, in sheerest desperation, taken refuge in the ports of Devon and Cornwall, and on November 29th he saw the queen and asked for protection—either naval escort to Antwerp or else overland transport of the cargo to Dover. This the queen granted, telling him that Admiral Winter, about to sail with a convoy for Bordeaux, had already moved to protect the Spanish ships and had indeed held off French attacks by force. Another Spanish ship, in danger off the Isle of Wight, was afforded similar protection at Southampton. So far the facts seem straight enough. But what happened next is not so clear. The English version is that when Winter announced that he must depart for France, the Spanish captains begged to have the treasure put ashore. The Spanish version, quite to the contrary, insists that it was against the captains' will that the treasure had been removed from their ships.[13]

The ambassador, hearing on December 18th that the money at Southampton had been taken into the town, hastened to court for an audience, only to be put off with excuses, and it was not until the 29th that the queen received him. On his request that the money be hastened on its way to Alva, whose letter of credence he presented, he was told by Elizabeth that the treasure was not in fact the legal property of the Spanish Crown but of certain Genoese financiers and that she herself proposed to borrow it from them. The English version of this part of the story was that they had heard from Antwerp merchants about December 16th that the money was not yet legally Philip's and upon investigation at the ports found it true. But—also according to the English story—the queen had told De Spes on the 29th that she would give him a definite decision on the money in four or five days.

The Spanish ambassador had already made up his mind as to what was going on and as early as the 21st was urging Alva to seize all English property and subjects in the Low Countries and to advise their king to do the same.[14] The duke acted on his advice on the very day that De Spes saw the queen although his action was not known in London until January 3rd. The English government was prompt to retaliate in kind by laying hands on all Flemish and Spanish property in the realm and seizing Spanish ships as they passed up the Channel. For good measure they placed De Spes under house arrest on the grounds that his secretary, on the way to Brussels, had caused the arrest of English merchants in Dunkirk and Bruges—presumably on his master's instructions.

The barrage of diplomatic interchanges in the next few weeks was, of course, meant to justify each side in its action; they do not clarify the course of events in England during December. Other evidence is scant but perhaps sufficient to sketch an approximate outline of developments. The initial reaction of the English was correct enough and the Spanish were given protection against the Huguenots, but probably from the first there were those who urged the seizure of the funds. Perhaps the first mover in this matter was William Hawkins of Plymouth. Early in December he heard from Admiral Winter the first hints of his brother's disaster in Mexico. John Hawkins, on his way home from another semi-piratical, semi-mercantile venture in the Spanish Indies, had met the Viceroy of Mexico's fleet in the harbour of San Juan de Ulloa and most of his ships had been destroyed. William Hawkins dispatched this news to London with a plea that Spanish goods be seized in retaliation; he also informed the Secretary that the treasure then in the western ports was not legally Philip's property; this latter information came through an Italian merchant resident in London, Benedict Spinola. Armed with this knowledge, the government determined on seizure. The evidence for their action lies in two letters, one from Vice-Admiral Champernoun in Devon, the other from Edward Horsey, Captain of the Isle of Wight.[15] On December 19th Champernoun wrote to Cecil, 'I have of late received from your honour a couple of letters both tending to one end, which was that I should under colour of friendship use all policy to recover such treasure of the King of Spain as is presently within our Western ports.' He describes the difficulties of accomplishing this without bloodshed and offers to take the blame of seizure upon himself, hoping that after storms of preliminary disavowal he will find the calm of royal favour. After all, it would be a great pity that such a 'butyn' should escape Her Grace. As for

Champernoun, 'I am of the mind that anything taken from that wicked nation is both necessary and profitable to our commonweal'. In any event the seizure seems not to have been attended with violence.

At Southampton the story was not much different since Horsey, following Cecil's direction, arranged to act with the Mayor; together they persuaded the Spanish captain that he must land his cargo lest the French ships lying outside the harbour seize it. The poor man had little alternative, for Horsey 'had so prepared as easily I would have had it whether they would or not'.

All this makes plain Cecil's intention to seize the treasure, by force if necessary, once he had a thin veil of legality to cover his moves. By his actions he provoked a serious crisis in Anglo-Spanish relations which brought the two sovereigns to the brink of open conflict. What immediately followed was not an actual break but an intense diplomatic crisis. De Spes, inept to start with and now beside himself with anger, proved a weak player for his side. The English had already taken one trick since Alva's proclamation of seizure had come out on December 29th, the very day that De Spes was being received by the queen to hear his plea that the money be forwarded on its way. Hence the Spanish could be accused both of bad faith and of initiative in aggression, while the English measures could be described as justifiable retaliation. Secondly, the ambassador had indulged himself in two foolish letters, both of which he knew would be seen by the Council.[16] In one he made insulting remarks about the English Councillors and declared that 'people, great and small, are discontented with the government'. In the second, drawing on the imagery of *Amadis de Gaula*, he referred to Elizabeth as Queen Oriana, himself as her prisoner, but declared all would end in a comedy. The English immediately took a high line, describing the second letter as offensive to their sovereign and the former as sheer malice.

In Brussels Alva kept a cooler head and refused to regard the English measures as prelude to inevitable war. Instead he sent over one of his Councillors, d'Assonleville, a man acquainted with England through previous negotiations, to sound out the queen's intentions. This agent, arriving in England, found himself treated with the greatest severity, detained at Rochester, denied access to the Spanish ambassador, refused audience by the queen, and kept under surveillance. Eventually, he was allowed to appear before the Councillors, Cecil, Northampton, Clinton and Mildmay. He found them determined to dredge up every possible issue, not merely those connected with the treasure but older matters such as Man's treatment in Spain or the book printed there containing matter offensive to the queen. Allegations were made about Alva's hostility to the queen and it was insisted that the English would negotiate only with someone accredited directly from the king. In short, every possible diplomatic red herring was dragged across the path, and it was made clear that England would cede nothing on the matter of the treasure. But, equally important, through the agency of Gresham, the queen made it plain that she did not want war.[17]

Reaction on the other side was prudently cautious once the English position was known. Alva doubted the advantages of war and urged on his master a conciliatory tone and a renewed approach after a decent interval. With due deliberation Philip arrived at the same conclusion, although initially he hoped for internal changes which would alter the English picture. De Spes was somewhat ambiguously encouraged to assist any movement against Elizabeth while Alva was given *carte blanche* to take any opportunity for aiding in the replacement of Elizabeth by her Scottish cousin. But by May 1569 Philip expressly ruled out war, dropped any reference to Mary, and ordered a mixture of gentleness and firmness, with the threat of possible military action being used as a spur to new negotiations. In these delicate but momentarily stable terms Anglo-Spanish relations remained suspended through the spring and summer of 1569.[18]

The dramatic events of mid-winter 1568, and the strong diplomatic line taken by the English Councillors in the weeks following, marked a dramatic and sudden shift in English foreign policy. The prudently defensive attitude which had prevailed ever since the Newhaven expedition in 1562–3 was now exchanged for one of unprovoked challenge and open defiance of the greatest European power. How is it to be explained? Who was responsible? This second question is easier to answer than the first. There can be no doubt that it was Cecil who pushed for bold measures; the Spanish ambassador thought so and what evidence there is in the English materials bears him out. It is fair to guess that Leicester, Clinton and Bacon were his active backers; Knollys, among the lesser Councillors, approved strongly. But motive and intention are more difficult to assay, for the materials are very slender indeed, and the most one can achieve is intelligent speculation.

The crisis, obviously, came unexpectedly; there was no premeditation in the English response. The initial reaction was diplomatically correct, neighbourly assistance to a friendly power. Perhaps for the moment, in the press of the Scottish queen's business, the magnitude of the occasion eluded the English ministers.[19] But the temptations were from the first very great, as De Spes sensed. The money itself—some £85,000—was a great consideration to a government short of funds and whose customs income had been reduced by the disturbances in the Low Countries. At stake was not merely the money but the possible effects of its seizure upon the whole European situation. At that moment the general Protestant cause stood in great peril. All his co-religionists might join in Lord Cobham's cry, 'God have mercy on His poor and weak flock who are ready to be devoured in all places'.[20] In France Condé was again in arms, but as always short of money and men, and since September Châtillon had been in England seeking aid. The Huguenot cause hung suspended in great uncertainties.

In Flanders the picture was darker still. Alva's campaign of extermination went forward apace; Egmont and Horn had gone to the scaffold in the summer; Louis of Nassau had taken up arms only to be disastrously defeated at Jemmingen in July; the Prince of Orange, after a futile attempt in Flanders, had fallen back on French soil in November and soon disbanded his forces.

Amidst these great convulsions abroad England's position worsened dangerously—or at least so Cecil thought. In a long state paper drawn up by him some time between January and March 1569,[21] the Secretary surveyed international affairs over the past decade; England, he argued, had remained relatively safe in those perilous years, more largely due to 'accidents of them that should have moved war, than by policy of any strength to stay war'. The sudden death of Henry II, Spain's distractions in the Levant and in the Maghreb, and the civil wars in France had shielded England from woe. But now, as he saw it, the whole situation was changing radically; Spain, free from her Turkish wars, could turn northward, while in France he gloomily predicted the approaching ruin of the Protestant cause. Then there would follow united action by the French and Spanish monarchs to carry out the will of the pope, restoring the ancient religion in the island and crowning Mary of Scots sovereign of England. Against this formidable combination England stood alone, bereft of allies, her weakness apparent to all. However exaggerated Cecil's gloom seems in historical retrospect, the fact remains that in this mid-winter season of 1568-9 he saw his country at a perilous, indeed a desperate, turning-point in her fortunes. Hence he was all the more ready to snatch at a heaven-sent opportunity to embarrass her enemies and reduce, even by a little, their too-great power. But, as his reflections make clear also, it must be done without actual war. Cecil was emphatic about England's martial weakness in comparison to her foes.

In December 1568 there was scant time to weigh the risks of action; the opportunity had to be snatched or lost. The English Council must have known the likelihood of Alva's retaliation against English commerce; almost certainly he acted faster than they anticipated. But as they balanced up their assets and liabilities, they might feel more confidence than the Secretary displayed in his memorandum. On the immediate issue of trade, they could reckon on offsetting losses of English merchants abroad by the treasure itself, by English seizure of Spanish and Flemish goods, and by additional booty from Spanish ships coming up the Channel. As for the immediate future, Cecil knew from the experience of the early 1560s that an embargo on Flemish trade was not necessarily disastrous to English commerce. Before January was out plans were being made to shift the Merchant Adventurers' base to Hamburg or Emden. Nor was the embargo by any means leakproof; English goods could move under Venetian or French guise or by way of Scotland. And indeed from the point of view of some Councillors—and quite possibly from Cecil's—a rupture in the old system of commerce through Antwerp was much to be desired. So thought Knollys in one of his frank letters of advice to the queen.[22]

On the larger issue of war, the English Councillors might well guess the reluctance of the Spanish to enter into hostilities at this juncture in their affairs. Early in the new year they heard of the Morisco revolt which had flared in Spain; in the Low Countries Alva's victory was by no means yet a certainty, and in any case the provinces were exhausted by the grave civil disorders of recent years. And the English may have had an inkling of the precarious situation of Spanish finances, of the heavy strain put upon them by the loss of the treasure and even more by the interruption of trade.[23] The arrival of d'Assonleville soon confirmed these assumptions and, immediate danger of war averted, they could settle down to slow and protracted negotiation.

But, in fact, most of these considerations were perforce *post hoc* ones. In the rushed days before Christmas, events overtook deliberation. Our knowledge of these events is very slight indeed, but it is a reasonable guess that queen and Council found themselves hurried into grave commitments with little chance for reflection or, perhaps, even for debate. Cecil, we know, was very deliberately going about the business of seizing the money; this he could hardly have done without royal approval; and that he probably was able to obtain once he had evidence that it was not yet the King of Spain's legal property. We may guess that the queen hesitated; the admonitory letter which Francis Knollys fired off from Bolton[24] urging her to listen to those faithful counsellors who wished her to defy 'the audacious boldness of the Duke of Alva' suggests this. Probably her hope was that by using the convenient legal ambiguities as to ownership, she could drag out negotiations to some length—postponing any fateful decisions to the latest possible hour. It is likely that Alva's embargo caught her unprepared and left her no alternative but to run the course whatever the risks. Cecil may have rejoiced at this turn of events; there were those in the Council who much doubted the wisdom of what was done.

Cecil, by his prompt action, had been able to seize an opportunity not likely to recur, but in so doing he had given a sharp turn to English foreign policy, suddenly wrenching an unprepared country into a stance of unprovoked but unabashed defiance towards an ancient and powerful ally. In retrospect his actions at this time can be seen as a great stroke of policy achieved with maximum damage to Spain and minimum cost to England. But in the immediate present he had every cause for concern, for these moves had helped to set in motion a highly dangerous and prolonged domestic crisis, so serious as to threaten not only his place in the state but the underlying stability of the Elizabethan regime itself.

Part Five

THE TESTING–TIME OF THE REGIME

12 The Norfolk Marriage

DURING THE tense months following the seizure of the Spanish treasure, disparate initiatives were taken at widely separated points on the political — and geographical — map of England which set in motion separate streams of events; their flooding confluence in the autumn and winter of 1569 was to shift many of the familiar landmarks of the English political order. They would also profoundly influence England's relations with her neighbours, for by no means all the actors in these events were English. The reckless Spaniard, De Spes; Leslie, Bishop-Elect of Ross, Mary Stuart's busy agent; and the sanguine Florentine banker, Roberto Ridolfi, were all to play main roles, while the more circumspect envoy of Charles IX, de la Mothe Fénélon, took a less active but perhaps not less significant part. Yet the prime actions which set all else in motion were backstage shifts among the English players, and the fulcrum of those shifts was the 'prisoner' at Tutbury, Mary Queen of Scots.

A year earlier in the late winter of 1567-8, just as the Earl of Sussex was returning from the futile embassy to Vienna, where he had hoped to solve the succession problem by concluding the Habsburg marriage, the unhappy Lady Catherine Grey had died, still under restraint; before the ensuing spring was out, Mary Queen of Scots had arrived in Cumberland. These two events, following in swift succession, gave a new and feverish vitality to the old well-worn problem of the succession. Catherine Grey, grand-niece to Henry VIII and beneficiary of his will, had been, so long as she lived, the strongest English claimant to the royal succession and the most probable rallying point of the Protestants in the event of Elizabeth's death. But the royal blood flowed too thin in the veins of the two boys born to her and Hertford to make them useful candidates for the throne, while Mary Grey's ludicrous match with the Sergeant Porter, Keys, effectually cancelled her shadowy claims.

And from May 1568 on, the strongest of all claimants was resident in the kingdom. The bizarre tangle of events in which Mary had been involved from the murder of Darnley onwards had grievously marred her prospects, but now, disembarrassed of Bothwell and free from the immediate entanglements of Scottish politics, her hopes might revive. Cecil and his allies had done their best in the proceedings at York, and afterwards at Westminster, to blacken her reputation beyond repair by stigmatizing her as her husband's murderess. But, as Cecil gloomily noted, 'the fame of her murdering her husband will by time vanish away or will be so by defence handled, as it shall be no great block in her way, to achieve to her purpose'. And by the spring of 1569 two high-placed courtiers, the Earl of Lennox and Sir Nicholas Throckmorton, were discussing the rapid revival of the Queen of Scots's prestige in both England and Scotland. In part, as Throckmorton pointed out, it rose from compassion for her misfortunes, and in part from the magnetism and personal abilities which even such an unremitting enemy as Knollys grudgingly admitted. But even more important was the conviction which by now hardly any of the English queen's servants could avoid – that Elizabeth would never marry. Cecil, in a state paper of early 1569, having pinpointed the absence of a royal husband and children as the very heart of England's weakness, remitted to prayer any hopes of the queen's marriage and went on to canvass those remedies which lay within the bounds of probable occurrence. The French ambassador wrote flatly of the general conviction among the magnates that the queen would never take a husband.[1]

Given this dismaying certainty, English politicians had to make their own best possible dispositions against the contingency of Elizabeth's dying. The ordinary chances of mortality were such that it would have been more than foolhardy to ignore them. The customary comment on the queen's health which prefaces so many letters written from her court was no mere polite form; it conveyed a most vital piece of political information.

Those who had put their hopes in a Habsburg marriage had no illusions left as to that possibility. What about that hardy perennial, the Earl of Leicester? The French ambassador recounts an interesting although certainly confused story.[2] According to Fénélon, Arundel persuaded Norfolk, as premier peer, to undertake the delicate mission of presenting a kind of ultimatum to the favourite. The duke told him that if he had still any hopes of marrying the queen, he would be given all possible support. But, if not, the earl should end his too familiar relations with the sovereign. Leicester, after an interval, saw the duke again, admitted the queen would not marry him, and thenceforth conducted himself more modestly. We need not take this story at its face value, but in a distorted way it probably represents the real situation. Leicester's hopes of marrying Elizabeth were dimmed almost to the point of extinction, although he was still plainly the favourite *en titre*.

The politically provident must then turn their attention to the next heir to the throne. As to who this was, few had any doubts, from the queen down. Fénélon was probably correct in writing of the queen's favourable view of Mary's claims, although, as he said, Elizabeth was interested in the preservation of her person, not of her honour. Even Cecil had to admit the 'universal opinion of the world for the justice of her title as coming of the ancient line'. And quite certainly the coterie of notables which clustered around Norfolk in the spring of 1569, and which included Leicester and Throckmorton, agreed on Mary Stuart as the second person in the realm.[3]

For Cecil and his allies in the Council—and for all committed whole-heartedly to the new religion—the position was a grim one. The Secretary was more convinced than ever that Mary was the prime enemy, whose goal was nothing less than the eviction of Elizabeth from her throne, the 'recovery of the tyranny of Rome' and the extirpation of the Protestants. She could not be destroyed; the queen would not consent; there was no leverage of evidence and as yet no possibility of exciting public outcry to coerce Elizabeth into such action. All that could be done was to keep her freedom of action to a minimum and see that nothing was done which would in any way further her cause. Cecil was dourly determined to face the hard facts of the English situation—the kingdom's isolation, the dangers of internal division and the menace of external interference. What remedies there were must be sought, inadequate though they might be; but however grim the situation, it was not to be an excuse for yielding one tittle to Mary's grasping ambition; there must be no compromise with the arch-enemy, no slightest concession to her claims, whatever their legal or historical force.[4] Behind Cecil stood a strong core of Councillors and the ever more self-conscious body of left-wing Protestant zeal.

But others in high political life read the situation in quite another light. For them Mary's claims were of incontestable legitimacy, and she would in all human probability be the next ruler of England. But here unanimity ended; as to what should be done there existed a whole spectrum of opinion. One body—a very influential one—saw the problem mainly as one of adapting Mary to fit into the English political scene with minimum harm to their royal mistress and maximum protection for their own interests. The Scottish lioness must be tamed to the more domestic habits of her future subjects south of the Border.

The views of this group are reflected quite clearly in two manuscript pamphlets of 1570 defending Norfolk.[5] The pamphleteer is strongly Protestant; he agrees with Cecil in assessing the grave dangers which threaten England from abroad and especially from a Catholic league. Elizabeth's marriage would, of course, be the best remedy of all; but, failing that, it is important that Mary be married to an Englishman. Her past life is glossed over; the fault was not hers; blame is shifted to Moray or to the other bad advisors who corrupted Darnley or dominated Francis II. As for her religion none could deny her papistry; but one could hope for her conversion. And in any case who could deny that 'the Gospel flourished in Scotland when her authority there bore greatest stroke'? Married to a Protestant Englishman, Mary was no menace to England's established religion.

The pamphlet goes on to take a strongly anti-Puritan tone. The latter are identified as those 'that will make the Gospel their buckler to maintain their own imagined devices' and paired with the Papists as threats to good order. Their intolerance towards all who disagree with them even on the smallest matters is held up to view; not even the bishops are warm enough for their liking since the latter wear caps and tippets. And all who differ from them are Papists. As for the writer, his view is that if men 'live in due obedience and observe the Queen's Majesty's laws, we take such to be no Papists'.

In short, the backers of this position saw the remedy as a very simple one; Mary had hitherto been unlucky in her husbands; let her find the right man, Protestant and English, and all would go well. Hints of this had floated about for some months and Sir Francis Knollys, no friend to Mary, had bluntly suggested that she be neutralized by such a marriage, preferably to someone near the queen in blood (on her mother's side). Specifically he mentioned Hunsdon's son, George Cary.[6]

The men of this stripe were straightforwardly Protestant in their views although lukewarm in their religious enthusiasm, at least by left-wing standards. But they did not see Mary's religious views as a stumbling-block to placing her in the succession; either by conversion or by agreement to differ, that could be got around. It was, as we shall see, a group of experienced and able politicians who took this line. But there were other adherents of the Scottish queen in England who saw the situation in a very different light. These men turned towards Mary not merely as a political convenience for easing the succession problem, but because she was a Catholic princess, and in her they saw at last some hope for a restoration of the old faith.

In June 1569 just a decade had elapsed since the coming into effect of the statutes which made the Roman Catholic mass an illegal rite in England. Virtually the entire episcopate and a sizable body of cathedral and university clergy had suffered deprivation rather than take the oath of supremacy. The bishops had endured a detention which varied in rigour, depending on political circumstance; the lesser clergy had either emigrated (to the Low Countries or to Rome) or else found refuge in some hospitable layman's protection.

But among laymen the confusion was such that the use of such a term as 'Catholic party' is inappropriate and indeed the term 'Catholic' itself is hard to define in this context. Since laity were not originally tendered the oath of supremacy in 1559 there was for them no clear-cut choice to be made. Most Englishmen were accustomed to accept the determination of religious forms as a matter for authority; only a small minority could yet conceive of the rights of private conscience, and the ancient source of authority in the medieval church – the pope – remained mysteriously silent about the new English ecclesiastical order. Some individuals – and to these the term Catholic may properly be applied – felt strongly enough about the recent changes to disobey the law, abstaining from attendance at the parish church, and, if they could afford it, sheltering a dispossessed priest in their own houses, to celebrate the now forbidden mass. A much larger number, uncertain and uneasy in their consciences, compromised the matter in various ways, by irregular attendance at church, by hearing Morning (or Evening) Prayer but not receiving communion, or by accepting the new service tentatively, meanwhile waiting passively on events. Many of these would end up faithful enough adherents of the Church of England although some would repent their ways and turn back wholeheartedly to the older faith.

But in no sense could they be called a party. There were eminent men among them, such as Lord Montague; there were foci for intrigue, such as Lady Lennox, but for nearly a decade there was neither organization nor action. Spiritual leadership was cut off by the imprisonment of the episcopate who courageously but passively waited for a martyrdom which never came. Possible lay leadership, from the rather large group of more or less pro-Catholic peers, never emerged. These noblemen preferred to wait upon events, hoping for a royal marriage – preferably with Archduke

Charles – which would reverse the religious weathercocks again, or, at least, open the way for some kind of tolerated exercise of the mass itself.

But most important was the lack of direction from Rome itself. At the beginning of the reign Spain's fear of French intervention had stayed Rome's hand. And, indeed, the papacy itself while the work of Trent was incomplete was reluctant to take severe action. The two abortive papal missions in 1560 and 1561 and Smith's conversations with the papal nuncio in Paris in 1563 were tokens of Roman conciliatoriness towards the English regime. Lastly, there was no eminent English Roman Catholic, no Cardinal Pole, at Rome to turn the attention of the overburdened Counter-Reformation pontiffs towards the lost provinces.[7]

As early as 1561 the English Catholic exiles at Louvain had begun agitation for direct papal denunciation of the queen and even for support of Mary Stuart as rightful sovereign, but a proposal mooted in papal circles for such measures brought angry objections from both Philip and the emperor. But on the delicate question of attendance at Anglican services, raised by English Catholics through the Portuguese and Spanish ambassadors, a Holy Office decision of October 1562 was emphatic. Attendance at such services was forbidden to the faithful. Later on an official authorization for reconciling those who had so offended was provided, but it is far from clear how much this was known in England itself, given the virtual breakdown of communication with Rome. By the summer of 1567 notarial attestations of the authorization were circulating in the island. Some exiled clergy were by now travelling about in the realm and by one such the Earl of Northumberland was reconciled to Rome in 1567. Thus some guidelines were being laid down for those faithful to the ancient religion, but there was still lacking any organization or any full-grown policy.[8]

The English government had displayed ambivalences of its own. The machinery attached to the act of 1559 to compel uniformity was clumsy and, given the queen's temperamental distaste for religious persecution, it was not worked with any great energy. On the other hand Cecil and his Protestant allies in the Council were alert for any sign of what might prove to be a Catholic resurgence, and, as in 1561, quick to use their powers ruthlessly and effectively. More power was given the authorities by the 1563 Parliament and pressure on Catholics tightened.

By 1568 the foreign ambassadors thought that persecution was definitely on the increase. Certainly religious tension was rising and for obvious reasons. The religious outbreak in the Netherlands in 1566, followed by the severe repression under Alva in the following years and coupled with the renewal of religious civil war in France, had profoundly disturbed English Protestants. The hopeful anticipations of the first years of the reign, when it had seemed that the new faith might triumph in France and Flanders as it had in England and Scotland, had grown dimmer. At home the mood of English Protestantism was more sombre but also more resolved and its attitude towards opponents harsher and more aggressive. In the early summer of 1569 Cecil was cogitating over a detailed memorandum from one of the committed Protestants. Aside from urging a strongly anti-Catholic foreign policy, the writer went on to propose a version of the Protestant association of 1588. The Privy Council was to take the initiative in drawing into a semi-secret bond the lay and ecclesiastical leaders of every county, by which they would swear to resist any attempt against the present order in Church and state, subscribing money to a special fund; any who refused upon invitation to enter this elite would be certified in the Council's records as a recusant. (Another book was to be filled with the names of those too doubtful even to be approached.) The plan was not then implemented, but it is an important indicator of mood, as each religious affiliation girded itself for head-on struggle with the other.[9]

On the Catholic side this same change of temper seems to have been felt; there was a sense of time passing and opportunities lost, a sense of action needed. If the end of the Habsburg negotiations finally closed one door, another had swiftly opened with the arrival of Mary in England. Her presence in the kingdom was a stimulus to bold and specific action by faithful Catholics. These men, unlike the cautious *politiques* considered above, were fanatics set upon advancing the cause of the Catholic faith and of Mary as its standard-bearer. What they sought was no careful readjustment of the political balance, but a revolutionary assault on the present order with no holds barred.

Response to the new opportunity which Mary's arrival offered was speedy and showed itself within a few weeks of her arrival at Carlisle. It came from two oddly assorted and widely separated quarters. In the North there was an immediate stir in the knot of ardent Catholic gentry who clustered about the Earl of Northumberland and who were unquestionably the most active community of Catholic laymen in the country. This was, of course, hardly surprising. But the other spurt of Catholic agitation arose in an unexpected way.

For at least a decade there had resided in London, in the half-world of continental merchants, a Florentine banker, Roberto Ridolfi. He was a familiar of the foreign merchant colony and of the Catholic embassies. (He was a pensioner of both the French and Spanish Crowns.) Through his banking activities he had access to the higher English social circles. He seems to have been an enthusiastic although not fanatical adherent of Catholicism; at some point Ridolfi entered into correspondence with Rome and became, at an indeterminable date, an agent for the pope in England. In the summer of 1568 he sent off to Rome a letter, no longer extant, but obviously containing a plan for the restoration of Catholicism in England. This was his first essay in this art; fuller opportunities for the exercise of his skills would soon offer.[10]

Hence, by the winter of 1568-9, when English affairs were severely jolted by the episode of the Spanish treasure, there were three nuclei of support for the Queen of Scots—of quite varying character. There were the 'moderates', numbering among them some of the major politicians of the court; the 'extremists', the northern hotheads; and the well-connected Florentine aristocrat-banker, ready to serve both parties. Within the next few months all were simultaneously very active in their separate endeavours; in the end their efforts were to merge, but for purposes of clear exposition they need to be dealt with separately. We may turn first to the 'moderates', the advocates of a 'suitable' marriage for the Queen of Scots.

There was a more eligible English suitor for Mary's hand than young Cary. Since September 1567 the sole duke and premier peer of England, Thomas Howard, Duke of Norfolk, had been a widower (for the third time). His almost princely rank and his ancient and noble lineage, supported by the greatest private fortune in the realm, placed him in a unique position among Elizabeth's subjects. In the days before the Darnley marriage when the two queens quibbled over a desirable British husband for Mary, Norfolk's name was on the short-list. It was hardly surprising that the idea of such a match sprang to mind again in 1568. It had come to Mary's ears even before the hearings at York began—quite probably from Lady Scrope, wife of the Scottish queen's keeper and sister to Norfolk.[11] Mary was in any case quite confident of a favourable hearing from the commissioners, since Norfolk's goodwill had been more than hinted to her; Sussex as the duke's friend would follow suit, and Sadler would be overawed by the two noblemen. To cap the matter Mary's friends, the Northumberlands, earl and countess, would be on hand to persuade the duke in her favour.

This happy picture was darkened when, through Maitland of Lethington, Mary was warned that the Regent Moray brought with him dangerous documents—the famous 'casket letters'—and would use them. Maitland undertook to deal with Norfolk to counter this danger. He did indeed see the duke and was followed by the Bishop of Ross (who saw Norfolk early one morning in an empty gallery before the other commissioners arrived); both sought to secure his promise of aid and both hinted at the marriage; the duke on his side spoke of his goodwill to the Scottish queen and there was discussion as to how to avert the danger of the casket letters (which Norfolk had by now seen). Finally, on an October Saturday afternoon Maitland and the duke rode hawking together out to Cawood, where almost certainly the subtle secretary used all his arts to lure the duke into the tempter's net of the marriage. Whatever was said, the results were useful to Mary. Norfolk was frank in the considered advice he gave her (which passed from Maitland to Ross and thence to Bolton Castle) as to Elizabeth's probable course of action and her own best response. Shortly afterwards the whole proceedings were revoked to Westminster, by Queen Elizabeth, possibly because she began to suspect Norfolk's soundness. As early as November 29th Fénélon was able to report gossip of Norfolk's softness towards the Queen of Scots and even rumours of an intended match. These rumours had certainly reached the queen's ears; and Norfolk, in alarm, went out of his way to disclaim to her any such ambition. He was in fact vehement in protestations of disgust at a match with a 'notorious adulteress and murderess'. Besides, he added boastfully, he was, by the queen's favour, as good a prince 'at home in my bowling-alley in Norwich' as Mary in her Scottish kingdom.[12]

The next scene was played out in January at Hampton Court. Moray was very uneasy over Elizabeth's indecisive course after she had encouraged him to divulge the casket letters. Worse still, he now became aware of a plot to assassinate him on his way home through the northern counties. Of his own accord he went to visit Norfolk. He had considerable talk with the duke, who made plain his serious intention of pursuing the marriage with Mary. Moray promised his support, provided she first divorced Bothwell and provided Elizabeth consented. The Regent received a safe-conduct through Yorkshire; Norfolk intervened with his brother-in-law, Westmorland, to squelch the Nortons' plot against the Regent. Moray heard no more until his agent, Wood, came to London in March, when the matter was broached by Norfolk, who made a firm offer to go through with the match if Moray would get his sister restored to Crown and honour. By now Mary was, of course, *au courant* with all these dealings and had given her consent to their going forward.[13]

In the meantime there was bustling activity within the English court. At various times during the spring Sir Nicholas Throckmorton, Lord Steward Pembroke, the Earl of Arundel and his son-in-law, Lord Lumley, entered into the matter of the marriage. Most important of all, the Earl of Leicester had been in the duke's confidence even before the Regent returned to Scotland. And at some point Ridolfi also became privy to the plans of this group. Who took the lead at this time is not clear; naturally, in their confessions afterwards, all sought to avoid the imputation. Norfolk represented Leicester as being the initiator; Throckmorton spoke of the duke as the ringleader. Norfolk seems to have needed little pushing at this point, but Leicester's interest was certainly keen.[14]

The lords mentioned above with their confidant Throckmorton were the inner core of conspiracy, although the matter seems to have been bruited about in wider circles. After considerable discussion, the principals in conclave solemnly resolved that, given the changes in France, Scotland and Spain, the 'tickell' state of the Regent Moray, and the queen's desire to restore Mary, if she could be sure of her, 'for all these causes, and other, the said earls and Sir Nicholas were of opinion that such good provision might be made by the Queen's Majesty and her council as by this marriage Her Highness and the realm might take commodity'. Norfolk protested that he was now in better estate than he would be married to Mary, but for the commodity of the queen and the realm, he was resignedly content to sacrifice himself.

Thereupon the Earls of Leicester and Pembroke, acting as brokers, formally wrote to the Queen of Scots proposing the match and setting forth the political terms which should accompany it – a Protestant establishment in Scotland and league between the two kingdoms. About the beginning of June, through the medium of Ross, the conspirators were able to obtain from Mary a commitment to a Protestant and Anglophile policy at home and abroad if she were restored. In the meantime formal courtship started with the sending and receiving of letters between the principals. The duke furthered his wooing by sending a ring and other tokens of his affection.[15]

In the meantime – in May – Queen Elizabeth had been brought to give approval to renewed negotiations for the purpose of bringing about a reconciliation between Mary and her subjects. Specific proposals were made for her return on conditions which would protect Moray and the infant James. This move was actively promoted by Norfolk and his friends in the Council, whose plans were in turn furthered by pressure from the French court. Given the very bad relations with Spain (over the treasure) and with France (over aid to the Huguenots) and the resulting threats of war with both powers, it was not difficult to persuade the queen to this conciliatory move.[16]

Thus the plot, as developed by late spring, was constructed in two stages. First the Regent Moray was to move for his sister's restoration in Scotland; he would be nudged into this action by pressure from the English court, promoted, as we have seen, by the Norfolk party, backed by the French ambassador. In the next stage the English queen was to be persuaded that her cousin's restoration could be most safely accomplished only if Norfolk accompanied her as an English – and Protestant – consort. The delicate task of convincing Elizabeth was to be left to Maitland, who was to come to England specially for this purpose.[17]

Moray, in this summer, was faced by the most exasperating uncertainties. Elizabeth, he knew, was under pressure within her Council and from France to make some settlement with Mary which would include her restoration, and he could not be certain she would not agree to a Norfolk match. He was himself, of course, also under pressure from Norfolk and his friends to forward their schemes by uniting the Scottish nobles in a programme for their sovereign's restoration. Caught in this squeeze, he played for time, dragging out negotiations with Elizabeth, while Norfolk and company were put off by his insistence that marriage precede restoration. It was not until late July that he agreed to summon a convention to deal with the restoration scheme. By the time that body met in early August, the earl's position in Scotland was so strengthened that he determined to make a stand. The convention politely but firmly declined to hear of the queen's return although agreeing to further discussions. Shortly afterwards Maitland was arrested on charges that he was party to the Darnley murder. These actions sadly damaged the whole Norfolk marriage scheme since the first stage of the two-stage ascent was now hopelessly crippled.[18]

Norfolk, in the meantime, had spent a busy summer drumming up support for his enterprise from various key figures. A messenger armed with letters went north in July to see the duke's old ally, Sussex, newly appointed Lord President at York, and the Earl of Derby in Lancashire; he was also to deal with the northern earls of Northumberland and Westmorland, who had already been dabbling pretty extensively in the Queen of Scots's cause. To each of them the proposal for the marriage

14

was broached. Northumberland rather dourly answered that he did not mislike the proposal, providing the queen assented; he thought it to the safety of both the realm and the sovereign. (He would have preferred a Spanish match, but at Mary's command went along with the Norfolk scheme.) Westmorland did not disapprove of the match, but feared that the duke might not be truly dealt with in the matter, that there might be some plot to ruin him with the queen. Derby flatly disapproved of the whole thing and urged the duke to leave the matter alone, warning him that some of his present backers might leave him in the lurch when he most needed them. Sussex refused to make a judgment but he also warned the duke that some of those who urged him on did not mean him well. At the same time Sussex told his deputy, Gargrave, of the proposal and expressed his fears for Elizabeth's safety were it proceeded with.*

By midsummer a good many other parties were also drawn into this ever-widening network of intrigue. The Spanish ambassador knew of it – doubtless through Ridolfi – by June 15th; the French envoy reported to his court in late July and asked for instructions. De Spes did not hear from his king on the matter for many months; not until November did that slow-moving monarch note his interest. Urging the greatest caution until Norfolk's true religious position was clear, he gave Alva permission to act as he chose and De Spes instructions to follow strictly directions from Brussels. Alva continued to remain contemptuously chilly to the whole project.[19]

Fénélon, on the other hand, received instructions promptly and hastened to put them into effect, entering into correspondence with the Bishop of Ross, and enthusiastically backing the match. Norfolk was appropriately grateful and declared that his devotion to the queen mother was surpassed only by his devotion to Queen Elizabeth. The ambassador thought the Spanish somewhat doubtful about the match since they would have preferred a Habsburg husband for Mary; this made Fénélon doubly anxious to promote Norfolk.†

* *Haynes*, 549–50; *CSPDom, Addenda, 1566–79*, 236, 402 fol.; Sharpe, *Memorials*, 193. Norfolk may have tried other noblemen as well. Ross (*Murdin*, 50) said that Norfolk had told him he had approached the Earl of Huntingdon, who had replied he would be the duke's friend in all matters except such a marriage. Sussex told Gargrave in July that he disapproved of the scheme as unsafe for the queen.

† *Fénélon*, 11, 194. The somewhat reluctant advice of De Spes that the Norfolk match be supported (*CSPSpan, 1568–79*, 189), when by late August it seemed inevitable, hints at these Spanish doubts. The Queen of Scots, through Ross, had told the ambassador that left to herself she would deliver herself into Philip's hands but now she was obliged to sail with the wind.

Bruits of the marriage were now spreading publicly in England and in Scotland. By early August Hunsdon at Berwick was hearing rumours both from court and from Scotland; by the 19th of that month he could report that the match was common gossip through the North and in Scotland. Cecil certainly had more than an inkling by mid-July. The time was fast approaching when the queen must be informed of the conspirators' plans or else she would find them out for herself. But before turning to the denouement of these actions, we need to look back to a parallel series of events which since early spring had involved many of the same participants and which was vitally related to the marriage scheme.[20]

This history is much more obscure than that of the marriage project; we can follow it only indirectly through the dispatches of Fénélon and De Spes. Both had good although not unbiased sources of information, probably within the Council or at least within its secretariat. Fénélon had a clear head and good judgment about English affairs; Philip's excitable representative saw what he wanted to see through the cloudy spectacles of his own prejudices. But together they give us a fair outline of the powerful attack mounted against Secretary Cecil in the spring months of 1569; it aimed at nothing less than his removal from office and imprisonment in the Tower; once there 'means to undo him would not be far to seek'.[21] The beginning of this story takes us back to the mid-winter crisis of the Spanish treasure. Almost certainly the outward appearance of crisp decision which the English government gave to its actions was belied by strong disagreements within the Council. Fénélon reported early in January that there was opposition from principal London merchants and that they had backing in the Council. Later he declared that De Spes's offensive dispatch (which the latter knew the Council would see) was purposely phrased thus in order to assist Cecil's opponents within it. Some of these lords had met at Nonsuch (Arundel's residence) to discuss the matter, with Cecil conspicuously absent.[22]

The leaders of the malcontents were in fact Norfolk and Arundel. As we shall see, they were already about to mount an attack within the Council, but they were also dabbling in intrigue with the Catholic ambassadors. De Spes could hardly contain his hatred for Cecil, and at the height of the seizure crisis had gone to the French ambassador with an excited proposal for a joint Franco-Spanish effort to overthrow the Secretary, coupling it with a joint embargo against England until Elizabeth accepted Catholicism. The Frenchman gave this proposal a very cool reception and advised his master to let the Spaniards try their hands alone. (The French government did in fact send Cardinal Guise to Spain with such a proposal in April only to have a cold refusal at Madrid.) De Spes was ripe for any action against the English minister, whom he regarded as his principal enemy.[23]

In February his hopes must have risen when Norfolk and Arundel, using the ubiquitous Ridolfi as intermediary, approached the ambassador, sending both a message and a cipher. In the former the lords expressed their dislike of the present policy towards the Habsburgs and their hopes of reversing it; they hoped soon to be strong enough to overthrow the present leadership among the ministers. As if this were not enough, they went on to talk of a Catholic restoration, to which they would bring the queen to consent.[24]

Fénélon was by now writing to the queen mother his expectation of a coming overturn, '*quelque mutation d'aulcunes choses en ce royaulme*', and by mid-March he had Ridolfi's full-blown version of what was to come. There would be, according to the sanguine Florentine, a restoration of Catholicism, accomplished by a bloodless revolution, led by Norfolk and supported by Derby, Shrewsbury, Pembroke, Northumberland, Arundel and Lumley. The initial step would be the removal of Cecil from office; for this purpose the all-important co-operation of Leicester had been secured, although he had been made privy only to the political, not to the religious, schemes of the conspirators. French co-operation was invited; Ridolfi was to travel to Rome (visiting Paris en route) to procure a papal brief on which the lords could act when the moment for revolution came.[25]

All this was sensational enough although probably owing a great deal to Ridolfi's scampering flights of imagination. But in the previous week Fénélon had transmitted a circumstantial account of a Council meeting in the queen's presence which displayed the real gravity of the internal crisis. He began by explaining that the discontent of those who distrusted both Cecil's monopoly of policy-making and his policy itself now had a focus for action. Popular discontent was rife, following the embargo in the Low Countries; adherents of the old faith were squirming under a new outburst of persecution; and public outcry was rising against the risky policy which seemed to be dragging the country into war with both France and Spain at a moment when matters hung so precariously in Scotland and Ireland—all these things together encouraged the noble malcontents in the Council to concerted effort. Most important of all, they now had Leicester on their side.[26]

Fénélon provided a graphic description of an Ash Wednesday meeting

of the Council with the queen (February 23rd). She had complained that
her Councillors could not be brought to resolve the most urgent matters
(Leicester had made a pretence of sickness and stayed away from previous
meetings). The favourite sharply replied that the principal part of her
subjects thought things so badly conducted that either the state would run
into grave danger or else Cecil would pay with his head for matters as
they now were. The queen retorted angrily to Leicester, whereupon
Norfolk, turning to his neighbour, the Marquess of Northampton, said in
a loud voice, 'See, my lord, how when the Earl of Leicester follows the
Secretary, he is favoured and well regarded by the queen but when he
wants to make reasonable remonstrances against the policy of Cecil, he is
frowned on and she wants to send him to the Tower of London. No, no,
he will not go there alone.' To which Northampton, hitherto a partisan
of Cecil, replied, 'Praise God, that you, who are the first subject of this
realm, want to show your virtue, whom I am ready to follow or aid with
all that I can, for I also am here to make my complaints.' There followed
a demand that Cecil make an accounting of his policy over the past eight
years; Cecil's appeal to Leicester that he would be involved in any such
investigation met with the cool answer that the earl had but followed
the leadership of the Secretary.[27]

How much accuracy there is to this story, we can hardly guess; Fénélon
had access to Council secrets but his informant may well have embellished
the episode in recounting it. It was, however, just at this time that Cecil
drew up his great state paper surveying English foreign policy over the
past eight years and laying down his own prescriptions for the future.
It does not seem to have been addressed to the queen. It may represent
his defence of his policy during this crisis; certainly it deals with the
questions apparently raised in Council.

It is not possible to know exactly what relation this attack on Cecil
bears to another one only obscurely recorded. Camden hints at a precedent
for assailing Cecil in an episode of the previous year, which concerned
money sent to the Huguenots, and a confused confession of 1572 recounts
a similar story which was going the rounds during Norfolk's trial.[*]

* Camden, *Annals*, 122; PRO, SP 12/85/20. The confession is dated January 1572 and
throughout Cecil is referred to as Burghley, but the reference to the £100,000 sent to La
Rochelle suggests the loan of £20,000 made in August 1568. The episode presumably predates
Cecil's peerage, and if we can follow Camden, probably has to be assigned to the autumn of
1568; Camden seems to date the attack on the question of the French loan as preceding the
episode of the Spanish treasure. There is an echo of this story in the rabidly anti-Cecilian
Treatise of Treasons published in 1572, 43d.

According to this account the duke had once charged Cecil at the council board with treason for sending one hundred thousand pounds to La Rochelle (presumably in the summer of 1568). The Secretary was so pressed that he was brought to his knees before the Council. Bedford, so the story goes, hastened to the queen and she herself appeared, demanding to know what was going on. The duke repeated his accusation and added that since Cecil ruled there had never been a peaceable or a quiet common-wealth. But the queen bade the Secretary rise, saying, 'I will give thee a quietus.' However confused, the story hints at the rising dissatisfaction with Cecil's leading role.

The attack on Cecil coincided with a very awkward passage in English foreign relations. There was now deadlock with Spain over the late seizure and the consequent embargo, and the English waited nervously for Philip's next move. At the same time additional support for the beleaguered Huguenots threatened a 'hot' war with France. Cecil and his supporters argued for continued aid to their co-religionists — even after the defeat and death of Condé at Jarnac in March — on the grounds that this was in England's best interest, her only defence. Their opponents pointed out the terrible risk of war with both France and Spain. To the latter argument the queen sensibly replied that there was too much animus between the continental sovereigns for them to unite, but she agreed with those who were anxious for peace, repeating over and over that she did not want war. For the time being affairs remained in suspense, England making no move, hostile or friendly, but waiting anxiously for a break in events.[28]

In late April the opposition party embarked on a new strategy. Be-lieving their support essential to the conduct of the state, especially in the face of so much popular discontent, they discussed the tactic of an Aven-tine withdrawal from the Council. Under this pressure, they believed, the queen would soon have to recall them and give them such full power as would enable them to exclude their opponents from office. But to make the tactic even more effective, they hoped for outside aid. Ridolfi was now urging Fénélon to a joint Franco-Spanish trade embargo; at the same time he was writing to Pius V, asking that this blockade be made general among all the Catholic powers; only the pope could accomplish this since he alone could overcome Habsburg–Valois rivalry.[29]

Through May, debate in the Council continued to rage around the issues of foreign policy, and the opposition's criticism of Cecil grew stronger. He was forced at least to the gesture of yielding some greater share in public business to other Councillors, although Fénélon believed the real centre of gravity still lay with the Secretary. During these weeks the opposition party gained sufficient strength to persuade the queen into a renewal of the negotiations for Mary's restoration. They continued to talk of a mass withdrawal from the Council, leaving Cecil alone with his mistress, but they were in fact still a minority in the Council on most other issues.[30]

Some time in June matters finally reached a climax. Both French and Spanish dispatches contain accounts, neither very clear, of what happened. According to De Spes there was actually a plan to arrest Cecil, but each time Norfolk and Arundel proposed to act, Leicester drew back; Cecil then found out about the plot and went to Norfolk, offering to meet his wishes and even proposing that the duke should go to Spain on a special embassy of reconciliation. In Fénélon's version, Cecil went to Norfolk, sought his protection, promised to follow his advice, and asked the duke to mediate for him with Arundel.

This crisis of events coincided with another set of circumstances. Norfolk's third duchess had died, leaving the duke guardian of her son by her first marriage, the young Lord Dacre. His death by accident in May 1569 threw open the awkward question of his inheritance. The duke claimed control of it as guardian for his three step-daughters, as co-heirs. He was opposed by Leonard Dacre, uncle to the little lord just dead, who claimed both the title and the estate of the Dacres. Leonard was one of the most ardent — and Catholic — adherents of Mary and an active worker in her cause. Cecil as Master of the Wards had a central although not decisive role to play in the hearing (June 12th) on the contested inheritance. His appearance on this occasion may well have forwarded the reconciliation between him and the duke. In any case the latter was victorious in his suit for the Dacre inheritance.[31]

From Cecil's own pen there remains dismayingly little for these highly critical weeks of his career, but enough to throw some dim light. On May 15th Sussex at York replied to a letter of Cecil's, full of dismay that the Secretary and Norfolk should 'stand on worse terms of amity than heretofore'. Cecil's answer of the 27th is in his most cloudy and verbose style and swells with aggrieved innocence. He laments Norfolk's unjust condemnation of him, declares his own good conscience and ascribes his troubles to 'secret reports of evil willers'. He ends on a note of resignation, looking forward to diminished power; 'I may percase use less diligence in service and gain more quietness.' But by early June the clouds had lifted. In a letter to his confidant, White, in Ireland, his mood is one of exultation; God has favoured him with His grace; His goodness has preserved the Secretary 'from some clouds or mists in the midst whereof I trust my honest actions are proved to have been lightsome and clear. And to make this rule more proper and special to be applied I find the Queen's Majesty my gracious good lady without change of any part of her old good meaning towards me.' 'And now whatever you shall hear to the contrary you may certify the same by this my own measure wherein if you shall be borne in hand that I am deceived yet surely I mean neither to doubt it nor to deserve the contrary.' His confidence was borne out by events; he was able to open up unofficial channels to Alva and thus to continue negotiations in that direction; in France, if things grew no better, they grew no worse, and so the summer wore on. But the drive to over-throw Cecil had now ground to a dead halt.[32]

In the meantime the scheme for the marriage lurched along on an in-creasingly erratic course. By the end of July Norfolk was nervously aware that the matter was becoming common talk and wanted to broach it to the queen, but the other conspirators insisted on sticking to the plan that Maitland should do the job. But Maitland, as we know, could not come, and there ensued a grim little comedy played out by the duke and the Earl of Leicester. The latter agreed to break the matter to their mistress, but nimbly dodged from excuse to excuse and delay to delay. The earl would arrange all, but today would not do; there were too many about the queen; but tomorrow did not suit either—and so it went, as the court moved at a leisurely pace through Surrey and Hampshire on the queen's summer progress.[33]

By now the Queen of Scots was inquiring what the duke would do if the queen refused her consent to the marriage, but Norfolk still desper-ately insisted that his mistress would not refuse. The wretched man was in fact now running from one confidant to another, seeking a cue, first from Leicester, then from Throckmorton, or even from Cecil (now in the 'secret').*

By now—early September—the queen had certainly had some inkling of the matter through her ladies-in-attendance and she began to drop

---

* *Murdin*, 44; Robertson, *History*, 11, Appendix 57, from which it appears that Cecil knew of the matter by July 20th. It was afterwards said that Cecil had encouraged Norfolk to go forward in the marriage (*Hatfield*, 451); his initial reaction was probably one of bland non-committal (*Cabala*, 155–6; *CSPScot*, 1563–69, 674). Throckmorton thought Cecil would fear to be left behind once he saw matters moving in favour of the match (Robertson, *History*, 11, Appendix 57).

unmistakable hints to the duke. Leicester chose this opportune moment
to disembarrass himself of the whole scheme, took to his sickbed and
there, with many sighs and tears, revealed all he knew to his mistress and
sought pardon. The court was now at Titchfield in Hampshire and there,
in the gallery, the queen summoned Norfolk, asked him the truth of the
matter, and received his halting acknowledgment that the marriage was
in train. Angrily she commanded him upon his allegiance to give over
all such matters. According to one account the duke, although alone
(Pembroke was conveniently in the country and Arundel at Nonsuch),
stuck to his guns, defended the marriage as sound public policy, and asked
for judgment by the Privy Council. The queen retorted that the Council
had nothing to do with it, but Norfolk persisted. A few days revealed his
true position at court; Leicester was chilly and reserved; the gentlemen
of the court refused even to be seen dining with the duke.

Thoroughly discomfited, he withdrew from court without taking leave
of the queen. He journeyed towards London, stopping off to see Pembroke
en route; while travelling toward the earl's house, the duke was met by
a servant of Arundel's who warned him that all the conspirators were in
danger and that some of his friends thought that for their safety the Tower
should be seized. The 'friends' in question were Lord Lumley, the Bishop
of Ross and Ridolfi, and the suggestion was made by the Florentine while
the three consulted in Arundel House. The duke mentioned this to the
Earl of Pembroke, who pooh-poohed the notion. Norfolk passed on his
anxious way to London and the shelter of Howard House. There he had
visitors, the Bishop of Ross (who now, instead of entering openly, was
smuggled in by a back way) and a messenger from Mary, who complained bitterly that she was now in the hands of her enemies Huntingdon
and Hereford, thanks to the duke's delays. It may have been on this same
occasion that Ross pressed him, by his mistress's command, to know what
the duke would do now that the queen had disapproved of the marriage.
The duke was bold in his reply; he would retire to his country house and
take counsel with Arundel and Pembroke and other friends. But, the
bishop objected, the queen would have him brought to court by force.
To which Norfolk boastfully returned, 'There would be no nobleman in
England accept that charge at her command, for he knew their whole
minds, especially of those in the North, who would assist him, and if he
might once have that open quarrel against the Queen, that she did first
pursue him ... he would have friends enough to assist him.'[34]

The political temperature was rising rapidly; the queen, thoroughly alarmed, had already taken measures to secure the Queen of Scots by sending the Protestant Lords Huntingdon and Hereford (the former a possible contender for the succession) to join Shrewsbury in guarding Mary. At the same time she dispatched a peremptory command to Regent Moray for an account of his share in these dealings. Norfolk himself was bidden to return from London to the court at Windsor.[35]

The duke stood at the moment of supreme decision. His intended bride pressed him to rise in arms to release her; his confederates in the North stood in tense expectation of his summons. Talk went about of two armies in the field, one led by Norfolk, the other by Leicester. But at Howard House the distraught duke, suffering from a migraine, fluttered uncertainly until the buzzing rumours that he was about to be sent to the Tower were confirmed by news from Leicester, and in desperation Norfolk suddenly bolted for his country house in Norfolk — Kenninghall — although he had just written to say he would come to court within three or four days. A queen's messenger, Fitzgarret, Lieutenant of the Pensioners, hastened after him to Norfolk with a royal command that the duke repair to court instantly. Norfolk, who had now taken to his bed, pleaded illness and asked delay.[36]

The court was now both angry and frightened. Some rumour of the talk about the Tower may have reached them, and Pelham, Lieutenant of the Ordnance, was put in charge there with added forces while the ports were hastily closed.[37] But the duke was now out of the royal clutches. In his own country, surrounded by the deferential gentry of Norfolk and Suffolk who had flocked to his presence upon his arrival at Kenninghall, the duke was, at least for the moment, unassailable if he chose to defy the government. The queen wrote to Lord Wentworth, the leading East Anglian peer after the duke, warning him of the circumstances and commanding him to get in touch with the sheriff to take whatever measures were necessary. But a surer measure of the court's temper was a conciliatory circular directed to the Lords Lieutenant to be sent on to the Justices of the Peace.[38] It begins by noting that the duke had gone to Kenninghall in fear of the queen's displeasure but adds that he has written he will remain a faithful subject 'and so we heartily wish and trust he will, considering there is not other cause. Yet for that we are not ignorant what inclination there is in evil disposed persons to take occasions upon small matters to move seditious bruits we have thought good to signify unto you that Her Majesty hath not meant any wise towards the said Duke of Norfolk any manner of thing to him offensive.'

The queen's only wish is to understand all the facts of the proposed match with Mary, which she does not allow, and to let the duke understand this in the presence of the whole Council. The duke is declared to be a 'just and true servant' to the queen; but knowing the risks of rumour, the Council orders all magistrates to keep close watch to check seditious words or deeds.

The duke meanwhile, from Kenninghall, sent off an exculpatory letter to the queen, expressing his fears that he would be imprisoned without a fair hearing, protesting that he had intended nothing without the queen's consent, and declaring his loyalty. He was at the same time consulting with the representatives of the leading East Anglian families. The duke was urged to return to court and when Fitzgarret returned with a second summons (of which there were apparently two versions, one gently persuasive, the other peremptorily harsh), the duke agreed to obey and set out for Windsor. It was from Royston while en route that he sent to the northern earls urgent advice not to rise, warning them it would cost him his life.

At St Albans he was met by two pieces of bad news. A messenger from Throckmorton warned him he must fend for himself; if he tried to blame his confederates, he could expect no assistance from them. The duke also learned that he was not to proceed to court but to be confined in a private house at Burnham, in Buckinghamshire, under Sir Henry Neville's surveillance, and separated from his own servants. Fitzgarret, as the agent who was to carry out this plan, was still apprehensive. If the duke balked, he still had about him nearly forty attendants while the lieutenant had but half a dozen. But this last crisis passed without difficulty; the duke was placed under restraint and within a week had been moved to the Tower he so dreaded. The government had been deeply frightened and, now that the duke was within their grasp, they hastened to secure him in the closest confinement. In the meantime, even before Norfolk came up from Kenninghall, civil invitations had lured the other offenders to court where they too had been placed in detention, although a much milder one than their noble confederate's.[39]

Pembroke, Arundel and Lumley were held at court and Throckmorton was in detention; the Bishop of Ross was being interrogated and Ridolfi was held incommunicado in the custody of Francis Walsingham. Leicester alone of the conspirators had emerged unscathed. In Cecil's bland words, ' — considering he hath revealed all that he saith he knoweth of himself, Her Majesty spareth her displeasure the more towards him'.[40]

The favourite's credit was large; the lapse was passed over, and restoration to grace came quickly.

The government pushed its investigations with vigour in the weeks before the outbreak of rebellion in the North distracted attention elsewhere. The lesser figures were treated leniently from the beginning. Pembroke was able to persuade the Council of his relative innocence within a short time and to win discharge to his house at Wilton. By December he was re-admitted to the royal presence and to his offices. During the rebellion he served as Lord Lieutenant of Wiltshire and Somerset, but on March 17th, 1570, died – none too soon if there is anything in Camden's mysterious hint. Arundel was more harshly treated, kept in detention until the beginning of December and then dismissed to an enforced residence at Nonsuch. Throckmorton was also required to remain in seclusion at his farm at Carshalton.[41]

But it was far harder to decide what to do with the greatest of the prisoners. The official line remained a muted one; Cecil wrote to Ambassador Norris in tones of sorrow rather than anger, treating the duke's behaviour as ill-judged rather than criminal. Sussex, in genuine distress, lamented that his own absence in the North had left Norfolk prey to bad advisors. A trial was considered, but Cecil warned the queen that the duke's actions as then known (he wrote in early October) hardly fell within the scope of the Statute of Treason; trial, followed by acquittal, would only increase the credit of the duke. The Secretary's shrewd advice was to find a wife for Norfolk as soon as possible, otherwise he would continue to hanker after the forbidden fruit of a Stuart marriage. But for the time being the duke remained in the Tower, although with some relaxation of his confinement.[42]

The most considerable storm of the reign, after darkening the political skies for months, accompanied by threatening flickers and rumbles, had dissipated itself in a gush of summer rain. But away in the provinces the clouds did not disperse so easily, as events in the North were soon to demonstrate. While the magnates of court and Council had conspired together to match the Scottish queen with Norfolk, that queen's well-wishers in the northern English counties had sought more direct ways by which to assist her.

13 The Revolt of the Earls

AT THE very first coming of Mary into England, the Earl of Northumberland had sought to reach her and had made an abortive attempt to secure custody of her person; balked in that, he had nevertheless kept in touch with her steadily. Among his confidants in these matters were Richard Norton and Leonard Dacre. The former, a Yorkshire gentleman of ancient family, had been out in the rising of 1537 and remained fanatically loyal to the old faith and in touch with the exiled clergy. (He was the only member of the Council of the North dropped at Elizabeth's accession.) His numerous family of sons were as enthusiastic in the cause as their father. Leonard Dacre, brother to Thomas, Lord Dacre, and cousin to Northumberland, was, since the death of his brother, senior member of a great Border clan, warmly Catholic and sympathetic to Mary.

These gentlemen were fertile in schemes to release the Queen of Scots. When Northumberland was summoned to court with the other earls at the Christmas of 1568 to hear the evidence against Mary, he took advantage of the opportunity to make a nocturnal visit to the Spanish ambassador. He suggested a marriage between Philip and Mary Stuart and in general sounded out De Spes, although without much success; he was also cognizant at the time when Norfolk was in York of the proposal to marry the duke to Mary, a scheme which he regarded with little enthusiasm, as he told De Spes.[1]

About the same time, while the Scottish queen was still at Bolton, Christopher Norton, one of the younger sons of that family, had access to her and various devices were talked of for getting her away—harebrained enough, but not more so than the trick which freed her from Lochleven. In the spring of 1569 Leonard Dacre took the lead, first in planning a scheme to carry off Mary from Wingfield (Shrewsbury's house in Derbyshire, where she was temporarily lodged) and later in dealing with De Spes for aid. Towards the first purpose he went so far as to reconnoitre at Wingfield, even speaking to Mary from the leads, but in the end he was convinced it could not be done. What his relations with De Spes were is unclear, but apparently in June 1569, after some previous messages, he told the ambassador that if Philip would send a force to England, Mary's friends would put fifteen thousand men in the field. Northumberland was aware of the plots to rescue Mary, so was Ross, and so was Norfolk. The matter became more complicated when the death of the little Lord Dacre made Leonard Dacre and Norfolk bitter enemies in the struggle over the Dacre inheritance. It was this enmity that caused the duke to warn Mary Stuart against Dacre's scheme for her escape. The gap between the northerners, who had always regarded the Norfolk match with suspicion, and the court conspirators was now widened. Nevertheless, as the larger conspiracy developed in the summer of 1569 they were constrained to go along with it since Mary herself wrote to Northumberland, urging his consent to her marriage with the duke. So, for the time being, the courtiers and the wild men of the North were brought into a doubtful collaboration. On the northerners' side the co-operation was reluctant; the duke was no more enthusiastic, but as first Moray and then Leicester failed him, he had perforce to turn to the northern earls.[2]

In the tense days at the end of September there was acute excitement in the North. When the duke left the court without leave and returned to London, the northerners believed the realm soon 'would be in a hurly-burly'. They saw events moving in their direction; the queen had refused her consent to the marriage, but the duke could hardly back down now. He would have to dance to their tune, and it would now be possible to aim at a 'reformation of religion' and the naming of a successor – the Queen of Scots – while leaving that princess free to make her own matrimonial choices. They expected the general support of the nobility and were at least hopeful of Spanish assistance from the Low Countries.[3]

They had sent again to the Spanish ambassador to ask for the aid of harquebusiers after they had released Mary; their messenger had an encouraging but indefinite reply from De Spes, who promised to refer the matter to Alva. In the meantime Westmorland had received a furtive messenger from the Duke of Norfolk, sent by the latter while he was en route back to court. The message was brief: the earls were not to move; if they did, his head was forfeit. The result was consternation mingled with baffled rage. Westmorland cursed the faintheartedness of Norfolk, but his immediate reaction was still to go on; the others urged inaction. There followed some weeks of uncertainty in which the conspirators

veered between boldness and despair, sometimes thinking of flight overseas and sometimes plotting to seize the Lord President, Sussex. There
were frantic conferences, divided counsel, recrimination, and paralysed
indecision. They turned to De Spes, to Mary Queen of Scots and to the
Bishop of Ross for advice. To the Spanish ambassador Northumberland's
messenger was instructed to say that the duke's weakness had wrecked
'the matter which was expected to have been done'. For the earl the choice
was 'to yield my head to the block or else be forced to flee and forsake
the realm for I know the Queen's Majesty is so highly displeased at me
and others here that I know we shall not be able to bear it nor answer it'.
The earl begged either twenty thousand crowns to finance a rising or else
guaranteed refuge in Flanders. The ambassador was willing to send a
messenger from the earls on to Alva, but for the present urged inaction
and, if necessary, flight. Before his answer reached the North, the earls
were in arms. The Bishop of Ross joined his advice to that of De Spes;
Ross's mistress at Tutbury wrote the earls not to stir for the present, but
her letters also arrived too late to do any good. Events and their own confusion of purpose had forced the hand of the northerners.[4]

The authorities, both in London and at York, were alert to the situation. Norfolk had hardly been lodged in the Tower (October 8th) before
the court had cause for apprehension. On the 10th the Lord President
reported the rumours which had swept through the North Riding and
the bishopric of Durham the preceding Thursday (October 6th) to the
effect that a rising was about to break out. The Duke of Norfolk, it was
said, had gone to his own countryside, and his friends the earls were about
to take arms to support him; the old religion would then be restored.
Rumour, for once, was fairly accurate, but, once the duke's capitulation
was known, out of date. Sussex took vigorous action to secure all strong
places and summoned the earls to York on Sunday, October 9th. They
appeared, acknowledged having heard the rumours, but swore they
would adventure their lives to prevent such a tumult. By now these
bruits had reached as far as Lincolnshire, whence Lord Willoughby sent
an alarmed express to the Council. The Lord President took a cheerful
view of the situation, assured the court that all was now quiet and suggested that no further investigation be pressed 'until winter, when the
nights are longer, the ways worse, and the waters bigger to stop their
passage, if there shall be any stir'. He even wrote hopefully of coming up
to London after Hallowtide.[5]

But the government was disturbed, probably the more so as they

examined Norfolk, his associates and his servants. On October 17th the
Privy Council issued orders for 'a general state' of each shire—a report
on its political and religious stability. This was followed up by an order
of November 6th that Justices of the Peace and ex-Justices take the oath
of supremacy. The bench of each shire was to send up the actual sub-
scriptions and reports of any defaulters to the Council. In the meantime
the queen herself, dissatisfied, wrote personally to Sussex demanding more
information as to what had happened and at the same time commanded
him to order both Northumberland and Westmorland to attend at
court.[6]

The Lord President sent for them to come to York, where he intended
to impart the royal order. Things now took a graver turn, for the earls
declined to venture even to the provincial capital. Northumberland sought
the excuse of business, but Westmorland bluntly declared, 'I durst not
come where my enemies are without bringing such a force to protect me
as might be misliked.' Sussex now began to write of the possibility of
rebellion, but he made yet a further effort to persuade the earls to come
to York. With Northumberland he almost succeeded, when an unlucky
rumour that local gentry were coming to seize him frightened that panicky
nobleman into flight.[7]

Neither of these peers had much stomach for fighting and both had spent
the last few days in virtual paralysis, indisposed either to obey the queen or
to take arms. Now, urged by their wives and their immediate entourage,
and driven by panic, in absolute desperation, they rode to Durham, and
there, on November 14th, pulled down the communion table in the
cathedral, scattered the English Bible and the Book of Common Prayer
on the floor, and commanded the celebration of mass. The Earl of Sussex,
hearing of their intentions, had the preceding day summoned the forces
of Yorkshire to Darlington and proclaimed the earls rebels.[8]

The eruption of open violence which had been threatening the realm
for months had now burst forth, but the explosion had come, not at the
centre, but at the extreme periphery. To some extent the whole political
structure of the nation felt the stresses, but the form which the outbreak
took was peculiarly local, and, in some respects, private in character.
Although the revolt erupted in the same northern world as the Pilgrimage
of Grace thirty years earlier, there were many important differences between the two risings. The first outbreak, preceded by an uprising south
of the Humber in Lincolnshire, had been centred in the most populous
areas of the North and had affected great reaches of England beyond Trent.

The Pilgrimage had brought together a welter of angry men of varying backgrounds and differing — often contradictory — interests. It had come near to welding these diverse grievances into coherent regional revolt. This second rising of 1569 had — in striking contrast — been narrowly restricted to the followers and to the lands of three great families, the Percys, the Nevilles and the Dacres. The areas affected were removed from the vital centres of northern life. The revolting dynasts had made some effort to enlarge the scope of their actions by identifying them with larger causes of religion and of state, hoping thereby to draw to their support broad regional backing, particularly from the gentry. But their pitiful efforts did not succeed in dignifying what remained a merely personal, or at best familial, enterprise.

Many men in this northern world were still traditionalist, even archaic, in their outlook. Some still gave their loyalties first to a Percy or a Neville, and only afterwards to the Crown; in religion most of them still adhered, more or less firmly, to the ancient faith. But in the generation since 1537 change had penetrated even here. The disasters of that year were by no means forgotten, and there had now been thirty years of strong royal government, embodied in the Council of the North. All observers agreed that the new faith had made little penetration anywhere within the ecclesiastical province of York, but attachment to the old, although tenacious, was passive. There was no leadership, clerical or lay, to give direction; the seminary priests had yet to arrive; the impulse of the Counter-Reformation was yet to be felt here. And in politics the power of the great families had shrunk; it barely encompassed their own dependants and did not provide wide regional leadership. Most important of all, the gentry, who played so large and active a role in 1537, now warily held back, waiting on events, or even, in many instances, rallying behind the Lord President.

The earls were not the kind of leaders to galvanize the discontents of the countryside into active revolt. Neither of them embodied the skills or the ambitious drive of Hotspur or the King-Maker. Northumberland had reason for thinking himself ill-used and distrusted by the Crown. At the beginning of the reign he had been removed from the office of Warden of the Marches, semi-hereditary in his line, then systematically excluded from any share in the royal government in the North, and finally, as he saw it, deliberately robbed by the will of the Crown of valuable mineral wealth which he believed was rightly his. These humiliations were not the immediate causes of his revolt, but they had set him on the

15

road of discontent, service to the Queen of Scots, unskilled intrigue and finally desperate treason. His uncertain religious convictions had been redirected to the old faith by the persuasions of the returned exile priest, Copley, in 1567[9] while his political inclinations were steadily prodded by his imperious and ambitious wife, daughter of the high-descended and Catholic family of Worcester. A wiser — or more fortunate — man might have accepted his fate and, like his neighbour across the Pennines, Derby, have settled down into the uneventful but not uncomfortable obscurity of a backwoods peer.

Westmorland had fewer reasons for resentment of the Crown, although he too was no favourite at court and he too had an ambitious wife, who was sister to Norfolk. But even more significant than any of these personal elements was the historical position which these men had inherited. They were descended from generations of turbulent Border war-lords, semi-independent in their frontier province and accustomed to using their power to maintain an eminence in national politics. The expectations of the world in which these two lords lived still cast them in this archaic role and looked to them to be quick in resenting any imputation upon their dignity and bold in asserting their ancient power. It was a corollary that they would also defend the historic church against the menace of heresy. Neither earl had either the temperament or the talents to sustain such a role; unluckily they also lacked the courage to eschew it altogether. Consequently they were all too vulnerable to the taunts flung at them, when the crisis came. They could not ignore Lady Westmorland's stinging words when they hesitated to act. She flung out at them that their country was shamed for ever and that they must seek holes to creep into.[10] Unfit either to fulfil or to cast off the role the past imposed on them, the earls stumbled forward into an act of rebellion from which they shrank with all their souls.

Their inadequacies were soon reflected in the course of action to which they turned. To liberate Mary Stuart and to 'reform religion' had been the goals these men held before themselves. The means they proposed to use were either desperate plots for kidnapping Mary or vaguely conceived hopes of aid from Alva, until the Norfolk scheme seemed to offer a better opportunity. But beyond the immediate goal of releasing the Scottish queen they seem not to have thought, and when Norfolk's failure of nerve shattered such plans as they had, they were left in a pitiable state of confusion.

At Northumberland's house of Topcliff, when the conspirators debated their course after Norfolk's defection, the question was asked on what grounds they should raise a standard of resistance. Dacre and the Nortons urged those of religion, but Westmorland was firm in his refusal, 'for such quarrels were accounted rebellion in other countries, and he would not blot his long stainless house'. They discussed, possibly also on this occasion, whether it was lawful to rise against an anointed prince, and here sharp disagreement arose. Against the scriptural prohibition it was argued that the queen was excommunicated by her own actions in refusing to receive the pope's nuncio and therefore outside the pale of Christian obedience. But this was not generally accepted among the conspirators and no solution to the problem was found.[11]

In the end, when they did take action, their public proclamations reflected their uncertainties. At Ripon, on November 16th, they revived the splendours of an older world in a procession through the town. Dressed in the traditional armour of crusaders and each wearing a red cross, they displayed the banner of the Five Wounds of Christ, the emblem of the Pilgrimage of Grace, along with the standards of Percy and Neville. Mass was celebrated in the collegiate church and a proclamation addressed to those of the 'old Catholic religion' was read out. Evil-disposed persons about the queen, it was said, sought to overcome 'the true and Catholic religion towards God', disordered the realm, and now threatened the nobility with destruction. They, the earls, had risen to restore the ancient customs and liberties to God's Church and this noble realm. 'If we do not do it ourselves, we might be reformed by strangers—to the great hazarding of the state of this our country.'[12]

But on November 28th they issued another proclamation, a copy of which they had sent across the Pennines to Lords Derby and Monteagle, inviting their participation. In this document a very different line was taken, evading the issue of religion and coming down heavily on the question of the succession. Defending their own resort to arms, the earls invoked the names of the 'high and mighty prince Thomas Duke of Norfolk', of Arundel, Pembroke and 'divers others of the ancient nobility of this realm' as their backers. Their purpose was declared to be to make known the true succession to the Crown, in which, they asserted, they were impeded by common enemies of the realm, close about the queen's person, whose malicious practice left them no alternative but the sword. Religion was barely mentioned, merely the consent of 'sundry the principal favourers of God's Word'. They ended on a characteristic note, 'God save the queen and the nobility'.[13]

Nevertheless, however ill-managed the rising was, its initial explosion was highly alarming both to Lord President Sussex and to his superiors at court. The Earl of Sussex's first impulse was conciliation, an offer of pardon if the earls would attend at court and then later a purge of the ill-affected (a tactic very like that used thirty years earlier). His early dispatches also emphasized the uncertain loyalties of the countryside, the slackness of response and the underhanded aid being provided to the earls. But by November 26th, a fortnight after the seizure of Durham, Sussex began to write in better heart; the country was slowly rallying to the royal cause. It was evident by now that no other northern lord would join the earls. They had made an appeal to the powerful Earl of Derby, the uncontested satrap of Lancashire and Cheshire, a nobleman thought to be of Catholic sympathies, and to his cousin, Lord Monteagle. Derby's response was to arrest their messenger and to send their letter to London with his own protestation of loyalty to the queen.

The Earl of Cumberland, husband to Dacre's sister, on whose assistance they had banked, remained cautiously aloof. He kept a man in their camp to watch proceedings, but before his death at the beginning of January co-operated fully with Lord Warden Scrope in actions against the rebels on the western Borders. Leonard Dacre, claimant to the Dacre land and titles, whose hopes had risen with the fall of Norfolk, was at court when the storm burst, and pledged his loyalty to the queen. This accident substantially reduced the forces the rebels hoped to field and wrote finis to their schemes for seizing Carlisle. Lord Wharton, once a Privy Councillor to Mary and a known Papist, when approached by the rebels offered to move if Dacre did so since the latter was the most powerful magnate in Cumberland. But long before Dacre belatedly took the field Wharton had thrown his weight behind the royal government. An opportune fall from his horse excused him from active participation. The other northern peers rallied either to Lord Scrope, Warden of the West Marches, or to Drury or Forster, the commanders at Berwick and in the Middle Marches, or to the Lord President.[14]

The government also reaped the benefits of a policy pursued for the past decade of filling the frontier posts with men loyal to the Crown. Berwick was in the hands of the queen's cousin, Lord Hunsdon, governor there and Warden of the East Marches since 1568, and of his capable lieutenant, the Buckinghamshire squire, Sir William Drury; the Warden of the Middle Marches was Sir John Forster, sworn enemy to the Percys, while the very pillar of northern government was the sage and experienced

Sir Thomas Gargrave, Vice-President of the Council in the North since 1555 (and Speaker of the 1559 Parliament). Lord Scrope, the Warden of the West Marches, was a northern magnate and brother-in-law to Norfolk but his loyalty did not waver, and working with the Bishop of Carlisle he kept the north-western counties in good order. This meant that all the centres of the North—York, Newcastle, Berwick and Carlisle—were firmly in government control; the rebels gained only the secondary towns of Durham and Ripon and the second-rate port of Hartlepool, its harbour dry at low tide.[15]

But at court the gravest cause of concern arose through suspicion as to the loyalty of the queen's Lieutenant-General in the North, the Earl of Sussex. Sussex had never concealed his warm personal attachment to the Duke of Norfolk. The latter had followed the earl's lead in politics, especially in antipathy to Leicester and the campaign for the Habsburg match. The earl was known to have been consulted by the duke as to his match with Mary Stuart during the previous summer. The conspirators themselves had had some hope of Sussex because of his friendship to Norfolk. The queen was displeased when he failed to secure the Earl of Northumberland just before the outbreak of rebellion, and wrote to him to say so. And busy tongues at court were not slow to cast suspicion on his doings, especially when his bastard brother, Egremont Radcliffe, went over to the rebels. The warm recommendations of Sir Ralph Sadler when he arrived in the North, the earl's service and the better face of events from December 1st onward, allayed suspicion, but even as late as February 1570 the members of the Council of the North were writing to affirm Sussex's innocence in the intrigues of the previous summer. It was not until the earl was able to return to court in March 1570 and have audience with the queen that he obtained her assurances of goodwill and trust. Who his detractors were is not quite clear; quite possibly Leicester, whose marriage with the queen Sussex had steadfastly opposed. Sussex's un-shaken loyalty to the Crown and his vigorous prosecution of war against the rebels were of untold value to the government. The slightest hesitation or lack of energy on his part might well have swayed the wavering opinion of the northern gentry toward the earls and produced such a groundswell of opposition as had overturned royal government in the North in 1537. Sussex's position, not only as Lord President, but as a member of the pre-Tudor nobility, and as a leading figure in promoting the Habsburg match—in short as an eminent 'opposition' leader—made his firm allegiance in 1569 and 1570 a fact of signal political importance.[16]

The campaign to put down the rebellion offered opportunities for many political notables to push their careers. Hunsdon was almost immediately dispatched northward to his command at Berwick, although he lingered about York and shared responsibility with Sussex at first; the greatest event in his career came when in February 1570 he beat Leonard Dacre's larger forces at Naworth in the sole battle of the campaign and won his royal kinswoman's affectionate commendation. The joint commanders of the relief army which was to make its way from the counties of the Trent valley were Clinton (Lord Lieutenant of Lincolnshire) and Warwick, the veteran of Newhaven. Neither of these noblemen distinguished himself in any action; but each rivalled the other in the widespread and indiscriminate plundering of the North which followed on the rebellion's collapse. Warwick's old wound plagued him and he had to return after a short sojourn in the North. The young Earl of Rutland was sent out by his anxious guardian, Cecil, to be blooded in his first campaign, and the Secretary also sent north his older son, Thomas, who enjoyed the rough and tumble of military life far more than he had his grand tour of the Continent in the early 1560s.

Bedford was made responsible for the West, although he probably did not go there, and even Pembroke, readmitted to grace, was to command an army to protect the queen's person if necessary. Sir Ralph Sadler, more knowledgeable in the affairs of the North than any other royal servant, was sent to do his usual efficient job as general nursemaid for administrative and financial matters. In the Midlands the Earl of Huntingdon and Viscount Hereford were kept busy moving the Queen of Scots to the safety of Coventry and keeping her under guard there while the threat of a rescue lasted. Alone among the political luminaries the Earl of Leicester assumed no special responsibilities; for a short time in January he was away from court at Kenilworth with his sister, the Countess of Huntingdon. No great reputations were made and none marred in the rising in the North; but both Sussex and Hunsdon were to benefit in the future from their good service; Huntingdon and Hereford, relatively young men, were now brought forward into the limelight and to the beginning of their public careers.*

---

* *CSPDom, Addenda, 1566-79,* 180, 195, 246; PRO, SP 12/59/23; SP 12/60/4; BM, Cotton MSS, Caligula B IX 382. Both Hereford and Clinton received advances in the peerage; to be Earls of Essex and of Lincoln respectively. The patent explicitly mentions their services in the North as grounds for promotion (*CPR, 1569-72,* 443). Hunsdon and Warwick had grants of land for their service (Ibid., 203, 212).

The queen could congratulate herself upon the enthusiastic rally of most of the peerage and of the great political figures to the support of the government, but there were at least two exceptions, apart from the northern earls themselves. These were two lords of unquestioned Catholic orthodoxy, Viscount Montague and his son-in-law, the young Earl of Southampton. At the beginning of December they consulted the Spanish ambassadors as to whether to take up arms or to fly to Flanders, and a few days later they did attempt to get across the Channel only to be turned back by adverse winds. Then—if the ambassadors had got hold of a true story—Montague went to court and was reconciled to the queen. In any case Montague decided against the earls; while they were still in the field, Leonard Dacre, his brother-in-law, attempted to persuade the viscount to send a message to Cumberland urging him to take arms, but Montague was resolute against this and advised Dacre to forsake the matter altogether.[17]

The rising itself was of brief duration. Before the beginning of the new year, both earls were refugees across the Border: Northumberland soon to be a prisoner in Scottish hands (at Lochleven), Westmorland to flee overseas to a life of exile in Flanders. Everything had gone wrong from the beginning; the ill-luck of Dacre's absence at court deprived them of his powerful assistance in the field and of the chance of seizing Carlisle, and of possible aid from Mary's adherents from the Western Marches of Scotland. It also probably chilled whatever sympathy the lords Wharton and Cumberland might have shown towards the rebels. Lack of money was a crippling disability from the beginning and their meagre supplies were quickly exhausted, leaving their forces either to turn to plunder or to disperse.[18]

The rebels had but one slim hope of a real success—getting through to Tutbury with a raiding force of cavalry and freeing Mary from her captivity. At first their cavalry was stronger than Sussex's and there was an outside possibility of success; a daring commander might have exploited it. But the time was very short, and by November 25th, ten days after their march on Durham, the Queen of Scots was safely lodged within the walls of Coventry, impenetrable by a mere raiding force of horsemen.[19]

The rebels had some expectation of help from the Marian party in Scotland, but here again they were disappointed, for the swift action of the Lord Regent in marching to the Borders and making a clean sweep through them disconcerted whatever plans were in making among the Border lairds. The death of Lord Moray in January freed these gentry to give aid to Leonard Dacre in the following month. Dacre had hoped to profit from Norfolk's downfall and, being at court in November, pledged his loyalty to the queen; but as soon as he reached the North, he began dealing with the earls, too late to help them but not too late to bring about his own ruin. By January the government knew more than enough about his dealings and the queen ordered his arrest on the 13th. This proved to be a difficult business since he lay in the family fortress at Naworth, deep in the snow-covered Border hills in the midst of a countryside loyal to the death to the Dacre name. But on February 20th Hunsdon's stout charge against the forces Dacre had collected, partly Scottish in make-up, sent the rebel scurrying over the Border, the first stage on the road to Flanders and permanent exile.[20]

The one faint hope to which the rebels had clung as their cause went down to shipwreck was succour from abroad. Northumberland had, of course, dealt with the Spanish ambassador when their hopes were high in September, and while De Spes reported himself to Philip as full of discretion and quite noncommittal, the ambassador had probably said enough to inspire hope among the northerners. Certainly the rank and file had some such expectation and the occupation of Hartlepool was meant to open a port of such aid. After the rising was under way, about the end of November, another agent was sent, first to see De Spes and then to go on to Alva (probably Northumberland's counsellor, Markenfeld). De Spes gave him a ciphered letter to Alva and sped him on his way. The insurgents also wrote to the pope before taking arms (November 8th) seeking help, but the letter did not, of course, reach Rome until long after the rebels were broken exiles: the pope offered money to be sent via Ridolfi.

They turned also to the French ambassador, who had been deeply interested in the Norfolk marriage and knew what was going on; some time about the end of November they sought aid from France (presumably the same harquebusiers they wanted from Philip II). Fénélon's malicious but understandable hope was that the fire now lighted in England might be the beginning of a conflagration not less widespread than that blazing in France. But he was carefully general in his answers to the rebels. He was narrowly watching the Spaniard, believing that the latter was seeking to advance an eventual Spanish match for Mary; since Fénélon, quite naturally, was a backer of the Norfolk match, he may have been all the cooler in any sympathies for the rebels.[21]

The English government soon came to know something of the overtures to Alva and became correspondingly suspicious. What they did not know was that Philip was at the most disposed only to a very cautious interest, authorizing Alva to give secret favour and money to the Catholics of the North. Alva had bestirred himself when the rising broke out to send a special messenger to Philip, but with characteristic scepticism added that he expected the whole enterprise to go up in smoke. He had little confidence in De Spes's judgment and was more concerned in unscrambling commercial relations with England than with dabbling in English politics. When the king knew more of the matter he too drew back (in late December) and ordered the ambassador to make no promises, referring the whole business to Alva.[22]

In any case the swift collapse of the rebellion ruled out foreign assistance. The rising died away amidst the miseries of a peculiarly harsh northern winter and a plundered countryside. Sussex and Hunsdon stumbled on over snow-choked roads through the Border wastes, while the earls and their followers sought refuge among the lairds of Liddesdale and Teviotdale, who regarded them as valuable pawns in the everlasting ebb and flow of Border banditry rather than as protagonists of some larger cause. Behind the Lieutenant and his forces came the southern militia under Clinton and Warwick, plundering and looting their way, the higher ranks clutching at the forfeitures of lands and offices, the lower putting their hands to whatever they could grasp. The queen's officers laid heavy punishment on the countryside, executing out of hand the humbler rebels while imprisoning those of higher status and confiscating their lands.

In the retrospect of history the rising of the earls emerges as an epiphenomenal event, the last gasping protest by the traditionalist society of the North against the encroachments of a new social and political order, or —in a slightly different aspect—as an ill-conceived and ineffectual effort of the suppressed Catholics to reassert their cause in England. But from a contemporary point of view this movement had been an attempted revolution against the existing order in state and Church, flaring up in the most sensitive region of the country, where the new regime was most fragile, where there was least loyalty to the dynasty, greatest discontent with all the royal government stood for and sullen hostility towards the new religion. The two earls and Dacre were the very embodiment of all these threats—regional war-lords who could overnight put a force of men in the field, and the only noblemen whose Catholicism was vital enough to move them to risk their lives on its behalf.

But now that the abscess of sedition had finally come to a head and burst there was deep cause for relief, for it was after all merely superficial. Only the tenantry and immediate dependants of the earls had actually appeared in the field; the bulk of the Northern gentry, however sympathetic, had in fact remained sullenly quiescent or reluctantly co-operative. The fire which the Catholics among the rebels hoped to light had fizzled out damply. The new regime had come to its time of testing and proved durable. Cecil could write, when news of the earls' flight reached the court, 'The Queen's Majesty hath had a notable trial of her whole realm and subjects in this time wherein she hath had service readily of all sorts, without respect of religion.'*

The rising must, of course, be viewed as part of the whole movement in politics which began in late 1568, a massive and fairly concerted effort to initiate a new general policy of state. The movement had begun with the scheme for the marriage of Mary and Norfolk. The combined skills of Secretary Maitland, the Bishop of Ross, and Nicholas Throckmorton had all been exercised in the shaping of this plot, but the two central figures in its execution were to be the Regent Moray and the Earl of Leicester. On the former depended the measures for arranging Mary's restoration in Scotland; if he could be prodded into playing his role and demanding from the English queen her cousin's return, Elizabeth would be hard pressed to refuse. Leicester in his turn would then have to step forward and do his part. How important that would be Throckmorton had warned the duke at the very beginning of their scheming; if he were to pursue the marriage, he must be a follower of Leicester's direction, 'for your own credit will never obtain the Queen's Majesty's consent thereunto'.[23] The weight of Scottish demands coupled with the persuasive-ness of the favourite would weigh the balance heavily in favour of the marriage; but would it be ponderous enough to offset the unwavering resistance of William Cecil to any scheme for Mary Stuart's advantage? It is here that the first plot – for the marriage – merges with the second – for the overthrow of the Secretary.

Clearly the conspiring lords feared that unless Cecil were altogether removed from the political scene – to the Tower if possible – their hopes for the marriage would go unrealized.[24] But to accomplish this they had

---

* *Cabala*, 159. There was one pathetic response. A mob at Kenninghall, Norfolk's palace near Norwich, was harangued by several artisan agitators, who vainly urged them to rise for ancient custom and the liberties of God's Church. See N. Williams, 'The Risings in Norfolk, 1569-70', in *Norfolk Archaeology*, XXXII (1961), 73-81.

to find another issue, a lever strong enough to oust the Secretary from the queen's confidence. Foreign affairs seemed to offer a happy opportunity. Cecil's urgings had led the country to the verge of war with Spain at a time when relations with France were dangerously strained, while Scotland stood poised in tense uncertainty. In thus shifting their ground they added new complications to their manoeuvre, since their attitudes towards foreign policy were in fact widely different. Arundel favoured a return to the old alignments of the 'Burgundian' alliance and was willing, perhaps even anxious, to accompany this switch by a reversal in religion at home. Norfolk went along with the first of these goals; his attitudes towards the second were ambiguous, but he did not altogether reject it. Leicester too wanted a reorientation of foreign policy, but what he sought was a working arrangement with France. He did not believe this to be incompatible with the promotion of an ever-more-radical Protestantism at home. All agreed in rejecting the independent, somewhat nationalistic, go-it-alone policy pushed by Cecil.

Apart from the confusion which these disagreements imparted to the common action of the conspirators, an assault on Cecil's foreign policy meant seeking the co-operation of the continental ambassadors. This in turn led Arundel and Norfolk into their first entanglements in the web of intrigue which Ridolfi was so industriously weaving and into courses of action very easily misconstrued by their jealous mistress. Moreover, the mechanical difficulties of the plotters were now multiplied since the machinery necessary to bring about Cecil's defeat included effective and well-timed pressure from the powers.

It is hardly surprising, therefore, that the anti-Cecil move dissipated itself ineffectually. First of all, the conspirators' calculations as to the powers' intentions proved quite wrong; Alva had no wish for war, indeed dreaded it, and was quick to respond to the unofficial feelers put forward by Cecil. The French government, well advised by its shrewd and clear-headed ambassador, held back from any decisive move to exploit English difficulties. The kind of overwhelming calamity which alone would have shaken the queen's confidence in Cecil did not materialize, and the minister further improved his position when he turned the enemy's flank by overtures to the pliable Norfolk and by assisting the duke to the Dacre inheritance. Leicester, put to the test, had refused to make a head-on attack on Cecil (if we may believe De Spes's story); more attuned than anyone else to the temper of his royal mistress, he probably sensed that even his credit was inadequate by itself to overthrow his rival, and declined to risk it under such unfavourable conditions. By early summer Cecil's position was secure and the marriage scheme, if it were to succeed, would have to allow for this fact of politics. The conspirators cheered themselves with hopes that he would be swept along by the general torrent of approbation for the match.[25]

The success of the match now turned on Moray's behaviour. If Maitland came down from the north armed with the backing of the Regent and the bulk of the nobility, his task would be rendered easier; it would be hard for the queen to deny such a request for Mary's release and the proposal to send her home with a Howard husband would be persuasive. At any rate, so the conspirators continued to hope. But the Scottish Regent's insistence that marriage precede restoration, and his veto on the proposals forwarded by the queen, were chilling news.

Moray had in fact found his way out of an intolerable position. He could not, under any circumstances, wish to see his half-sister restored to her throne; it could only be to the severe damage of his position and that of the faith he served. But, as he wrote to Cecil in explanation, 'We here have not always followed our own course when as we could not see our example with you, that we must needs follow.' Seeing Elizabeth apparently determined on some kind of restoration, 'I could not think it profitable to lose the benevolence of such as seemed bent that way, having no taste of Her Highness misliking of the purpose, but rather daily proof of the contrary'. But once his own position in Scotland was assured, as it was by the agreements of June and July which brought most of the greater peers, including Huntly and Argyll, to an acknowledgment of the Regent's regime, Moray felt freer to take a firm stand against any suggestions of a Marian restoration.[26]

Thus, on the critically important Scottish front, the campaign for the marriage was stalled by midsummer and Norfolk was driven inexorably towards the 'direct-action' party of the northerners, although for a time he could hope that Leicester's persuasive intervention would bring the queen around to an acceptance of the match. That hope gone, the duke could only make an agonized and humiliating retreat – or, risking all, take up arms.

As Moray was the indispensable man in Scotland, so Leicester was in England. Leicester's role remains the most ambivalent among all those involved. Did he aim 'dissembling and cunningly, for the overthrow of the duke'?[27] Camden could not make up his mind, and the evidence is little clearer now than it was then. The earl's attitude was probably in fact a good deal more subtle. His own position had changed a great deal in the last few years. In the early years of the reign his behaviour was necessarily that of a gambler, playing for the highest stakes—playing, in his case, for all or nothing. But circumstances had changed for him now that that dangerous bauble, a crown matrimonial, had almost certainly slipped beyond his reach. In place of that bird in the bush, he had in hand substantial prizes of great worth. He was still the queen's favourite, but he was also a great magnate in the land, lord of Kenilworth, with a widespreading network of property and interests. His ambitions were coming more closely into line with those of his fellows in the Council; like them he had much to lose if there were a time of trouble. He had to think of a future when Mary might sit in Elizabeth's place and when Norfolk would be a great figure in a new court.[28] And not only his personal future was at stake but also the future of the left-wing Protestant cause of which he was now the grand patron; nothing could be so damaging to it as a Catholic and foreign match for the heiress to the English throne. These motives, we may reckon, were strong enough to move Leicester to join in the enterprise of the match.

His motives in joining the attack on Cecil are not so easily accounted for. No doubt he would have rejoiced to see the fall of his only real rival for the queen's confidence, especially since the Secretary had been an unremitting, if covert, enemy to a match between the favourite and the monarch. Moreover, since he was preparing to back the Marian succession, he clearly had to join in the elimination of the most implacable opponent of that policy. One must also reckon that Leicester's confidant and advisor during these months was Throckmorton, whose disappointed but still powerful ambitions could be gratified only if the Secretary were removed from power.[29]

Lastly, Leicester may have not quite abandoned hope of the marriage he had so long hoped for. If Mary were safely married to Norfolk, opposition to the earl's own match with the queen would diminish. The surmise is based on the doubtful assumption that the queen herself wished marriage. All the evidence, however, suggests that she was now committed to the single life and content to maintain the present relationship with her favourite.

But Leicester chose—just precisely when we cannot be certain—to abandon the intrigue and to leave Norfolk to his fate. He had had ample opportunity to assess the most essential element in the whole scheme, the queen's reaction. The conspirators had counted on her yielding to the combined pressures which they hoped to bring to bear. It is just possible that in the tense, worrying spring months, when the country seemed to hover on the brink of hostilities with each of her great neighbours, the queen's resolution wavered. Cecil seems to have thought the threat to his position was real enough. But whether or not this is so, it is certain that in June she threw the whole weight of her authority behind him. It may have been this development which chilled Leicester's interest in the Norfolk match; by midsummer he began to evade the duke's importunities to broach the scheme to the queen. Moray's defection may have settled the matter for the favourite. He must have calculated that his mistress would yield to nothing less than the united pressure of the English and Scottish magnates. This was now clearly impossible, and Leicester had no intention of squandering his own credit on a certain failure. In his unique position the earl had a talisman possessed by no other courtier, which he could use at will to cancel out any liabilities accrued in such a venture as this most recent one. All he had to do was to make his humble confession, acknowledging his fault and revealing all he knew, to win the royal forgiveness and re-admittance into grace. The venture had been a gamble worth taking; it had failed, but the earl had made his retreat with skill and expedition, and was none the worse for it.

The other conspirators were not so happily placed. The unlucky northern earls had gone beyond the point of retreat and had to lunge on to a doom they could read for themselves. But they at least had been willing to face the necessity for using force, and the cause they struggled for seemed worth a risk. That risk had seemed reasonable so long as they could count on Norfolk; his defection destroyed them, but that too was one of the chances of the field.

The rest of the conspirators were variously situated. Arundel and Pembroke, the courtier earls, had played a special kind of game. The former, a disgruntled and sullen politician, had been sulking for years, deeply embittered that a Fitz-Alan should have to play second fiddle to such upstarts as a Cecil or a Dudley. He was a traditionalist in domestic and foreign politics and in his faith, and more and more deeply committed to a reversal of all that had happened since 1558. The most revolutionary of the conspirators in his aims, he came off very easily indeed since by the spring of 1570 he was readmitted to the Council. Paradoxically he probably owed this leniency both to his eminence of rank and to his political impotence. His restoration to the Council was a reassurance to conservatives throughout the political classes. It was a sop to their alarms in the tense months just after the rising; but it cost little, for without his over-mighty son-in-law beside him he counted for little in the Council and the court.

Pembroke is another story. If Arundel was the high tory of this action, Pembroke was the trimmer. A parvenu, a 'raiser of his own fortunes', he had turned to that task with single-minded purposefulness, avoiding ideological commitment and, as he said, 'leaning on both sides the stairs to get up'. By Elizabeth's accession his place was established and the foundations of an immense fortune laid, but Pembroke was a nervous politician and a timid one. Still at work on the structure of land, office and influence he was building for himself and his posterity in Wiltshire and South Wales, he was terrified by the prospects of a contested succession. When the marriage scheme failed, his retreat was precipitous and abject, his first anxiety always the protection of his estates and the inheritance of his children.[30]

Throckmorton's role was of yet another genre. Although not on a par with his noble fellows in the conspiracy, he probably played a large part in the actual business of the plot. Since his mission to Scotland in 1567 he had had no important post in government and had been passed over in appointments to the major household offices and for a place on the Council. Viewing Cecil as the enemy who stood in the path of his advancement, Throckmorton had latterly linked himself closely with Leicester; he had also gradually moved to support of the Marian succession. For him the success of the scheme was all-important; it would either lead on to the great place he so eagerly coveted; or, if it failed, leave him in hopeless obscurity.

The last and greatest of the conspirators is a more complex case. Norfolk was, in so many respects, the child of the gods. His great station was matched by personal endowments of high order. He was a man who excited genuine admiration and affection among his contemporaries. He seems to have had the ideal temperament to play the part of the grandee, open, amiable, winning all men's hearts but never lacking in dignity or poise. Yet his position, for all its splendours, was an exacting and even dangerous one, and required an uncommon range of skills to maintain it. The very fact of being the sole duke in the realm demanded that he assume a principal place in national political life, as a permanent member of the inner circle of power, or at least a leader in important actions. At the beginning of the reign his commission in the North seemed to promise the opening of such a role, but he was instead half-forgotten at court for the next couple of years, the era of Dudley's first ascendancy, and called into the Council only to provide a nominal balance when the favourite was given the same advancement. The coldness that grew up between him and the queen and his dislike of Leicester had gradually cast the duke as a kind of leader of the opposition – or, to put it more precisely, as the leader of a pressure group outside the Council whose aim was to persuade the queen to marriage. Under Sussex's able tutelage (and acting with Cecil's approval) he had been foremost in pushing the Habsburg marriage. This was acceptable conduct within the existing political framework and might have been successfully exploited by a subtler man. Adapting a great position in the country – a position in some degree autonomous of the court and of royal favour – he could have sustained a role as a focus of public opinion, as a responsible spokesman for loyal disagreement with some aspects of Crown policy. (A man of real political flair might have displaced Leicester as patron of the Puritans.) But such a course required great discretion in the choice of causes for which to speak and acute sensitivity in sounding the permissible limits of action. This was peculiarly difficult for a duke, for the premier peer of the realm was always in the glare of great publicity and under the watchful regard of the Crown, and what in a lesser person might be dismissed as foolish indiscretion was likely to be taken more seriously in a duke.

When Norfolk fumblingly attempted to transfer his advocacy of the failed archducal marriage to the cause of the Stuart succession, his short-comings as a political leader became quickly and dismayingly apparent. Within a short time he had dangerously compromised himself, first with the Scottish queen and then with the militant Catholics. It may be argued that in both instances it was all too easy to be misled by ambiguities which the queen herself had fostered. Even the much more acute Moray was half-convinced that Elizabeth really did intend a restoration of Mary and in both the Habsburg negotiations and again, later, in the Anjou wooing of 1571, the queen allowed the possibility of permitted nonconformity to the state religion to be discussed. But the very mark of Norfolk's inepti-tude was his failure to understand just how delicate both these matters were, how much patient and cautious reconnoitring was necessary before so much as putting a foot forward. The duke, by lightly plunging into seditious intrigue with a hostile ambassador and affiancing himself to the queen's most dangerous rival, took advanced positions from which the possibility of safe – or at least dignified – retreat was slight.

But even had Thomas Howard been a man of greater political ability, he might well have come to grief in the pursuit of a career in public life. His misfortune lay ironically enough in the golden spoon of his inheritance. It had in fact given him all that he could hope for or aspire to without his lifting a finger; his position in the state was so great that any ambition on his part would be suspect to the Crown, for he could augment his place only at its expense. Hence he must strictly ration his ambitions, eschewing political activity except in the limited and cautious terms suggested above, or else turn his energies in some other direction altogether. Here again the duke was unlucky in his generation. His grandson was to win distinction as a discriminating patron of the arts; and in another generation still, the options within which a duke could respectably live up to his station would be yet wider; he could cultivate the arts or his lands, buy pictures or build houses, patronize poets or improve his farms; or lead a merely social existence, a glittering court fixture. But in the 1560s these things were yet to come, and although Thomas Howard was destined to become a victim in large part of his own mistakes, they were errors liable to be made only by one placed in his unique and perilous eminence.

The duke, of course, might also have tried his fortune at arms. His contemporaries expected him to do so in September 1569, and he earned the contempt of many when he failed to make the attempt. In the last analysis this was a personal failure of nerve; Norfolk lacked the metal out of which effective political leadership is forged. In 1569 and again in the following two years he was to display the same fatal character defect, the stubbornness of a weak man, which led him into an exposed position where he froze, unable to retreat or to advance, until inevitable disaster overtook him. But his ruin was also in part a consequence of changes in the larger political system.

The conspirators of 1569 set out consciously to provide a new solution for an old problem—that of the succession. Unintentionally they very nearly stumbled into what might have been major civil conflict—revolution or civil war. But they set out on a familiar enough path. For a decade, politically conscious Englishmen had been preoccupied with the haunting problem of the succession. Commons petitions, clandestine pamphleteering, endless discussion up and down the land, had revealed sharp divergences of opinion on many aspects of the matter but unanimous conviction that the matter must be settled. The elemental need to safeguard the foundations of social order and to provide some security for the future was self-evident to all. Much the most preferable way to secure these ends

would be a royal marriage—and royal children—as both Lords and
Commons did not cease to press upon the queen, but without effect, and
now it seemed almost certain that there would never be either husband
or children. What then could be more persuasive than a match, which,
while securing the future to the Queen of Scots, would bring her into
dependence upon Elizabeth during the latter's lifetime? The scheme
seemed to offer satisfaction to all parties concerned. The conspirators could
reasonably feel that the queen's obstinate refusal to face whatever personal
risks the establishment of a successor might mean to her was countering
the needs of the nation and that their enterprise was therefore an entirely
legitimate and proper one.

Yet from the beginning the scheme was shot through with ambiguities
which even the principals hardly admitted to themselves. In all their
planning everything was made conditional upon Queen Elizabeth's assent
(with the implication that she could hardly refuse any proposals so eminently reasonable). But in fact they were busy at work constructing a plot
which would coerce the queen into acceptance by leaving her no alternatives. Gentle persuasion was to be backed by the demands of Scotland
for the return of its queen, by the near-unanimous voice of the whole
Council and peerage, and by discreet but unmistakable prodding from
the continental powers. She was to be brought to agree not only to the
marriage but also to the dismissal of her most trusted minister. The whole
tenor of English politics under the Tudor dynasty was to be shattered by
the introduction of a kind of dynastic politics in which the putative heiress
to the throne and the near-royal dynast, Norfolk, were to be made poles
of counter-attraction to the Crown.

The confusion implicit in the thought and action of these men bears
witness to the inchoate and contradictory assumptions of the political
system within which they lived. In theory the queen was an inviolable
autocrat, placed above all human judgment by divine decree and exer-
cising an unrestricted play of her will. In practice the political system
was gradually coming to allow a widening but uncertain range of free
discussion of public questions. The mechanism of parliamentary petition
opened the Crown to the respectful but forthright pressures of public
opinion. The principal difficulty of such a system was the very narrow
range of manoeuvre within which pressure could be brought to bear upon
the sovereign; worse still were the uncertainties as to what were the permitted boundaries of such manoeuvre. Every Parliament presented a
demonstration of these difficulties: sometimes the queen seemed to yield;

sometimes an offending M.P. went to the Tower; on other occasions she forbade any further discussion of a subject; or, more rarely, she might give way and promise redress. But the tendency, within and without Parliament, was for a continuing pressure upon those boundaries by an ever more aggressive political community. This was what the backers of the Norfolk marriage were up to; they intended to mobilize every means of pressure at their disposal to force the queen to their desires. The risk in such a manoeuvre was that they would overstep the all-important boundary between a contest of wills and a contest of force – or, to put it another way, the line between intrigue and open violence.

This was precisely the crisis that rose in the late summer of 1569. The resources of intrigue had been exhausted: Cecil had survived the attacks in Council; Moray had evaded their blackmail; Maitland was in Edinburgh Castle; and finally Leicester opted out and made his peace with the queen. Norfolk had to make his resolve, whether to abide by circumstances, recognizing failure of the plot, or to mobilize an army. His decision was a fateful one not only for himself, but for the whole course of English politics. Contemporaries waited tremblingly to see what he would do, for open war seemed near. To us, looking back, his decision seems a predestined one. The commitment to civil order, the habit of obedience to constituted authority, by now ran very deep throughout English society. All that was said between the duke and the East Anglian gentry who attended on him at Kenninghall we do not know. They included some eminent Roman Catholics (Cornwallis, Morley, the younger Jerningham)[31] as well as Protestants of great local eminence. He did at least broach the possibility of defiance, but he seems to have had nothing but discouragement from all those who surrounded him. It was unlikely that a gathering of well-to-do East Anglian squires would willingly risk their lives and estates in such a cause. They had been willing enough to defend Mary Tudor's rights two decades earlier, but they had then acted in the name of their legitimate sovereign and to avoid civil strife. The very grounds on which the duke proposed marriage to the Queen of Scots were the avoidance of future civil war over the succession; but in fact to take up arms now would be to invoke deliberately the same disaster in the immediate present. And whatever role religion played, it took second place to loyalty to the existing political order. As Protestants had risen to support Mary Tudor in 1553, so now Catholics rallied around her half-sister. Even in the over-heated political atmosphere of the North, the circle of Catholics around the earls solemnly debated the lawfulness of their proposed action and came to no conclusion. Even in that sullen province, the habits of obedience were deeply ingrained.

The victory of the Crown was beyond doubt; on every front the queen had triumphantly repelled all attacks; and when the North had taken to arms the unhesitating response of the nation had vindicated the sovereign. Yet the crisis had been real and frightening enough to contemporaries. The Tudor political order was a peculiarly fragile one since it rested on the intangible cement of habit, of custom, and, to a degree, of consent. Since 1558 the Crown had pursued policies which were novel, in some respects radical, and unsettling to important fractions of the political nation. Cecil was acutely aware that the religious polity of 1559 was but coldly regarded by a portion of the aristocratic classes; their acceptance of it was at the best passive. He knew too that a smaller but important body of public opinion regarded with distrust what they thought a dangerously risky foreign policy. Hence he had dreaded the coming of just such a crisis as this one, which would strain the delicate network of loyalty. But the test had come and the fabric had proved stronger than the minister had dared hope. Loyalty to the Crown, far from being shaken by the new religious polity, was stronger than ever, and the committed Protestants in the Council might begin to feel for the first time that their faith was sinking deep roots. They had been a 'minority government' during the first years of the reign, holding the reins of power but feeling a fearful precariousness in their hold. Now they could breathe easier, knowing that their opponents had made a grand-scale assault and failed.

Their failure had also cleared away the last lingering uncertainties which had clouded the central question of religion. The passage of time had swept away the survivors of the older generation, whose pliable religious views stemmed from the first epoch of reform. Cecil and his contemporaries among the Councillors were, with some personal variations, irrevocably committed to the new faith. But there had yet lingered in the minds of many Englishmen the notion that reversion to the old religion was still a possibility—a possibility, that is, within the range of legitimate political activity. Northumberland's somewhat naive hope was expressed in homely terms. He hoped that Cecil 'with his singular judgment' would be 'blessed with godly inspiration to discern cheese from chalk ... and bring Her Majesty to the truth'.[32] Many others, both ardent Catholics and those more lukewarmly sympathetic to Rome, would have echoed these views. The foreign ambassadors had thought such a change possible in the earlier 1560s; De Spes still entertained the notion that under pressure the queen could be brought to such a reversal; that notion was probably put in his mind by Arundel. In retrospect these may seem mere foolish fantasies, but to contemporaries—at least to some informed contemporaries —a Catholic restoration under the queen seemed a possibility. The events of 1569 cleared the air of such ideas. The Catholic cause became, by force of circumstance, identified with open rebellion; henceforth it could be advanced only outside the bounds of legitimate politics, by conspiracy and ultimately by force. Men like Montague were driven to make the choice of open and unlawful resistance, of flight (which he apparently contemplated) or of complete withdrawal from politics into quietist seclusion. He chose the last.

Finally, within the inner circle of politics, a shift of balance had occurred. The plots for the Norfolk marriage and for the overturn of Cecil had displayed the possible range of manoeuvre open to a skilful practitioner. Roughly speaking, in the immediately preceding years Norfolk, Sussex and Arundel had, with the tacit support of Cecil, united their influence against the ambitions of Leicester. He had in turn cultivated the more radical Protestants. But the 'reversal of alliances' which brought the duke and the favourite together (almost certainly through Throckmorton's intervention) had shown that political expediency was stronger than personal animus. Cecil had for a time been left in uncomfortable isolation. The coalition had gradually broken up during the summer of 1569. Thenceforth Cecil held the loyalties of the more or less Puritan element in the Council, his brother-in-law Bacon, Knollys and Mildmay, and was soon to have a strong conciliar ally in Sussex, a man more principled and more astute than Norfolk and very unlikely to enter into any understanding with Leicester. The favourite, in turn, found himself once again without strong allies on the Council and hence driven back to a more or less lone hand. He still possessed the magic talisman of royal favour, but he had now to abandon any prospect of dislodging Cecil from his place in court and Council. The favourite had had his last and most dangerous fling at personal and conspiratorial politics. It had failed and henceforth he had to subside into political sobriety and to learn to live within the bounds set by courtly civility and official propriety.

In a larger sense the whole problem of faction, which had loomed so frighteningly for a few years, was now fading away. The worst possibility —nation-wide faction founded on religious difference, as in France—was now excluded by events. Court faction, based on animus among the greater courtiers, had seemed to threaten, especially as the hostility towards

Leicester grew in intensity. This was kept in bounds by the queen's care not to lavish her favour on Dudley too freely, by her willingness to listen to others than the favourite and by his own political skills. Probably only the threat of actual marriage would have set off open conflict. What was frightening in 1568 and 1569 was the possibility that irritation over the succession issue would lead to a coalition of erstwhile rivals strong enough to coerce the queen and to break Cecil. This foundered, in the first instance, on Dudley's ultimate unwillingness to gamble his assets of royal favour in such a cause. Even after his withdrawal there was the possibility that a combination of Norfolk and the northern earls would be the match to set ablaze civil conflict. This possibility disappeared partly because of Norfolk's own failure of nerve, but also because he no longer possessed the power to raise a whole province in the Howard name against the Tudors. However deferential the gentry of East Anglia might be towards this great potentate, their prime allegiance now lay with the Crown. Regional politics had given way to national, although the disappearance of old habits had been a silent and gradual change. Even in the North the earls' magic held good only within the limited circle of their own tenantry. England had quietly passed a great landmark in her political history, a basic and lasting change of habit and outlook.

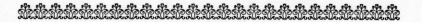

14 *The Aftermath of the Storm*

THE LONG-TERM consequences of the northern rising still lay hidden in the future; at the moment the dispersal of the earls' forces seemed but a respite, and a short one at that, since even before Dacre had been put down a fresh and jolting misfortune befell the English government. On January 23rd the Regent Moray was assassinated by one of the Hamiltons at Linlithgow; all the affairs of Scotland, which during the last year had been shaped into some rough coherence by the strong will and arm of the Regent, were now again set adrift. For England the death of Moray was catastrophic. With Scotland under his guidance there seemed to be some real possibility that the harmony of policy between the two island kingdoms which Cecil had looked forward to a decade earlier might actually be realized. It was not only that the Regent was firmly Protestant and that his circumstances bound him to a close dependence upon England, but his abilities seemed to promise a Scottish government strong enough to master endemic anarchy and to pursue a consistent policy. Above all, Moray, as the declared enemy of Mary, could hold her party in check and collaborate with Cecil in hindering all moves made by the Scottish queen or her allies.

Now all was to do again. There was no successor to Moray as regent; all was in confusion; and the Marian party within Scotland took heart. Still strongly based on the Hamilton fortress of Dumbarton and on the Huntly domains in the North, their leaders now reasserted their authority as the legal government of Scotland by Mary's commission. They also sought foreign intervention by either France or Spain. Just at the moment when the failure of Mary's English friends seemed to have crushed her hopes, a new and fair prospect opened up for her in her native country.

Abroad the balance also turned in Mary's favour and against England. The Huguenots had received a severe setback at Moncontour in October and negotiations for a settlement began at mid-winter. Although they were inconclusive, the government of Charles IX was relatively stronger and freer to take a stronger line abroad. Already in the preceding summer Fénélon had eagerly followed up his instructions to encourage the Norfolk match. France wished to stir up troubled waters in England, possibly to the point of civil dissension, and to keep Mary Stuart out of Spanish hands. Fénélon continued in close touch with the Scottish queen and with Norfolk through the winter and spring and did what he could to encourage the duke to remain faithful to Mary.[1]

Nearer home there was much to vex, to irritate, and even to alarm the English government. Westmorland and Leonard Dacre, along with a substantial number of mounted followers, had escaped into the Scottish Border dales, and with the Regent dead there was no one to restrain the sympathetic assistance they received from the borderers. Northumberland was in custody in Scotland but obviously it would be difficult – and expensive – to obtain surrender of his person, and in the meantime he might escape.

At court too there was cause for malaise. In October the Councillors had pressed their investigations into the events of the preceding summer; now, as prisoners came in, they sought to probe into the ramifications of the northern rising. At this point the government knew both too much and too little – too much for their own peace of mind, but too little to act effectively to relieve their fears. They more than suspected the involvement of foreign powers, especially Spain; they were uneasily suspicious that not all the roots of the Norfolk scheme were yet uncovered nor even all the branches cut down.[2] The Councillors' fears were not relieved when in late winter a pamphlet appeared in Paris, '*A discourse of troubles newly happened in England in October with a declaration made by the Earl of Northumberland and other great lords of England*', which defended the actions of Norfolk and his friends (in which were included Sussex). There are extant at least two manuscript copies of a defence of Norfolk's plan to marry Mary Stuart (one dated March 15th, 1569–70) and also a printed pamphlet condemning the duke (and not sparing Mary).[3]

The defence of the duke is strongly Protestant in tone; it defends the duke's soundness in religion, and points out that the Gospel never so thrived in Scotland as under Mary. The opponents of the marriage are attacked as self-seekers who had already discouraged Queen Elizabeth from the three matches she might have made and were interested in nothing except protecting their own positions of power. The argument was substantial and aimed at just such uncommitted men of the middle road who were more concerned about an unsettled succession than the cause of right religion.

These were signs that the match was not yet a dead issue—or perhaps that Norfolk was still a live centre of political activity. According to the French ambassador the duke had for some time resisted attempts to get him entirely to forswear the match. He certainly had friends at court, and even before the outbreak in the North there were rumours of a lighter confinement; by mid-winter agitation for some relief—and ultimate release—was growing. Unless some firm ground of indictment could be uncovered in the wreckage of the northern uprising, the government, sooner or later, would have to liberate the premier peer of the realm.[4]

But most immediately Scotland was the matter which required attention. Since the death of the Regent Moray there was virtual anarchy in that unhappy country. There was also the possibility that the English fugitives, with the assistance of the Marian party and some support from abroad, would launch a renewed offensive. Elizabeth's first act was to send her former envoy to Scotland, Randolph, northward to reassure the Scots lords that she would not take any steps towards Mary's restitution without first hearing their case.[5] But beyond these bare assurances the English queen was not prepared to go.

English policy reflected the acute distaste with which the queen faced the Scottish situation. The fiction that Elizabeth did not recognize James as King of Scotland had been maintained throughout; it had obvious diplomatic advantages; moreover, it suited the queen's intense dislike of revolutionary regimes. Now she refused to accept James's party as her allies, and withheld English backing for any particular candidate for the regency. The Marians took heart and acquired new support while the king's party dwindled.

The English government met the problem of the fugitives by the simple expedient of sending an army under Sussex across the Border to suppress the Border lairds who sheltered the English rebels. Throughout April the English forces ravaged the Scottish dales and seized the principal strongpoints.[6]

But in the meantime the situation complicated itself; the French, freer to act than for many months past, now took action. An envoy was sent to Scotland and in March they let it be known they were amassing a force to send to Dumbarton; in early April Charles IX directly demanded the withdrawal of the English forces in Scotland. The object of this manoeuvre was to force the queen into serious negotiations for the restoration or at least the release of Mary Stuart, and the threats were too real to be ignored, especially since the queen feared that Spain would join France in this enterprise.[7]

Elizabeth was deeply reluctant to concede anything to the Queen of Scots, but the pressure was now very intense. Sussex was directed to give just enough encouragement to James's party to ensure their continued existence, but no promise of outright recognition. The queen still hesitated to spend money on the greedy and unreliable Scottish nobles or to commit herself to whole-hearted backing of an Anglophile party in Scotland. Sussex, more anxious than his mistress to back the king's party, took advantage of his instructions to patch up a working arrangement with them and to advance to Edinburgh with the intention of disarming the opposition lords assembled at Linlithgow.[8]

This move was eminently successful; the Marian lords fled from Linlithgow to Glasgow and thence northward over the Clyde. Led by the Earls of Morton and Lennox, the king's forces burned the castle and palace of Hamilton and wasted the adjoining lands. But before Sussex could assist them in the capture of the Hamilton fortress of Dumbarton, the gate through which foreign assistance might enter, Elizabeth countermanded his advance and ordered his return to the Border. She was frank with Sussex; if she continued to support James's adherents, there must needs ensue a 'kind of war' between her and Charles IX. To that king she now offered to withdraw from Scotland (on condition the French sent no forces) and to open negotiations with Mary. To this proposal Charles IX responded with alacrity and on June 10th wrote that he had countermanded the dispatch of his forces from Brittany.[9]

To these decisions of the great powers the Scottish lords of both factions grumblingly submitted, while the Queen of Scots's agents began to bustle about in expectation of better things to come. In July the king's supporters, headed by the Earl of Morton, came together at Edinburgh to elect Lennox as the new regent. The Marian party refused to acknowledge his authority, and both factions jockeyed uncertainly through the summer while Randolph and Sussex strove vainly to bring them to agreement. But at least for the time being James's government was established in some sort of security. The English rebels were now mostly gathered around Aberdeen under Huntly's protection; from there they began to slip off one by one across the seas to Flanders. Dacre and his followers still haunted the West Marches of Scotland and in late August Sussex again crossed the Border to ravage that area and smash potential support for the rebel. The

Marian lords agreed to abandon support of the English rebels early in September and most of them had left Scotland by the end of November. By mid-September an uneasy truce prevailed in Scotland as both sides girded for the round of negotiations about to begin in England.[10]

The revival of the Queen of Scots's cause had not come to pass without great travail in the English Council. The causes of Scotland, of its queen, and of Norfolk all merged in bitter debates which shook the Privy Council from January onward. The evidence for this struggle comes almost solely from Fénélon, who clearly had a source of information within the Council or its secretariat. Fénélon was generally well-informed on English affairs and usually sound in his judgments. The details of his reports may not always be accurate but their general tenor is likely to be so.

The ambassador had reported the existence in the Council of a 'moderate' faction, friendly to Norfolk and favourable to Mary Stuart, opposed to an 'extremist' group, urging upon the queen harsh treatment of Roman Catholics and continued assistance to the Huguenots. What next to do about the Queen of Scots was under discussion by March, with her friends arguing for restoration to her throne as the queen's safest policy. The threats of French intervention in Scotland which began to be pushed by Fénélon at this point were forcing the issue to a head. But the 'moderates' joined this matter with others in pushing a general policy of appeasement—settlement with France and with Flanders and a pardon for past offenders. One immediate goal was the freeing of the previous autumn's prisoners. Pembroke, already free and returned to Council, was an advocate for those still detained. Lumley was by now free, Arundel still confined to Nonsuch.[11]

In late March Leicester, friendly towards Mary and Norfolk throughout the winter, lent his powerful influence towards efforts for Arundel's release, and on Good Friday the earl kissed hands and was accepted again in the court; Ross, too, confined since February in the Bishop of London's house on suspicion of involvement in the northern rising, was released after Easter. Fénélon saw these moves as a gain for the 'moderate' party and a token of retreat by Cecil and the 'extremists', and credited them to Leicester's support. May saw the two factions wrestling manfully in their efforts to persuade the queen each to its own proposals. She had almost given way to Mary's sympathizers when Bacon skilfully raised the issue of Ross's book on the succession. This gave the queen opportunity to delay and to accede to Sussex's march to Edinburgh. As we have seen, Sussex and his lieutenant, Drury, had by this time scattered the Marian forces effectively, but the threat of French intervention now became so real that Elizabeth bowed to outside pressure, and ordered the Lord President to fall back while at the same time agreeing to negotiations with Mary.[12]

According to the French ambassador, these decisions were arrived at only after prolonged and heated debate in the Council. At one point, he related, the Lord Keeper staged a kind of strike by refusing to attend at the board; at another, when Cecil passionately opposed restitution of Mary, both the queen and Leicester attacked him for inconsistency and deceit and the queen ended by asserting, 'Whatever it may be, Mr Secretary, I want to get clear of this affair and to understand what the king [of France] sends me and not to involve myself any longer with you and your brothers in Christ.' On another occasion the queen, angry and upset, lamented that they put her in great danger by giving such opposing counsel.[13]

The Bishop of Ross's indiscreet involvement with the Catholic Earl of Southampton reawakened Elizabeth's distrust of him and slowed down negotiations, as did the arrival of Pius V's bull deposing the queen, and the discovery of a plot for an uprising in Norfolk. They also prevented the other object of the 'moderates', the release of the Duke of Norfolk from the Tower. But by June 25th the ambassador could write that Cecil and his supporters now saw the queen was determined on a settlement with Mary and accepting that fact had now come forward with a set of conditions.*

At the beginning of August, after several false starts, the Duke of Norfolk was at last delivered from the Tower, where the plague had now broken out, and allowed to retire to Howard House in the city, still under some restraint and not allowed to leave his residence. He had of course signed a submission. Earlier that summer the duke's home countryside had been disturbed by an abortive attempt at a rising. The conspirators, minor local gentry, had at first used the slogan of 'out with the foreigners' (i.e. the Flemish exile weavers). This met with no response; so they tried again with a cry against evil advisors around the queen and a proposal for calling on Alva's aid. They do not seem to have used Norfolk's name or called for his release. The conspiracy was easily suppressed by the local

---

* *Fénélon*, III, 214. Ross met Southampton in Lambeth marsh after dark and held a long conversation with him (innocent enough in the bishop's account). As he wryly observed to Cecil, had he intended harm to the queen, he would have made use of a 'more grave sort' than the earl (*CSPScot, 1569–71*, 203, 218).

magistrates, but the government was worried and investigated closely.[14]

The long debate of the spring and summer of 1570 bore some resemblances to that waged a year earlier, since in both cases a party in the Council was urging a major reversal in the direction of English policy, and in both instances Leicester was a leader in the drive for change. But circumstances were in other respects quite different. In 1569 the enemy was Spain, embodied in Alva, and the issue one directly between England and Spain. In the following year France was the antagonist but the issue at stake was not only a matter of Anglo-French relations but also the future of the Queen of Scots and the larger questions which hung upon her fate.

The argument was at least in part conducted at the level of high policy considerations. The anti-Marians urged the general hostility of Catholic Europe towards the queen, brought up the old bogy of a Guise plot, insisted on the irreconcilability of the queen's religious opponents at home and overseas, and urged strong measures at home, in Scotland and abroad to uphold the Reformed interest. Only by supporting her natural allies could she protect herself. England—it was argued—could take a chance on French intervention since the ships could be stopped before they reached Dumbarton; and Elizabeth was reminded of her father's boldness when faced by foreign aggression. As for Mary some went so far as to hint her life should not be spared, and all urged the queen not to let go free a competitor for her own Crown.[15]

Against these arguments their opponents asserted that France had no basically hostile intentions against England if her just complaints were met (and they emphasized the danger from French power, especially now that the religious wars were damped down). They were able to point to the approaching defeat of the Moriscos in Spain. Elizabeth's sardonic hit at Cecil about his 'brothers in Christ' suggests that they had played too on the queen's distaste for sectaries, whether of domestic or of foreign origin, and when Cecil and his supporters called for the courage of Henry VIII, Arundel bitterly reminded them that Henry was protected by the now shattered umbrella of the Burgundian alliance. In short, they struck all those chords which they hoped would alarm a queen so little disposed to war and so well aware of the fragile position of her state. They probably encouraged Maitland in his opposition to English policy, giving him good hope that they would sway the queen to Mary's side.[16]

This time Cecil's good luck, which had served him so well a year ago, deserted him. Foreign events played into his opponents' hands as they had played into his the previous spring. The Huguenots' protracted negotiations with the court were concluded in an armistice in July and a definitive peace at St Germain in August. The Moriscos' revolt was at last being crushed in Spain, and in the summer English nerves were tried first by the arrival of the papal bull of deposition in June and then by suspicious massing of shipping in the Flemish ports. Allegedly Alva was preparing a fleet to escort the new Queen of Spain home to her husband, but Englishmen feared the ships might descend on Scotland to bring aid to Mary's party. The discovery of the plot in Norfolk in July was worrying evidence of discontent at home. All these factors helped to swing the queen away from the policy of the forward party to a position of compromise.[17]

The contest was not only a policy debate but also a personal struggle, primarily between Leicester and Cecil. The favourite, after abandoning the Duke of Norfolk to his fate in the preceding September, had chosen to stand by his friend – and Mary's – through the months that followed. Presumably Leicester reckoned that the Queen of Scots and the duke were still potent enough in English politics to be worth his continued attention. At any rate he was willing to back them against Cecil in Council. The rivalry with the Secretary was bitter, but beyond that the earl still saw the problem of Mary as one of adjusting her to English political life by fitting her into some scheme satisfactory to English needs. For the time being her restoration to Scotland, under strict terms, seemed much the safest policy. There was no necessary conflict with his commitment to the Puritans; Mary had – as the pamphlet of 1570 pointed out – peaceably coexisted with Protestantism in her northern realm. Probably he calculated that by the time she reached the English throne the Protestant order would be strong enough to make terms with her. He still thought of her as the heir, with whom he must establish a working relationship for the future. His belief that Cecil would back a Hertford succession was probably an additional factor in his attitude.

Even more important was Leicester's reading of the European situation. As he saw it, the best interests of the Protestant cause demanded Anglo-French collaboration against the Habsburgs. The latter posed a grave threat – for different reasons – to both the Protestants and to France. Hence, in spite of religious differences, there was gound for common action between England and France. This, in turn, meant, for the time being, support for Mary Stuart. The next heir to the English throne must be kept at all costs from embracing the Habsburgs as her protectors.

Hence to preserve the link between Mary and the French government might be useful to English purposes at this juncture. An accommodation with France on this issue might lead to other measures of collaboration.[18]

The earl's friendship towards Norfolk is less explicable; but he may have reckoned that the duke's influence, temporarily diminished, was too great to perish altogether, and especially in a Stuart court the princely Howard would necessarily be a great figure. Leicester's policy brought him into collaboration with a strange bedfellow—Arundel. The latter was playing a lone—and eccentric—game, more and more committed to extremist causes. He had contemplated flight to France in the spring and confided to Fénélon his hopes for a renewal of the earls' rising, with Scottish aid, and the eventual restoration of the old religion.[19]

Cecil's position was clear enough; he never wavered in his views of Mary Stuart; he believed that her goal was to attain both the island Crowns; restored to Scotland, she would seek continental aid, and Cecil was gloomy enough to fear that were invasion to come, it would be doubtful how much of English force could be relied on since the Queen of Scots's adherents were to be found in every corner of England.[20]

Sir Ralph Sadler echoed the same outlook. 'God has delivered her to your hands', and the queen should not hesitate to keep Mary prisoner; more hopeful than the Secretary, he reckoned on the internal divisions of the Scots (the Hamiltons really cared only for themselves, not for Mary) to neutralize her supporters there; while he counted on a general international situation fluid enough to give the queen room to find allies. Along with Lord Keeper Bacon, these men fought against any dealings at all with Mary. 'God send Her Majesty a good issue of this Scottish matter whereinto the entry is easy but the passage within doubtful and I fear the end will be monstrous.' So Cecil summed up their position in May.[21]

But the queen was not prepared to run the risks of such a course. She dreaded war, even the unofficial kind being waged in Scotland by Sussex. Her expenses for that expedition had been heavy and it had been necessary to send out Privy Seals for a loan. The Spanish ambassador told his master—and for once he may have been right—that Elizabeth was afraid to call a Parliament because they would insist on discussing the succession. But if real war broke out, there would be no alternative. Moreover—for the moment—Mary had a clear tactical advantage. She had acceded to the harsh terms laid down as conditions for negotiation, including the transfer of the young James to England, and, as Elizabeth admitted to Sussex, it was difficult to see under these conditions how with honour and reason she could continue to keep Mary under restraint.[22]

Somewhat the same considerations probably prevailed in Norfolk's case, once he had made his formal submission and promised not to marry Mary Stuart. Cecil probably felt little enthusiasm about freeing the duke. In July, after Norfolk had made his submission but when there was still no final decision about his release, Leicester was putting about the story that it was Cecil who was dissuading the queen from proceeding, and the Secretary felt compelled to sign a rather curious document in which he formally denied such charges. But at the same time he was secretly keeping watch on the duke and—although the letter is very obscure—may have had some inkling of the duke's continued interest in Mary Stuart. There remains a memorandum critically analysing the submission and ending with, 'His Grace may mean well but he has not said well enough'. The Secretary may have agreed with Bedford's restrained comment: 'The duke's liberty I should like well of, praying God it may in all things be such as it should be for God's glory, the Queen's honour, and that his meaning be as he saith.'[23]

Norfolk passed to his London mansion; the plague-ridden summer drew to its close; and in September, amidst a flurry of preparations on all sides, Cecil and his coadjutor, Sir Walter Mildmay, finally received their commission to proceed to Chatsworth to conduct negotiations with Mary Stuart. Reluctantly Cecil took up his task: 'I am thrown into a maze at this time, that I know not how to walk from dangers. Sir Walter Mildmay and I are sent to the Scottish queen ... God be our guide, for neither of us like the message.'[24]

Nevertheless, Cecil and his allies had contrived a schedule of articles to be demanded of the Scottish queen at which she might well blench. Mary was to confirm the Treaty of Edinburgh, by which she surrendered any claim to the English succession during Elizabeth's life (or the lives of the latter's issue). Scottish foreign policy was to be subordinated to English since Mary could have no league with another power without Elizabeth's consent. Moreover, the young James was to be brought to England to live. There were other provisions, less important but hardly less humiliating and, to cap it all, Mary was to agree that if she violated any of the terms of the treaty she would forfeit all claim to the English succession, and it would then be legal for Elizabeth to use all possible means to place James back on the Scottish throne. For these concessions Mary was to be allowed to return to Scotland to a throne hedged about with numerous capitulations which would secure to Mary's enemies every important office and every major stronghold in the realm.[25]

Had either party the slightest intention of entering seriously into treaty? Cecil clearly intended to do his best to prevent the conclusion of any arrangement whatever. It is hardly coincidence that the charge of negotiations was given over to the Secretary and to his confidant and ally, the strongly Protestant Chancellor of the Exchequer, Sir Walter Mildmay.[26]

On the other side the view taken was probably that of Maitland of Lethington. Smarting under the defeat which his party had suffered at Sussex's hands and brimming over with bitterness against the Queen of England – of whom he wished he might hear she had gone *ad patres* – he nevertheless counselled going forward with the treaty and accepting what terms were offered, because the great point – to be won at all costs – was Mary's liberty. 'I speak all to this end – that her liberty be procured whatsoever the conditions be. Press it the best. If we fail we must accept the worst.' 'Yield to all rather than she remain prisoner, because interim "I think her life ay in danger".' Mary herself, as will be seen, had better hopes for the future, but she was prepared to deal with Cecil and Mildmay and to make the most of what was offered.[27]

The negotiations began at Chatsworth and dragged on at tortoise pace through the winter. Occasions of delay were endless, especially since the king's party in Scotland was determined to block the whole proceeding. Morton, the moving spirit among these lords, saw no way to bind Mary so as to secure Elizabeth's safety and feared that Mary's return home would mean ruin and destruction for his whole party. It was easy enough for them to spin out discussion month after month, raising interminable difficulties. By February 1571 Cecil was speculating how Mary might be retained prisoner and by March he had sketched out a programme for accomplishing this end. A convenient excuse for postponement of the whole matter was found in late March when James's commissioners insisted that they could not act without special warrant from the Scots Parliament. Their opponents objected to such a body as illegal under present conditions, but Elizabeth decreed on March 23rd that all further dealings would be postponed until May, after the meeting of the proposed Parliament.

Before that date various events had occurred; the Regent Lennox had surprised Dumbarton and hanged the Hamilton Archbishop of St Andrews; while Grange, the captain of Edinburgh Castle, had seized the city and driven out the Regent and his government, but refused to declare for either side.[28]

17

An even more decisive factor was the new Anglo-French amity in-augurated by the proposal for Elizabeth's marriage to the Duke of Anjou. This drastically diminished Mary's already dwindling stock of assets; her negotiating position, strong in the spring of 1570, was now, a year later, a very weak one. Worse was to come, for in April the English government stumbled on to the first clues to the Ridolfi plot. The seizure of letters from Flanders to the Bishop of Ross led to investigation and to the deten-tion of the bishop on May 13th. The denouement of this story was delayed for some months; but when it came, it would strike at the heart of Mary's cause.[29]

In the meanwhile, during the trying months of negotiation with Mary and the Scottish factions, the English Councillors were called upon to give their attention to an even more important, and potentially far more fruit-ful, proposal. The whirligig of French politics had spun around in an unexpected way in the summer of 1570. The queen mother, in her tireless struggle to dominate the factions, had made peace with the Huguenots and admitted them to a share in her confidence. In this new situation at the French court, the Vidame de Chartres, one of the Protestant leaders who had spent much time in England and knew the English scene well, obtained Catherine's ear and was able to titillate her ambition for her sons with a fanciful but not wholly unrealistic scheme. Let her match her second son, Anjou, with the Queen of England, and the Valois might well rival the Habsburgs. The two brother kings could unite their forces to seize the Low Countries for the French dynasty; this done, there would be no force capable of preventing the reassertion of French power in Italy—where a Crown might be found for the third son, Alençon.[30] A general council could then be summoned under French leadership and France, England and Germany (i.e. the Protestant princes) would impose a universal religious order to which other powers would have to conform.

Catherine was not likely to be carried away by such fantasies, but she did perceive certain solid and obtainable advantages in a marriage between Anjou and Elizabeth—a Crown for her second son, and the possibility of successful intervention against the Habsburgs in the Low Countries. Hence the vidame's proposal, made sometime in the autumn of 1570, received a favourable hearing at the French court. He and the Cardinal Châtillon had already prepared the ground at the English court through conversations with Cecil. Here also there was a favourable atmosphere and Elizabeth herself opened the matter with the ambassador, Fénélon. These events coincided with the dispatch of Francis Walsingham as the new English ambassador to France. For some time Walsingham, Cecil (Lord Burghley since February), Leicester and Thomas Sackville, Lord Buckhurst, the special ambassador sent to the royal French marriage, were the only Englishmen party to the discussions; gradually others were drawn in. Informal discussions became formal negotiations as the spring advanced and these were protracted into the following autumn.[31]

From the perspective of posterity Elizabeth's recurrent courtships take on the quality of somewhat tasteless comedy; we can be quite certain that in 1571 she had no intention of taking the Duke of Anjou or anyone else as her husband and the details of the abortive treaties which accompanied the courtship seem hardly to claim our serious attention. But for her contemporaries the question was a deadly serious one. They too, of course, suspected her sincerity from the very beginning of discussion. Endless time and effort were wasted in attempts to solve the conundrum of the royal intentions—all vain, of course, since it was both her pleasure and her policy to conceal this vital information. Once she had indicated her maidenly interest in hearing 'of motion and suits for marriages with princes and great estates', her advisors had no alternative but to set in motion the whole diplomatic machinery; yet throughout the protracted discussions which followed, the interminable wrangling over niceties of protocol and the solemn considerations of state policy, no one could quite shake off the feeling of dreamlike unreality that hovered over them. For the English Councillors it was especially difficult to render judgment or give advice when every political equation contained this floating, unknown and unknowable component.[32]

There was a good deal to recommend negotiation from a purely diplomatic point of view. Since 1568 England had been—as the English ministers constantly lamented—in an uncomfortable isolation, at odds with both France and the Habsburgs. The diplomatic weapon of a royal marriage had become seriously blunted and Elizabeth herself at a discount in the international marriage market. Now an unexpected turn of the wheel had opened up novel prospects. After some months during which the English watched with some dismay the approach of a religious peace in France, they were pleased to find the posture of affairs favourable to English interests and their queen once more a marketable commodity in diplomatic commerce. There was every reason to exploit this opening; Mary Stuart's hopes would be effectually dimmed by focusing French interest upon the English queen and England would acquire new bargaining power in dealing with Spain. At the very least a breathing space could be obtained by spinning out discussion with France for as long as possible.

But looking beyond short-term advantage, politicians had to do some awkward sums in the arithmetic of national policy. Theoretically the great desideratum, the grand solvent of all difficulties, was a royal marriage – with royal issue to follow. The many advantages hardly needed to be enumerated, most of all the sense of peace and security among her subjects which would bury 'curious questions of succession, now the ground of all mischief'. But the realization of all these much-to-be-desired goods turned on one condition – that there be an heir. Elizabeth was thirty-seven years old, her bridegroom-to-be of the sickly Valois stock; the chances of a royal child were not high. Might not the price to be paid exceed the value of the goods to be received? (Cecil morbidly considered the possibility that a widowed Anjou, having shortened the queen's life, would then marry Mary and unite the British Crowns in his person.)[33]

Moreover, the specific match in hand had serious flaws. Since Philip, no foreigner was likely to win much favour with Englishmen, and all the old fears of being dragged into unwanted and irrelevant foreign war, as in 1557, came crowding back along with the darker nightmare of becoming a mere satellite of some continental sun. The prince in question was near the throne; should he succeed his brother, there was too good a chance, as Cecil feared – echoing his words of 1565 – that England would become a mere Brittany.[34]

A new note, however, was struck by the new man involved in these discussions – Francis Walsingham. Like his predecessor at Paris a decade earlier – Throckmorton died early in 1571 – the new ambassador was an evangelical imperialist. Foreseeing a Spanish war of revenge on England and deeply dreading the fifth column of malcontents within England, he urged offence as the best defence – a concerted attack on the Low Countries and a division of spoils among England, France and the Prince of Orange. Or in a more pious but no less militant mood, he called for alliance with France against the Papist Burgundian house, enemies of the Gospel; even if the temporal benefits were small, the alliance was worth making.

These conflicting extremes of unreasoning fear and unreasonable hope reflect the grave perplexity of English statesmen faced with so major a shift in the whole structure of England's domestic and international position. Amidst these confusing claims, the royal Councillors had to pick their individual ways as best they could. Convention required that all courtiers should vie in promoting their mistress's marriage. Their actual feelings in the matter naturally varied. Cecil's ill-wishers asserted that he *'qui est roy plus qu'elle'* opposed this or any marriage; the Secretary in his turn managed to insinuate that Leicester's enthusiasm was insincere. Publicly the earl threw himself with great energy into the negotiations and chose to appear as the principal promoter of the match. Cecil did his best to wear the same guise although Fénélon remained unconvinced.[35]

Cecil's attitude was in fact complex. Always prone to bleak views of the future, he feared a French association in which England would be an earthenware pot, ill-suited to travel with a brass companion. Yet, on the other hand, there was the long-deferred hope of a marriage. As he wrote in March 1571, 'If God should order this marriage or any other to take place, you may judge no time would be wasted otherwise than honour may require; I am not able to discern what is best, but surely I see no continuance of her quietness without a marriage.' In the end he came down decisively on the side of the match and struggled for it through the summer. But when the possibility of an alliance without a match began to emerge, doubt again came to the fore in the Secretary's mind. Without the cement of matrimony to give co-operation permanence, he feared the French would 'make us ministers of their appetites and these fulfilled, cast us off'.[36]

Leicester was publicly all enthusiasm for the match. But in Council he was quick to magnify those obstacles—such as religion—which hindered it. And he was counted among those who favoured alliance without matrimony. No doubt, he was, as always, opposed to the queen's marrying, but he did nevertheless seriously seek the completion of a French alliance. He shared with Cecil a deep aversion to the Habsburgs, as the grand promoters of European Catholicism. But unlike the Secretary, who displayed a wary reluctance to any foreign entanglement, the earl looked to a France where the new religion was at least tolerated as the best hope for the future of English—and European—Protestantism.[37] He had been consistent for some years past in promoting the interests of the Huguenots when they were struggling for survival, and now, when they were at least halfway inside the citadel of French power, he was anxious to strengthen them by bringing English and French monarchs into close collaboration.

The comings and goings of negotiation, the alternations of doubt and optimism, and the formal exchange of proposed terms, consumed the months from New Year of 1571 to midsummer. In fact neither of the principals was seriously interested in marriage. Besides the difficulties which Cecil foresaw, Elizabeth's own observation made her sceptical as to the future of the quicksilver politics of France. The other principal, Anjou, vain and ambitious and at that time under strong Catholic influences, was not nearly so anxious for the match as his mother or brother. He professed his devotion to 'the rarest creature that was in Europe these five hundred years', but stubbornly insisted on the rights of his conscience. To Elizabeth's offer of mere external conformity to the English service, he retorted that she wanted him to be little better than an atheist. As the summer went on, both principals hardened in their stands and hope of any workable compromise dwindled away.[38]

As with Elizabeth's other courtships, one cannot pinpoint its termination; Walsingham was writing of the marriage as unlikely by July, but the queen mother was unwilling to give up entirely. In August de Foix crossed over to England as a special ambassador to deal in the matter, 'to conclude either marriage or some streight amity between the two crowns', and after that the character of the discussions gradually changed; yet the ghost of the marriage proposal continued to haunt the English court as late as December.[39] But during the autumn of 1571 the English court was so preoccupied with the great matter of the Ridolfi plot that the French negotiations for a time receded into the background. The possibility of alliance still awaited discussion and decision.

Given our advantages of hindsight, we become impatient in focusing our attention on these intricate, inconclusive and ultimately abortive negotiations over the fate of Mary Stuart or the match between Elizabeth and Anjou. But it is important to recover a sense of the deep anxieties of contemporaries. In spite of the failure of Norfolk and the ruin of the northern earls, Mary's potency in English politics was by no means exhausted. Leading English political figures were still in acrimonious disagreement as to her future, and she was still an important counter in relations with other powers. Her hopes ran high and she remained a focus of disturbance in the English court until the unforeseen swing in French political alignments opened the way for Anglo-French rapprochement. Mary's consequence diminished rapidly; in her dismay at this turn of events she took to desperate courses. In the meantime the English Council gradually realigned itself around the new issue of a French marriage. Disagreement and uncertainty there were, but the disagreement was not nearly so dangerously divisive as that produced by the Queen of Scots. Indeed, there was enough common ground to allow Leicester and Cecil to combine in grumbling co-operation on a major goal of policy.

15 The Ridolfi Plot

THE YEARS 1571-2 were marked by a series of conclusive events which ended much of the worrying uncertainty of the previous two years. The fierce anti-Marian feeling of the 1571 Parliament cut off the hopes of the Scottish queen even before the uncovering of Ridolfi's plot to bring foreign aid to her support. The revelations of the plotters brought Norfolk to the block and ruined Mary's last prospects of building up an English following. Indeed, if Parliament had had its way she might have followed the duke to the same fate. Finally, the conclusion of the Treaty of Blois brought England out of her precarious isolation, and substantially strengthened her hand in international affairs just as they took a new and important turn. All these events rounded off the prolonged crisis which had begun in 1568; the enemies of the regime had been struck down one by one, and its supporters could look forward to the future with an assurance and hopefulness which they had not previously enjoyed.

During the busy weeks when the Councillors were deeply engaged in the Anjou negotiations, and nervously watching the jockeying of the Scots factions, they had to deal with another, more familiar, kind of problem. After a lapse of five years a new Parliament had been elected and met at Westminster on April 2nd. Sovereign and ministers probably felt some nervousness about this gathering. It had been said that a year earlier the queen forbore summoning Parliament for fear they would demand to discuss the succession.[1] In truth relations between 'executive' and 'legislative' were beginning to be awkward because the behaviour of Commons was becoming, in one sense, unpredictable, and in another, all too predictable. Now that a focused and coherent public opinion on the great questions of the day was finding voice in the lower House, it was quite certain in advance that the House would have much to say on these issues. The uncertainty arose from the government's inability to sample or estimate the intensity and direction of public opinion in the intervals between Parliaments. The last Parliament had occupied itself with the questions of the succession, the royal marriage and religion. The pre-occupations of the M.P.s of 1571 are a measure of the rapid and power-ful currents which were carrying the political classes into hitherto unexplored reaches of the religious and political landscape.

The new Parliament was the first which sat under the act requiring subscription to the oath of supremacy. There was at least a sprinkling of men who had links with the Norfolk–Arundel circle, Ferys of St Albans and Barker, one of the duke's secretaries, and Henry Goodere, a Staffordshire gentleman, who was among those arrested in the following autumn. But in general it was a Parliament in which the left-wing Protestants had if anything a more powerful voice than before, as events would soon demonstrate. The government had lost a leading spokesman in the Commons by the promotion of Cecil to the upper House, but the experienced Sir Francis Knollys, seconded by Mildmay, and less ably by the new Comptroller, Croft, was there to speak for the Council.[2]

From the point of view of the government, the gentlemen of the House had been summoned from the counties and boroughs to transact certain necessary business of the commonwealth – to vote a grant of taxes and to pass some legislation rendered necessary by recent events. But the mem-bers, while prepared to do what was required of them for the public service, regarded the meeting as an opportunity for airing their views on a number of great public issues and, if possible, of turning these views into statutes. The relative infrequency of Parliamentary sessions meant that there built up in the intervening years a perfect powder magazine of passionately held convictions, which exploded with great force when the fuse of a royal summons was applied.

In the spring of 1571 the government's legislative programme, aside from the inevitable subsidy, included an additional treasons Act to meet new situations, and some subsidiary legislation to deal with the importa-tion of papal bulls and the problem of Catholic fugitives. Besides this the government was prepared to accept some ecclesiastical legislation; the Parliament was to consider 'whether the ecclesiastical laws concerning the discipline of the Church be sufficient or no'. It was this latter subject which was to engage so much of the Parliament's attention and to reveal such embarrassing divergences between the views of the Commons and those of the queen.[3]

There were, as we shall see, very specific differences of opinion in this sensitive area, but more important still were the underlying attitudes with which Councillors on the one hand and members on the other approached the issue. Both parties agreed on the central importance of religion to civil society, but in the Councillors' view it took its place among other major concerns. In the years since the settlement of 1559 the problem of religion had almost always presented itself to them in its most secular — and political — guise as a facet of foreign affairs, the succession problem, or domestic faction. But many of the impassioned country gentlemen in Commons saw the matter in quite another light. One earnest and anxious M.P., speaking for a goodly number of his fellows, put it thus. After lamenting that causes of such great moment should be so slenderly dealt with, he went on: 'These causes ... be God's. The rest are all but terrene; yea, trifles in comparison. Call ye them never so great, or pretend ye that they import never so much; subsidies, crowns, kingdoms, he knew not, he said, what they were in comparison of this. This, he said, he knew, whereof he thanked God: *primum quaerite regnum Dei et caetera omnia adjicientur vobix*.'4 When this soul-felt zeal encountered the discreet hesitations and the calculated reservations of ministers there was bound to be a sense of embarrassed strain.

Beyond these general considerations, there was what amounted to a major disagreement between the queen and the more radical portion of the House of Commons. The queen's position on the religious question had been fully laid out in two statements issued in 1570. The first, and longer, drawn up just at the close of the northern rebellion, was a general justification of royal policy, but particular attention was given to drawing out the royal view of religion.5 While asserting her authority as next under God to direct all estates 'to live in faith and the obedience of Christian religion and to see the laws of God and man which are ordained to that end to be duly observed', she was emphatic in repudiating 'any superiority in our self to define, decide or determine any article' of the Christian faith or any ancient ceremony used by the apostolic church or to use any function belonging to a minister of the Word and Sacrament. She went on to declare that no subject should be put to examination or inquisition in any matter of faith so long as they accepted the authority of Scripture and of the Catholic creeds, and 'in their outward conversation showed themselves quiet and conformable and not manifestly repugnant and obstinate to the laws of the realm'. This proclamation was directed to be read in every parish church in the land.

In June following, the Lord Keeper in his annual allocution to the judges in the Star Chamber was ordered to repeat substantially the same doctrine, reasserting that the queen would not bother any who attended service as prescribed by law nor molest man's consciences so long as they kept within the letter of the law.[6] This latter was probably intended as a riposte to the papal bull which had just been tacked up on the Bishop of London's door. When Parliament met in the following year, Elizabeth was prepared to expand the law so as to bring within its penalties those who disseminated any papal bull and to penalize those who, by fleeing beyond the seas, sought to evade the law. In effect the queen's *politique* proposal was to invite the Roman Catholics to stay out of politics, to cultivate their own gardens and in return to be left unmolested.

Contrast this attitude with that exhibited in the first bill to be introduced into the Commons, which proposed to stiffen the recusancy fines but, much more important, to compel the taking of communion at least once a year, under penalty of a fine of one hundred marks. After prolonged debate and some notable speeches in favour of a free conscience, the bill passed through both Houses only to receive a royal veto. But it is clear that a majority of both the radical Commons and even the more conservative House of Lords (four lay peers voted against it) were in favour of this measure. Another bill over which the Commons laboured long was one 'for conservation of order and uniformity in the Church', which probably imposed some kind of religious test on laymen and which had as companion a measure compelling the surviving Henrician and Marian clergy to subscribe to the Articles of Religion. (These were to be statutorily confirmed by the first bill.) This bill perished in the House of Lords when the queen sent a message saying she preferred the Articles to be published under royal rather than parliamentary authority.[7]

In these instances the hot crusading zeal of anti-Catholicism had outrun both the Council's purely political concern to safeguard the realm's security and the queen's marked distaste for ideological tests. But the government was to be embarrassed again over one of its own measures — the treasons bill, which was meant to compass offences likely to be committed through the incitement of the papal bull, such as calling the queen a heretic, a schismatic, or not legally monarch of the realm. On the first reading of this bill, Thomas Norton, that articulate and fiery radical, moved another measure, to be tacked on to the government's, which would deny the succession to anyone who claimed or had claimed the Crown during Elizabeth's lifetime or denied her lawful right as queen or refused to acknowledge her as undoubted sovereign. Further, he would extend the exclusion to the heirs of such a person. Any supporter of such a person, or anyone who denied the right of the queen, with Parliament, to determine the succession would be a traitor. After vigorous discussion within the lower House and friction between the Houses, the measure was softened so as to remove its retrospective provision and to delete reference to the heir. It was also left to the queen to proclaim such a person by name before he (or she) became guilty of treason. So amended it was acceptable to the queen and passed on to the statute book.[8] The radicals in the lower House had in this case been able to persuade the government into a bill which, while not acceptable to it, went further, in its pointed reference to the Queen of Scots, than the Council had intended. Here, for those who cared to read it, was a clear enough index of public feeling about that princess.

But apart from these questions of current policy where the sentiment of Parliament, particularly of the representative House, far outran the government's intentions, there was revealed a breach of generations and the emergence of a new impulse in the history of the English Reformation. The parliamentary session of 1571 proved to be a hinge event in the fortunes of English Protestantism. In part the activities of the religious radicals in the Commons carried on the programme they had set in motion in 1566; they revived the bills of that year against pluralities, absenteeism, nonpreaching clergy and so on; there was also brought forward once more the *Reformatio Legum*, Cranmer's corpus of Reformed canon law; and an effort was to be made to reform the Book of Common Prayer by dropping a number of ceremonial requirements although with only minor amendment to the text of the liturgy. These proposals were logical extensions of the work of 1559, the carrying forward to its conclusion of the work of reform; they had been consistently advanced by the left-wingers for over a decade. Almost without exception these bills failed because of government intervention in one form or other at the royal bidding. Gradually the parliamentary reformers must have begun to sense what the queen's servants already too well knew — her implacable hostility to the content of such measures and her anger at the impertinent invasion of the prerogative which she saw in them.

But the character of the left-wing party was itself in the process of radical change as the new generation of Cartwright and Field began to push to the front. Tokens of a new position were not lacking in this Parliament. In the discussions over the bills to enforce subscription to the Articles of Religion it became apparent that there was a shift in the radical position; five years ago their representatives in the House of Commons had striven together with the bishops to persuade the queen to give statutory confirmation to the Thirty-Nine Articles of Religion. Now the radicals were no longer willing to accept all these articles; some at least of the non-doctrinal ones, such as those on homilies or the consecration of bishops, seemed to them not agreeable to the Word of God. Their insistence on this position speedily brought them into disagreement with the bishops. The prelates themselves with a strong element of Marian exiles among them were by no means reactionary, but they were the officers of the establishment who for more than a decade had borne responsibility for the governance of the Church under the terms of 1559. Unconsciously they themselves, once rebels, were becoming defenders of the status quo. Furthermore, like the Councillors, they had good reason to know the strength of the queen's resistance to further reform measures. But the younger generation were firm in their convictions, and firmer still in their contention that decisions on matters of faith were not solely the business of the clergy, even of the bishops. 'That', as Peter Wentworth told them, 'were but to make you popes.' The radicals stood on the brink of a directly anti-episcopal move which would mean a confrontation with the Crown; but that was still a little in the future.[9]

Yet when this Parliament was dissolved on May 29th, the government could take some satisfaction not only in legislation passed, but in a more harmonious, less dangerously obstreperous session, than in 1566. The crisis of 1569 had drawn men into more anxious dependence upon the throne and more lively loyalty. The question of the succession, so tender in 1566, had reshaped itself. It was no less dangerous, perhaps more so, in light of recent events. Mary was proving to be a pole of strong magnetic effect, drawing some to devoted service to her, but with equal force repelling many others. The anti-Marian forces were already becoming a party in themselves; hatred for the Scottish queen had become a focus to draw men to common action—and this before the Ridolfi plot was revealed or even suspected by more than a few. The flaw, the fatal flaw, in their position lay in the mortality of their sovereign: alive, Elizabeth drew men's burning loyalty, but were she to die, where were they to turn? Such thoughts must have been much in the minds of the English Councillors in the autumn of 1571 as, thread by thread, they unravelled the Ridolfi plot.

The government's first inkling that it was sitting on a huge, but as yet unexploded, mine came in April and May of 1571 when the marriage treaty with France was barely initiated. One of Lord Cobham's officers at Dover was so earnestly pressed to pass certain packages that he became suspicious and consulted his master. The bearer, a Gallicized Scot named Charles Bailly, a servant of the Bishop of Ross, was seized and his baggage examined. Almost immediately it was discovered that Bailly carried a new edition, printed in the Low Countries, of a book in favour of the Queen of Scots; but he also carried certain curious letters. Even after his seizure these might not have come to the government's knowledge, since the Lord Warden allowed himself to be persuaded by his ne'er-do-well brother, Thomas, not to pass the letters on to Lord Burghley. The younger Cobham declared the letters would ruin Norfolk, and in the end the Lord Warden sent a substitute package to the Secretary and delivered the actual letters to Leslie, insisting they be opened in his (Cobham's) presence. The wily bishop was able to persuade the Lord Warden that their contents were harmless.[10]

Nevertheless Burghley came to a knowledge of these letters. Bailly was put into the Marshalsea, and by tapping the letters which passed between the imprisoned messenger and his master, and by putting a counter-spy into contact with Bailly, the government was able to penetrate the initial mysteries of the Ridolfi maze. It was not difficult to frighten Bailly into revealing not only the existence of the letters but the gist of their contents, to wit, a conspiracy, sparked by Ridolfi and involving, with papal and Spanish co-operation, an invasion from the Low Countries. According to Bailly, there were two letters addressed in cipher, one to '30' and one to '40', each of whom was an English nobleman. Taxed with this, the Bishop of Ross, who had been taken into custody on May 13th, went so far as to admit to the letters, but declared that '30' was the Spanish ambassador and '40' his own mistress, adding that he had destroyed the letter to her. The English government, thoroughly alarmed but unable to penetrate further into the mystery for the present — the ambassador and Mary naturally denied everything — put Ross under restraint in the Bishop of Ely's custody, allowing him to accompany that prelate down to his diocese. Ross passed a not unpleasant summer with Bishop Cox, hunting, studying the ancient tongues and civilly debating questions of theology with his host.[11]

While the government continued its anxious but unavailing probing into the luxuriant foliage of the Ridolfi plot, they were also exploring the mushroom growth of lesser plots which had sprung up around the Queen of Scots. One of these flourished in the remote countryside of Lancashire, a county notorious for its recusancy, and was centred on the Stanley family, although neither the Earl of Derby nor his eldest son was involved.

Sir Thomas Stanley and Sir Edward, younger sons by a second wife, were the doers in this.

In the summer of 1570, leagued with two other Lancashire squires and a former servant of the Earl of Shrewsbury (now in service with Viscount Montague), they had schemed for the liberation of Mary from confinement. Their plan – or rather plans, for there were variants – was to spirit her away to the Lancashire coast and thence to the Isle of Man or to Scotland, although sometimes they spoke of proclaiming her Queen of England. Some of them met with Mary's steward, Beton, on the high moors above Chatsworth and they exchanged a cipher with the Scottish queen, but it came to nothing. They talked vaguely of finding two hundred men to carry her off safely but admitted this would soon end secrecy; they acknowledged that they lacked arms and munitions and seemed to expect her to provide money. Mary probably did not take them quite seriously and in any case at this time was hoping for the success of her negotiations with Elizabeth. The son of one of these Lancashire squires, Rolleston, was a Gentleman Pensioner and, once he was told of the schemes by his father, revealed all to the authorities. The plot came to the attention of Guerau De Spes, who with his customary inflation of facts reported to his master that the Stanleys could raise ten thousand men and that Montague, Southampton, Lumley and Arundel would join them. As a matter of fact both Norfolk and Montague had turned thumbs down on the plot. In December the Stanleys and Gerard were summoned to court, where they were examined by the Council but let off with a scolding and in February allowed to return home.[12]

In the spring of 1571 there had been another flurry of activity when the meeting of Parliament brought men together in London. Sir Thomas Stanley was approached by a Gentleman Pensioner, Powell, who had a year or so earlier talked with servants of Lumley and Arundel about the possibility of an escape, and who now wished to draw Stanley into another such scheme. This same Powell also got in touch with Sir Henry Percy, the brother of the exiled Northumberland, and held several conversations with him about the possibility of spiriting the Scottish queen away to the east coast. These vague conspirings never got beyond the stage of talk and faded away when Parliament went home. They gradually became known in full to the government after the capture of one of the Lancashire conspirators, Hall, at Dumbarton; he was duly turned over to the English by Regent Lennox and his examination in June 1571 opened the way to further discoveries. These investigations were still going on when the

Ridolfi plot was broken open in September, and a link between the lesser and greater plots was soon uncovered once the Bishop of Ross loosed his torrent of confession. All of the schemes for Mary's liberation had at one point or other come into the bishop's hands and most of them had been passed on to Norfolk for approval. Many great names emerged in these revelations – two earls, Arundel and Southampton, the Lord Lumley (all of whom were confined) and Viscount Montague (who was not). The revelations of this autumn also brought into discredit the Cobhams, thanks to the intrigues of the family black sheep, Thomas, and the weakness of his brother, the Lord Warden. Both were in confinement for a time.[13]

These plotters – or would-be plotters – were a singularly ineffectual lot, talkers – and indiscreet talkers at that – and not doers; and even their talk was wildly impractical. Nevertheless, it was unnerving to the government to uncover this network of intrigue reaching across the country and touching so many sensitive points, involving one of the greatest noble families, servants of the court, and a hitherto reliable and hard-working frontier official, Henry Percy. It gave the government a feeling of profound unease to discover the unreliability – or corruptibility – of men in important posts or of high rank who might all too easily be lured into the shadowy borderlands between loyalty and treason. Above all, it heightened their feelings towards the Queen of Scots, who more than ever seemed to be a kind of centre of infection, a germ-carrier, from whom there rippled out one epidemic of seditious conspiracy after another.

The Council, deeply uneasy, tried in vain to persuade the queen to forgo her summer's progress, especially as their intelligence from the Low Countries recounted the exiles' boasts of an early return under the auspices of a Spanish army. At the very time when the queen was visiting Norfolk's own house at Walden and favourably considering his pleas for final release from constraint – 'even then was it found by a good hap' that the duke was sending money through his servants in the northern Dacre lands to the Marian party in Scotland. The money in this instance came from Mary's ambassador in France, and it was Fénélon who had pressed Norfolk to aid in forwarding the money. It was this episode, quite accidental in character and irrelevant to the Ridolfi plot proper, which offered the government the long-sought clue into the intricacies of that scheme. The intercepted letters to Scotland led the authorities to an examination of Higford, the duke's secretary, who was secretly arrested and taken to the Tower. Under pressure he soon gave way and his revelations opened the way to investigations which within a few weeks laid out to view the whole extent of Ridolfi's schemes, of Mary Stuart's actions over the last several years, and of Norfolk's hidden participation in them not only in 1568 and 1569 but in the interim since.[14]

What was revealed to the eyes of the queen and her ministers was probably not entirely surprising but certainly quite dismaying. First, there was the knowledge that Norfolk, in spite of all the events of the year 1569 and in spite of all his protestations to the contrary, had never severed the link with the Queen of Scots. Communication with the Bishop of Ross had begun even before Norfolk had gone to the Tower—when he lay at Burnham at the beginning of October 1569. Direct correspondence between the duke and Mary had been initiated in the autumn of 1569, and at Christmas and again at midsummer 1570 Norfolk sent a ring to Mary. She was strong in her affirmation of continued attachment and he responded accordingly. There was constant exchange of information and consultation, in which Arundel, Lumley and Throckmorton also participated. They advised Mary on what line to take in the negotiations of 1570 and she gave her counsel on Norfolk's submission to the queen in that summer. The correspondence went on briskly enough while Norfolk was in the Tower but gradually fell off once he was home again in Howard House. Matters thus hung on between the two, the duke always professing his devotion to Mary but refusing on every occasion which presented itself to take any risky action on her behalf and always counselling patience.[15]

Early in 1571 the Queen of Scots gave events a sharp new turn. Since the death of the Regent Moray she had been content to pursue a policy in which she relied upon the French to apply pressure both in Scotland and in England, while looking for the release of Norfolk and the renewal of her party in England itself. Committed to this general line of action, she had entered into the negotiations with Elizabeth, hopeful of winning her own liberty. By January 1571 she began to lose hope in this strategy as the negotiations lost themselves in a morass of petty dispute which did not conceal the favoured position of Mary's enemy, Morton, now the leader of the Protestant party in Scotland. More important still, the new constellation of French politics and Elizabeth's marriage negotiations with Charles IX was robbing Mary of effective aid from France. The Queen of Scots had come to expect little initiative from Norfolk, but in the strategy on which, at Ridolfi's urging, she was about to embark, the duke had an important part to play.[16]

The Scottish queen's decision to turn to Alva, Philip and the pope for assistance of course played into the hands of Ridolfi. That hopeful schemer had passed unscathed through the storms of 1569 and in fact gradually won the confidence of the government to the point where he had audience with the queen in the spring of 1571. After Ridolfi was released by the English government in November 1569 he revealed to the Bishop of Ross that he had a commission from the pope as the latter's agent in England. When Pius V issued the bull *Regnans in Excelsis* deposing Queen Elizabeth, Ridolfi had arranged for printing copies of it for distribution in England, and he was the agent through whom the papal gift of twelve thousand crowns for the English exiles in Scotland reached England.[17]

During 1570 Ridolfi was busy with proposals for action. In July he was urging on Pius V his old favourite scheme of a Catholic embargo of England, backed up now by the authority of the bull against Elizabeth. In September he was reporting that 'some of these lords' have promised Alva they would rise if he provided arms and money and asked that the pope send money to Flanders for this purpose.[18]

In January 1571 Ridolfi received dispatches from the papal nuncio in Paris, to be transmitted to Mary, which promised that, should the treaty with Elizabeth fail, the pope would provide the money and Philip the troops for an invasion of England in her behalf – provided that the queen's friends in England would rise to assist the invading force. Mary seems to have hesitated, still hoping for something from the treaty, but by March those faint hopes had perished and she now wrote to the Bishop of Ross commanding him to see the Duke of Norfolk; she armed him with a letter to that peer from her.

This document contained a shrewd review of her situation, in which she drew up her political accounts. France, she saw, was interested in her largely as a pawn in their negotiations for an English alliance; her own fate interested them only to the extent of blocking any match she might seek with Don John of Austria (here Norfolk was useful to them). Spain, on the other hand, although interested in an accord with England, would be very loath to see a Scottish settlement which utterly ruined the Catholic cause in Britain. Hence it was to Philip that she must turn. But here came the crucial turn in her argument; Spain would support her only so long as her cause was that of Catholicism. She could of course meet this condition by marrying Don John, but this she would not do – having faith that the Roman Catholic faith in Britain would be restored by Norfolk. She ended by commending Ridolfi as the fittest agent to deal with the Catholic powers.[19]

18

A somewhat hesitant Ross now put pressure on the very reluctant Norfolk to see the Florentine, and two clandestine interviews at Howard House ensued. The duke agreed to summon his friends if Alva sent over ten thousand troops (including three to four thousand cavalry) to land at Harwich. Ridolfi then insisted on letters of credence to carry to Alva, Philip and Pius V. Norfolk balked at this, refusing to sign anything but sullenly agreeing to verbal assurances (confirmed to the Spanish ambassador through the duke's secretary) of his assent to the plea for aid. In the document which reached the pope, Norfolk says—or is made to say by Ridolfi—that he is himself a Catholic (previous behaviour to the contrary), that he wishes to restore the ancient faith in England and that he will prepare either Harwich or Portsmouth for the reception of Philip's forces.[20]

Armed with these potent documents Ridolfi, having paid his respects to Queen Elizabeth at Greenwich around Eastertide, set off cheerfully for Brussels. It was his optimistic reports of his interview with the Duke of Alva, in letters to Norfolk ('40') and Lumley ('30') which were intercepted by the English authorities in April. In fact Alva had done nothing but dispatch Ridolfi on his way to Rome and Madrid. The pope recommended him to Philip and, in a letter smuggled to Norfolk by Ross, promised aid. But Pius V warned the duke that nothing could be done during the current year. In Madrid Ridolfi got a hearing, but it was July before Philip gave a very cautious and conditional approval to further consideration of the proposal. Before that month was out the Curia knew that some part of the plot had been discovered, and warned Ridolfi not to return to England. Later the king received dispatches from De Spes detailing the whole catastrophe to Catholic hopes, and by November all the king could do was to instruct his new viceroy in the Low Countries to hold all action in abeyance, reserving the two hundred thousand crowns allotted by Philip for an English enterprise for some future opportunity.[21]

Ridolfi was still dabbling in English matters at Brussels in the autumn of 1571,[22] but soon, with the same wonderful inconsequence with which he had entered on the stage of English affairs, he departed, to be heard of no more in the island. (He died in Florence in 1612 after many peaceful years in his native city.) Of his successes and failures on the Continent the English government knew little, but the very full confessions which they had 'bolted out' of Bishop Leslie and the duke's secretaries laid open quite fully enough the schemes of the Queen of Scots and the follies of her would-be husband.

The former's actions were those of a frantic woman, angry, frustrated, almost despairing, who, seeing her enemies blocking up every path of action, turned now to more desperate courses than she had hitherto pursued. Up to this point Mary had pinned her hopes on a manipulation of events within Britain which would lead to her liberation from Elizabeth's clutches. With the necessary added leverage applied by France, she had high hopes of being once more her own mistress. But the resolute intervention in Scotland, planned by Cecil, executed by Sussex and backed, for once, by their mistress, wrecked all hopes of an effective Marian revival in that country, while the sudden turn of events in France had offered Mary's enemies an opportunity which they eagerly grasped. And in England itself the weary irresolution of Norfolk, without whom no other magnate would budge, had dimmed her once bright hopes of effective support within the kingdom.

Under these harrowing conditions, irritable and impatient, she had entrusted her fortunes to a man whom she had never met and of whom her ambassador in London thought little, whose recommendations were slight, and whose past experience in matters of high politics was modest.[23] What she did not know was that while his motives were above reproach and his actions all well-meant, he possessed a fertile, indeed a boundless, imagination and the slenderest judgment. (Surely one of the most astonishing elements in this whole wilderness of muddled intrigue is the willingness of both Mary Stuart and Pope Pius V to entrust such grave issues to so inadequate an agent—and one known to neither of them. Ridolfi's powers of self-promotion must have been staggering.)

Mary had chosen badly in her reliance on Ridolfi; more important, she had taken a decisive step on the long, downhill road to her own destruction. In English politics she had always had to act from the periphery, using men over whom her mastery was but fitful and uncertain and methods which were hardly within the accepted rules of the political game, while she was buffeted by events over which she could exercise little or no control. Nevertheless, she had continued to operate within the regular orbit of English (and Scottish) politics. Now, with her commitment to the Ridolfi plot, she was deliberately—although perhaps desperately—embarking on the veering uncertainties of foreign conspiracy with the view of driving her rival from the throne of England by armed Spanish intervention. From this road there was no turning back; henceforth any hope of manipulating British politics to her advantage by purely domestic means was closed to the Queen of Scots; she could gain her ends only by invoking the intervention of foreign arms from outside the island.

For the unlucky Norfolk the situation was an even more desperate one. He was brought at last to that 'marvellous streight'[24] which the contradictions of his position had always threatened. Hitherto he had refused to face these furies, but now they were upon him and not to be denied. He had failed to use his own power and that of his friends within the realm to procure Mary's delivery by treaty; now he must turn to foreign princes to accomplish this, and their aid was to be bought only at the price of the mass. No longer could he straddle the fence betwixt Catholics and Protestants, calling himself one of the latter but wooing the former. The duke had to take the fatal plunge which placed him outside the English law and placed in mortal jeopardy not only his own life but the whole future of the house of Howard.

The duke had brought himself to this pass by no conscious decision or deliberate commitment. Initially he had allowed himself to be lured into the prospective match with the Queen of Scotland; in the fateful September weeks of 1569 his own irresolution had destroyed the greatest – and most dangerous – opportunity of his career. There had followed the bitterest humiliation. From that time on, lack of will had paralysed any action towards the relief of Mary, while obstinacy and pride had kept him sullenly but unyieldingly loyal to her person. To every scheme which was advanced for her escape he found objection; and he seemed to offer the impatient prisoner at Tutbury little more than advice to be patient and wait upon events.

But Norfolk remained very susceptible to aspersions upon his own character and very open to the pressures which those wily plotters, Mary, Leslie and Ridolfi, knew how to bring to bear upon him. Mary had no hesitation in throwing up to him the lost opportunities she and hers had passed by at his urging. Ridolfi even more bluntly spoke of the duke's honour, lost by his faintheartedness in 1569 or by his betrayal of the northern earls, matters to be undone only by bold actions now. Otherwise – Ridolfi and his mistress both hinted – there were other, braver, champions, Don John or the Duke of Anjou, waiting to play St George to the distressed Queen of Scots. All this was infinitely galling to the senior peer of the realm and an all-too-effective goad to force his acquiescence in Ridolfi's plans.[25]

Once the government had at its disposal the full burden of evidence it was not slow in taking action against the duke. But the Howard name still had a credit balance to draw on, and the Council moved with caution. There had been popular sympathy for the duke when he was taken to the Tower a second time; and he still had friends at court, even at the time of his trial. The discoveries of the early summer had not involved the duke's name, and his long confinement in Howard House for an offence officially forgiven over a year earlier may have made him seem a mistreated man in popular estimation. In any case the government took care to make its case against him generally known before the actual trial, first at a gathering of noblemen in the Star Chamber and later at a Guildhall meeting when Recorder Fleetwood gave a full account to the Londoners.[26]

With tension already running high, it was again augmented by the discovery of another plot. About a fortnight before the opening of the Norfolk trial, Burghley received through the London post a mysterious communication warning him of a plot—in which the anonymous writer was involved—upon the Secretary's life. Burghley was probably already put on to this conspiracy through his ubiquitous spy, Herle. At any rate, by mid-January two loose-tongued and woolly-headed desperadoes, Edmund Mather and Kenelm Berney, were in custody and had confessed their intended misdeeds. Both were Norwich-born, of good families. Mather had fled to the Continent to escape the consequences of a brawl in Norwich; Berney had served in the English embassy in Paris as a secretary. Both had returned to England in the summer of 1571 expecting to serve in a rebellion which would place Mary on the throne.

They talked together about the plight of the Duke of Norfolk and had gone so far as to post a writing of Mather's (Berney tacked the papers up) in various prominent spots which they hoped would discourage an immediate trial of the duke. Their motives seem to have been principally self-seeking, the hope that a grateful duke might help them to some advancement. In the end they talked themselves into graver matters and began to consider ways of killing either (or both) Lord Burghley and the queen. At some point Herle came into their counsels, and all was soon up with them.[27]

The whole business seems to have been one of two empty-headed, large-mouthed and needy rogues. The one more alarming feature of it was the conversations which Mather had had with the Spanish ambassador and the latter's secretary in which vague but unmistakable encouragement had been given by the secretary to Mather's murderous thoughts. The ambassador was already on his way—under escort—to the coast, expelled for his share in Ridolfi's activities, but the government hauled the secretary back to London for questioning. The episode had its grotesque absurdities, but there was always an outside chance that such lunatic fringe activities would succeed. In any case it served to raise the political temperature yet another degree or two.

The trial itself came on in January before the court of peers meeting under the Lord Steward's chairmanship. That high office, which sprang to life only on these solemn occasions, was filled by George, Earl of Shrewsbury, Mary Stuart's keeper, the holder of one of the realm's most ancient titles, a great Midlands magnate and widely respected for his integrity and uprightness. The twenty-six peer-judges numbered nearly half the whole body of nobles. The next senior peer after Norfolk, the octogenarian Marquess of Winchester, was excused, but virtually all the earls were there; the absentees (the imprisoned Arundel and Southampton apart) included only Derby, now in the last months of his life, and the young earls of Rutland, Oxford and Cumberland. All the peers of the Council sat, but so did a senior surviving Catholic nobleman, the Earl of Worcester. It could reasonably be said to be a wide representation of the English peerage.

The government was probably anxious to avoid the imputation that still lingered around the condemnation of Norfolk's father, Surrey, that he had been done to death for very light causes. The case against the duke was prepared with care; three main charges of treason were alleged against him: (1) that he conspired to overthrow the queen and alter the constitution of both state and Church; (2) that he succoured the northern rebels while fugitives in Scotland; and (3) that he aided the queen's enemies in Scotland—Hamilton, Herries, Hume, et al. The first charge was clearly the heaviest and was made to include both the scheme for marrying Mary and the Ridolfi plot.[28]

Although the evidence the Crown could adduce against the duke in his dealings with Ridolfi would surely have been damning enough, the government went out of its way to introduce the marriage scheme of 1569 and to construe it as treason. The Crown's lawyers argued that Mary unlawfully laid claim to the throne in her own right, that Norfolk knew this, that he sought her hand solely with the intent of furthering Mary's claim to England, that he meant to do this by force—and 'all these matters considered, the seeking of this marriage in this form must needs be high-treason within compass of the Statute of 25 of Edward III'.[29]

The argument may have been a bit strained, and certainly it was casuistical to turn the duke's own contemptuous phrases about Mary, which he used to excuse himself to Elizabeth in December 1568, into a demonstration showing that it was neither for her charms nor for her kingdom of Scotland that he sought her hand. Nevertheless from the government's point of view it had the satisfactory aspect of exposing the entire course of both the Scottish queen's actions and those of her suitor from the time of the York hearing onward. The trial afforded an opportunity, which the government exploited with skill, of laying before the assembled peers a detailed account of the Queen of Scots's actions almost since her arrival in England. Extensive documentation was provided; details were spelt out fully and her dealings, not only with Norfolk but with the northern rebels, and now with the pope and the Habsburgs, were exposed at length and with convincing proofs. She was spared nothing in the proceedings, being referred to as the 'late queen of Scots', who 'falsely, wickedly, and unjustly usurped the style, title, and regal name of this kingdom of England'.[30] In short the occasion became as much a trial of the Scottish queen as of the Duke of Norfolk.

The duke undoubtedly suffered from this, being presented as a more deliberate traitor than the facts of his feckless behaviour really justified. The duke faced the usual grave disabilities of a sixteenth-century Englishman accused of treason, yet by contemporary standards the trial was not outrageously unfair in its conduct. But it was naturally devised to show the duke as a man who proposed to 'endeavour a change and alteration of the sincere worship of God, well and religiously established in the said kingdom' and 'to subvert and destroy the whole constitution of the said state, so happily instituted and ordained in all its parts' and to do all this by the use of 'divers aliens and foreigners'.

The evidence presented was full, detailed and weighty enough to convince an impartial hearer of the duke's voluntary—although increasingly half-hearted—participation in plots dangerous to the established order. In his defence he relied heavily on bare denial and even more on the imputation that the witnesses against him were men of too little weight to convict a duke. 'He is a Scot', was his contemptuous dismissal of Leslie's evidence, but as Sergeant Barham retorted, 'A Scot is a Christian man'.[31] As for his servants, even though they were not able to spend five marks a year, yet the credit of their testimony was sufficient for the purpose at hand. The duke was plainly told, 'You may not stand upon your honour and difference of degree and thereby limit how far they are to be credited.' There is a hint here that throws some light on many of the duke's actions.

However foolish or however dangerous he knew his actions to be he could never quite believe that a high-born Duke of Norfolk could be brought to account for them. While acknowledging the just rights of the Crown or the limits set out by the law, he could not quite believe that he should be made to suffer the punishments for disobedience laid down for lesser men.[32]

So he stood condemned by the voice of his peers; but he was not yet to meet his end. There were still voices about the queen urging her to mercy. At the end of January, a fortnight after the trial, the queen actually signed the death warrant on a Saturday night but cancelled it on Sunday evening. Fénélon wrote that the Countess of Surrey and Henry Howard, the duke's brother, had been to beg for his life; Burghley wrote mysteriously of secret causes for the stay of execution. The queen herself spoke of his high degree and his nearness in blood to the throne.[33]

Among Elizabeth's advisors there was virtual unanimity of opinion as to the duke; he must die for the safety of the sovereign and of the state. Burghley in a characteristic memorandum set forth with almost scholastic precision a demonstration of this harsh necessity. Mercy shown the duke would only purchase increased danger to 'the Queen's Majesty's party' since the 'adverse party' needs must increase when they saw justice forborne against the duke. 'What more hope can be given to the evil than to see impunity which some interpret to fearfulness of the Queen, some to lack of power in her hand, by God's ordinance; yea, some to the Scottish queen's prayers and fasting.' Sadler had made up his mind even before the trial; Hunsdon from Berwick and Smith and Walsingham from Paris added their voices. Even the conservative Shrewsbury, whose voice had broken as he read the sentence against his fellow peer, could only pray that the queen might 'use that to the duke that may be most for Her Majesty's own quietness and surety to her'. Nonetheless the queen continued to waver; the order for execution was again given and withdrawn in February. By March sermons were being preached against the duke. Late in the month the queen was very ill, a frightening experience for her court at any time; at this juncture, a traumatic one.[34]

It was just at this point that writs were issued for a new Parliament (March 28th). Although there is no direct evidence, there is a strong probability that the queen gave in to Council pressure to call the Houses together.[35] She herself was increasingly reluctant to meet that body, and the usual occasion for summoning Parliament, the need for money, did not exist at this time. We may suppose that the united pressure of her

Councillors and the rising clamour outside the court pushed the queen into grudging consent. In any case it bought time for her, and perhaps the half-conscious hope that she could shift the responsibility for Norfolk's death on to the shoulders of the Houses.

Rumours flew about London that Parliament would meet to confiscate the goods of rebels, to take measures against Spain, or, in regard to Ireland, to ratify the treaty with France, but all assumed that something would be done about the succession; possibly the queen would ask power to leave the Crown by will like her father.[36] Speculation turned towards the Hertford children, towards the young James (or even his uncle, Darnley's younger brother); Huntingdon and Leicester were spoken of again. It was said that the queen had most trusted Leicester during her recent illness (he and Burghley had watched by her bed for three nights).

The opening speech of Lord Keeper Bacon on May 8th gives at least some clues to the queen's intentions and throws light on the state of mind of the government in the wake of the previous autumn's discoveries. Both the Privy Council and the rest of the wisest persons in the realm — the Keeper said — agreed that existing laws were inadequate to deal with the great treasons and notable conspiracies recently revealed through the providence of God. No clearer guidance than this was given at that point; but the Speaker, Robert Bell, was more explicit in his disabling speech when he declared that there was a person in the land whom, many thought, no law could touch. He was bold in asserting that any person, of any condition, committing felony within the realm should die for the same. But although the law could deal with the matter, it was best to have the consent of Parliament, to wipe out the error that the Queen of Scots (he never mentioned her by name) was above the English law and to consider remedy. This speech may very well have echoed — or indeed reproduced — the views of the leading Councillors. There can be little doubt from their later comments that they hoped for nothing less than the destruction — i.e. the death — of Mary Stuart through the action of Parliament.[37]

The course of events in the session is interesting. The first step was the appointment of a joint committee of both Houses to deal with 'the great cause' now before them. Its first action was to arrange for a long report to the Commons by Thomas Wilbraham, Attorney of the Court of Wards, who had been one of the principal Crown prosecutors in the duke's trial. He was called upon to rehearse in a longish speech the whole burden of the case against Mary Queen of Scots. With great thoroughness he went back to the beginning of the reign, to the quartering of the

English arms by Francis and Mary in 1558 and 1559. The point of all this ancient history was, of course, to draw out the implication that the marriage scheme had aimed at displacing Elizabeth from the throne. He was to display the Scottish queen as a contestant not merely for the succession but for the incumbency of the English Crown. The details of the Ridolfi plot in all its ramifications were laid out in full.

The debate in Commons which followed left no doubt as to the sentiment of the articulate members; one followed another in denouncing the Queen of Scots and in demanding not only her exclusion from the succession but also her life. There were a few voices raised in favour of the Queen of Scots, raising doubts about Parliament's jurisdiction over a sovereign queen, or arguing that at the least she should be given a hearing. These men had some difficulty getting a hearing in a restive House, but the one indiscreet burgess – Arthur Hall – who bluntly reminded them that the Queen of Scots might one day be their mistress – 'You will hasten the execution of such whose feet hereafter you would be glad to have again to kiss' – was arraigned before the House for his lewd speeches and forced to submit.[38] In many members' minds to speak in favour of the Queen of Scots was an act dangerously close to treason.

In the midst of this warm discussion, Sir Francis Knollys rose to give the House a hint as to the most profitable line of action by warning them off any attempt to establish the succession; there was little prospect of winning royal consent to any proposal of that kind. He further urged them against formal petition, suggesting instead a more informal statement of their opinion. The House agreed to this although Norton tried to persuade them to the stronger alternative of petition. The joint committee now came forward with formal proposals. Their own wish was to attaint Mary of high treason and by a second bill to declare her incapable of succeeding to the throne. But the queen, they were informed, wished to defer the first proposal and to proceed for the present only with the second; the perils of the plague in the London summer and the imminent arrival of the French embassy for ratification of the Treaty of Blois were reasons for the speedier procedure of a disabling bill.[39] But the thoroughly aroused M.P.s balked at so milk-and-water a proposal and insisted upon proceeding to attainder.

The queen now more formally asserted her wishes to the House through Sir James Croft, that they proceed only with the disabling bill, setting aside attainder for the time being. But the House once again returned to their previous position. Desperately fearful for the future and ruthless in

their determination to sweep away the great source of all their fears, they
one after another begged the queen, for the weal of all, to proceed to the
last merciless extreme against her Scottish cousin. In the end the House
resolved to go forward with the attainder bill, joining to their resolution
a request that Norfolk be brought to the block before the end of the
present session of Parliament. The Lords joined in the determination to
go forward with attainder of Mary although, as it was their membership
which had already judged the duke, they felt they had already spoken on
that subject.

The next move was to draw up a petition to persuade the queen to their
way of thought. This was to be in the form of a treatise; the first part
written by the bishops adduced an oppressive abundance of biblical (largely Old Testament) precedents. The laity added their contribution in suitably secular terms. Picking up the dispute which had ranged discursively
over the last decade as to the Scottish queen's rights in the succession, they
flatly declared that 'we do take it for a known truth that both by the laws
and statutes in this land now in force she is already disabled'. Then, in
nakedly Machiavellian terms, they pointed out to the queen that her only
security for the future – and theirs – lay in the death of Mary. Nothing
else would keep the latter from 'her malicious intent to subvert Your
Majesty and to give a push for the Crown come of her what will'.[40]

This time the queen summoned a delegation of the House to court and
again thanked the Commons for their goodwill and zeal, admitted the
weight of their advice, but urged that given present circumstances a bill
of attainder should be deferred while an act on Mary's title should be
carefully drawn up; in the meantime she forbade any more discussion on
the matter in either House.[41]

The Commons, balked on one front, now swung back to attack their
other enemy, and a rising clamour for the immediate execution of Norfolk
filled the House day after day.[42] Once again a Machiavellian note was
sounded in the crisp arguments of Thomas Dannet, a minor official figure
and connection of Burghley. Mercy or justice could be used by a prince
in dealing with enemies, but once the latter had been allowed its course
and condemnation had taken place, only severity served. 'Mercy, coming
after honour stained, irritateth rather than appeaseth.'[43] It was a shrewd
comment on the condemned duke's behaviour. The agitation of the
House was now rising to a crescendo; in the last days of Whitsun-week
Knollys was barely able to restrain them from too-insistent pressure on
the queen. They adjourned for the week-end; early in the morning of

Monday, June 2nd, before they reassembled, the duke finally went to his fate on Tower Hill.

One goal, at least, had been achieved. In the meantime the Lords received a bill on the Queen of Scots's title, acted rapidly on it, and passed it on to the Commons. They, in spite of government prodding towards speed, took their time in debate so that Parliament had to be adjourned for thirteen days during the reception of the French embassy of ratification. The bill laid before them—a bill with conciliar backing—began with a preamble which recited at length the case against Mary (a repetition of Wilbraham's report) and continued with a petition that the queen act as soon as possible to punish these treasons. Its clauses of enactment declared Mary incapable of any interest or title in the Crown of England, and provided that any claim on her part during Elizabeth's lifetime or any attempt by Mary's supporters would result in the Scottish queen's indictment for high treason. And after Elizabeth's lifetime, any attempt to claim the English Crown by Mary would put her outside the law. It was to be made treasonable to support the Marian claims in any way. Additional clauses ascribing the agitation for Mary to Rome made it treasonable to do anything with the intent of re-establishing papal authority in the realm, and finally—a vain gesture towards the future—there was an indemnity clause for all actions or speeches against Mary.[44]

The debates in the House centred largely about the implication in the bill that Mary had a claim to the throne of England. One member after another was insistent in denying that such a claim had ever existed—and so, clearly, wanted to make explicit the implicit exclusion of James. The result of this was the addition of a proviso that nothing in the bill should be expounded to affirm any title in the succession to any person.[45]

In the steady succession of speakers who rose one after another to condemn Mary and all her works, only one interrupted the litany of condemnation—Francis Alford, whose courageous intervention in behalf of Mary's civil rights won him the ill will of the House. Protesting that he thought her 'as vile and as naughty a creature as ever the earth bare', he insisted that nonetheless she should not be condemned unheard nor denied the protection of the law. Norton's characteristic retort was that Mary had already committed overt treason and only the queen's lenity protected her from present penalty. The bill with its proviso and other amendments was passed by the House of Commons, approved in its altered form by the Lords, and so awaited the royal decision on the final day of the session, June 30th. That came in a curious form. The queen was resolved not to accept the bill, yet she felt compelled to temporize at least in form. Hence, while using the traditional formula of veto – '*la royne s'avisera*' – she explained that the phrase was to be taken in its literal sense, that she partly approved, partly disapproved, of the measure so that no final action was implied. Parliament was to stand prorogued until the next All Saints Day.

The bill was almost certainly a Council measure, not so extreme as most of them would have wished but probably representing the maximum they thought acceptable to the queen. It impugned Mary Stuart's title as thoroughly as the law could devise and brought her as close to the effects of an attainder as was possible without the real thing. Shrewdly the bill avoided any precise statement as to where the succession did in fact lie (even the Commons' proviso did not touch that). The *cri de cœur* to which Cecil gave vent to Walsingham expresses the bitter disappointment of the Council at its failure to persuade the queen at least to the disablement of Mary from the succession.[46]

They could take some comfort in the fact that Mary's most dangerous instrument within England, the Duke of Norfolk, was now permanently removed and no Englishman seemed likely to come forward to fill his place. But the nightmare which intruded itself on their consciousness in March during the queen's illness had still to be lived with. One speaker after another in the recent Parliament had laboured the obvious point – that all the legal prohibitions the lawyers of England could devise were fragile barriers against Mary's claims should Elizabeth die. Just what the Councillors – or M.P.s – did intend, even if the queen had accepted the proposed statute against Mary, is far from clear. It is noteworthy that nothing seems to have been said in Parliament, either in 1571 or in 1572, on the question of marriage, although two different matches, with Anjou or with Alençon, were under active consideration.

In all probability most men first of all despaired of Elizabeth's marrying and, second, were sceptical, even in that unlikely event, of the appearance of an heir. In other words their hopes must have been centred now on the succession. But what did they hope for? Foreign ambassadors most often spoke of the Hertford children as favoured, and Burghley was frequently referred to as their adherent. But there was opposition to that claim and to others no better or no worse. A few perhaps began to think of James of Scotland, but he was only six years old and the chances of Scottish politics were far too uncertain to bank on his survival, let alone his future religious and political orientation. In fact the English politicians found themselves in a frustrating, even infuriating, kind of impasse. The whole thrust and weight of opinion in the House of Commons was almost hysterically anti-Marian, and there is little doubt that it represented the majority of the political classes, but they had no alternative towards which to turn as a focus of action—either as a husband for the queen or as a successor. Something of the irritability of their frustration spills over into their venomous antipathy for Mary.

This Parliament was too preoccupied with the great issue before it to have much time left over for other matters. Nevertheless, the indefatigable spokesmen of the religious left managed to bring forward a measure of really audacious character. This bill began with a preamble which strongly criticized the Book of Common Prayer and slightingly implied that it was pabulum fit for the weak digestions of 1559 which were now ready for stronger food. It proposed to allow an individual parish to deviate from the text of the Prayer Book—in a Protestant direction, of course—if the bishop approved; it would even be open to the minister to employ the service of the French or Dutch congregations.[47] The ostensible reason for introducing it was that parsons were being prosecuted for any slight deviation, such as the wrong scriptural reading or the like. The bill got favourable hearing and reached third-reading stage before royal intervention occurred; Knollys and Speaker Bell had already interfered to soften its provisions so as merely to meet the alleged grievance rather than to bring in a revolution in the Church of England by the back door. But the queen would not even accept this mild measure, and her prohibition on any religious bills which had not received episcopal approval held.

Before Parliament was prorogued, the famous manifesto of the Puritans, *The Admonition to Parliament*, had been issued, too late to have any direct influence upon proceedings but the token of an important shift in English religious history. The Puritan effort in the Parliament of 1572 had probably been, in the nature of things, a makeshift one, but their success in drawing the House with them showed an easy command of manoeuvre and the strength of their appeal to a large part of the membership. More important still, it was another evidence that in religious matters there was now an initiative coming from outside government circles, an impulse to political action which owed nothing either to the Crown or to the Council (although there were Councillors not unsympathetic to this particular measure). It was another symptom of the broadening base of political life within a nation stirring to new self-consciousness.

The meaning of these parliamentary transactions was plain enough for those who had eyes to read. Whatever claims of right Mary Stuart had to the English succession meant little or nothing to the angry country gentle-men at Westminster. The Queen of Scots's cause, which had seemed to Cecil so strongly based in 1569 when he feared she would win the backing of all moderates and lovers of a settled future, was now fatally flawed. The very men whose defection Cecil had dreaded were now numbered among her bitterest enemies, joining in the clamour for her head. Henceforward the surest check to the ambitions of Mary in England was the deadly hatred she excited in the most influential ranks of the English gentry.

While the liquidation of the Ridolfi plot cleared away the last traces of the domestic crisis which had begun in 1568–9, and the Queen of Scots was safely neutralized in her Midlands prison, English foreign relations took a new turn of major consequence with the conclusion of an alliance with France. Negotiations had dawdled during the crowded autumn of 1571 as the possibility of marriage faded, but they were kept alive and there was talk of a special English envoy to Paris. By the time he was appointed in December important changes had occurred at the French court. In October the Spanish had won their world-resounding victory at Lepanto. Philip, freed at least for a time from his preoccupations in the eastern Mediterranean, was able to turn westward again. The French court looked with some restlessness at this shift in power relationships. The king, although never so enthusiastic about his brother's aggrandize-ment as their mother, was strongly anti-Spanish in feeling. And now the appearance at court of the Admiral Coligny, the grand master of the Huguenot party, offered a bright prospect for the English. Walsingham wrote with unaccustomed cheerfulness that the English could have any-thing they wanted while their friends were in power at court. Coligny's major move was to arrange the marriage between the young Henry of Navarre and Catherine's daughter, Marguerite, but he was also disposed to push the cause of an English alliance.[48]

In December Sir Thomas Smith went as special ambassador to France, instructed to deal confidentially with the Admiral and empowered to seek a defensive alliance with France. (Walsingham was ill and away from the French court for some months.) Alliance without marriage had been mentioned as long ago as August, and had from the beginning had a warm adherent in Walsingham. Sir Francis argued that during the great days of the Burgundian alliance England had been the stronger power in the partnership; now that Burgundy was transformed into Austria the situation was reversed. Moreover, the Habsburgs had a grudge against England as well as being its religious enemy. To these reasons for a French alliance he added his concern about the Low Countries where, he foresaw, France would soon intervene. Alliance between Elizabeth and Charles IX would at once check Spanish revenge against England and counter French ambition in Flanders.[49]

Burghley was less hopeful once it became evident that there would be no match, but mere alliance. The queen too seemed unenthusiastic about an alliance, nominally because she declared the French were uncooperative over the marriage. Even when Smith was sent off, Fénélon thought she preferred to remain unattached to any foreign power. But circumstances, he suggested, were turning her towards France. He meant the revelations of Spanish involvement in the Ridolfi plot. More important still, from the English point of view, was the growing possibility of intervention in the Low Countries by a France whose policy was being guided by the Protestant Coligny. This prospect cheered and excited Leicester and Walsingham; it made Elizabeth and Burghley acutely uneasy. French control of these provinces would be no better—in some ways, worse— than Spanish.* But all could agree—although for differing reasons—on the advantage of an alliance. Leicester hoped for Anglo-French co-operation in the Low Countries; Burghley saw the possibilities of using the alliance to check France there.

In January the proposal for the Anjou match, moribund for some months, was formally buried; and the French then proposed the youngest Valois, the Duke of Alençon, as a substitute for his brother. The queen was only mildly interested in this, though willing, as always, to encourage talk of a courtship. But the marriage and the alliance were now made separate matters of discussion, and the latter was proceeded with in a serious fashion. Once under way, negotiations moved with businesslike speed, and by early April the main outlines of a treaty were agreed on. What emerged was a defensive league in which each promised specified aid to the other in case of a demand by the other partner. By a special exchange of letters between the queen and Charles IX, it was agreed that an attack on either country because of religion should be included among the causes for making operative the pact. Scotland was a thorny problem and no clear formulation proved possible. In truth the French were no longer seriously interested in Mary Queen of Scots and were interested

---

* Digges, 129; CSPSpan, 1568–79, 331, 384; Fénélon, IV, 251, 306, 376; Wernham, Before the Armada, 315. In a memorandum of 1569 (Hatfield, 457, also in Haynes, 588 but with vital clause omitted) which outlines dangers facing the state and their possible remedies, Cecil lists as one danger 'the imperfection of alliance and treaties with other princes'. Alone of the dangers listed this one has no remedy suggested.

in Scotland itself mainly as a diplomatic weapon against England. The treaty confirmed Mary's worst expectations and drove her more effectively than ever into the arms of Philip. (In March her ambassador to Alva, Lord Seton, was shipwrecked on the Essex coast, and although he escaped his papers fell into the hands of the English authorities and revealed much of his dealings with Alva.)[50]

The treaty was formally signed at Blois on April 19th. It is hard to estimate just how seriously English leaders took it. Leicester was, of course, enthusiastic and was eager to be appointed special ambassador for the ratification, an honour which the queen accorded to Lord Clinton (newly made Earl of Lincoln), reputed a close associate of Leicester's in forwarding the treaty. Sir Thomas Smith, one of the signers, writing to the queen a couple of days after the signing was matter-of-fact in his tone. He thought that Charles 'went as sincerely and *tam bona fide* as any prince can' in the matter. If Spain threatened England, the treaty would be an effectual discouragement. On the other hand, if the Habsburgs wanted peace nothing in the treaty hindered that.[51]

Perhaps Burghley would have agreed with this. The treaty really involved minimal commitments by England while offering her a diplomatic weapon in dealing with Spain. But Burghley remained anxious not to close any doors to reconciliation – or at least to civil relations – with Philip and took informal but effective steps to get in touch with Philip, indicating his friendly feelings and those of the queen. The latter went out of her way to back Burghley in this gesture by public acknowledgment of the merchant, De Guaras, who was the intermediary. Burghley remained as warily suspicious of dependence on any foreign power as he had ever been.[52]

*　　*　　*

The turbulent years from 1569 to 1572 witnessed a quiet, almost routine, alteration, far less dramatic than the events which then filled the foreground of change, but in some ways more important. A change of generation was going forward at the top levels of politics. In March 1570 in the aftermath of the rebellion, William Herbert, Earl of Pembroke, died and was buried with due solemnity at St Paul's, attended by his fellow Councillors, a delegation of courtiers and the gentlemen of Wiltshire and South Wales.[53] Within the next two years there followed him to the grave two more noblemen of the Council, Parr, Marquess of Northampton, who died at Ambrose Dudley's house at Warwick on

October 28th, 1571, and the aged Marquess of Winchester, Lord Treasurer for nearly a quarter of a century, who had ended his days at Basing in the preceding March.

Two more earls died during these years; Cumberland, in whom the northern rebels had placed great hopes, held to his allegiance but barely survived the rising, dying on January 2nd, 1570. The greatest surviving regional magnate of the North, Edward, Earl of Derby, an ill man for some years past, survived to see his son's disgrace; his death occurred in October 1572. The wardship of the young Earl of Cumberland passed to Bedford, who undertook to 'avoid him from such Popish wasps and bees as will be buzzing in his ears to confirm in him a deafness to true religion'.[54] The new Earl of Derby was less affected to the old religion than his father and had kept his skirts clean of his brother's plotting.

Outside the ranks of the nobility, death carried away in these years Sir William Petre, long-time Councillor and civil servant, who had gone into virtual retirement in 1570 and died in 1572 at the age of sixty-seven or sixty-eight. Sir Nicholas Throckmorton, a much younger man, only fifty-six in 1571, died suddenly in Leicester's house on February 12th of that year, still in disgrace at court.*

All this mortality made for far-reaching change in the higher personnel of politics.' The reshuffling began, rather surprisingly, in the bleak January following the rising in the North, when Sir James Croft underwent political resurrection after a decade of oblivion with his appointment to the comptrollership of the Household and to the Privy Council, while Vice-Chamberlain Knollys was shifted to the treasurership of the Household. At about the same time Sir Thomas Heneage, member of a courtier family, was made Treasurer of the Chamber.[55] Croft's appointment was something of a mystery since he had been quite out of favour ever since his disgrace in 1560. However, he was an enemy of the fallen Norfolk but thought friendly to the Catholics and was certainly pro-Habsburg.[56] Elizabeth had a tendency to make balancing appointments and in her efforts to conciliate and soothe her Roman Catholic subjects—note the declaration of policy of these same weeks—may have chosen Croft deliberately as a sop to their feelings. His appointment meant that the friends of the Queen of Scots and the advocates of a conservative and pro-Habsburg policy would continue to be represented on the Council.[57]

Additional changes in the make-up of the Council did not come until the very end of the year (Arundel had returned to his seat in the spring,

* Dr Nicholas Wotton had died in 1567.

but Norfolk, of course, never sat again). On December 30th, 1570 the Earl of Sussex was sworn to the Council. He was not to be relieved of his northern presidency for more than another year (the Earl of Huntingdon was appointed to York on December 1st, 1572); but Sussex's residence in the North was no longer so urgent and his attendance at Council during 1571 was quite regular. Nearly a year later, in December of 1571, Shrewsbury was also sworn to the Council, but his onerous duties as perpetual warder of the Queen of Scots made his attendance rare and his appointment virtually an honorary one.[58]

The death of Winchester brought additional change, since the great office of Lord Treasurer had now to be filled. There could hardly be much doubt as to who would succeed, since Burghley had been Winchester's alter ego in fiscal matters since the beginning of the reign and was a close collaborator with the 'permanent under-secretary', Mildmay, Chancellor of the Exchequer. The French ambassador heard, almost certainly inaccurately, that Sussex was in competition for it and later was told, very probably by Leicester himself, that he (Dudley) had declined the office because it required special knowledge. In any case Burghley's patent of appointment was dated September 15th, 1571. He had been a baron of the realm since the preceding February.[59]

Burghley did not immediately vacate the Secretary's office; although rumour assigned that post to Sir Thomas Smith from April 1572 on, he did not actually assume it until July 13th.[60] Smith's Edwardian career as Secretary had been wrecked by too close association with Somerset, and his recovery under Elizabeth had been very slow. He had served a term in France as ambassador from 1563 to 1566 but after his return no other regular employment was found for him until he entered the Council in March of 1571. He was assigned as a principal investigator in the Ridolfi affair and that was followed by a return engagement in Paris, as joint negotiator with Walsingham of the Treaty of Blois. Walsingham's appointment in Paris was an important one. He had hovered on the fringes of official life for several years, performing small missions for the government. His assignment to the French capital placed there, for the first time since Throckmorton's departure, a man of vigorous opinion, a Protestant of the left, and a statesman who shared Throckmorton's vision of a Protestant internationale. Another confirmed Protestant of the left received high office when the Earl of Huntingdon went to York as Lord President of the North in the autumn of 1572.

In September of 1571, when Burghley took up his new office, the queen made two promotions in the peerage, elevating Lord Admiral Clinton to the Earldom of Lincoln just before he was dispatched on an embassy of honour to Paris, and raising the Viscount Hereford to the dignity of Earl of Essex. The former was being rewarded for a long career of service dating back to the 1540s; the French ambassador regarded him as a close friend of Leicester,[61] but in fact he seems to have stayed aloof from faction during the past several years. Hereford, a young man of about thirty, had come into some prominence as joint keeper, with Huntingdon, of Mary Stuart during the emergency of December 1569; he had married into the courtier clan of the Knollys in the early 1560s.

One final change within the court was the retirement of the queen's great-uncle, William, Lord Howard of Effingham, Lord Chamberlain since the accession. He resigned that office and shortly afterwards was appointed Lord Privy Seal in August 1572 (with a salary of one pound per diem), an office vacant since the death of Mary.[62] He lived only until the following January. His successor in the Chamberlain's post was Sussex (appointed in July 1572).

The net effect of these many changes was important. Of the generation of seniors who had surrounded the queen at her accession few were now left, the most eminent of them the Lord Admiral (born in 1512) and the Lord Keeper (born in 1509). With the death of her uncle, Howard, in 1573, Clinton, Sadler (the same age as Bacon) and Knollys (born in 1514) were the last links with the court of her father. It was the heyday of the middle generation, mostly a few years older than the queen—Burghley (born 1520), Bedford (born 1527), Sussex (born 1526), Leicester (a year older than the queen), along with Smith (born 1513), the veteran Knollys and Croft (Leicester's contemporary) form the core of the working Council of 1571–2. Mildmay (the same age as Cecil) and Sadler, infrequent attenders at Council, were important as the government's chief professional civil servants. At the same time a younger generation began to emerge into the limelight of politics.

Walsingham was now about forty; the new Lord President of the North, thirty-seven; Hereford, whose promising career was to be cut off untimely in Ireland in 1576, about thirty. Sir Richard Sackville's son (Baron Buckhurst since 1566), born in 1536, was now being employed in the negotiations with France; Charles Howard, an exact contemporary, the late Chamberlain's son, had commanded the horse in 1569 and the ships which met the Queen of Spain's convoy in 1570 and was employed on other tasks for the government. The queen was taking more and more notice of another younger man, Christopher Hatton, thirty-two in 1572 when he was appointed Captain of the Guard.

The high political world of the early 1570s exhibited certain obvious characteristics. The elimination of Norfolk and Arundel had removed the two chief representatives of the 'old' as against the 'new' nobility; more important, it had left a Council whose members were more concordant among themselves in their general political outlook than had hitherto been the case. Sussex, once the close collaborator of the fallen 'conservatives', was now won to the other side. The total effect was probably a slight shift to the left. All agreed in their determined hostility to the Queen of Scots and her claims. On other policy there was less unanimity; over the French proposals there had been division between those who (with Burghley, Bacon and Sussex) wanted marriage first and alliance afterwards and those who opposed the marriage but desired the alliance (Leicester, Clinton and Knollys).* This division was reflected in domestic affairs. Leicester was now very openly the great patron of left-wing Protestantism, and Bedford, Knollys and Mildmay shared this enthusiasm. Certainly Burghley was no enemy to Puritan ideals but as always he took a more cautious view about the initiation of change, especially when the impulse came from outside official circles.

But most important was the general agreement on policy which now prevailed in the Council. Croft apart, there was no one left to argue in support of the Queen of Scots or to oppose a strong anti-Catholic policy. Henceforth the grandees of the Elizabethan regime were men thoroughly committed to a central loyalty to the new religion established by law — although they were still to disagree as to the best means for advancing the Protestant cause, at home and abroad.

The interval between the crushing of the Northern rebellion in midwinter 1570–71 and the signing of the Treaty of Blois in April 1572 was filled with unfinished pieces of business left over from the great events of the preceding year. These proved awkward to handle and were cleared up only very slowly. The Queen of Scots was obviously still a dangerously attractive element in English politics; so shrewd a politician as Leicester

---

* CSPSpan, 1568–79, 331; Digges, 116 (for Leicester), 129 (for Burghley) and those who opposed the marriage but desired the alliance (Leicester, Clinton and Knollys). The line-up reappears in the spring of 1572 (CSPSpan, 1568–79, 384). De Guaras, reporting to Philip, listed the Council as divided five to seven on the question of settlement with Spain over the seized goods. Favourable to settlement he included Burghley, Bacon, Sussex, Howard and Croft; opposed, friendly to France, Leicester, Bedford, Clinton, Sadler, Knollys and Mildmay. His informant was probably Croft.

was still prepared to bet on her future and to back her cause in Council. Norfolk, however battered his reputation, still possessed great reserves had he known how to utilize them. The duel between Leicester and Cecil continued, albeit somewhat muted in tone. Relations with France and Spain remained precarious.

What might have been the outcome of these turgidly confused circumstances is not clear. Cecil showed great skill in protracting endlessly each negotiation with Mary, and these wearing tactics helped to tip the balance in her decision to plot with Ridolfi. The new and unexpected Anglo-French amity left her with little alternative. In any case this decision to go ahead with the Florentine's scheme, and the series of accidents which revealed the whole plot to the government, solved their problem for them. With full information in hand, the way was open for Cecil and the Councillors working with them to smash Norfolk once and for all and to drive Mary Stuart into the political wilderness. The phase of the succession question which had opened with the first scheming at York in the autumn of 1568 was over and the major threat to the regime which it posed totally liquidated.

In the process of liquidation a major shift in the balance of political power imperceptibly took place. In the 'sixties Cecil enjoyed the royal confidence but hardly stood on the same footing as Robert Dudley. A good deal of his time and energy went into blocking the moves of the favourite, and to do this he had to work in collaboration with Norfolk and Sussex. In 1569 the sudden shift of alliances over the succession question which brought Leicester and the Howards together left Cecil politically isolated, and he very nearly fell victim to a concerted conspiracy against him. He was saved by the queen's intervention and by the success of his risky foreign venture. The events of 1568–9 drew him into a working alliance with the queen, more intimate and more harmonious, one may guess, than they had hitherto enjoyed. During 1572 he received substantial tokens of royal favour, grants of land (some from the estates of the late Marquess of Northampton) and, more valuable still, two of the coveted licences to export goods without paying full customs. There was one for twelve thousand undressed cloths and another for four thousand tuns of beer. Licence to export cloth was rarely given by the queen and only to an inside circle of favourites.[63]

She was obviously willing to back his daring yet carefully measured 'brinkmanship' in the seizure of the treasure and in relations with the Huguenots. He assumed a prominence in policy-making and execution which he had not known for some years past. The unexpected turn of events in France, which gave temporary preponderance to the Châtillon faction in that court, offered a new scope for English action. It also affected the relations between Cecil and Leicester. The old rivalry was again apparent during the marriage negotiations, but their differences of opinion – marriage versus alliance – were really ones of means not ends. They were moving towards a *modus vivendi* which would allow for fairly broad areas of general co-operation. The old questions which had sharply divided them were now largely dead, while the new ones just emerging found them much closer to one another in their points of view.

But the great rewards bestowed on Cecil by his mistress by his elevation to the peerage and the Lord Treasurership, and the definitive successes of the causes which he stood for in Council, measurably shifted the balance between him and the favourite to his advantage. The queen's steady support for Cecil at the height of the attack on him had revealed the limits of Dudley's influence. And the events of 1569–72 had weakened the earl's position in many ways. His old allies, Pembroke and Throckmorton, were dead; his new friend, Norfolk, soon followed them to the grave. In the Council as it was constituted by 1572 Leicester's influence had perceptibly shrunk. By virtue of office, rank and experience Burghley now stood pre-eminent while he was surrounded by colleagues, such as Sussex, Smith and Mildmay, who looked to him as their guide. Dudley's position as favourite and as a magnate was not diminished, but his wings had been clipped; his political mobility was reduced; and his relative political influence lessened.

16 *Conclusion*

THE EVENTS of 1569–72 had been a testing-time for the regime which had come into being a decade earlier at the queen's accession. The problem of the succession had erupted into intrigue dangerous to the state; the dreaded Scottish rival had made her determined bid for a place in the English political firmament; an attempt had been made to restore the old religion. Armed revolt and conspiracy to bring in a foreign army had followed. And all these domestic convulsions had taken place while the Protestants of the Continent had passed through a time of troubles which bade fair utterly to destroy them. Yet the regime had not only survived, it had triumphantly struck down each successive challenge. Better still, the clear evidence of a strong base of enthusiastic loyalty on which it could now be seen to rest gave to the government a sense of self-confidence and of achievement which would serve it well in the difficult years which lay ahead. The fortunes of continental Protestantism were still very uncertain; in France the Huguenots were, in the spring of 1572, enjoying an unprecedented but fragile ascendancy at court. In Flanders the prospects of the opposition, at once Protestant and nationalist in nature, seemed very bleak until the revolt of the Sea-beggars in April suddenly altered the whole picture. But England's uneasy relations with Spain and France were appreciably eased. For nearly three years she had waged a species of 'cold war' with each of them, but now she had achieved open alliance with France and a brittle but viable armistice with Spain.

The Elizabethan regime had begun its career under auspices so obscure as to render the future altogether uncertain to any observer. The queen had inherited the misfortunes of a disastrous war, an empty treasury and a bankrupt foreign policy while facing the threat of a contested succession. Yet she had also been endowed with a generous share of fortune's goods. The rivalries of Habsburg and Valois had stood her in good stead in the first dangerous weeks of her reign and brought both the great powers to accept, and in the Spanish case to back, her. Two unexpected deaths in the

French House within the next two years distracted the attentions of that dynasty, and there followed the first ominous eruptions of religious civil war. Philip's departure for Spain and his long preoccupations, first with the problems of the Mediterranean world and then with the grave discontents of the Flemings, left England free from any serious attention on his part for nearly a decade.

In 1558 much of western Europe had stood near the flash point as the two great religious parties grimly girded for open battle. The first phases of the Reformation – triumphant Protestant revolution and stunned Catholic confusion – were past; the papacy's counter-measures were well in hand and there was a renewed sense of confidence within Catholic ranks, while Protestants were rapidly becoming aware of the magnitude of the struggle they now faced. England might reasonably have feared the same catastrophe of religious civil war which did in fact soon erupt in Scotland, France and the Low Countries.

But here again the queen was singularly fortunate; the season of her accession saved England from a great calamity. Mary's death came just early enough to place Elizabeth upon the throne at a time when it was still possible to control the course of events in England. The point of combustion had not quite been reached. English Catholicism, sluggish and complacent under the benign protection of its royal patroness, was taken by surprise at her death, still lacking either the self-awareness or the organization necessary for the coming struggle. To the episcopate the only alternative seemed to be martyrdom, and this they faced courageously; but the laity shuffled on in a dazed confusion, altogether uncertain what road to follow.

The English Protestants had sharpened their wits and hardened their determination in the days of exile and persecution, but they were by no means an organized faction in the kingdom as yet. They themselves were far from clear what their own goals were – beyond the abolition of Roman jurisdiction and the prohibition of the mass. Their coherence was just great enough to enable them to jostle the queen into accepting the Second Prayer Book of King Edward, but not sufficient to overawe the Crown or to make it the instrument of a doctrinaire confessional policy. Hence the Crown remained the arbiter of religious polity in the realm, within the limits of the acts of 1559 which committed it to an anti-Roman position but not to any clear-cut version of Protestant orthodoxy.

Unprepared and unorganized, the English Catholics remained paralysed while Rome, distracted by many other problems and not without hopes of Elizabeth, remained silent. The English Protestant leaders, for their part, lost no time in taking advantage of the situation. They were speedily entrenched in possession of the whole apparatus of state power and fortified by the prestige of statutory enactment; the queen did not sympathize with all their aspirations and there were moments of frustration and anxiety, but she was in large measure tied to alliance with them. For the immediate present the important thing was that civil conflict was avoided; only through outright rebellion could the Catholics hope to assert their cause, and since neither the imprisoned Marian hierarchy nor distant Rome counselled this, the English lay Catholics were content to wait in uneasy passivity upon circumstances.

Hence the most dangerous of all possibilities — all-out religious civil war — was eliminated. Extremists, both Catholic and Protestant, were shuffled off the stage and politics left in the hands of men who, while committed to the new settlement of Church and state, tended to see it in a political rather than a religious light. English politics in the 1560s were not to be dominated by the exigencies of doctrinaire strife. Instead, they were to be shaped by a series of contingencies in which deliberate initiative by any English group played a relatively small role. The new leadership — once the initial decision of 1559 was taken — was more anxious to conserve and consolidate than to innovate. Moreover, it was very much at the mercy of external contingencies. Scottish developments — first the civil war of 1559–60 and later the protracted excitements which began with the Darnley match in 1565 and lasted until Mary's flight in 1568 — inevitably involved England. They touched closely on the home-bred problems arising from Elizabeth's unmarried state — marriage and the succession. These were issues too sensitively linked to the basic conditions of English security to be ignored.

Most of the circumstances which shaped English politics in this decade did not arise from English initiative, but English responses in each of the successive episodes were moulded by the actions of a few dominant and very powerful personalities. In each episode the centre of decision is to be found in the powerful but opaque personality of the queen. In the first few months of her reign a good deal could already be predicated about the new ruler. She was clearly her father's daughter; she had displayed the same personal qualities: courage, determination, a quick intelligence, a somewhat overpowering charm, a sardonic wit and a commanding — indeed, an imperial — presence. Like Henry she had little interest in the more creative ranges of statesmanship, although she possessed the same shrewd capacity for selecting advisors such as Cromwell or Cecil who did possess these qualities.

But she soon showed the sharp differences which set her off from both Henry VIII and Mary Tudor. She shared neither Henry's zest for theological disputation nor her sister's simpler, but more potent, piety. There was in her a complete absence of the rather conventional ambitions of her father; obviously, she could not seek the laurels of a great commander, but, unlike her cousin of Scotland, Elizabeth entertained no ambitions for a marital alliance which would lift her to a greater throne than that of England. She was quite content to be Queen of England and Ireland, and no more. Nor did she seek to magnify English power. In this she disappointed those enthusiasts who cast her as the English Deborah and — like Throckmorton — longed to see her mingle the glories of a Protestant champion with those of a renewed English leadership in western European affairs.

More startling still was the absence in the queen of any marked dynastic sense. As there was no urge to magnify the dynasty's power, so there was none to perpetuate it. The lack of this particular motive, so dominant a trait among her predecessors and such contemporaries as Catherine de Médicis, set off the English sovereign in an unusual way from her continental peers. It gave to her political outlook a certain detachment and freed her advisors from some of the most vexing preoccupations of continental ministers. On the other hand this very lack of ambition, dynastic or personal, left a kind of vacuum in her political attitudes since they were not oriented towards the usual goals of action. Nor did she share the religious enthusiasms which were the springs of action in so many of her contemporaries. She was in fact coldly — at times, hostilely — indifferent to religious concerns, pietist or *politique*.

The queen was, of course, deeply and happily involved in politics. She had an intensely political personality and loved the business of politics. She throve on the thrust and riposte, the matching of wits and the confrontations — either on paper or face to face — which made up the everyday matter of political life. But her enjoyment stopped short at the door of the council chamber. Once the focus of action moved to the distant frontiers of Scotland, or worse still beyond the seas, she was seized with doubts, anxieties and hesitations. Necessarily such actions could be carried out only by men; the limitations of her femininity came unpleasantly home to her at these times.

This sense of her limits of control was one of the factors which made

Elizabeth in many respects a profound conservative, since it caused her always to long to contain events within the range of her immediate power as far as possible. There were other elements; her education was, in a sense, old-fashioned; she was as firm, though less learned, an exponent of divine-right monarchy as her Scottish successor. Monarchy, to her, was an instrument for protecting a standard of certainty in a political universe always threatened by instability. Certainly she did not see it as a tool for the selective and purposeful exercise of power. These views heightened the instinctive feelings for the unique dignity of her great office and its inviolability which worked steadily in her. Hence she was deeply resentful of any attempts to guide, to push or even to persuade, since they seemed to impugn her capacities to fill that office. Open and independent initiatives such as those of the left-wing Protestants of course awakened her bitterest anger. And perhaps underlying this jealousy for her power was the suspicion that her masculine courtiers never quite believed in the royal capacities of a mere woman. This deeply buried sense of insecurity added another stratum to a complex character.

All these things working together made of the queen a ruler reluctant to act and suspicious of change. She always preferred to wait on events. At the best this produced an intelligent, cool-headed opportunism, which offset the sometimes over-excited nervousness of her ministers to the benefit of the state. At the worst it led to a kind of *immobilisme* and a dangerous absence of imaginative leadership at the topmost level—the kind of leadership which goes out to meet a crisis, or at least prepares alternative solutions in advance.

In any case the conception and initiation of policy was frequently left to the royal Councillors; it became their business to devise the best possible mode of proceeding in each individual contingency of state. It remained for the queen to accept, reject or modify their proposals; there could be no question that final decision remained a royal prerogative. Often the result was a somewhat spasmodic working of the state machinery. In 1559–60 Cecil propounded the scheme for countering the French in Scotland; it took months of unwearying patience to jog his mistress step by weary step along the path of action. At the worst, English policy came near to paralysis, as in the troubled months after Mary Stuart's fall when the queen's instincts, profoundly outraged by the Scottish nobles' treatment of their ruler, led her to insist on a policy which cut athwart all other considerations of English interests at this point. Her deep-rooted abhorrence of all rebels against constituted authority—monsters in nature

—made for a constant bias in her attitude in a whole series of major decisions. Co-operation with rebels, Scottish, French—or later Dutch—went too much against the grain of her beliefs to make such policies easy for her. Yet this complex royal personality included not only an element of high-flown, metaphysical dogmatism but also the easy flexibility and moral neutrality of the practising politician.

For the latter role the queen possessed great qualifications. First of all—a very masculine attribute—was the sheer force of her imperious personality, which she used ruthlessly in subordinating to her will both court and Council. She thus made effective her unchallenged control of all decisions. Yet by itself this might not have served had Elizabeth not also displayed two other traits. One was a self-mastery which enabled her at crucial moments to put political goals ahead of personal preferences. The great testing-time for this quality came in 1560–61 when she tacitly turned away from marriage with Dudley. But that mastery was not always complete. In her relations with Mary Stuart, for instance, personal biases alternated uncertainly with political calculation, and her ministers had always to reckon with the influence of these half-buried but intensely felt instinctive reactions.

Secondly there was the keen political acumen which the professionals of her court came to appreciate. They continued to be dismayed and exasperated by what seemed to them a lack of seriousness about the ultimate goals of politics. But they came to have confidence in her as a virtuoso in the game of politics. They trusted her judgment as a player in making individual moves on the board. This respect for her professional skill made possible a working relationship between the queen and her ministers, although it did not remove altogether their mutual misunderstandings. She, on her side, had no comprehension of their ideological involvements or of the goals which they pursued. They, on theirs, could not understand what seemed to them an ultimately wayward frivolity about the highest ends of state. Nevertheless, the combination of awestruck fear and professional admiration which the queen commanded in the highest political circles stood her in good stead when her control of policy was seriously challenged in 1569. It was the foundation of the political stability which obtained in the years to follow.

That same challenge in 1569 threatened the career of the ablest of her ministers. On the first day of her reign Elizabeth chose as her principal political confidant Sir William Cecil. She was not to withdraw her confidence—in spite of occasional bouts of coolness between them—for the forty years he spent in the royal service. Giving her confidence to him by no means meant accepting his advice, as Cecil had frequent occasion to complain, but his mistress never lost respect for his judgment or doubted his reliability. Cecil, in many respects, remains as opaque and impenetrable a personality as his royal mistress; like her he never found a friend to whom he entrusted his confidences. In many ways he was a very ordinary man of his time and place, conventionally ambitious for himself and his family, a parvenu, a climber and a snob, busily but prudently engaged in the accumulation of wealth and the attributes of rank—houses, patronage and suitable alliances for his children. Yet among sixteenth-century English statesmen, Cecil's only peer is the great Henrician minister, Thomas Cromwell.

Elizabeth's secretary was as a man probably less imaginative and certainly as a domestic statesman less creative than his predecessor. Cromwell's talents had lain in his abilities to reshape and to modernize the structure of English administration, and to carry through with a steady hand the managed revolution of the Henrician Reformation; in his approach to English foreign policy he had shown a less sure and skilful touch. Cecil's domestic policy was in most respects conventional and cautious; he pursued the traditional Tudor goals of paternalistic regulation with consistency and some vigour, but he seldom innovated, certainly never on the grand scale of the Henrician statesman. On the vital question of religion his stand, once he came to power, was one of irrevocable commitment to the new faith. Under Mary he had conformed to the old; he was a private person then and by his lights had no option but obedience to constituted authority. But in office he was a strong and sometimes ruthless protector and promoter of the Protestant religion established by law. His religious feelings were not deep; there is no evidence that the Protestant faith ever touched him personally in any profound way, yet we need not question the sincerity of his adherence. He viewed Protestantism in coolly secular terms and its most attractive features to him were its rejection of a foreign ecclesiastical jurisdiction and the concomitant subordination of clerics and of all ecclesiastical questions to the royal government's control. His attitude towards the older faith was not founded on an abhorrence of spiritual or moral error but rather on distaste for an outmoded superstition and deep distrust of a fallacious social and political theory.

It was in the management of foreign relations that his forte lay, and it was there that his talents were most conspicuous. Here he displayed a certain detachment and a very uncommon clarity—one might almost say, purity—of political vision which enabled him to isolate, to understand and to act upon a concept of English national interest as distinguished from that of the monarch and quite unclouded by his own personal ambitions. Without ever setting forth any statement of such a principle, he thought, wrote and acted in those terms. Furthermore, he took for granted the peculiarly English character of the state he served; this feeling was an unselfconscious one which required no theory of nationalism to justify or explain it. Cecil proceeded simply from common-sense considerations and from a knowledgeable understanding of English history. For him no spelling out of the identity and the autonomy of the English realm was needed, and all of his political genius was focused on its needs and its future.

In his voluminous papers the most impressive items are the coolly lucid analyses of the international political situation and its relevant domestic circumstances, detached, objective, magisterial, almost always couched in pro/contra form, a kind of simplified scholastic *quaestio*. His analyses were dominated by a vision of foreign policy which was near-isolationist in character. Maximum autonomy for England in international affairs, minimal entanglements or commitments abroad, and the corollary conception of a kind of Monroe doctrine for the British Isles were the columns on which all his policy rested. Cautious and wary as he was, Cecil was ready enough to take risks—great risks—on those rare occasions when he was certain the occasion justified them. The French menace to England's security and the assertion of the Stuart claim to the throne had left him with no doubts at all in the dangerous winter of 1559–60; and again in December 1568 he was prepared to take considerable risks through the seizure of the Spanish treasure. (He may have somewhat miscalculated the speed of Alva's reactions on this second occasion.) In such instances he acted with a cool head and a skilful manipulation of diplomatic instruments. But more commonly Cecil was to be found on the side of watchful inaction or, at the most, cautious backstage intervention, and in this respect he echoed something of the conservative instincts of his mistress. He certainly developed, as time went on, an 'official' attitude, a jealousy of amateurs who, outside the inner circle of politics, dared to press their views on matters of state. He clung to the view of statesmanship as a 'mystery' in the old-fashioned sense of that word. In this respect he stood rather apart from Leicester's sympathy with the broad movement of left-wing Protestantism in the country. It was not that he disapproved of the general moderate Puritan position, but he found it hard to sympathize with their eagerness to take the initiative in great matters of state instead of leaving them to the judgment of the professionals. With the years he developed a certain *gravitas* of demeanour, a mask of judicious, dispassionate, noncommital omnicompetence which made him the minister *par excellence*, almost the embodiment of public wisdom and selfless service to the Crown.

Nothing distinguished him more sharply from the third member of the Elizabethan triad of power than this posture of public rectitude. Leicester, both by circumstance and by temperament, played his part with a panache, even an abandon, which usually placed him in brilliant contrast to the sober figure of the Secretary. In many respects the earl is an even more mysterious person than either Cecil or their mistress since he has left so little direct, personal evidence. His own letters are few and on the whole not very interesting or revealing. Contemporaries envied the upstart favourite, and although they gave him lip-service praise their real feelings break out in such poisoned polemics as the famous libel, *Leycester's Commonwealth*, or in such outbursts as Cecil's angry – but private – memorandum of 1566. Posterity has tended to accept his detractors' account and has shrugged him aside as too slight a figure to be taken seriously in his own right.

The record of the years we have been dealing with hardly seems to bear out these disparaging judgments. What kind of man Dudley was as a private person remains quite unclear; one may guess that he lacked the complexities and inner stresses of both Elizabeth and Cecil. He was in many respects a conventional courtier, remarkable neither for intellect nor for taste, but fortunate in his physical and psychological attractiveness to the queen. But as a politician he demands close and serious consideration. From the beginning of the reign he had had an exceedingly difficult role to play and a treacherous road to travel. He was descended from a singularly ill-fortuned house. His grandfather, a parvenu of obscure origins – whatever the claims to a connection with the Lords Dudley – had gone to the block as the scapegoat for the shabbier political sins of Henry VII. John Dudley, his father, was a sinner on a far grander scale, and contemporaries were not likely to forget that he had committed the highest of all treasons in his attempt to displace the Tudors from the throne.

This was bad enough, but one must add to it the peculiarly rancorous jealousy which the young queen's unconcealed preference for him excited in all male breasts. Beset from without by this bristling jealousy and from within by the obvious temptation to flaunt his favours in the face of the court, Dudley walked with uncommon discretion. Not that he put on a false humility or hesitated to exploit his position for as much as it was worth, but he remained watchfully aware of the limits which his jealously regardful mistress set and acutely conscious of his relations with fellow-courtiers. Early in the reign he began to build up credit wherever he could by using generous drafts on his own reserves with the queen so that he became an intermediary in many appointments or grants, especially those connected with the Church. At the same time, as we have seen, he carefully cultivated every possible connection in the court and in the embassies.

Up to about 1564 Dudley was no doubt playing for the biggest prize of all – marriage and a Crown. As has been argued above, at some point in the years 1563 or 1564 a subtle change came over his relationship with the queen when, after having come almost to the brink of matrimony, she drifted away – without, however, lessening her preference for Lord Robert. They began to move, ever so slowly, into an easier, more relaxed, yet also more complex, relationship, harder to define, but durable and strong. This was perhaps the greatest testing-time for Dudley. As the half-conscious realization of this change gradually dawned upon him, he responded with unusual adaptability and skill. He began more and more to establish for himself a new position which, while based on his special relationship to the queen, was one of more independence. He sought and gradually obtained a political position of his own. Once on the Council, he showed himself diligent and attentive and took care to be associated with every major piece of public business. From this time too dates his increasingly deliberate patronage of the Puritan party. Nothing was better calculated to give him a prominent and a strong position in the kingdom than the championship of a cause so vigorous, so appealing to the newer generation and so attuned to many of the strongest feelings of an ever more self-conscious public. In short, Leicester made the transition from a position as the favourite of dubious origin, dancing attendance on his mistress's whims – the queen's horsemaster as Catherine de Médicis once contemptuously called him – to that of a premier magnate, singled out by royal confidence and approval, but standing also on his own feet as a great territorial lord and as the patron of a cause widely popular and only partially within the permitted bounds of political correctitude.

As has been suggested, the circumstances of this flamboyant career set Leicester in sharp contrast to his colleague and rival, William Cecil. The

20

latter embodied all that was correct, all that was conventional, in the Elizabethan world. The son of a minor court official, university-trained, the protégé of Somerset who yet emerged unscathed from his patron's fall; the epitome of public gravity and official discretion, measured in his judgments, close-mouthed, he manoeuvred his way through the intricacies of court politics with a stiffly correct dignity. There is about Leicester, on the other hand, an air of the outrageous, of the slightly disreputable — the adventurer, gambling his career on dangerous uncertainties, flirting with Catholic intriguers or Puritan agitators, and even in his more respectable days prepared to risk himself in the quicksands of the Norfolk marriage. In a sense he represents the underside of Elizabeth's character. She was careful of her dignity, jealous of her royal privileges and insistent upon a splendid decorum in her household, but she liked to flirt with the faintly improper, mildly to scandalize the Spanish ambassador or Puritan zealots; and there had been a moment when she would have flouted all the conventions and given herself up to the delights of infatuated dalliance with her lover. To these submerged elements in her personality Leicester appealed strongly. The important thing, of course, is that both of them learned how to play this game without risking the kind of reaction which Mary provoked in Scotland by her affair with Bothwell. This instinct in the queen saved her from grave errors of judgment; the same instinct in Dudley was perhaps at the root of his successful transformation from favourite to statesman.

The wide differences between Cecil and Dudley were reflected in the policies of state which each advocated. Cecil's views, as already indicated, were cautious, limited, publicly neutral and privately noncommittal; in foreign affairs almost isolationist; and in all things stiffly 'official'. Leicester had not hesitated to play the delicate role of protector to the Catholics early in the reign or to risk royal disapproval by courting the Puritans later in the decade. It was a characteristic gesture of the earl publicly to take communion in the French church in 1568. Unlike Cecil he had no hesitations in sympathizing with 'non-official' causes, or encouraging movements of opinion outside the court circle — even, of course, in intriguing with Mary Stuart and the Duke of Norfolk. He was prepared to be venturesome, even daring, for lesser causes, and for personal advantage, where Cecil economically husbanded his stock of boldness for carefully calculated occasions when the national interest was closely touched. Gradually Leicester developed a coherent set of ideas about national policy, which he followed with increasing consistency. Its main features were his advocacy of a French alliance and his patronage at home of the Puritan party.

In the beginning the favourite doubtless took up the French cause as self-protection against a Habsburg alliance; but, as time went on, he expanded his vision in a way consonant with his backing of the Puritans at home – a policy which may have reflected Throckmorton's influence on him, since it was in a modified form that which Sir Nicholas himself had pushed when an ambassador. Support of the Huguenots coupled with a mediatory role in French politics would open the way, he hoped, to a working arrangement between the English and French courts against a common enemy, the Habsburgs, a threat to both the French dynasty and English Protestants. A common fear would bridge the ideological gap and lead to at least minimal collaboration. The advent of the Coligny party to favour at Paris promised an even more hopeful future. Such a policy contrasted strongly with the cautious isolationism of Cecil, although, as events proved, their common Protestantism and the fear of international Catholic conspiracy provided a ground for collaboration in 1572.

The course of events during these years reflected in large part the attitudes of these three great actors; it was they who shaped the pattern of English development. The queen was almost always content to wait on events, to play for time and run as few risks as possible; Cecil, pessimistic but resolved, brooded watchfully, ready to pounce when the opportunity offered; while Leicester became the spokesman of the activists, pushing for involvement and commitment. The bold gamble in Scotland in 1559–60 which paid off so handsomely was largely Cecil's doing. But it was Dudley who was responsible for the intervention in Normandy two years later; an unwise speculation which ended in failure, but there was no harm done to vital interests of the English Crown and no liabilities for the future were contracted. There followed some years of quiet isolation from continental matters, a state of affairs which suited both the queen and her Secretary. But in 1568 Cecil believed that impending dangers to English security made it absolutely necessary to resume the initiative and persuaded his mistress into the risky gamble of seizing Alva's treasure. The crisis that followed was frightening and for a moment in the succeeding spring royal confidence in the Secretary may have wavered. But his skill in carrying through a policy which conceded nothing to Spain and yet avoided war assured the advancement of his career. Thereafter, in relations with France, Dudley once more came to the fore as the leading exponent of Anglo-French co-operation, but the final achievement of alliance involved Leicester and Burghley in a common enterprise.

At the very moment of agreement on the Treaty of Blois the revolt of the Sea-beggars in Holland opened a new phase in English relations with the Low Countries, Spain and France, but it found England in a relatively strong and advantageous position vis-à-vis all parties concerned. Relations with Scotland were also about to enter a new stage. In May 1573 the Regent Morton, using artillery provided by the English, battered his way into Edinburgh Castle and smashed the last remnants of Marian power in Scotland. The final victim of the Stuart enchantress, Secretary Maitland, met his tragic end in the wake of this event. Scotland's future was as un-predictable as ever, but at least the present situation was one which the English government could regard with some satisfaction.

At home the queen's preference for Dudley had skewed the shape of politics for many years. Even after she turned away from marriage with the favourite there was a long duel between him and his enemies. Cecil played a discreet but important role in their plan to find a husband for their mistress, preferably the Austrian archduke. Their failure to achieve this had been followed by privy conspiracy of a mischievous kind – the effort to provide for the succession by marrying Mary and Norfolk. In this scheme the favourite in a characteristic move switched alliances and played a key role, this time as a backer of the match and co-conspirator in a plot to ruin Cecil. The failure of this scheme, the suppression of the earls' rising and the successful detection of the Ridolfi plot had proved the enduring vitality of the regime and confirmed beyond all question the queen's sovereign control over English politics. Leicester had survived his adventures essentially unscathed, but reduced in importance and thoroughly tamed to a more domestic mode of political action than he had pursued in the past. Burghley had grown mightily in political stature, obtained new office, and risen to a new height of dignity and influence. Each rival had successively failed to dislodge the other, and each now was driven to an armistice and to tacit acceptance of the other's political existence.

Out of these events emerged the re-establishment of basic political stability, such as England had not enjoyed since Henry VIII's conscience was first troubled at the end of the 1520s. There had been at least two major causes for that prolonged instability. One, more urgent but essenti-ally more superficial, had been felt only since the death of Henry in 1547. This was the absence of effective leadership at the very top. The political machinery of the English state was geared to operate only under firm royal direction, and this had been lacking under the boy-king Edward and his half-sister, Mary. And even though Elizabeth's personality was an imperiously commanding one, there was through the first decade of her reign an underlying lack of confidence in the political future. The second obstacle to renewed stability was more complex and far more difficult to surmount. It arose from a new phenomenon in English political life — the presence of a large body of organized, coherent and very articulate public opinion on the great political questions of the age, shaped by the new faith and shared by a large segment of the aristocracy, which it was impossible either to ignore or effectively to control.

The first problem, although the simpler of the two, was far from easy to deal with. During Edward's time it became clear that the royal power of the Tudors could not be safely delegated during the incapacity of the monarch. The bitter in-fighting among the rival Councillors led to conspiracy, coup d'état and ultimately to Northumberland's attempt to replace the dynasty. Mary's swift recovery of power was reassuring, but she failed in the long run to win the enduring confidence of the political elite and by the end of her reign royal control was shaky and a real threat of civil strife shadowed the future.

Elizabeth reasserted effective royal control over the court and the aristocracy, but the terrifying uncertainties of an unsecured succession, the plausible ambitions of Mary Stuart and the ambiguities of the wider European religious and political scene made for continuing malaise and lack of confidence. Elizabeth's own flirtation with Robert Dudley did nothing to reassure those who were apprehensive of feminine rule, especially since the experience of Mary's reign. Deep unease arose from the unmarried condition of the sovereign. Men looked to the marriage of the queen not merely as a normal incident of her personal life but also as a necessary condition for effective royal leadership. Only a man could provide the weight of personality, the decision and the judgment which would win general loyalty and trusting obedience. And only a man would display the ambition and driving energy which would give direction and purpose to political life. Elizabeth surprised her courtiers by the range of masculine qualities which she commanded, but, effective as her personal leadership was, it still lacked that very element of personal or dynastic ambition which men thought an essential ingredient in serious politics. For a long time they expected her to take a husband; until that event took place all political calculations seemed to them to have a merely provisional character.

In the end a partial but workable solution was found. The queen did not marry but she acquired surrogate husbands. Her collaboration with Cecil and Dudley – and to a lesser extent with the whole Council – served to fill out the missing dimensions of effective leadership. Leicester no doubt provided some of the personal emotional support which the queen would have found in actual marriage with him. But both Secretary and favourite came to act in the less personal, the public and official roles, which a royal consort would have played. By providing those masculine elements of ambition and of drive towards a goal which even their versatile mistress could not encompass, they became a good deal more than mere ministers, offering advice and executing commands. They became in fact sharers in supreme power. In the total process of decision the queen was very much the first person in this secular trinity, but if the final choice was hers the ingredients which went into it, the specific contents of decisions, were the ministers'. By this oblique participation in supreme power they slowly bent the shape of English policy into forms of their desiring.

The arrangement was a makeshift one and subject to strain. It depended on the co-operation of three powerful personalities, and, as we have seen, two of these, Cecil and Dudley, devoted much of their energy in the 1560s to attacking one another. The queen's steady but measured support, first of Dudley in the years when the Howard clan sought to oust him, and then of Cecil in the crisis years of 1569 and 1570, finally steadied the triple relationship and made regular the orbits of movement of the two lesser lights. The Elizabethan political world now had about it an air of permanence and predictability which had been lacking for the past fifteen years. The queen would not marry, but her confidence in Burghley and Leicester was now a reliable landmark. Men could make their political calculations accordingly, possessing at last a political map which was clearly marked. They knew which were the thoroughfares to favour and advancement and they knew that these highroads would be open so long as the political principals remained alive.

The second great obstacle to a stable political order was of a different magnitude from the first; nothing less than a mutation in the very nature of English politics. At the end of the fifteenth and the beginning of the sixteenth centuries its characteristics had seemed fairly fixed. The powerful Yorkist and Tudor kings had re-established stability by eliminating the feuding regional war-lords and successfully resuming the traditional role of the medieval monarchs. In this role these kings had used all their resources to provide stability and security for society, to maintain public order and to protect private property. The monarchy had been the conserving force, the ordering principle, which defended men against the endemic disorder of medieval society, which, in short, was the great balance-wheel of society. Since the work of government had been done largely by the monarch himself or by his chosen and dependent ministers, he had unrivalled command of the political scene. The subjects' main political obligation had been obedience; their political role, service. It was the climax of dynastic and patriarchal polity; by the 1520s it was already archaic.

It was Henry VIII who for the first time used the enlarged power of the Crown in a different way, not as a conserving but as an innovating, indeed as a revolutionary, instrument, to make a break with the past and to effect a fundamental reorganization of society. The separation from Rome proved also to be the blow which shattered the mould of the patriarchal political world. In accomplishing his revolution, Henry took into his service men whose eagerness to break with the past far outran the king's intentions. Some among them were ardent religious reformers, anxious for a radical moral and spiritual reawakening in individual men and a corollary reordering of society. In others, the solvent forces of the age worked most strongly. Touched as much by Renaissance humanism as by the Reformers' enthusiasms, they were radicals of a different stripe, coolly secular-minded, sceptical and disillusioned as to the received orthodoxies, but open-minded towards the future. This latter breed derived from Italian humanism a keen interest in the political dimensions of social reformation.

Men who blended in varying proportions elements from this spectrum of ideas inherited Henry's power in 1547. In the six brief years of Edward's reign this party of change shattered not only the ancient fabric of religious life but also the received political tradition of the nation. Henry had used the state power as an instrument for social change; they adapted and developed this mode of action in important ways. His goal had been primarily the protection and continuation of his dynasty. Theirs was a mixture of aims both more noble and more crass. Some sought to renew the spiritual life of the inner man by the institution of new religious forms and by recasting religious institutions. Others were merely using the opportunities of a royal minority to scramble for place and fortune. But the whole process was a strong stimulus to the growth of robust new political appetites.

It was a truism that if true religion were to prosper the state must back it. The novelty which arose in the decade after Henry's death lay in the conviction that the standards which regulated the state's action towards this end were to be determined neither by solely sacerdotal nor by solely royal authority. Judgment on these great matters was to be made by a much larger range of the community. The leaders of change, drawn from all the segments of the aristocracy, were determined to share fully not only in setting up the guide-posts of a new religious establishment but in the corollary decisions of domestic politics and foreign relations which vitally affected the Protestant interest. The ultimate touchstone of right political action was no longer solely in the royal grasp.

For men touched by the impulses of the new faith, politics came to assume new and vast dimensions. Its purposes soared beyond the merely personal or dynastic – even beyond that extended and national conception of dynasty which the Tudors had sedulously cultivated. The aims of Christ's true religion ought to dominate all other considerations, as the radical ideologues saw it. Foxe, for instance, in his great work on the martyrs, displayed God's purposes at work in past and present English history and pointed out the great task to be done by His elect nation. Not all Protestants could share Foxe's high intensity of vision, but even the more tepid were moved by the political elements in it.

These radicals were quite content to leave the active government of the realm to the traditional authorities, the Crown and its servants, but they reserved to themselves the right of judgment as to its actions and implicitly the rights to propose and to oppose – to press change upon the Crown, or, more rarely, to dissuade it from some intended course of action. This meant there was now a focus for action within society which could rival the Crown in the loftiness of its aspirations and in its appeal to men's loyalties. Old habits of obedience to the monarch were still very strong, but they were now subject to new and dangerous strains. Under Mary they came close to the snapping point; the close of her reign was filled with ominous signs of threatening civil conflict.

The formulation of a full-blown theory of legitimate disobedience to the monarch was long in coming. Goodman, Knox and Ponet were skirting the frontiers of such a theory at the very end of Mary's reign, but the timely accession of Elizabeth averted a direct confrontation between Protestants and Catholics. It thus became irrelevant to pursue such a line of argument. Outright doctrines of justified resistance to constituted authority were to thrive only where there was a head-on collision between Catholics and Protestants, as in France.

In Elizabethan England the situation was curiously ambiguous. In 1559 the Crown and the forces of innovation were in approximate agreement. But this harmony was not long-lasting. Even under a Protestant monarch the rift in the body politic was evident. Advocates of a forward move, eager for additional religious change and for a vigorous collaboration with foreign Protestant movements, were at odds with a monarch strongly resistant to action, conservative in her very instincts, and coldly indifferent to their ideological enthusiasms. These men constituted something more than a faction, something less than a party. Their cohesion arose not from loyalty to a particular leader or family but from a common body of shared opinion. The word 'opinion' is important for it was not doctrinal formulation which bound them together but something more diffuse. There was agreement on a theologically radical Protestantism which took concrete form in the Thirty-Nine Articles in 1563. But this was not the primary focus of their attention. It was the political and institutional aspects of Protestant ideology which concentrated their energies. Opinion was transmuted into action by such matters as the Prayer Book in 1559, clerical attire in 1565, the treatment of the Catholics throughout the decade, or the explosive issue of the succession from 1563 onward. Cecil's tussle with Alva in 1568–9 and Leicester's advocacy of alliance with France in 1571–2 stemmed from the same body of convictions. The common thread through all this was the protection or the advancement, at home or abroad, of the Protestant interest. It was increasingly evident that the ideological core of the movement gave it a coherence, an articulateness, and a continuity which mere personal leadership or partisanship could not have achieved. It provided a common field of action for men of diverse personalities and clashing ambitions, so that what might have been a formless flux of competition for power and place came to have some rough shape and coherence. And it brought together under a common standard of reference the diverse day-to-day problems of political action.

This is not to say that individual personalities and personal loyalties did not play a large role. Leicester's advocacy with the queen, Bedford's careful utilization of parliamentary patronage and Burghley's steady support in Council were central to the movement's life. So were the forceful and often well-organized interventions of left-wing M.P.s in successive Parliaments. But it was the cause rather than the men who ultimately counted. The very pervasiveness of active Protestant partisans in Council, Parliament, court and country made a formidable political problem. It had no special class or regional focus since its supporters included great noblemen, Councillors and a great host of wealthy and influential country gentlemen and their merchant and lawyer cousins.

The problem which required attention was how to regularize relations between a conservative and traditionalist monarch and those determined advocates of a forward policy. By an ironic turn of history the political activism which the queen's father had introduced to the English scene when he used the royal power to overthrow Rome's authority was now taken over by a political elite which, while loyal to the Crown, drew its strength and convictions from sources quite independent of the monarchy. The Crown in its turn had reverted, under Elizabeth, to a conserving and balancing role in society, consolidating the general position which Henry had secured rather than moving towards any new ground.

The risks of open defiance of the Crown were limited by the ironclad necessity which bound the queen and her Protestant subjects in permanent embrace. Neither could do without the other; for her there was no turning back from the decisions of 1559, however much she would have liked to blur the fact. For them she was the only possible occupant of the throne. Nevertheless, the radical Protestants did not allow even their rejoicing in Elizabeth's providential accession to hinder their determination to have their own way on the religious settlement. In 1563 they made themselves felt in Convocation, where they were narrowly defeated, and in 1566 in Parliament. They were unremitting in their efforts to obtain harsher anti-Catholic laws and further reform of the English Church. They also took up a determined stand on the succession and were resolved to block Mary's claims. After 1559 they never were very successful in securing additional religious reform, but they jostled the government into an ever-more extreme anti-Catholic stance and effectually checked Mary Stuart's hopes for the succession. In the Habsburg wooing they made clear their disapproval of a marriage which would exempt the royal consort from the penal laws. In all these things what is important is their cheerful determination to oppose their judgments to the queen's whenever their convictions so dictated. The traditional view that great decisions of state were solely the business of the Crown was being shunted firmly aside.

Elizabeth's responses to these pressures varied from haughty rejection of their demands to politic evasion, but she took few pains to conceal her dislike for the religious reformers and rarely shared even the *politique* Protestant enthusiasms of Burghley. In addition she resented what seemed to her an assault on her inviolable prerogative by these clamant, self-appointed counsellors, thrusting their proposals on her at every possible opportunity. Since neither side was likely to yield much in its views, there seemed to be an impasse.

What imperceptibly evolved was an arrangement characteristically makeshift, clumsily intricate and just workable. The Council eventually provided the necessary bridge. That body, as it was constituted by 1572, had a good deal of homogeneity. All its members—save Croft—were committed adherents of the new religion and agreed with one another on the major lines—if not the details—of national policy. They were dominated by the two major figures of Burghley and Leicester. This relatively harmonious and compact body enjoyed the full confidence of the queen; most of its members were her own choice; the Lord Admiral was by now the sole hold-over from her sister's reign. But they were also men who had close and sympathetic relations with the countryside and most particularly with the gentry of an advanced Protestant outlook. With the possible exception of Smith, none of them was solely a courtier or a bureaucrat; each had his landed base and regional status—Leicester in Warwickshire, Burghley and Mildmay in Northamptonshire, Bedford in the West, Knollys in Oxfordshire, to cite only a few. They were thus ideally suited to serve as transformers between the high political voltage of many of Elizabeth's more prominent subjects and the very low political voltage of the queen herself. They were able to mediate between the cool indifference of the monarch and the ardent Protestant activism of her subjects. The two centres of initiative within the nation—the Crown and the party of the new faith—were brought into a clumsy but viable working relationship. The presence of such outspoken supporters of the advanced Protestant cause as Leicester, Bedford or Knollys, or of the more discreet but no less committed Burghley, gave a sense of confidence to the gentlemen of left-wing persuasion in the counties.

This cumbersome arrangement had relatively narrow working limits; in the next generation even the more moderate Puritan hopes for reform were doomed to disappointment. But that lay in the future; in 1572 reformers could afford to be more cheerful. There was a line of communication between the Crown and a restless, opinionated elite. So long as the Privy Council retained a broadly representative function, so long as it was not solely a 'court' body but also in some sense a 'country' one as well, there would be some protection against a dangerous rift between the rival foci of loyalty and action—the Crown and the Protestant interest.

The years between 1568 and 1572 were crowded with melodramatic events, tumbling one upon another in rapid succession, bewildering and alarming to spectators. Yet, veiled by their turbulent confusion, a number of clear-cut and far-reaching changes were rapidly taking place. What was most visible to contemporaries—and most comforting to them— was the fact that the new regime had finally won through to a hopeful prospect of lasting stability. Rather more slowly they came to realize that the longer and even more dangerous era of instability which had opened when Henry VIII led the country into the Reformation was now past. Lastly, an even greater shift in the deep currents of English political life was just beginning to make itself felt as England moved out of the classical age of dynastic politics. The nation was leaving behind the relative simplicities of a time when the great decisions of state had been determined largely by the interests and ambitions of the royal house. Ahead lay a troubled time when royal authority would be challenged by opinionated and ambitious subjects with their own strong views on national policy. It was the beginning of the long and painful transformation from personal monarchy into an aristocratic parliamentary polity. In this new era the traditional currents of personal and family interest would be crossed by the strong tides of ideological conviction.

But in 1572 what was most immediately apparent was that the Elizabethan regime had at last attained its majority. Its most urgent difficulties had arisen from the political uncertainties created by an unmarried queen and an unsettled succession. No solution had been found to either of these problems; nevertheless, a kind of stabilization had finally been attained. The queen, after contemplating marriage with Dudley, had resolved against taking any husband at all and, lucky in events, had successfully evaded her subjects' importunate solicitations until the passing years rendered the matter more or less irrelevant. Circumstances favoured her since pressure for marriage diminished as the succession problem also drifted into stalemate. The hapless Grey sisters effectually ruined their prospects by their marital indiscretions. That more formidable claimant, the Queen of Scots, squandered her chances through her own persistent fecklessness, although the steady growth of Protestant feeling would probably have been a formidable obstacle in any case. At any rate by 1572 Englishmen had little option but to resign themselves to a problematical political future. The murk of uncertainty was lightened for them by their growing trust in their queen and her good fortune and by their sense of confidence in the men who now held uncontested leadership in her Council.

Not only were the anxieties of the immediate past less acute now but the government had also surmounted some longer-standing obstacles to the political stability of the nation. The essential decision of the Reformation had been taken in 1559 with surprising ease and minor disturbance, but it was not until the early 'seventies that men could begin to feel some sense of its permanence. In 1569 the last forces of traditional English Catholicism had been liquidated with minimal effort and negligible damage to the political fabric. More important still, those restless magnates who, while not themselves Catholics, were willing to flirt with those who were loyal to the old faith, had been eliminated. The committed Protestants had triumphed over those internal foes who might have challenged their dominance. A workable arrangement between the Crown and the pushing Protestant elite in the country had been developed. All this promised a run of settled political weather ahead, while this very control over the political structure gave time and opportunity for the working of those deeper currents of change which were giving the whole national ethos a deeply Protestant tone.

These achievements marked the close of a long chapter in English political history; but – although contemporaries were hardly aware of it – another had already opened. The injection of ideology into politics occasioned by the events of the Reformation would be a central theme in this new chapter. Already the number of active participants in the political game was vastly increased. The initiatives of the 1560s drew in the whole membership of the House of Commons and agitated some sizeable segment of their constituents in the larger boroughs and in the shires. The range of political topics with which they concerned themselves had broadened astonishingly. Above all, religion was providing a matrix within which men could form a long-term, coherent and unified conception of politics. For the time being – for so long as the present protagonists lived – the makeshift arrangements of the Elizabethan political system would be adequate to contain the ferment stirred up by the new conditions. The long lives of the principal actors would extend this epoch of political stability into the next century. But the basic conditions for the transformation from an age of dynastic politics to one of national politics had been laid down. Elizabeth's reign was to serve as prologue to the long political drama of that transition, a drama on which the curtain would not fall until the eighteenth century.

Reference Notes

1 PROLOGUE TO A REIGN

1 For interesting discussion of this problem see A. Ferguson, *The Articulate Citizen and the English Renaissance* (Durham, North Carolina, 1965) and Michael Walzer, *The Revolution of the Saints* (Cambridge, Mass., 1966).
2 See William Haller, *The Elect Nation* (New York, 1963).
3 See Lawrence Stone, *The Crisis of the Aristocracy, 1558–1641* (Clarendon Press, Oxford, 1965).

2 THE MAKING OF A GOVERNMENT

1 PRO, SP 12/1/7, 8.
2 *APC*, VI, *passim* for Council attendance.
3 *Hatfield*, 154, for the blame laid on Paget for the war.
4 Biographical details, unless otherwise noted, are taken from the *Dictionary of National Biography* and the *Complete Peerage*.
5 PRO, SP 11/19; Lawrence Stone, *The Crisis of the Aristocracy, 1558–1641* (Clarendon Press, Oxford, 1965), 138, and Appendix VIII.
6 For Clinton's grant as Admiral see *CPR, 1557–58*, 2. Arundel appears in the *APC* of Mary as Lord Steward until the summer of 1557; from his return to the Council in January 1558 he is listed simply as Lord Arundel; in Elizabeth's reign he is first called Lord Steward December 23rd, 1558 (*APC*, VII, 27).
7 *The State Papers and Letters of Sir Ralph Sadler*, 3 v., edited by Arthur Clifford (Edinburgh, 1809), I, 388; Stone, *Aristocracy*, Appendix VIII.
8 J. A. Froude, *History of England* (London, 1875), V, 390, 398, 500, 528.
9 BM, Lansdowne MSS, ix, f. 49.
10 *CPR, 1558–60*, 59.
11 See F. G. Emmison, *Tudor Secretary* (Longmans, London, 1961) for a biography of Petre.
12 PRO, LC 2/4/2 and 2/4/3.
13 For Englefield, *APC*, VII, 29; Parry, *CPR, 1558–60*, 60; Southwell, *CPR, 1558–60*, 320; Sackville, *CPR, 1558–60*, 56; Mildmay, *CPR, 1558–60*, 57; Cobham, *CPR, 1558–60*, 103.
14 Perry Williams, *The King's Council in the Marches of Wales under Elizabeth* (University of Wales Press, Cardiff, 1958), 249, 251–2.

15 Rachel Reid, *The King's Council in the North* (Longmans, London, 1921), 186–7. Sir Henry Percy, Sir Henry Gate, Christopher Estoft, John Vaughan and Richard Corbett, all royal officials, and several of them lawyers, were added. The Catholic, Richard Norton, was dismissed.
16 PRO, Baschet Transcripts, June 7th, 1559.
17 Bodleian Library, Tanner MSS, 90, f. 197.
18 'Sir Nicholas Throckmorton's Advice to Queen Elizabeth on her Accession to the Throne', edited by J. E. Neale in *English Historical Review*, LXV (1950), 91–8.
19 PRO, SP 12/1/3.
20 *CPR, 1558–60*, 60–61, 321, 324.
21 PRO, SP 12/2/19.

3 THE OPENING MONTHS

1 PRO, SP 12/1/9.
2 *CSPFor, 1558–59*, 30, 54; *CSPRome, 1558–71*, 1.
3 Amos Miller, *Sir Henry Killigrew* (Leicester University Press, 1963), 38–48; R. B. Wernham, *Before the Armada* (Cape, London, 1966), chapter 28.
4 *CSPFor, 1558–59*, 137–9.
5 Ibid., 156–7, 163–4, 178.
6 PRO, SP 12/2/10.
7 For Throckmorton's advice see *English Historical Review*, LXV (1950), 91–8; for Goodrich see PRO, SP 12/1/68, 69; for Waad see SP 12/1/66; and for the Device see John Strype, *Annals of the Reformation* (London, 1824), I (2), 392–8, copied from Cottonian MSS, Julius F VI 53. For an epitaph ballad on Goodrich, who died in 1562, see *Broadside Black-letter Ballads Printed in the Sixteenth and Seventeenth Centuries*, edited by Thomas Richards (London, 1868), 29–30.
8 For information on the membership of this Parliament not included in *Returns of Members of Parliament* I am greatly indebted to the History of Parliament Trust, who have been generous in assistance, most particularly to Miss Norah Fuidge.
9 On Bedford see unpublished London M.A. thesis by John C. Roberts, 'Parliamentary Representation of Devon and Dorset, 1559–1601'; on Norfolk see Neville Williams, *Thomas Howard, Fourth Duke of Norfolk* (Barrie and Rockliff, London, 1964).
10 J. E. Neale, *Elizabeth I and Her Parliaments, 1559–81*, 2 v. (Cape, London, 1953–7; Cape Paperback, 1965), 51–84, and his article, 'The Elizabethan Acts of Supremacy and Uniformity', in *English Historical Review*, LXV (1950), 304–32.
11 Strype, *Annals*, I (2), 408–23, 431–56.
12 See E. Jeffries Davies, 'An Unpublished Manuscript of the Lords' Journal', in *English Historical Review*, XXVIII (1913), 531–42.

4 THE SHAPING OF THE REGIME

1 *CSPFor, 1558–59*, 518; *Sadler Papers*, I, 375; Gilbert Burnet, *History of the Reformation of the Church of England* (London, 1715), III, 283, Appendix 54; BM, Lansdowne MSS, iv, f. 9; Cotton MSS, Caligula B X 84.

2 Conyers Read, *Mr Secretary Cecil and Queen Elizabeth* (Bedfordshire Historical Record Society, London, 1955; new edition, Cape Paperback, 1965), 142; *CSPFor, 1558–59*, 365.

3 Read, *Cecil*, 166–7.

4 *CSPFor, 1558–59*, 519; BM, Cotton MSS, Caligula B X 78–84; PRO, SP 12/6/34.

5 *CSPFor, 1559–60*, 94, 165; J. E. Phillips, *Image of a Queen* (Cambridge University Press, 1964), 18–19.

6 *CSPFor, 1559–60*, 103, 135. See also the Treaty of Berwick, 414.

7 *CSPFor, 1559–60*, 72.

8 Ibid., 71, 72, 112. There was still much uncertainty in the Councillors' minds. In a letter of November 14th the Privy Council warned Sadler that no final decision had been made and ended on a very doubtful note, 'For indeed alterations and changings of things that may hap here may give to you there other occasions of proceedings than presently we here determine' (BM, Cotton MSS, Caligula B X 48). It is to this period that we must also assign Cecil's letter of resignation (BM, Lansdowne MSS, cii, f. 1, printed in *CSPFor, 1559–60*, 186), in which he declares that since the queen finds his advice on Scotland unacceptable, he must request to have nothing more to do with the whole matter.

9 *CSPFor, 1559–60*, 54, 197, 221; BM, Harleian MSS, ccliii, f. 83b.

10 See the dispatches of this envoy in Victor von Klarwill, *Queen Elizabeth and Some Foreigners* (John Lane, London, 1928), 1–171.

11 *CSPSpan, 1558–67*, 95, 97, 111.

12 Ibid., 115; *CSPFor, 1559–60*, 154 and also Cecil to Sadler and Crofts, 171.

13 *CSPSpan, 1558–67*, 107, 113, 117.

14 Read, *Cecil*, 168; PRO, SP 12/12/1; *Haynes*, 295.

15 *CSPScot, 1547–63*, 367, 369.

16 Patrick Forbes, *A Full View of the Public Transactions in the Reign of Queen Elizabeth*, 2 v. (London, 1740), I, 454–7; PRO, SP 12/12/21; *Hatfield*, 221.

17 Forbes, *Full View*, I, 500–501.

18 Ibid., 501; *CSPFor, 1560–61*, 87.

19 Ibid., 104.

20 *Haynes*, 342; *Hatfield*, 244.

21 BM, Cotton MSS, Caligula B X 96; Thomas Wright, *Queen Elizabeth and Her Times*, 2 v. (London, 1838), I, 30; *CSPFor, 1560–61*, 184–5.

22 PRO, SP 12/1/66.

23 Reid, *Council in the North*, 192.

24 Rachel Reid, 'The Rebellion of the Earls, 1569', in *Transactions of the Royal Historical Society*, n.s., XX (1906), 177, 180n.

5 THE EMERGENCE OF DUDLEY

1 *CSPFor, 1560–61*, 222, 226–7, 262, 274, 287.

2 Ibid., 262.

3 Ibid., 433.

4 PRO, SP 12/13/21, 21 (1).

5 *CSPFor, 1559–60*, 171; *CSPSpan, 1558–67*, 141; *Relations politiques de la France et l'Espagne avec l'Écosse*, 5 v., edited by A. Teulet (Paris, 1862), I, 54.

6 Dudley MSS, Longleat House, i, *passim*; *CSPSpan, 1558–67*, 106, 109.

7 PRO, SP 12/11/14; SP 12/13/12, 14; SP 12/6/35; Dudley MSS, i, 54.

8 Ibid., i, 21, 161.

9 *CSPSpan, 1558–67*, 95, 96, 107.

10 Ibid., 118; *CSPFor, 1560–61*, 350; Dudley MSS, i, 204.

11 On Amy Dudley's possible malady, see Ian Aird, 'The Death of Amy Robsart', in *English Historical Review*, LXXI (1956), 69–79.

12 Read, *Cecil*, 199, quoting Stow MSS, f. 180b and SP 70/17. See also Winchester's letter, *Haynes*, 361.

13 *CSPFor, 1560–61*, 376–7; *CSPSpan, 1558–67*, 176–7; *Hatfield*, 252, 253.

14 *CSPSpan, 1558–67*, 176, 178.

15 *CSPFor, 1560–61*, 398; BM, Additional MSS, 35830, 74.

16 Ibid., 66; *Hardwicke*, I, 163–9.

17 *CSPFor, 1560–61*, 467, 475.

18 *CPR, 1560–63*, 44.

19 *CSPSpan, 1558–67*, 178, 180, 181–3.

20 *CSPSpan, 1558–67*, 187–9; BM, Additional MSS, 35830, 74; *CSPFor, 1561–62*, 23.

21 *CSPFor, 1560–61*, 443, 492, 505, 565, 579; *CSPSpan, 1558–67*, 186.

22 Ibid., 186, 189; *Relations Politiques des Pays-Bas et de l'Angleterre Sous le Règne de Philippe II*, 11 v., edited by Kervyn de Lettenhove and L. Gilliodts van Severen (Brussels, 1882–1900), I, 547.

23 *CSPFor, 1561–62*, 82–8, 104; *CSPSpan, 1558–67*, 193, 195; Read, *Cecil*, 210.

24 Lettenhove, *Relations Politiques*, I, 553; PRO, SP 12/16/55, 66–8; SP 12/18/7, 8, 19; *CSPFor, 1561–62*, 104.

25 PRO, SP 12/17/1; *CSPFor, 1561–62*, 93; *Hardwicke*, I, 180.

26 *CSPSpan, 1558–67*, 180; *CSPFor, 1560–61*, 478, 587.

6 THE NEWHAVEN ADVENTURE

1 *CSPFor, 1561–62*, 277; *Hardwicke*, I, 176; PRO, SP 12/19/31; SP 12/21/39, 55.

2 *CSPFor, 1561–62*, 163, 204, 248; *CSPScot, 1547–63*, 542.

3 BM, Additional MSS, 35831, 119, 191, 205; *CSPSpan, 1558–67*, 208; *CSPFor, 1561–62*, 418.

4 *CSPSpan, 1558–67*, 224–5.

5 *CSPFor, 1561–62*, 237, 355–9, 410; *Hardwicke*, I, 174, 179; *Hatfield*, I, 262; *CSPScot, 1547–63*, 565.

6 *CSPFor, 1561–62*, 362, 389; *CSPScot, 1547–63*, 577, 595, 640.

7 BM, Additional MSS, 35831, 37; PRO, Baschet Transcripts, July 11th, 1562.

8 *CSPSpan, 1558–67*, 227.

9 *CSPFor, 1561–62*, 608, 609.

10 *CSPSpan, 1558–67*, 219, 226.

11 *CSPFor, 1562*, 21, 22, 36.

12 *CSPFor, 1561–62*, 404; *1562*, 36, 80, 129.

13 *CPR, 1560–63*, 189–91 (lands); 244 (cloth licence); 270 (renewal of sarpler licence); 310 (Constable of Windsor Castle); 361 (£1,000 annuity).

14 Ibid., 291, 330.

15 Forbes, *Full View*, II, 2; *CSPFor, 1562*, 170; Read, *Cecil*, 243–9.

16 *CSPFor, 1562*, 363.

17 Ibid., 268, 306.

18 PRO, SP 12/24/21; Baschet Transcripts, July 21st, 1562; *CSPFor, 1562*, 292. The French wished that Lord Grey were with him; Throckmorton hinted that Croft might be well employed in this service.

19 See *The Life and Death of William Whittingham*, printed in *Camden Society Miscellany* (London, 1870), VI, 14–19; *CSPFor, 1562*, 575, 577; Patrick Collinson, *Letters of Thomas Wood, Puritan, 1566–77* (Special Supplement, No. 5, *Bulletin of the Institute of Historical Research*, 1960), ix; PRO, SP 12/19/36.

20 See Dudley MSS, I, *passim*; Collinson, *Thomas Wood*, xxi–xxiii.

21 Miller, *Killigrew*, 87.

22 *CSPFor, 1561–62*, 404; see Mary Dewar, *Sir Thomas Smith* (Athlone, London, 1964), for full biographical account.

23 *CSPSpan, 1558–67*, 263; Forbes, *Full View*, II, 188.

24 *CPR, 1560–63*, 533–43.

25 Read, *Cecil*, 257.

26 Ibid., 255.

27 *CPR, 1560–63*, 127.

7 SUCCESSION AND MARRIAGE: THE FIRST PHASE

1 *CSPSpan, 1558–67*, 262–4. On the whole succession question, see Mortimer Levine, *The Early Elizabethan Succession Question* (Stanford, 1966).

2 *Hardwicke*, I, 187; see Claire Cross, *The Puritan Earl: The Life of Henry Hastings, Third Earl of Huntingdon, 1536–95* (Macmillan, London, 1966).

3 PRO, SP 12/28/20; *CSPSpan, 1558–67*, 321.

4 *CSPFor, 1562*, 615 (dated 1560); *CSPFor, 1560–61*, 415; *CSPSpan, 1558–67*, 176; *Papiers d'État ... relatif à l'Histoire de l'Écosse au 16e Siècle*, 3 v., edited by A. Teulet (Bannatyne Club publication, 107, Paris, 1852–60), I, 400.

5 *CSPSpan, 1558–67*, 135; *CSPFor, 1562*, 12–16, 23.

6 PRO, SP 12/23/6; *CSPFor, 1563*, 273, 415, 463.

7 PRO, SP 12/19/4; F. C. Dietz, *English Government Finance, 1558–1641* (New York, 1932), 19; *CSPFor, 1562*, 141–2.

8 BM, Lansdowne MSS, cii, f. 13, 18, 20; Neale, *Parliament, 1559–81*, 116–17; BM, Cotton MSS, Vespasian C VII (Wotton to Challoner, October 13th, 1562); *CSPSpan, 1558–67*, 259, 295; *CSPFor, 1562*, 423; Strype, *Annals*, I (I), 555; Wright, *Elizabeth*, I, 127, 129. See also *CPR, 1566–69*, 63, 65. For this last reference I am indebted to Professor J. E. Neale.

9 BM, Lansdowne MSS, cii, f. 24; Neale, *Parliament, 1559–81*, 91, 93, 121; *CSPFor, 1563*, 186; Strype, *Annals*, I (I), 475 fol.

10 BM, Lansdowne MSS, cii, f. 18; *CSPSpan, 1558–67*, 273.

11 BM, Lansdowne MSS, cii, f. 22.

12 *CSPScot, 1547–63*, 667.

13 *CSPScot, 1563–69*, 8, 22; *CSPSpan, 1558–67*, 308–15; Maurice Lee, *James Stewart, Earl of Moray* (New York, 1953), 114–15. See also Cecil's memorandum of July 20th, 1562 in Forbes, *Full View*, II, 2.

14 *CSPScot, 1563–69*, 8, 19, 20, 22; *CSPSpan, 1558–67*, 338.

15 *CSPScot, 1563–69*, 27, 31–3; *CSPSpan, 1558–67*, 313.

16 *CSPScot, 1563–69*, 32, 51, 54, 55–9.

17 Ibid., 81.

18 Ibid., 44.

19 *CSPFor, 1563*, 415; Lee, *Moray*, 123–4.

20 *CSPScot, 1563–69*, 60, 68, 75, 76–7, 83; Lee, *Moray*, 125.

21 *Memoirs of Sir James Melville of Halhill*, edited by A. F. Steuart (Routledge, London, 1929), 88–9, 92, 98; *CSPScot, 1563–69*, 124; *CSPFor, 1564–65*, 247; BM, Lansdowne MSS, cii, 66; William Camden, *Annals of Queen Elizabeth* (London, 1688), 75; *Original Letters Illustrative of English History*, edited by H. Ellis (London, 1827), 2 ser., II, 294.

22 Wright, *Elizabeth*, I, 179, 187.

23 *CSPScot, 1563–69*, 141–7; according to the French ambassador (Teulet, *Papiers d'État*, II, 195–6 and Baschet Transcripts, May 2nd, 1565) the other noblemen mentioned were Norfolk and Arundel.

24 *CSPFor, 1561–62*, 189; *1562*, 67–9; *CSPSpan, 1558–67*, 238–49.

25 Ibid., 259–60, 276, 280, 293; *CSPFor, 1563*, 32.

26 BM, Cotton MSS, Vespasian C VII 224–6.

27 *CSPSpan, 1558–67*, 297, 321.

28 BM, Lansdowne MSS, cii, f. 89, 93, 102, 193; *Hatfield*, 290. Hales's book was not printed until 1713.

29 BM, Lansdowne MSS, cii, f. 93, 102, 103; *CSPFor, 1564–65*, 190; *Hatfield*, 291.

30 *CPR, 1563–66*, 59; *CSPFor, 1564–65*, 145.

31 BM, Lansdowne MSS, cii, f. 103.

8 SUCCESSION AND MARRIAGE: THE SECOND PHASE

1 BM, Lansdowne MSS, iv, f. 6; see A. Woodworth, *Purveyance for the Royal Household of Queen Elizabeth* in *Transactions of the American Philosophical Society*, n.s., XXV, Part I (1945), 12.

2 See John Nichols, *The Progresses and Public Processions of Queen Elizabeth* (London, 1788); E. K. Chambers, *The Elizabethan Stage*, 4 v. (Oxford University Press, 1923), IV, 75 fol.

3 BM, Additional MSS, 35831, 169.

4 *CPR, 1563–66*, 320.

5 Ibid., 16.

6 *CSPFor, 1564–65*, 58.

7 *CPR, 1563–66*, 85, 87, 259.

8 *CPR, 1560–63*, 476.

9 PRO, SP 12/20/24.

10 Ibid., 12/21/26.

11 *CSPSpan, 1558–67*, 446.

12 *CSPFor, 1563*, 493.

13 Wright, *Elizabeth*, I, 130.

14 For these various meetings see *CSPScot, 1563–69*, 150 (dated May 1st, 1565); *CSPFor, 1564–65*, 384–7 (dated June 4th); BM, Cotton MSS, Caligula B X 299–308 (dated June 2nd–4th); Caligula B X 350d–53 (written after the marriage); and 354–9 (dated September 24th–26th); Lansdowne MSS, cii, f. 112 (dated June 3rd and 12th).

15 *CSPSpan, 1558–67*, 393, 398. See *A Collection of Original Letters from the Bishops to the Privy Council, 1564*, edited by Mary Bateson in Camden Miscellany IX (London, 1895). Out of 852 names listed, 431 are favourable to the new religion; 264 are set down as neuter, indifferent, or not favourable; and 157 are counted as hostile. These are the results of a survey ordered by the Council on October 17th, 1564. There had been two new commissions of the peace for the entire country in 1562 (*CPR, 1560–63*, 433 fol.) and in June 1564 (*CPR, 1563–66*, 19, fol.), but no changes were made in the wake of the bishops' reports.

16 *The Correspondence of Matthew Parker*, edited by John Bruce for the Parker Society (Cambridge, 1853), 223–7; Richard W. Dixon, *History of the Church of England*, 6 v. (Oxford, 1902), VI, Chapter 37.

17 Strype, *Annals*, I (2), 129; *Parker Correspondence*, 237, 243, 245; John Strype, *Life and Acts of Archbishop Parker*, 3 v. (Oxford, 1821), I, 308, 314.

18 *CPR, 1563–66*, 259.

19 BM, Lansdowne MSS, cii, f. 121; *CSPFor, 1564–65*, 458, 478, 481.

20 BM, Lansdowne MSS, cii, f. 114; *CSPFor, 1564–65*, 215; Teulet, *Relations Politiques*, II, 233.

21 BM, Cotton MSS, Caligula B X 350–3; Teulet, *Relations Politiques*, II, 235.

22 *CSPFor, 1564–65*, 415, 475, 500, 504; *1566–68*, 27–31, 33; BM, Cotton MSS, Caligula B X 352; Lansdowne MSS, cii, f. 121.

23 *Hatfield*, 283, 285; *CSPFor, 1563*, 558; Wright, *Elizabeth*, I, 207; Klarwill, *Elizabeth and Some Strangers*, 172–257.

24 PRO, Baschet Transcripts, February 16th, February 17th, May 10th, 1565.

25 Ibid., May 20th, June 6th, June 18th, 1565; Teulet, *Relations Politiques*, II, 217; BM, Lansdowne MSS, cii, f. 114.

26 *CSPSpan, 1558–67*, 434; Klarwill, *Elizabeth and Some Strangers*, 237.

27 *CSPSpan, 1558–67*, 382, 438, 517–18, 544, 575–6; PRO, SP 12/39/31; Klarwill, *Elizabeth and Some Strangers*, 259–64.

28 *CSPSpan, 1558–67*, 431, 521, 524; *CSPFor, 1566–68*, 8.

29 BM, Lansdowne MSS, cii, f. 121.

30 Camden, *Annals*, 79; PRO, SP 12/36/66; *Murdin*, 760; *CSPSpan, 1558–67*, 445–6.

31 Ibid., 450, 453.

32 BM, Lansdowne MSS, cii, f. 121; *CSPSpan, 1558–67*, 511, 554, 563, 564; *Murdin*, 761; *CSPVen, 1558–80*, 382 (which probably confuses this quarrel with that of the preceding summer); Read, *Cecil*, 332–3, quoting SP 63/18/19.

33 *CSPSpan, 1558–67*, 575–6; Chambers, *Elizabethan Stage*, IV, 82; PRO, Baschet Transcripts, August 6th and August 12th, 1566.

34 *CSPSpan, 1558–67*, 365; PRO, Baschet Transcripts, July 3rd, 1565; BM, Lansdowne MSS, cii, f. 110, 121.

35 Ibid., cii, f. 110, 121; *CSPSpan, 1558–67*, 377.

36 *APC*, VI, 314; *CPR, 1566–69*, 137; S. E. Lehmberg, *Sir Walter Mildmay and Tudor Government* (Austin, Texas, 1964), 48n., 65.

37 *Haynes*, 444.

38 *CSPSpan, 1558–67*, 409.

39 Ibid., 557, 560; Melville, *Memoirs*, 114–19, 133; *CSPScot, 1563–69*, 286.

40 Camden, *Annals*, 79.

41 *CSPSpan, 1558–67*, 466.

42 BM, Cotton MSS, Caligula B X 472; *CSPScot, 1563–69*, 310.

43 *CSPSpan, 1558–67*, 450, 473, 483, 485, 497–9, 507–8, 516–17, 523; *CSPScot, 1563–69*, 198, 210, 272.

44 Ibid., 278, 294, 457, 627–8.

45 PRO, Baschet Transcripts, September 22nd, 1566; *CSPSpan, 1558–67*, 577, 580; PRO, SP 12/40/68.

46 BM, Harleian MSS, 555, f. 11–16 (Browne); *Allegations against Surmised Title of the Queen of Scots and the Favourers of the same* (London, 1565); Cambridge University Library Gg iii, 34, pp. 107–17; Dd ix, 14, 64–70; Bodleian, Ashmolean MSS, 829, f. 31–36. See also M. Levine, 'A "Letter" on the Elizabethan Succession Question 1566', in *Huntington Library Quarterly*, XIX (1956–7), 18–38.

47 BM, Egerton MSS, 2836, ff. 37–71.

48 *Sadler Papers*, II, 556–71.

49 BM, Cotton MSS, Caligula B IX 255–65.

50 BM, Egerton MSS, 2836.

51 National Library of Scotland MSS, 571–2, La Forêt to Charles IX, October 21st, 1566. I have used a transcript made available through the kindness of Professor J. E. Neale.

52 See Neale, *Parliament, 1559–81*, 145–50.

53 Ibid., 158–60; PRO, SP 12/41/28, 29.

54 Dietz, *English Public Finance*, 22–4.

55 PRO, SP 12/41/36.

9 THE DOWNFALL OF MARY STUART

1 *CSPFor, 1566–68*, 232, 252; *CSPScot, 1563–69*, 336, 340, 342.

2 Ibid., 348.

3 Ibid., 348–9, 366–7, 378–9; *CSPFor, 1566–68*, 290, 295.

4 Melville, *Memoirs*, 165; *CSPSpan, 1558–67*, 655, 659, 669, 674; *CSPScot, 1563–69*, 361, 385; *CSPFor, 1566–68*, 324; *Cabala sive Scrinia Sacra* (London, 1691), 128–30.

5 PRO, SP 12/43/36, 39.

6 *CSPScot, 1563–69*, 378–9, 385–6, 389; *Cabala*, 130.

7 *CSPFor, 1566–68*, 383.

8 *CSPSpan, 1558–67*, 610, 626, 640.

9 PRO, SP 12/44/23.

10 *CSPSpan, 1558–67,* 616, 626–7, 628.

11 Ibid., 459, 605, 616, 623, 631, 656, 670, 686–7.

12 *CSPFor, 1566–68,* 257; *CSPSpan, 1558–67,* 636–7.

13 *CSPFor, 1566–68,* 360, 361.

14 PRO, SP 12/44/53; BM, Cotton MSS, Titus B II 328; for Norfolk's letters see Historical Manuscripts Commission, *Calendar of the Manuscripts of the Marquess of Bath Preserved at Longleat, Wiltshire,* 3 v. (London, 1904–7), II, 17–19. PRO, SP 12/44/42, 46; *CSPFor, 1566–68,* 377–8, 382; Wright, *Elizabeth,* I, 265.

15 For Sussex's views see *CSPSpan, 1558–67,* 461; for Cecil's, 580, 611.

16 Ibid., 459; Neale, *Parliament, 1559–81,* 147.

17 Collinson, *Thomas Wood,* xii–xiii, 1–2.

18 Dixon, *Church of England,* VI, 149; *Journals of the House of Lords* (London, 1834), I, 641.

19 Wright, *Elizabeth,* I, 209.

20 Dixon, *Church of England,* VI, 152; *CSPSpan, 1558–67,* 606; PRO, Baschet Transcripts, March 25th, 1568.

21 *Haynes,* 444.

22 *CSPFor, 1566–68,* 431.

23 *CSPScot, 1563–69,* 407–9.

10 MARY IN ENGLAND

1 *CSPScot, 1563–69,* 410, 412, 413; *CSPFor, 1566–68,* 469, 473; BM Cotton MSS, Caligula B IX 290; Wright, *Elizabeth,* I, 272; *Memorials of the Rebellion of 1569,* edited by Cuthbert Sharpe (London, 1840), 340–41.

2 *CSPScot, 1563–69,* 414, 416; PRO, Baschet Transcripts, May 22nd, 1568.

3 *CSPScot, 1563–69,* 463, 469.

4 Ibid., 424–7, 431–5, 459; Camden, *Annals,* 110; Teulet, *Relations Politiques,* II, 369–70; *CSPSpan, 1568–79,* 35–6.

5 *CSPScot, 1563–69,* 438.

6 Ibid., 418–19.

7 *Hatfield,* 358; *Haynes,* 467–8; *CSPScot, 1563–69,* 421, 438, 451–2, 459–60; BM, Harleian MSS, 6990, 78.

8 *CSPScot, 1563–69,* 462–3, 470–71, 509.

9 Ibid., 492, 510.

10 PRO, SP 12/47/36.

11 Ibid., 12/46/62, 65.

12 Ibid., 12/47/36; *CSPScot, 1563–69,* 492, 510–11.

13 *Hatfield,* 369; *CSPScot, 1563–69,* 529, 536–8, 540.

14 Ibid., 520, 523, 529, 532.

15 Ibid., 527, 528, 551; Lodge, *Illustrations,* I, 458–64; *Hatfield,* 369.

16 *CSPScot, 1563–69,* 533–4.

17 *Hatfield,* 365–6; *Haynes,* 487–8.

18 *CSPScot, 1563–69,* 552, 554–5, 560, 563, 569 fol.

19 Ibid., 581, 583, 590.

20 Ibid., 589–92, 594, 604; *Hatfield*, 384; *Haynes*, 497.
21 *CSPScot, 1563–69*, 529, 534, 540; *CSPFor, 1566–68*, 570.
22 *Fénélon*, I, 17–18.
23 Ibid., 79.
24 *CSPScot, 1563–69*, 595.

11   FRENCH PROTESTANTS AND SPANISH GOLD

1 *CSPFor, 1566–68*, 373, 434; PRO, Baschet Transcripts, March 25th, 1568.
2 Ibid., August 28th, September 16th, October 16th, October 25th, 1568; *CSPFor, 1566–68*, 533, 545, 548, 555, 560.
3 Ibid., 551, 561–2, 573; *Hatfield*, 364; PRO, SP 12/47/92; *Cabala*, 143; PRO, Baschet Transcripts, October 31st, 1568.
4 *Fénélon*, I, 24, 45, 77–8.
5 *CSPSpan, 1568–79*, 10.
6 *CSPFor, 1566–68*, 20 (instructions for Man dated February 20th, 1566); *CSPSpan, 1568–79*, 30.
7 Ibid., 30.
8 Ibid., 10.
9 Ibid., 3.
10 Ibid., 19, 36–7, 40.
11 Ibid., 27, 33, 43, 52, 61; *Hatfield*, 371; Wernham, *Before the Armada*, 291–5.
12 *Cabala*, 143.
13 *CSPSpan, 1568–79*, 90, 91, 101, 102, 114; Lettenhove, *Relations Politiques*, v, 253; Conyers Read, 'Queen Elizabeth's Seizure of Alba's Pay Ships', in *Journal of Modern History*, v (1933), 443–64.
14 *CSPSpan, 1568–79*, 90.
15 PRO, SP 12/48/50, 60, 62.
16 *CSPSpan, 1568–79*, 98; BM, Cotton MSS, Galba C III.
17 *CSPSpan, 1568–79*, 104, 122; Lettenhove, *Relations Politiques*, v, 262, 273, 274, 277.
18 *CSPSpan, 1568–79*, 108, 109, 132, 150.
19 Ibid., 83. De Spes rejoiced that initially the business of the ships was left to the Clerk of the Signet, Bernard Hampton, fluent in Spanish and once secretary to Philip II; Cecil was otherwise occupied.
20 *CSPSpan, 1568–79*, 85; PRO, SP 12/47/32.
21 *Haynes*, 579–88; it can be dated by references to the Spanish embargo and to the death of Condé, who was killed in March.
22 *CSPSpan, 1568–79*, 135, 153; *CSPFor, 1569–71*, 119; Lettenhove, *Relations Politiques*, v, 250. Alva regarded the Treaty of Bruges as favourable to the Low Countries (*CSPSpan, 1568–79*, 216); Wernham, *Before the Armada*, 283–5.
23 For Philip's views see *CSPSpan, 1568–79*, 150, 177.
24 Lettenhove, *Relations Politiques*, v, 250.

12 THE NORFOLK MARRIAGE

1 *Haynes*, 548, 581, 586. Leslie, the Bishop of Ross, had published his *Defence* of Mary's claim in 1569. See also *Fénélon*, II, 122.

2 Ibid., II, 120–21.

3 Ibid., II, 123; *Haynes*, 580. See Throckmorton's unconvincing denial that such a decision had been made (*Haynes*, 548). The ex-ambassador gave himself away in the exchange with Fitzgarret, by his angry accusation that the latter was a partisan of the Hertford children's claim.

4 *Haynes*, 579–87. Cecil was alleged by his opponents to be a favourer of the Hertford claims (Camden, *Annals*, 122), but there is no direct evidence of this.

5 BM, Cotton MSS, Caligula C II 551–64; Julius XI 22–41. The latter is dated March 15th, 1569–70. The basic text is the same in both but there are many variations.

6 *CSPScot, 1563–69*, 530, 534–5, 540; *CSPFor, 1566–68*, 570–72.

7 J. H. Pollen, *The English Catholics in the Reign of Queen Elizabeth* (Longmans, London, 1920), 73 fol.; *CSPRome, 1558–71*, 371.

8 Pollen, *English Catholics*, 77–8, 101, 104–6. See *A Bull Issued by the Pope to Dr. Harding* ... (London, 1570); this pamphlet, probably written by Thomas Norton, contains both an English and a Latin text of the bull of 1567. See also C. G. Bayne, *Anglo-Roman Relations, 1558–65* (Oxford University Press, 1913), 176, 296; *CSPDom, Addenda, 1566–79*, 407; Sharpe, *Memorials*, 280–82.

9 *CSPSpan, 1568–79*, 4–5, 10, 14, 17, 22; PRO, Baschet Transcripts December 6th, 1567; SP 12/51/6.

10 Pollen, *English Catholics*, 131; *CSPSpan, 1568–79*, 163; *Fénélon*, I, 258; *Murdin*, 42; *CSPRome, 1558–71*, 302. Fénélon refers to him as accredited by the pope in the spring of 1569; Ross in his confession says that it was only after being released in the autumn of 1569 that Ridolfi showed him authority from the pope.

11 *Murdin*, 52; *ST*, I, 978.

12 *Murdin*, 45 (misplaced and misdated under 1571), 52 fol.; *CSPScot, 1563–69*, 533; *ST*, I, 975–8, 988; *Fénélon*, I, 17–18; *Haynes*, 574.

13 *Murdin*, 51; *Haynes*, 574–5; W. Robertson, *The History of Scotland* (London, 1759), II, Appendix 58–61; *ST*, I, 979–82; *CSPScot, 1563–69*, 693–4.

14 *CSPScot, 1571–74*, 33–4; *Haynes*, 541. Leicester knew of Norfolk's hopes as early as January. He was in the duke's confidence before Moray returned to Scotland (Robertson, *History*, II, Appendix 58–61).

15 Haynes, 542.

16 *CSPScot, 1563–69*, 642 fol.; *Fénélon*, II, 6–7.

17 *Murdin*, 106; Robertson, *History*, II, Appendix 57.

18 *CSPScot, 1563–69*, 659, 664, 666.

19 *CSPSpan, 1568–79*, 167, 189, 209, 210; *Fénélon*, II, 126–7; Lettenhove, *Relations Politiques*, V, 438.

20 *CSPFor, 1569–71*, 109, 119; *Cabala*, 155–6; Robertson, *History*, II, Appendix 57.

21 Camden, *Annals*, 122.

22 *Fénélon*, I, 96–7, 114–15. See also Lettenhove, *Relations Politiques*, V, 297–8 for a report that the price of woollens had fallen 15 per cent to the great discontent of merchants. Trade with France was under a French embargo in the late winter.

23 *Fénélon*, I, 69–70.

24 *CSPSpan, 1568–79*, 111; *Fénélon*, I, 233, 258 fol.

25 Ibid., I, 204, 233, 258 fol.

26 Ibid., I, 233–4. See also Lettenhove, *Relations Politiques*, V, 331–3.

27 *Fénélon*, I, 235–6. See also Lettenhove, *Relations Politiques*, V, 307, n. 1, where a variant of the same story is told in a letter attributed to Ridolfi.

28 *Fénélon*, I, 217–23, 322; Lettenhove, *Relations Politiques*, V, 333 fol., 360.

29 *CSPSpan, 1568–79*, 142; *Fénélon*, I, 330; *CSPRome, 1558–71*, 302; Lettenhove, *Relations Politiques*, V, 366, 384.

30 *Fénélon*, I, 409–10.

31 *CSPSpan, 1568–79*, 166; *Fénélon*, II, 51–4; Williams, *Norfolk*, 117–18.

32 *Hatfield*, 409; BM, Cotton MSS, Titus B II 336; Lansdowne cii, f. 143.

33 *CSPScot, 1571–74*, 35–7.

34 Camden, *Annals*, 129–30; *CSPScot, 1571–74*, 36; *ST*, I, 989, 994–5; *Fénélon*, II, 236; *Hatfield*, 541; *Murdin*, 23, 44, 50, 126. The suggestion may have been Leslie's; according to his testimony it was Ridolfi's, but Lumley (*Hatfield*, I, 541) mentions the bishop.

35 *Haynes*, 521–7.

36 *Murdin*, 225–6; Camden, *Annals*, 131; *Haynes*, 528–9; *Fénélon*, II, 247–8, 272. See Lettenhove, *Relations Politiques*, V, 451, 456, 458–9 for De Spes's confused account of what he hoped was going on.

37 *Fénélon*, II, 258; *CSPSpan, 1568–79*, 197; *ST*, I, 990.

38 *Haynes*, 531–2.

39 Ibid., 528–30, 533, 539–40, 596. *CSPScot, 1571–74*, 38; *CSPDom, Addenda, 1566–79*, 404; Sharpe, *Memorials*, 195; *Hatfield*, 430; Camden, *Annals*, 131; *Cabala*, 157; *CSPSpan, 1568–79*, 198–9.

40 *Cabala*, 156–7.

41 *Haynes*, 571–2; Camden, *Annals*, 145; *Fénélon*, II, 379.

42 *Cabala*, 156–7; *CSPDom, Addenda, 1566–79*, 84; *CSPScot, 1563–69*, 684.

13   THE REVOLT OF THE EARLS

1 *CSPDom, Addenda, 1566–79*, 402; *CSPSpan, 1568–79*, 96; Sharpe, *Memorials*, 189–90, 192, 194.

2 PRO, SP 12/67/59; *CSPDom, Addenda, 1566–79*, 274, 403; *Murdin*, 30; *CSPScot, 1563–69*, 487; *CSPSpan, 1568–79*, 167; R. Reid, 'The Rising in the North', in the *Transactions of the Royal Historical Society*, n.s., XX (1906), 171–203; Sharpe, *Memorials*, 192, 193. Fénélon seems to have got hold of a tag end of this proposal or one related to it; and so may the English government (*Fénélon*, I, 325, 398).

3 *CSPDom, Addenda, 1566–79*, 406; PRO, SP 12/85/33; *Murdin*, 215; *CSPSpan, 1568–79*, 196, 199; *Hatfield*, 469; Sharpe, *Memorials*, 201.

4 *CSPSpan, 1568–79*, 196, 199, 208; *CSPDom, Addenda, 1566–79*, 404–5, 413; *Haynes*, 596; *Murdin*, 217, 226–7; PRO, SP 12/67/59; BM, Cotton MSS, Caligula C I 514; Sharpe, *Memorials*, 195–200; Lettenhove, *Relations Politiques*, V, 479, in which Alva advises De Spes that the earls should flee to the Low Countries.

5 CSPDom, Addenda, 1566–79, 85, 89, 93, 95; BM, Cotton MSS, C I 472; Haynes, 550.

6 PRO, SP 12/59/20; SP 12/60/18; CSPDom, Addenda, 1566–79, 89.

7 Ibid., 98, 99, 101; Hatfield, 470; Sharpe, Memorials, 10–15.

8 CSPDom, Addenda, 1566–79, 104–5; Sharpe, Memorials, 24–5, 36, 50–51.

9 CSPDom, Addenda, 1566–79, 407; Sharpe, Memorials, 204.

10 CSPDom, Addenda, 1566–79, 405; Sharpe, Memorials, 199.

11 CSPDom, Addenda, 1566–79, 403, 407–8; Sharpe, Memorials, 193, 196, 204.

12 R. Reid, Transactions of Royal Historical Society, n.s., xx, 197; CSPDom, Addenda, 1566–79, 111; Sharpe, Memorials, 39–42, 184.

13 BM, Harleian MSS, 6990, 89; Haynes, 564.

14 CSPDom, Addenda, 1566–79, 108, 111–12, 114, 119, 148, 225; Sharpe, Memorials, 81, 210–11; Haynes, 563–4; Derby had already declared his loyalty to the queen, even before the earls' letter came (PRO, SP 12/59/28).

15 Reid, Transactions of Royal Historical Society, n.s., xx, 177; CSPDom, Addenda, 1566–79, 146; Sharpe, Memorials, 78–9.

16 CSPDom, Addenda, 1566–79, 86, 89, 113 (Sussex's warrant as Lieutenant-General was dated November 15th, 1569), 114, 119–20, 123–4, 187, 235; CSPScot, 1563–69, 674; PRO, SP 12/67/59; Haynes, 553; BM, Cotton MSS, Caligula B IX 375, 382, 398; Hatfield, 465; also in Lodge, Illustrations, I, 500–3.

17 CSPSpan, 1568–79, 214, 218; Fénélon, II, 379, 385–6; Murdin, 38, 39; Montague appears on the list of Lords Lieutenant issued November 20th (Haynes, 560 and PRO, SP 12/59/24) but not on the list in SP 12/59/60 (only the Lord Chamberlain appears for Sussex/Surrey). Note the cryptic marginal note by Cecil on SP 12/60/4, December 4th—'Lord Montague'. The refugees abroad had hoped that the two lords would join Alva, bringing the Cumberland heir with them (CSPFor, 1569–71, 212).

18 CSPDom, Addenda, 1566–79, 276; Sharpe, Memorials, 285.

19 CSPScot, 1569–71, 9.

20 Ibid., 54; CSPDom, Addenda, 1566–79, 193, 241.

21 Ibid., 134, 274; Sharpe, Memorials, 285; CSPSpan, 1568–79, 211; Fénélon, II, 348, 351, 424; CSPRome, 1558–71, 326–7. See CSPDom, Addenda, 1566–79, 171 and Sharpe, Memorials, 122–3 for English suspicions of Spanish intentions.

22 CSPSpan, 1568–79, 186, 217, 224.

23 CSPSpan, 1568–79, 184; CSPScot, 1571–74, 33; Camden, Annals, 122; Haynes, 548.

24 Camden, Annals, 122.

25 Robertson, History, II, Appendix 57.

26 CSPScot, 1563–69, 695; 1569–71, 166; Robertson, History, II, Appendix 58–61.

27 Camden, Annals, 127.

28 Fénélon, II, 124.

29 Camden, Annals, 122; Haynes, 548, 577.

30 Camden, Annals, 145; David Lloyd, State Worthies (London, 1670), 552; Fénélon, III, 29.

31 Hatfield, 438–40.

32 CSPDom, Addenda, 1566–79, 407.

14 THE AFTERMATH OF THE STORM

1 Fénélon, II, 355-6; III, 45, 76.
2 CSPScot, 1569-71, 366; Haynes, 594-6.
3 PRO, SP 12/66/55, which was almost certainly written by Francis Walsingham. See C. Read, Mr Secretary Walsingham, 3 v. (Clarendon Press, Oxford, 1925; Archon, 1967), I, 63-4. For pro-Norfolk pamphlets see BM, Cotton MSS, Julius F XI f. 22-41; Cotton, Caligula C II 551-64. The printed pamphlet, which is bound in with the manuscripts in Caligula C II 284-91, seems to be earlier in date.
4 Fénélon, II, 302, 336, 355-6.
5 CSPScot, 1569-71, 87.
6 Ibid., 196.
7 Fénélon, III, 144 fol.; CSPFor, 1569-71, 217; CSPScot, 1569-71, 137.
8 Ibid., 171.
9 Ibid., 182, 183, 189, 191, 204.
10 Ibid., 438 (Châtelherault to Sussex).
11 Ibid., 103; BM, Cotton MSS, Caligula B IX 395; Fénélon, III, 95.
12 Ibid., III, 43, 194, 123, 154-61; CSPScot, 1569-71, 182, 189; Cabala, 162; CSPSpan, 1568-79, 239-41.
13 Fénélon, III, 188.
14 Haynes, 597.
15 Fénélon, III, 95, 123, 139, 162, 189.
16 CSPSpan, 1568-79, 256; CSPScot, 1569-71, 172-3.
17 CSPFor, 1569-71, 302-3; CSPScot, 1569-71, 283, 288, 322; CSPSpan, 1568-79, 256. See CSPSpan, 1568-79, 216-17 for Alva's pessimistic assessment of Spain's situation vis-à-vis England. On the Norfolk rising see N. Williams in Norfolk Archaeology, XXXII (1961), 73-81.
18 Fénélon, III, 100, 123; CSPSpan, 1568-79, 229; BM, Cotton MSS, Julius F XI 22-41; Caligula C II 551-64.
19 Fénélon, III, 76, 102.
20 See memorandum dated December 1570 (CSPScot, 1569-71, 455), but applicable to earlier months of 1570.
21 Sadler Papers, III, 332; PRO, SP 12/63/16; Cabala, 167; see CSPScot, 1569-71, 358 for the queen's views.
22 Expenses from April 1570 to January 1571 totalled £43,071. See Hatfield, 492; CSPScot, 1569-71, 358-9.
23 Hatfield, 473, 474, 475; CSPScot, 1569-71, 261; Haynes, 599.
24 CSPScot, 1569-71, 364, 366.
25 Haynes, 608, also CSPScot, 1569-71, 363-4; Fénélon, III, 308, 328-9.
26 Ibid., III, 321.
27 CSPScot, 1569-71, 309 fol.
28 Fénélon, IV, 14, 51; CSPScot, 1569-71, 484, 501, 511.
29 Ibid., 530.
30 E. Lavisse, Histoire de France, 9 v. (Paris, 1900-11), tome 6me., I, 114-15.
31 Fénélon, III, 358, 417.
32 Ibid., III, 461; IV, 11, 41, 59; Digges, 62-3.
33 CSPDom, Addenda, 1566-79, 328-32; CSPFor, 1569-71, 383-4; PRO, SP 12/80/17.

34 *Fénélon*, IV, 12.
35 *Digges*, 33, 72, 127–8; *Fénélon*, IV, 9–10, 23.
36 *Digges*, 55, 129.
37 Ibid., 72, 100–1, 104, 133–4; *CSPSpan, 1568–79*, 331.
38 *CSPFor, 1569–71*, 384, 453, 454; *Digges*, 85, 90–2, 97–9, 100–1.
39 *CSPFor, 1569–71*, 496, 502; *Digges*, 119–20, 138–9, 153–4.

15 THE RIDOLFI PLOT

1 PRO, SP 12/66/42. Cecil was considering the summoning of Parliament in February 1570.
2 *Murdin*, 43.
3 Neale, *Parliament, 1559–81*, 186, 225.
4 Ibid., 199.
5 *Haynes*, 589–93.
6 PRO, SP 12/71/16.
7 Neale, *Parliament, 1559–81*, 192, 204, 206, 215.
8 *Statutes of the Realm* (London, 1810–28), I, 526–8.
9 Neale, *Parliament, 1559–81*, 205.
10 *CSPScot, 1571–74*, 9, 12, 88.
11 PRO, SP 12/85/11; *CSPScot, 1569–71*, 529, 538–9.
12 *Hatfield*, 504–72, passim; *CSPSpan, 1568–79*, 274, 288; *Fénélon*, III, 401, 422–3, 458; PRO, SP 12/74/41.
13 *Hatfield*, 533, 572 (Percy); 544, 549 (Powell); *CSPScot, 1571–74*, 9; *Fénélon*, II, 295; *Murdin*, 118–20.
14 PRO, SP 12/85/11; *Fénélon*, IV, 261; *Murdin*, 28.
15 Ibid., 26, 27, 37, 42, 76, 81, 82, 135. (At Christmas 1569 and again at midsummer 1570 Norfolk sent a ring to Mary [*Murdin*, 138].) For specimens of the Norfolk–Mary correspondence see *CSPScot, 1569–71*, 385–6, *Hardwicke*, I, 190–4 (all in 1570) and BM, Cotton MSS, Caligula C II 70, 72, 73 and Caligula B IX 315 (from Coventry) and *Fénélon*, II, 301–2 for Norfolk's promise to persevere in the match. For a Marian view of the situation in March 1570 see Ross's letter to the Archbishop of Glasgow in *CSPRome, 1558–71*, 330–2.
16 *Murdin*, 24, 94; Camden, *Annals*, 156–7; BM, Cotton MSS, Caligula C II 518.
17 PRO, SP 12/85/11; *Murdin*, 26, 37, 42, 65; *Hatfield*, 555.
18 *CSPRome, 1558–71*, 338, 349.
19 *Murdin*, 24, 56; Camden, *Annals*, 154, 162–3; BM, Cotton MSS, Caligula C II 518.
20 *CSPRome, 1558–71*, 393–400.
21 *Murdin*, 113; *CSPSpan, 1568–79*, 323, 349. Ridolfi acknowledged that Alva was a great obstacle to the enterprise (*CSPRome, 1558–71*, 464–5). Ross had heard from Rome in April that nothing would be done during the present year because of the Turkish matter (*Murdin*, 100, 113).
22 *CSPRome, 1558–71*, 463–6.
23 *Murdin*, 100, 116.
24 Ibid., 26.

25 Ibid., 126, 127, 142.

26 Camden, *Annals*, 163, 164; *Fénélon*, IV, 338. See *The Effect of the Declaration made in the Guildhall by M. Recorder of London concerning the late attempts of the Queen's Majesty's evill, seditious and disobedient subjects* (London, 1571). Note that the Recorder did not specifically name Norfolk, Mary, or the other conspirators, but he painted a picture of invasion by Alva, backed by the pope, and aimed at harming the queen. See Bodleian 9772 (Perrot 7), 12–14, a similar document, probably for Irish distribution. See also *Hatfield*, 543, for a French version of the same. See *Murdin*, 196, for mention of a printed *View of Treasons*. BM, Harleian 4627, ff. 1–9 has the draft of a letter from 'R. G. to his brother-in-law' with an additional official account of the Norfolk–Mary affair from 1569–72, written at the time when the Lord Mayor and aldermen were summoned to hear the story, October 13th, 1571. This was printed as *Salutem in Christo* (London, 1571).

27 *Murdin*, 194, 208–10; *CSPFor, 1572–74*, 32; Williams, *Norfolk*, 231–2.

28 Camden, *Annals*, 78; *ST*, I, 959–65.

29 Ibid., I, 991.

30 Ibid., I, 960.

31 Ibid., I, 978.

32 Ibid., I, 1022, 1023.

33 *Digges*, 165, 166; *Fénélon*, IV, 359.

34 *Murdin*, 212; *CSPScot, 1571–74*, 85, 113; *CSPFor, 1569–71*, 571; *1572–74*, 72; *Digges*, 199; Camden, *Annals*, 177; *Fénélon*, IV, 410–11.

35 Neale, *Parliament, 1559–81*, 242.

36 *Fénélon*, IV, 426.

37 Neale, *Parliament, 1559–81*, 244; *Digges*, 203, 218.

38 Neale, *Parliament, 1559–81*, 253, 261.

39 Ibid., 258.

40 Ibid., 263, 268, 272.

41 Ibid., 274.

42 Ibid., 280.

43 Ibid., 279.

44 BM, Cotton MSS, Caligula B VIII 240–6.

45 Neale, *Parliament, 1559–81*, 286.

46 *Digges*, 218.

47 Neale, *Parliament, 1559–81*, 298; PRO, SP 12/86/45, 46, 47, 48. Consent for any deviation was to be given by a majority of all bishops; any provisions for use of alternative services were deleted. (Neale, *Parliament, 1559–81*, 302.)

48 *Fénélon*, IV, 223; *Digges*, 139–40; *CSPFor, 1569–71*, 538, 551–2, 557–8.

49 *Digges*, 120–1, 127–8, 152–3; *Fénélon*, IV, 305.

50 *Fénélon*, IV, 355–6; *CSPFor, 1572–4*, 86.

51 *CSPFor, 1572–74*, 88.

52 *CSPSpan, 1568–79*, 36, 381.

53 PRO, SP 12/67/64; for a printed epitaph for Pembroke see *Ballads and Broadsides Chiefly of the Elizabethan Period*, edited Herbert L. Collmann (Horace Hart, Oxford, 1912), 94.

54 *Haynes*, 599. For an epitaph on Derby see Collmann, *Ballads*, 101.

55 *Sadler Papers*, II, 98; BM, Cotton MSS, Caligula B IX 382. In the *Sadler Papers*, Kennedy is probably a miscopying for Heneage.

56 Croft immediately offered his services to De Spes and was a regular informant of the ambassador in the year following (*CSPSpan, 1568–79*, 227).

57 See letter in Bodleian MSS, 10576, f. 104.

58 For Sussex's appointment see *APC*, VII, 408. For Shrewsbury see *Hatfield*, 571, and PRO, SP 12/83/33.

59 *Fénélon*, IV, 410, 437.

60 Dewar, *Smith*, 123.

61 *Fénélon*, IV, 440.

62 PRO, SP 12/89/2.

63 *CPR, 1569–72*, 269, 407, 426, 473, 480. Dudley also had some of Parr's lands and a modest assortment of other leases or grants during the same year.

Index